Crisis in the Caribbean

edited by Fitzroy Ambursley and Robin Cohen

HEINEMANN
KINGSTON · PORT OF SPAIN · LONDON

Heinemann Educational Books Ltd
22 Bedford Square, London WC1B 3HH

PO Box 1028, Kingston, Jamaica
27 Belmont Circular Road, Port of Spain, Trinidad
IBADAN   NAIROBI
EDINBURGH   MELBOURNE   AUCKLAND
SINGAPORE   HONG KONG   KUALA LUMPUR   NEW DELHI

ISBN 435 98020 3

543632
BSB.

Filmset in Monophoto Garamond 10/11pt by
Northumberland Press Ltd,
Gateshead
Printed in Great Britain by
Richard Clay (The Chaucer Press) Ltd,
Bungay, Suffolk

Crisis in the Caribbean

To Walter Rodney

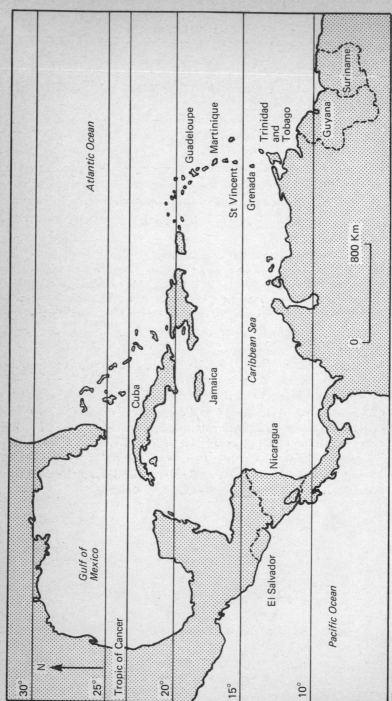

The Caribbean Basin

Contributors

Fitzroy Ambursley is a Jamaican Ph.D. student at the University of Warwick.

Jean-Pierre Beauvais is a journalist working for *Rouge*, a radical weekly published in Paris. He has written extensively on political events in Latin America and the Caribbean.

Philippe Alain Blérald is Senior Lecturer at the Centre Universitaire Antilles-Guyane (Martinique).

Robin Cohen is Professor of Sociology at the University of Warwick.

James Dunkerley is the author of *The Long War: Dictatorship and Revolution in El Salvador*.

Sandew Hira is a Surinamese student doing research in Holland. He is the author of *Van Priary tot en met De Kom. De geschiedenis van het verzet in Suriname, 1630–1940* (From Priary to De Kom. The history of the struggle against colonialism in Suriname, 1630–1940). He is a member of the *Beweging van Surinaams Links* (Movement of the Surinamese Left).

Philip Nanton is a regular contributor to *African Business* and is co-editor of *Melanthika: An Anthology of Pan-Caribbean Writing.*

José Miguel Sandoval is a Chilean who has been lecturing at the University of the West Indies, Trinidad, since 1977. He studied in Chile and at the University of Sussex.

Clive Y. Thomas is Professor of Economics and the Director of the Institute of Development Studies (Guyana). He is the author of *Dependence and Transformation: The Economics of the Transition to Socialism* and *The Rise of the Authoritarian State: An Essay on the State in the Capitalist Periphery*.

Henri Weber is Senior Lecturer at the Université de Saint-Denis (France). He is the author of *Nicaragua: The Sandinist Revolution*.

Acknowledgements

We would like to thank the following individuals for the encouragement, assistance or critical comments they provided during the preparation of this book: Dennis Bartholemew, Christine Brown, James Currey, Mike Davis, James Dunkerley, Richard Hart, Winston James, Susan Lowes, Philip Nanton, Marion O'Callaghan, Jenny Pearce and Rod Prince. A special mention should also be made of our two translators, Patrick Camiller and Selina Cohen, both of whom helped with some of the editorial work.

Contents

Contents

List of Tables

ONE

Crisis in the Caribbean: Internal Transformations and External Constraints

Fitzroy Ambursley and Robin Cohen

This book draws together analyses of some of the most salient political developments to have taken place in the circum-Caribbean during the last few years. In this period we have witnessed a qualitative heightening of class contradictions in most countries and a growing crisis of US foreign policy in the region. The Grenadian revolution of March 1979 and the overthrow of the Somoza dictatorship in Nicaragua four months later were the decisive elements in the overall situation. These popular struggles shaped the context of subsequent events, such as the military coups in El Salvador and Suriname, the political turmoil during the October 1980 elections in Jamaica and the murder of Walter Rodney in Guyana. Indeed, one could say that 1979 opened up a new period in the Caribbean, a period exhibiting four main characteristics:

(i)   The consolidation of revolutionary governments in Grenada and Nicaragua, providing a more radical model of political transformation than that of either the former Manley regime in Jamaica or of the present government of Forbes Burnham in Guyana.

(ii)   The political impact of the Grenadian and Nicaraguan events in bolstering the strategic position of the Cuban state and providing it with more consistent and durable allies in the Caribbean.

(iii)   The emergence of the oil-based economic power of Venezuela and Mexico as a new and complicating factor in the determination of US foreign policy in the region. While the growing influence of these two countries is viewed, quite correctly, with some apprehension by smaller countries in the Caribbean basin, Mexico and Venezuela have also adopted a posture which, on certain key questions, clashes with the policies of the US State Department. The opposition which both regimes, along with other members of the Organization of American States (OAS), expressed to any direct US intervention during the revolution in Nicaragua was the most important example of this. On the other hand, the huge external debts that Mexico had incurred by mid-1982 will limit the extent to which it can continue to oppose the US.

(iv)   The strengthening of political and military ties between Washington and the traditional pro-imperialist parties in the region in the wake of events in Grenada and Nicaragua. Electoral contests and political debate in a number of the smaller territories have evinced a much sharper polarization between radical and conservative programmes. At the same time, the contradictions of dependent development continue to manifest themselves even in more stable and economically 'successful' territories such as Barbados, Trinidad and Tobago, and Puerto Rico.

While Washington's counter-offensive against its own deteriorating position has already scored certain victories (the most significant being the electoral success of the Jamaica Labour Party (JLP) in Jamaica), the general context remains quite explosive with the possibility of further revolutionary advances on the Central American isthmus in El Salvador and Guatemala. Hence, whatever the vicissitudes of the political situation from month to month and from country to country, the contemporary crisis in the Caribbean is going to be both protracted and fraught with a good deal of uncertainty.

The countries selected for this book have been chosen to convey the full dimensions of the regional economic and political crisis. We have therefore included studies from each of the four principal linguistic domains and, other than those countries that have hit the international headlines, have provided investigations of three ostensibly stable territories (St Vincent, the French Antilles and Trinidad and Tobago). Another set of countries (Jamaica, Guyana and Suriname), while being prone to a good deal of internal violence or dramatic shifts in government, have none-theless undergone no radical structural transformations. Finally, the book compares those countries in the region (Cuba, Grenada, El Salvador and Nicaragua) that have experienced a revolutionary trajectory of some signi-ficant degree.

All the essays are informed by a Marxist methodology, while the fundamental issue addressed by each of the contributors is the problem of socialist transformation. Our authors are concerned with unravelling the mechanisms being used by imperialism to dominate the region and, at the same time, with posing critical questions on the political strategy and institutional forms necessary to effect an authentic transition to socialism. This introductory chapter partly integrates the theoretical and political arguments of the contributors. But it also operationalizes the concept of 'crisis' which we use in the title of the book and provides a discussion of the primary impediment to any revolutionary trajectory in the region—US foreign policy.

Internal transformations

The locus of underdevelopment

Most of the case studies in this volume seek to explain Caribbean under-development mainly in terms of class relations and of the insertion of these countries into a subordinate relationship with the capitalist world economy. As such, they offer more complex and multiform explanations of the region's impoverishment than those offered by 'plantation-economy' theory. Although one of its protagonists, Beckford, has moved beyond this framework in recent years (Beckford and Witter 1982), the paradigmatic basis of much Caribbean scholarly writing was set by this perspective (Beckford 1972; Levitt and Best 1978). The plantation-economy thesis is, in essence, a Caribbean version of dependency theory. Many studies based on it contained valuable material on the misallocation of resources engendered by estate production for export, while a number of writers in this school made acute observations about the exploitative nature of the connection between the periphery and the metropole. But such studies were often vitiated by their failure to take into account the role played by indigenous bourgeois classes in propping up and defending the dependent capitalist system. Moreover, as a number of the studies contained in this volume indicate, there has been a progressive shift by the dominant classes of the Caribbean, and by the metropolitan interests that supported these classes, away from purely agricultural production. Thus, an attempt to conceptualize these societies primarily in terms of the plantation unit bears little relation to the dynamics of capital accumulation in the region.

The parasitism, the retrogressive and surrogate nature of the local ruling class are stressed, in particular, in the chapters on El Salvador and on Jamaica by Dunkerley and Ambursley. In criticizing the political programme of the Partido Comunista de El Salvador (PCS), Dunkerley points to the absence of an independent industrially based national bourgeoisie. He argues that the economic boom of the 1960s was sponsored by the landed oligarchy in concert with foreign capital, but that the continued hegemony of the oligarchy and its direct control over the state apparatus have thwarted attempts at land reform and have frustrated plans to increase consumer demand through income redistribution.

A similar line of argument is put forward by Ambursley in his assessment of the Manley era in Jamaica. He highlights the critical role that foreign investment in bauxite has played in the Jamaican economy and the extreme dependence of the local bourgeoisie on inflows of capital, raw materials and fuels. Although Manley's attempt to renegotiate the terms of the island's domination by imperialism could hardly be thought of as radical, it nonetheless unleashed a chain reaction which pitted the local capitalist class against the People's National Party (PNP). Ambursley again emphasizes the importance of the character of the ruling class in explaining the sustained depression of the Grenadian economy under Gairy. He draws attention to the preponderance of the comprador bourgeoisie and shows how its pre-eminence was cemented by the lending policies of foreign-owned commercial banks, by tourism and by the stagnation of domestic agricultural production. The corrupt and idiosyncratic nature of the Gairy regime merely added a new dimension to the inertia and limited horizons of this class. Thus, while there is an evident crisis of accumulation in the region, it stems as much from the underdeveloped, compliant and frequently corrupt nature of the local ruling classes, as from a structural and largely outdated abstraction like 'the plantation economy'.

The crisis of the state

The central feature of the state in the Third World is that it provides the basis for primitive accumulation for the native bourgeois classes, since both the internal social structure and external capital limit the scope of independent development in the productive spheres. The expanded role of the state in numerous countries of the capitalist periphery does not necessarily reflect any radicalization of these regimes, but corresponds rather to the exigencies of national capital accumulation and to the realities of the present-day world economy. While, on the one hand, the local capitalist class can only develop with the assistance of the bourgeois state, on the other hand, foreign capital has increasingly adopted a strategy of allying itself with the local bourgeoisie through 'joint ventures' patent and licensing agreements, loans and credits. Four of the chapters in this volume address themselves specifically to this question. Thomas explains how the expansion of the state sector in Guyana, to encompass some 80 per cent of the local economy, was the outcome of two distinct but complementary stratagems: firstly, an aspiration on the part of the petty-bourgeois elements inside the People's National Congress (PNC) to use the state apparatus as an instrument of 'class creation'; and, secondly, a move by the multinational sugar and bauxite-alumina companies to alter the terms of their domination of Guyanese society. The net result of the government's commercial 'repurchase' of these companies was to turn national assets into a national foreign debt. A heavy premium was thereby placed on all subsequent foreign-exchange earnings. Thomas sharply criticizes commentators who saw the growth of state control as a move to the left by the PNC regime. His principal thesis is that the advent of state capitalism led ineluctably to an increase in government repression, since it was basically designed to foster the development of the petty-bourgeois and bourgeois forces aligned to the PNC. Nanton's chapter on St Vincent also focuses on the increase in dependency that is brought about by the expansion in the activities of the peripheral capitalist state. He shows how the increase in state intervention brought out unintended and far from beneficial consequences, even for the incumbents of state. The economy in general, and the agricultural sector in particular, have been badly mismanaged, while government ineffectiveness triggered a growth in labour unrest, a brief separatist rebellion and a significant political challenge from the left.

The chapter by Blérald on the French Antilles addresses itself partly to the crisis of capital accumulation and the attempt by the colonial state to resolve this crisis by restructuring and re-orientating the economies of Martinique and Guadeloupe. This is being effected mainly through a redistribution of income and a massive increase in public expenditure. Blérald, however, isolates a number of obstacles to the state's modernization drive. These include the vigorous opposition that has been mounted by the monopoly transport companies and the comprador bourgeoisie, the disastrous effects which a rationalization policy would have on the already high level of unemployment and the limitations which the capitalist world recession has imposed on the state's ability to increase public spending. Blérald also points out that while the granting of autonomy to the two *départements* would facilitate the consolidation of the industrial wing of the bourgeoisie, this option is ruled out because of the dependence of the ruling class as a whole on metropolitan France for the instruments of state coercion.

Finally, the chapter by Sandoval on Trinidad and Tobago, the most dynamic economy in the Commonwealth Caribbean, traces the role played by the state in promoting capital accumulation by both local and foreign interests. He points out how the spectacular increase in oil revenues after 1973 permitted the implementation of a strategy of industrialization devised in the 1950s, but which, until the oil bonanza, had encountered numerous difficulties. The principal effect of the oil boom was to enable the state to enter into joint ventures with the multinational companies which dominated the oil and natural gas industries, and, at the same time, establish autonomous enterprises of its own. Local capital was also drawn into the process. Several established trading firms developed important manufacturing and assembly activities, and managed to extend their operations into the neighbouring islands through Caricom. Sandoval concludes his chapter by pointing out that the recent reductions in income from the oil sector now place a big question mark over the government's economic strategy.

Given that Sandoval has concentrated his discussion on economic factors, the social and political tensions apparent in Trinidad and Tobago are accordingly de-emphasized. His attention to the modern period also presents the 1970s as a sort of *belle époque* in the country. This was not the case. The oil boom itself generated a number of contradictions, the most notable of which were economic bottlenecks, an exhaustion of infrastructural capacity, corruption, mismanagement and, perhaps the most ominous of all with respect to the long-term prospects of the state, the burgeoning of a radical labour movement. The crisis of the state in Trinidad and Tobago began long before the difficulties in the oil industry.

Culture, race and national identity

The racial and cultural heterogeneity of Caribbean societies and their long years of subjugation by European powers have made ethnicity and national identity important foci of the class struggle. This dimension has also been integrated into several of the case studies, which counterpose a Marxist treatment of this subject matter to the thesis of cultural pluralism—the theoretical premise of much academic writing about the Caribbean. (For the *locus classicus* of this tradition, see Smith 1965.) Ambursley's chapter on Jamaica contains a brief discussion of Post's work, which has made a seminal break with the prevailing literature on this and many other questions. Ambursley also proposes that the PNP's ideology represented a bourgeois adaptation of popular Jamaican racial and cultural motifs, which were interlaced with Fabian and nationalist shibboleths.

The issue of national identity and cultural imperialism is, however, most acutely addressed in the French islands, much of Blérald's chapter being anchored upon an analysis of the ideological–cultural system of oppression. He points to the material basis of the French state's policy of 'genocide by substitution', whereby Antilleans are encouraged to emigrate to France, ostensibly as a solution to the unemployment problem, only to see Europeans take up key posts and settle in the Antilles. Blérald argues that the cultural sphere constitutes the terrain where the crisis in the relations of oppression is most marked and lists the gamut of publications and organizations that have emerged in opposition to assimilationism. The reassertion of a unique cultural identity can be considered (more negatively) as a displacement of a classical nationalist struggle or (more positively) as the expression of a political challenge in a context where the objective basis for economic independence is limited.

Hira's chapter on Suriname is also concerned with the cultural level, in that he draws attention to the overlapping of racial categories with class boundaries, and examines the effects that his has had on the tenor of class struggle. He too mentions the mass exodus of people to Holland on the eve of Surinamese independence. His explanation of this phenomenon as solely an expression of the 'disillusionment of the masses in the economic and political system' could, however, be extended. For example, it takes no account of either the debilitating effects of the colonial incubation, or the internalization of Western lifestyles and consumption patterns by the Surinamese populace. Despite this shortcoming, the chapters mentioned do at least show the outlines of an alternative form of cultural analysis to that presented by pluralist theorists.

Pitfalls of the 'non-capitalist path'

The downfall of the PNP government in Jamaica, the revolutionary victories in Grenada and Nicaragua and the army officers' coup d'état in Suriname, all raise a number of theoretical issues concerning class alliances and revolutionary strategy in the Caribbean. Initially, we wish to introduce this topic by considering the theory of 'non-capitalist development' or 'socialist orientation', which is adhered to by the official communist parties and their supporters in the region. The theory has also influenced (or at least provided an ideological sanction for) parties such as the PNP and the New Jewel Movement (NJM). Contrary to the assertion made by its principal Caribbean advocates (Gonsalves 1981; Jacobs and Jacobs 1980) and even certain writers who have made valid criticisms of it (Thomas 1978; Halliday and Molyneux 1981), the theory of non-capitalist development has no real basis in the writings of Marx, Engels and Lenin. As Löwy (1981) has recently pointed out in his philological study of their texts, Marx and Engels's theoretical prognoses on the bypassing of capitalist development in Russia during the 1880s envisaged this process taking place only under proletarian hegemony and linked to a proletarian insurgency in the advanced capitalist countries of Western Europe. Likewise, Lenin's deliberations on the possibility of averting capitalist development in backward countries, made at the Second Congress of the Comintern and in other writings, stressed the necessity of establishing independent organs of the working class and poor peasants. He also noted the importance of material assistance from more advanced countries under the dictatorship of the proletariat (Lenin 1971; 1971a).

In short, the modern theory of non-capitalist development may use quotations from the works of Marx, Engels and Lenin, but it arrives at conclusions that are wholly at variance with the major content of their arguments. Elaborated in the 1950s and 1960s by the Soviet theorists Ulyanovsky (1974), Solodovnikov and Bogoslovsky (1975) and Andreyev (1977), it raises the objective possibility of superseding capitalism in contemporary underdeveloped countries, yet suggests that in order to accomplish this, a new stage of development must be traversed that is neither capitalism nor a transition to socialism. Furthermore, this allegedly non-capitalist path can involve, as Ulyanovsky in effect concedes, a long-term strategic alliance with the local bourgeoisie (Ulyanovsky 1977: 26).

As Löwy (1981) points out, the real origins of official communist 'stagism' as required by the theory of non-capitalist development are the neo-Menshevik theses advanced by Stalin during the 1920s. Whereas Stalin's writings did, however, have a certain logical consistency, in that the injunction to enter into a broad strategic alliance with the bourgeoisie was justified as a means of consummating the bourgeois democratic revolution, the theory of non-capitalist development mystifies the objective nature of the process it describes with vague talk of 'bypassing the capitalist stage'. Indeed, such have been the contradictions involved in the application of the theory that it has undergone a semantic evolution and is now called 'socialist orientation'. Halliday and Molyneux (1981: chapter 7) have explained how the reversals suffered by Soviet foreign policy in Egypt and Somalia (two of the countries that were considered to be classic examples of the non-capitalist road) led the Soviet theoreticians to re-examine the theory and suggest a refinement which they termed the 'states of socialist orientation'. A perusal over the list of countries Halliday and Molyneux identified in Soviet literature as 'socialist orientated', however, would suggest that, as with the non-capitalist path, the terminology is reserved for dissident Third World regimes with close economic and political ties with the Soviet Union, whatever the objective basis for such a label might be. (The list includes, for example, such diverse countries as Ethiopia, Guinea, Benin, Malagasy, Congo, Tanzania, Angola, Mozambique, Guinea-Bissau, Cape Verde, São Tomé, Algeria, Syria, South Yemen, Libya, Afghanistan, Burma,

Nicaragua and Grenada.) The emphasis in the theory of socialist orientation upon such factors as 'the relative autonomy of the state', 'the revolutionary potential of military officers' and 'popular committees' serves merely to occlude the objectively capitalist nature of most of these countries and their continued symbiosis with the capitalist world economy (for a more extended critique of the theory see James 1982).

Within the official communist movement, the decision to designate a country as non-capitalist or socialist-oriented is taken by the Central Committee of the Communist Party of the Soviet Union (CPSU). But apparently no such decision was taken about either the Manley regime in Jamaica or the Burnham government in Guyana. Nevertheless, at least three Caribbean proponents of official communist orthodoxy (Gonsalves 1979: 2; Jacobs and Jacobs 1980: 83) have actually placed these regimes in this taxonomy. Moreover, the official communist parties in both these countries pursued a political line fashioned largely by the ideological parameters of the socialist-orientation thesis. In his chapter on Jamaica, Ambursley argues that given the innumerable ties that bound the Jamaican bourgeoisie to foreign capital, the Workers' Party of Jamaica's (WPJ) search for a 'national patriotic bourgeoisie' was illusory and only led the party into becoming loyal but mistaken supporters of the PNP regime. In its endeavour to 'push' the PNP along a non-capitalist path, the WPJ refrained from mounting any serious opposition to Manley, even to the point of joining PNP henchmen and security forces in breaking up a mass protest movement in 1979.

The PNP experiment in 'Democratic Socialism' was a tightly controlled affair. It sought to ameliorate some of the more naked forms of oppression of the Jamaican working class and attempted to accomplish this by redistributing a greater proportion of the surplus value extracted by foreign capital towards a particular fraction of the local bourgeoisie. The socialist and anti-imperialist pronouncements of the PNP, Ambursley argues, were designed to increase its appeal among the oppressed and provide a camouflage for its pro-capitalist policies. In the theory of non-capitalist development it found a ready-made ideology which the left wing of the PNP integrated into its populist rhetoric. Manley himself preferred not to use this particular terminology and in his recent book depicts the PNP's abortive development strategy as a 'third path'. This, he claims, was a distinct and median course between the Puerto Rican model and the Cuban revolution (1982). Manley's contention that his removal from office was due to a CIA conspiracy is a matter of the truth, but not the whole truth. And it ought not to evoke too much sympathy, coming as it does from a man who was baptized into Jamaican politics in 1952 as the willing accomplice of a US-inspired operation that decapitated the Marxist tendency in the Jamaican labour movement. The economic policies of the Manley regime could in no way be construed to have represented a serious challenge to the local capitalist class or to foreign domination. Most of the battered remnants of the PNP's reform programme still in existence in 1980 were discarded by the Seaga regime without significant popular opposition. On balance, Ambursley argues, the WPJ strategy of alliance with the PNP only facilitated Manley's unprincipled balancing act between the classes. It also left a gaping hole for the JLP to build a right-wing opposition movement and carry out its electoral coup d'état.

We have already mentioned Thomas's warning that the extension of state control in Guyana should not mislead us into thinking of the Burnham regime as left-wing. Yet here too the advocates of the non-capitalist path made precisely this error. The main proponent of the notion that the regime was undergoing radicalization was the Guyanese CP, the People's Progressive Party (PPP). In 1975, the PPP adopted a policy of critical support for Burnham and this helped consolidate the PNC regime. The pusillanimity of the PPP's politics, indeed, promoted the emergence of the Working People's Alliance (WPA), which offered a more resolute and proletarian-anchored strategy of political opposition to the PNC. The PPP's pursuit of an alliance with the PNC is now greeted with a good deal of scepticism, since it is widely acknowledged that the Burnham regime is the most repressive and despotic in the English-speaking Caribbean and, in 1980, was responsible for the brutal murder of one of the region's leading revolutionary thinkers, Walter Rodney.

Class alliances and revolutionary strategy

The chapters by Weber and Dunkerley, on Nicaragua and El Salvador respectively, highlight a number of pitfalls in the official communist practice of seeking to establish long-term inter-class blocs. Weber (1981) points out how the Partido Comunista de Nicaragua (PCN) was out-flanked on the left by the Frente Sandinista de Liberación Nacional (FSLN), because of the former's step-by-step overtures towards the Somoza dictatorship. A similar fate also seems to have befallen the PCS in El Salvador. Dunkerley explains how the PCS's desperate search for reformist elements within the various client military regimes and its dogged commitment to electoralism led the party into a political impasse. The principal guerrilla movements (the Fuerzas Populares de Liberación (FPL), the Fuerzas Armadas de Resistencia Nacional (FARN) and the Ejército Revolucionario del Pueblo (ERP), either emerged out of, or developed their politics through, a sustained critique of the policies of the PCS. The PCS has now been obliged to abandon its gradualist strategy and has joined with guerrilla groups in forming the Frente Democrático Revolucionario (FDR) and its military wing, the Frente Fara-bundo Martí para la Liberación Nacional (FMLN). Dunkerley suggests that the PCS is, nevertheless, still pursuing a stagist orientation within the revolutionary camp. Both Nicaragua and El Salvador thus provide a certain parallel with events in Cuba during the 1950s, where the official CP (the Partido Socialista Popular (PSP)) was supplanted by the July 26 Movement as a result of its conciliatory attitude towards Batista.

The popular insurrections that took place in Grenada and Nicaragua pose a number of complex questions about class alliances and revolutionary strategy. This is because both events were led by political formations other than orthodox CPs and yet, in both cases, political alliances were entered into with the bourgeoisie which remain intact to this very day. Of course, the official communist movement is not the only protagonist of class alliances with the bourgeoisie in the capitalist periphery: such ideas have been peddled in various complexions by a plethora of bourgeois and petty-bourgeois currents. Indeed, the attraction of particular tenets of official communism to a host of Third World regimes has its basis in a political convergence with respect to the complex issue of class alliances. Hence, in the case of Nicaragua and Grenada, our analytical task would appear to be to ascertain whether the popular-frontist pronouncements of either the FSLN of the NJM have led to a neo-bourgeois or petty-bourgeois deflection of the revolutionary process. Both in his book (Weber 1981) and in his chapter included here, Weber advances the view that FSLN alliance politics are different from those of the Stalinist front, in that they are based on conflict and on FSLN hegemony. In spite of the non-Somoza bourgeoisie retaining its economic power and its ties with foreign capital, a transition to socialism is in progress because of the FSLN leadership's commitment to such a course and because of the control the revolutionary movement has over the coercive apparatuses of the state. Dunkerley, however, in his chapter on El Salvador, takes issue with what he considers the subjectivism of Weber's analysis. He regards the possibility of a state capitalist ossification of the revolution as equally, if not more, likely than a transition to socialism. In any event, he perceives great dangers in the revolutionary movement of El Salvador adopting the 'Nicaraguan model' and characterizes the Sandinista regime as a popular front.

Ambursley's chapter on Grenada is somewhat more definitive in arguing that the alliance with the bourgeoisie has congealed and considers the New Jewel Revolution as already having been 'interrupted'. Essentially he revises a more tentative analysis that he put forward in a study of the first year of the revolution (Ambursley 1982). Ambursley's thesis is that the Bishop regime's proclamations of 'socialist orientation' represent only one strand of the ideology of the NJM, which is by no means the dominant one. The social and economic policies pursued by the NJM during its first three years in office, while an obvious advance on the trauma of Gairyism, do not challenge the basis of class rule in Grenada. They could, therefore, hardly be described as preparing the ground for an ultimate transition to socialism. Ambursley is thus critical of the proponents of 'stagism' in Grenada and of those writers who, even more implausibly, have argued that a socialist revolution is taking place.

In his recent book, Manley points to the 'mixed-economy' approach being followed in Grenada and Nicaragua as a vindication of the development path that he tried to chart, since, despite the armed seizure of power that took place in these two countries, the NJM and the FSLN have also seen fit to align themselves with the private sector. He argues that the difference between these two processes and the PNP strategy is mainly a matter of emphasis (Manley 1982; *Socialist Challenge* 9 July 1982). Manley would seem to have a better appreciation of what is taking place in these two countries than a good number of Marxist writers, though his claim that these developments somehow represent an *ex-post-facto* verification of 'Democratic Socialism' is not very convincing. Moreover, it is clear that the FSLN and the NJM do not represent the same class interests as did the PNP, and that the Sandinista and Bishop regimes already have been able to effect a greater degree of popular participation than the PNP achieved at any time during its eight years in office. Nevertheless, in so far as these regimes do not cross the Rubicon to socialist revolution, a progressive degeneration along the lines of the PNP would seem to be inevitable.

In showing that the main impetus for the February 1980 coup d'état in Suriname came from the industrial wing of the bourgeoisie, the chapter by Hira indicates an additional dimension to the problem of class alliances and revolutionary strategy. The bourgeois forces grouped in the Partij Nationalistische Republiek (PNR) (Party for a Nationalist Republic) had for some time expressed dissatisfaction with the comprador-bourgeois government of Henk Arron and had conspired with a dissident caucus of non-commissioned army officers to seize state power. The right-wing origin of the military putsch immediately became evident as the new regime moved to impose press censorship, curfews and a ban on political meetings. The radical inclinations of the army officers have, however, given rise to tensions within the insurrectionist fraction of the bourgeoisie and this has saddled the National Military Council regime with an element of marked instability. The regime's attempt to make economic concessions to the masses, in an extremely unfavourable international climate, has added fuel to the government's crisis. Suriname thus presents a significant divergence from Grenada and Nicaragua, for although a component of the bourgeoisie supported the uprisings that took place in these two countries, unlike in Suriname, the primary thrust came from revolutionary 'Jacobin' forces which mobilized the working class and poor peasants.

Finally, to conclude this section on class alliances and revolutionary strategy, a word on Soviet and Cuban foreign policy in the Caribbean is in order since, on the one hand, the Cuban model (or elements thereof) have been embraced by various political formations and, on the other hand, all radical developments in the region have been regarded by US strategists and their supporters as emanating from Moscow and/or Havana. On the contrary, our chapters have shown that the principal challenge to the neo-colonial status of the region has not in fact come from the official parties tied to Moscow. Soviet policy, as carried out by these parties, has neither been subversive nor expansionist. Furthermore, Ambursley argues in the case of Jamaica, there is evidence that the Soviet Union advised Manley to remain in the Western camp because of its unwillingness to provide him with economic assistance.

Equally, Cuba has for the main part supported the strategy of the CPs in the region. The precise international policy to be pursued by a revolutionary government with the geo-political and economic circumstances facing Cuba is undoubtedly a complex matter. Nevertheless, it is necessary to stress that since the period 1968–70, Cuban foreign policy has undergone a distinct shift away from unconditional support for revolutionary movements in Latin America and the Caribbean and has evolved around three specific axes. Firstly, an alignment with the basic international orientation of the Soviet Union. Secondly, an opening towards reformist bourgeois governments which the Cuban leadership has described as 'anti-imperialist' and 'revolutionary'. And finally, an abandonment of the strident criticisms that Castro himself made of the official CPs of Latin America and a growing rapprochement with these parties. Resolutions adopted at the Havana conference in June 1975 sanctioned these shifts of policy (Castro 1972; Petras and Laporte Jr. 1971: 331–371). This evolution was certainly facilitated by Cuba's growing economic ties with the Comecon countries and by the sustained isolation of the revolution in the American hemisphere, but we do not believe that it was inevitable. In any event, Cuban foreign policy in the Caribbean has been laden with contradictions and cannot adequately be described as consistently internationalist—as has recently been argued by Taber (1981).

In his report to the Second Congress of the Cuban CP held in December 1980, Castro expressly used the notion of 'socialist orientation', and the political ramifications of this theory appear to have underlined much of Cuban policy in the region. Both Michael Manley and Forbes Burnham were given the José Martí award and eulogized by the Cuban regime as 'revolutionary leaders'. The Cubans also endorsed the alliance strategy of both the WPJ and the PPP. Events in Grenada and Nicaragua have, of course, met with an enthusiastic response from the Cuban leadership and this has deepened the rift between Havana and Washington. The Cuban government is, however, using its not inconsiderable influence in these two revolutionary states to underscore a strategy of class alliance. Equally, according to Dunkerley (1982: 212), the Cuban intervention in El Salvador is designed to coax the guerrilla movement into establishing a long-term bloc with the reformist opposition. Surprisingly, the Cubans themselves also seem to be the source of a currently fashionable misconception that the Cuban revolution itself went through a process of 'non-capitalist development' (Gonsalves 1981: 31; Halliday and Molyneux 1981: 276). But this is entirely erroneous. Within the space of less than a year, the alliance between the *Fidelistas* and the bourgeois wing of the July 26 Movement had proved untenable. In the face of Castro's determined effort to introduce revolutionary socialist measures, the Cuban bourgeoisie turned to counter-revolution and is now found in Miami, Florida.

In summary, then, it is true that the revolutionary experience of Cuba and the accomplishments of the Castro regime have provided a source of inspiration to political forces throughout the region. But the main radical developments in the Caribbean cannot be attributed either to Soviet or to Cuban foreign policy, which in theory and practice seems to have a restraining influence.

The transition to socialism and socialist democracy

Despite our foregoing remarks on Cuban foreign policy, Beauvais's chapter on Cuba registers some of the social and economic advances that a planned collectivist economy can bring about in the Caribbean. It also highlights a number of contradictions and tensions inherent in the Cuban attempt to build socialism. He takes care, however, to separate those objective factors that militate against the development of the Cuban revolution, from the impediments that he sees as resulting from the economic and political decisions of the Castro leadership. Beauvais's analysis, in effect, represents a more nuanced version of the 'Sovietization' thesis, advanced by writers such as Mesa-Lago (1974), Gonzales (1976) and Gouré and Weinkle (1972). According to this line of argument, the qualitative strengthening of Cuba's external links with the Soviet Union, particularly after the political and economic setback of 1970, led to the wholesale Sovietization of Cuban society. Previously distinctive aspects of socialist transformation in Cuba have either been discarded or refashioned in the image of the Soviet Union. Beauvais, like the Sovietization theorists, is cognizant and critical of the growing use of Soviet economic doctrines in Cuba and considers that the adoption in 1975 of the new System of Management and Planning in Cuba provides fertile ground for the reproduction of some of the deleterious aspects of Soviet planning. Nevertheless, while there is definitely an objective trend towards bureaucratization, Beauvais argues that a bureaucratic caste, which has interests that are antagonistic to those of the masses, has not yet consolidated itself in Cuba. He cites the democratic aspects of the Cuban political system, *poder popular*, as well as the high level of political consciousness and mass mobilization, as evidence that the Cuban revolution has not regressed to the level of the 'degenerated workers' states' of Eastern Europe. Nevertheless, he views the organization of power in Cuba as paternalistic and feels that it is unlikely to guarantee any genuine exercise of power by the masses. It is above all the absence of democratic planning, self-management of the units of production and distribution, free public discussion and the possibility of open debate within the party and mass organizations that has given rise to the 'low economic consciousness of the workers'. He argues that the technical reforms introduced in the 1970s, although an improvement on some of the inefficiencies of the early years of the revolution, provide no real alternative to a democratic self-organization of the proletariat. Beauvais thus arrives at a different conclusion from that of Fitzgerald (1982) who has made an interesting critique of the Sovietization thesis. Fitzgerald's submission is that the introduction of Soviet-derived planning mechanisms has not only made Cuban society more functional, but has also afforded greater and more stable participation by the masses.

The question of socialist democracy is also touched on in the chapters by Weber, Ambursley (Grenada) and Thomas. Like Beauvais, Weber and Ambursley consider the Cuban system inadequate as a method of proletarian rule and express reservations about the FSLN and the NJM emulating certain aspects of this system. Ambursley, however, stresses that the Bishop regime's failure to break with the dependent capitalist system presents an even more formidable obstacle to socialist democracy than the limitations of the Grenadian conception of popular power. Significantly, Thomas concludes his chapter on Guyana with a quotation from Rosa Luxemburg, the legendary communist leader of the Polish and German labour movements who, perhaps more than any other classical Marxist thinker, ruminated upon the relationship between socialism and democracy. We may reflect that in Guyana, as in many states of the Caribbean basin, the choice facing the masses will increasingly be posed in terms of socialist democracy or no democracy at all.

External constraints

Foreign domination of the Caribbean

Whatever choices are open to the people of the Caribbean, they are tightly constrained by the current and historical domination of the region by external forces. During the mercantilist period, the islands were little more than plantation outposts of the core economies, the effective control of the area being determined by the relative strengths of British, French, Dutch, Portuguese, Spanish and, in the Virgin Islands, Danish, mercantilism.

Despite the general success of the movements towards independence and self-government in the post-war period, the process of dismantling external hegemony is far from complete. Puerto Rico passed from Spanish hands to US control in 1898, the Danish Virgins were simply purchased for $25m by the US in 1917, while US Marines occupied Haiti for twenty years (1915–35). While general decolonization has been effected by the British, the UK continues to govern the Turks and Caicos and the Cayman islands, though these are seen as residual and minor colonial responsibilities, which are seen as best shed, rather than shouldered. Although this is the prevailing view in the British Foreign Office, the case of the Falklands/Malvinas shows how even the faintest prospect of colonial vainglory in the remotest spot can be used to stir reactionary and chauvinist sentiments, when that will turn to the advantage of a discredited politician.

As far as the territories in this book are concerned, the French Antilles have, if anything, been more tightly integrated into the web of metropolitan control, having the status of a department of France. The material advantages of this status have constantly dogged the attempts by progressive elements in Martinique and Guadeloupe to advance their case for political independence. Consequently, as we have indicated, Blérald's contribution to this book depicts the struggle for socialist transformation in the French Antilles as much in cultural as in political or economic terms. The political struggle has also been much blunted by the successive apparent concessions to 'autonomy' and by Mitterand's public disagreement with Reagan at such events as the Cancum summit in Mexico. Mitterand both rejects the notion of development through private capital transfers and unfettered market forces and advances the cause of a 'North–South dialogue' and a 'New International Economic Order'. For all that, Guadeloupe and Martinique remain as firmly under Paris's political thumb as they ever were.

Unlike the French Antilles, Suriname has held some independent status since 1975 and, technically, enjoys a similar relationship to the kingdom of the Netherlands as does Holland, but the country is critically dependent on Holland for aid, technical expertise and investment. Holland also continues to dominate the former Dutch Caribbean on such critical matters as defence, foreign affairs and definitions of nationality and citizenship. So powerful was the ideological grip of the metropolitan power that virtually half the population of the country went to Holland as the country approached independence. Despite a careful attempt to install a pro-Dutch ruling group at independence, it was difficult constantly to prop up the discredited regime of Prime Minister Arron whose government, as Hira shows in his contribution, was constantly under the threat of collapse from its own decline in morale, following a wave of corruption charges and the growing strength of the left in the army, the trade unions and other popular forces. In the event, the right in the army has temporarily triumphed in a pre-emptive coup designed to nip the movements of the left in the bud.

In the case of St Vincent, Britain continues to have an influential voice in the island's affairs, despite the discarding of the status of an associated state in 1980. The regime's dependence on foreign aid was particularly manifest during an emergency following a volcanic eruption on the island. As Nanton shows, the ruling party was able to use its connections with its 'special friends'—Canada, the United States and Britain—to ensure its electoral victory. By the same token, Cato's ruling party was able to tar his opponents on the left (organized for the most part under the banner of YULIMO) as tools of the Soviets or the Cubans and ready to propel St Vincent along the much-feared path of Grenada.

The US imperial tradition

Though we have described the continuing importance of French, Dutch and British influence in the Caribbean, there is no doubt that the major foreign threat to the Caribbean comes principally not from the European powers, but from the US, whose policies in the region both follow a long imperialist tradition and show some recent alarming shifts. The most rabid imperialist doctrines were openly advanced by Roosevelt (Beale 1956: 39) at the turn of the century, while the cases of Haiti, Puerto Rico and the Virgin Islands, already mentioned, show that the US had little hesitation in acquiring new territories or intervening when it felt its regional interests to be threatened. The cavalier treatment of the peoples of the region by the US was later to be followed by military interventions (for example, in the Dominican Republic and Nicaragua), occupation (for example, of the Panama Canal), attempts to destabilize regimes through covert means and finally, the use of international agencies (like the IMF in Jamaica) to undermine the legitimacy of reformist governments. Even in the period before the Second World War, when the right of the Republican Party under Senator Taft advanced the notions of 'Splendid Isolation' and 'Fortress America', as Davis (1981: 32–36) makes clear, what the right really wanted was isolation from European squabbles. The doctrine of 'Manifest Destiny' was always applied to the Caribbean and (to a lesser extent) in the Pacific. Kennedy's adventurist and abortive invasion of the Bay of Pigs in 1961 and the invasion of the Dominican Republic in 1965 were thus part of a long tradition of wielding a big stick in the area whenever US economic or strategic interests appeared to be threatened.

Why then has the Caribbean occupied so central a place in the expression of US imperialism? First, as Maingot has argued, parts of the US are in fact *in* the Caribbean even if not precisely *of* the Caribbean. This has meant that the US has always conceived the Caribbean as *mare nostrum*. Second, in its strategic definitions of thirty-one essential trade routes, several of the major routes pass through the Caribbean and all the busiest border Cuba. In particular, Trade Route Number 4 (so designated by the Merchants' Act of 1934) makes heavy use of the windward passage between Cuba and Haiti (Maingot 1979: 255, 256).

But if these two factors may be seen as determining the long-standing strategic significance of the region to the US, since 1959 a number of new economic and political factors have increased the US sensitivity to its interests in the area. The US military and naval control of the area had been much extended during the Second World War when Churchill abandoned naval bases in the area in return for US strategic support in the Second World War. In addition, the Second World War had marked the period when British capital effectively collapsed as the dominant force in the region and American capital became predominant. This, however, was not sufficient to stop the July 26 Movement in Cuba. The US was unable to invade Cuba successfully, subvert it internally or assassinate Fidel Castro (though CIA attempts were numerous and often bizarre, including the issuing of a 'contract' to the Mafia). So the first new factor in the Caribbean/US equation was the successful emergence of Cuba as a socialist state in the region—and one that was to have considerable influence on progressive forces. Second, US investments in the area began to expand and currently constitute some $4.5 billion (excluding Puerto Rico). By the 1970s, 55 per cent of Caribbean exports and 43 per cent of imports went to and from the US. In terms of value, the US exported goods worth $2 billion in 1977. Though this level of economic investment and trade is relatively small in world-wide terms, it is nonetheless disproportionately great if we bear in mind the relatively minor economic importance of the region in the world economy (Maingot 1979; Palmer 1979). Third, since 1973 the issue of Caribbean oil has become a matter of vital concern. There are major oil refineries in Mexico, Venezuela, Puerto Rico, Trinidad and Curaçao, all of which refine oil, often not from the region, for the US market. So if the Middle East and the Gulf are important in respect of oil supplies, the Caribbean is an equally sensitive zone in terms of the sea routes through which oil is imported and the refining capacity of the region. Fourth, the first two named countries, Venezuela and Mexico, also have an increasing stake as oil producers in their own right. Prior to 1973, when Venezuelan oil was expensive in relation to Middle Eastern oil, this was of no great importance. However, since 1973, Venezuelan oil has become competitive in US markets and it is only since that date too that Mexican oil reserves (thought to be well in excess of Saudi Arabia's) have come on stream on any large scale. This has given to Venezuela and Mexico a certain degree of strategic leverage in the region though, in the case of Mexico, this is limited by its huge accumulation of debts to Western, and particularly American, banks. Both countries have nonetheless played an important mediating role (insofar, for example, as Mexico provides diplomatic and economic support for Cuba) and both show a certain capacity to intervene in their own right— as 'sub-imperial' powers. Fifth, American concern for its Caribbean borders reflects regional shifts within the US away from the north-east and towards the southern rim. This shift in power was recently engagingly described by Sale (1979). The leisure industry, defence and space programmes, agri-business and new manufacturing industries have all become increasingly concentrated in the southern rim and lent a new significance to the Caribbean ports and industrial areas of New Orleans, Miami and Houston. At a political level, so Sale's argument runs, Nixon and Carter's elections to the presidency (and, we may add, Reagan's) all symbolize the 'power shift' he describes. It is not without significance to the evolution of US policy in the Caribbean basin that the coalition of southern business interests set up overseas branches in Guatemala and Nicaragua and were influential in seeking to torpedo the Panama Canal legislation (Black, forthcoming).

The liberal phase and its demise

By the time of Carter's accession to power, the stage was set for the US not only to uphold its traditional interests in the area, but also to advance them in new and more pervasive directions. Carter's foreign policy was, however, dictated by more complicated ends than simply wielding a big stick. The failure of US attempts to unseat the Manley government in 1976 played an important role in pushing the Carter administration to introduce changes in its foreign policy in the Caribbean. In that year a Caribbean Task Force began functioning in the State Department. Its fundamental brief was to keep West Indian experiments in socialism from drifting to the radical left and to do so through political, rather than military, means. This approach was also supported by the House Sub-Committee on Inter-American Affairs headed by Dante Fascell, the Democratic representative from Florida. In addition, the liberal foreign-policy group, whose views were reflected in the Linowitz Report, favoured such a policy. The report reflected some new foreign-policy imperatives: the need to respect diversity and ideology and economic and social organization, the independent role of Latin American and Caribbean nations in international fora and the global significance of US Latin American and Caribbean relations. The report emphasized co-operation with Latin American nations and the provision of aid to development agencies. Less emphasis was placed on bilateral aid. In spring 1978, a 'Group for Co-operation in Economic Development' was launched to implement such a multilateral approach in the Caribbean under World Bank sponsorship. Various international agencies (the IMF, the Caribbean Development Bank and the Inter-American Development Bank) were to co-ordinate aid activities in the region (Maingot 1979: 298). This softly-softly approach was to be reflected in other ways too. Foreign service in the Caribbean had traditionally been a repository for political appointees, but Carter soon began to appoint career diplomats, particularly to the ex-British Caribbean. In 1977 Andrew Young visited the area and emphasized Carter's doctrine of human rights and the USA's new concern for the area (Khan 1979: 29–53). In that year, too, there was a growing entente with Cuba, with hints of the possible establishment of diplomatic relations and a more relaxed attitude to the Manley regime in Jamaica. This phase of American policy in the region was not to last long, but was perhaps best expressed by Terrence Todman, the Assistant Secretary of State for Inter-American Affairs.

We no longer see the Caribbean in the same stark military security context that we once viewed it. Rather, our security concerns in the Caribbean are increasingly political in nature. The threat is not simply foreign military bases on our doorstep. It is possibly an even more troublesome prospect: proliferation of impoverished third-world states whose economic and political problems blend with our own (cited Maingot 1979: 293).

This more sophisticated view of the region was to be dealt a death blow by three events. The first was the victory of the revolutionary forces in Grenada on 13 March 1979. While a meeting of the Caribbean foreign ministers held the next day denounced the revolutionary change in government in Grenada as 'contrary to the traditional methods of changing governments in the region', it nevertheless 'reaffirmed that the affairs of Grenada are for the people of the territory to decide and accordingly there should be no outside interference' (*Trinidad and Tobago Review* May 1979). This stance by American allies restrained direct US intervention for the meanwhile. The second decisive event happened only four months later, when the revolution in Nicaragua reached a decisive phase. Again, the OAS restrained the US from mediating, but this time the patience of the US for 'diversity in economic and social organization' was wearing thin. Finally, Carter's human rights policy came under strong attack from the right as the Cuban refugee crisis escalated. At first, the administration were able successfully to use the refugee crisis to score a propaganda victory over Cuba. But Castro was able to turn the tables initially by announcing that all who did not agree with the aims of the revolution would be free to go and second, by emptying the prisons of Cuba and sending minor criminals to the embarkation point. The large numbers of Cubans involved soon aroused the wrath of racist interests in Florida, while the poor conditions under which many refugees were admitted and housed turned the propaganda victory rather sour. Under the weight of the Grenadian, Nicaraguan and Cuban crises, Washington's policy took a massive lurch to the right.

Its first move was to provide greater economic and military assistance to its traditional allies and at the same time strengthen its capacity to undertake rapid military action. In July 1979 the State Department's AID authorized $8.4m as a loan on soft terms to the Barbados-based Caribbean Development Bank. This money was designed for the ailing economies of the small territories of the Caribbean—St Lucia, Dominica, Antigua and so on—and was intended to prevent 'another Grenada' (*Financial Times* 17 July 1979). Next, using the pretext of the discovery of Soviet troops in Cuba, a military task force was set up in Key West Florida, while US marines were deployed at Guantanamo Bay, Cuba, in October 1979. This was followed by the Solid Shield exercises in May 1980. State Department officials warned that co-operative security arrangements would be necessary in the region and that the failure to effect these would 'leave the field open for Cuba' (*Caribbean Contact* July 1980). Barbados, the Bahamas, Guyana, Haiti and the Dominican Republic received particular attention from the so-called International Military and Education Training fund. Barbados was identified as a special friend in the region and there was even talk of that country becoming a sort of Iran in the Caribbean. This message was received with some unease by the Prime Minister, Tom Adams, who pointed to the fate that befell the Shah. However, Barbados did indeed act in a minor way in this capacity in December 1979, when it responded to a request from Milton Cato to put down a rebellion in Union Island in the St Vincent Grenadines, an event described by Nanton in his chapter in this book.

Economic sweeteners and 'security assistance'

The outlines of a much tougher stance towards the Caribbean basin were thus already present in the last year of the Carter administration, but with Reagan's accession to power the attempts to secure a policy consistent with Reagan's campaign themes of 'Resurgent America' have accelerated. It is perhaps important to emphasize that Reagan has not entirely subordinated the 'liberals' in the foreign-policy establishment; Haig's departure caused some strains and there are considerable unresolved tensions between various business, military and political lobbies with interests in the Caribbean, some of which are mentioned below. Nonetheless, the main lines of US foreign policy in the area are now clear. For those countries which appear to be 'soft on communism' or linking themselves to the Soviet Union or Cuba, immediate economic and diplomatic sanctions are applied. By contrast, Washington's 'friends' are provided with special economic packages and privileged access to the US market, even though in conformity with the doctrine of Reaganomics, private capital should be predominant in effecting this economic relationship. Finally, for those countries which are held to be fighting the communist menace, military assistance is provided irrespective of the means whereby popular insurrections or democratic dissent are contained.

The pattern of economic sanctions directed against regimes that were held to be adopting the wrong international stances again predate Reagan's election, though in the case of Jamaica this pressure gained renewed emphasis with Carter's demise. In fact the IMF, whose lendings were essentially influenced by the US, started proffering its poisoned chalice to Jamaica as early as 1976; by 1980 an attempt to swallow its contents had resulted in the destabilization and electoral defeat of the Manley government. The IMF made eight major demands to the Jamaican government over the period: (i) an attack on excessive wage increases; (ii) pressure to change what they saw as an overvalued exchange rate; (iii) pressure to reduce the fiscal deficit; (iv) pressure to reduce monetary expansion; (v) an attack on Jamaica's trade restrictions and payments; (vi) pressure to reduce state intervention in the economy; (vii) pressure to reduce price controls; and (viii) pressure to increase business confidence (Girvan et al. 1980: 118–119).

It is doubtful whether any reformist Third World government with the basic economic problems that Jamaica experienced would have been able to resist such an onslaught, particularly since it is questionable whether Manley's regime had any consistent or continuous mass support for its programme. In the event, it vacillated, resisted some measures, partially accepted some, but was ultimately forced to go along with all the principal IMF demands. The assault on living standards for the working class, not to mention the related problems of violence and insecurity, propelled a significant section of the urban poor into the hands of Seaga's populist Jamaican Labour Party. Seaga lost no time in linking himself firmly to the tougher US line. He called for closer co-operation in Caricom to 'halt the expansion of communist imperialism' and again dwelt on this theme at a conference of US businessmen held in Miami on 23 November 1980. 'Like minds', he said, should fight 'Marxist adventures' in the region (*Latin American Regional Reports* 5 December 1980). Six months later the *rapprochement* with Jamaica was complete. If the US government did not want to fund some of Jamaica's economic programmes directly, it was sufficient that Reagan gave the go-ahead to private US interests. As Seaga (a former US-trained economist and IMF official) stated to *Newsweek*, 'I knew the President was strapped for money ... but his connections with the US business community were an untapped resource'. Apparently that community was responsive. According to one 'involved' businessman, 'with names like Rockefeller and Reagan singing duets about how wonderful Jamaica is, those wallets should be there and open in no time' (*Newsweek* 20 July 1981).

While the US had little difficulty in gaining the unswerving loyalty of Seaga, other economic sweeteners appeared to be more difficult to package. The creation of a so-called Mini-Marshall plan for the region, drawing in the regional powers of Mexico, Venezuela and Canada, although trumpeted with a great flourish, ultimately ran into difficulties. The plan was fully unveiled in a meeting in the Bahamas in July 1981 between General Haig and the foreign ministers of Canada, Venezuela and Mexico. It followed an intervention made to Haig, by Prime Minister Seaga in January 1981 who argued that the small, weak, dependent territories of the Caribbean would fall 'like dominoes' to Cuba's influence, unless some $3 billion was poured into the area each year (a trebling of the previous level of aid). The plan ran into some immediate difficulties, largely occasioned by Haig's heavy-handed demands. The Venezuelans and Mexicans had separate and somewhat contradictory interests to advance. The Canadians refused to go along with American insistence that Grenada should be cut off from all aid and indeed have agreed to provide a considerable level of aid to the island. The attempt to isolate Grenada even aroused the wrath of the twelve members of the Caribbean Economic Community, including Jamaica and Barbados, who attacked the US for offering a $4m grant to the Caribbean Development Bank, only on condition that none of the money be used in Grenada. In addition to these difficulties, there were reported inter-agency tussles in Washington as to how the Mini-Marshall aid should be allocated and spent (*Financial Times* 1 July 1981, 10 July 1981, 14 July 1981). By February 1982, even the nomenclature had changed—'Mini-Marshall' had been replaced by the Caribbean Basin Initiative (CBI). It appears that by the time the CBI had been diluted by congressional lobbies, the total aid package of US$350m will be spread more thinly, with the special interests of Puerto Rico partly protected, a maximum of US$75m established for each recipient and other restrictions (*The Weekly Gleaner* 11 August 1982; *Financial Times* 27 May 1982). While not a completely damp squib (the package could well buy the loyalties of some smaller territories in the Caribbean archipelago), the emergency relief included for those countries with foreign-exchange difficulties is of little significance where (as in Central America) the ration of foreign debts has grown twice as fast as the GDP or where (as in El Salvador) medium- and long-term loans have grown at ten times the GDP (Black, forthcoming).

Reagan's policies for the 'Caribbean basin' are not, however, simply confined to opening up the area for a dose of 'Reaganomics'. The new administration has clearly signalled a fundamental reassertion of the USA's mission to contain the spread of 'world communism'. Perhaps the most blatant expression of this was made by Jeane Kirkpatrick, Washington's ambassador to the UN, who derided the ridiculous idea that 'forceful intervention in the affairs of another nation is impractical or immoral' (cited Chomsky 1981: 150). Like a diviner reading the entrails, one can also discern shifts in foreign policy and gain an insight into the mentality of planners, by examining a key article that appears from time to time in the journal *Foreign Affairs*, the publication sponsored by the establishment's Council on Foreign Relations. Just such an article was Robert W. Tucker's 'The Purposes of American Power', which Chomsky has dissected in a recent analysis (Chomsky 1981). According to Tucker (1980/81), a scholar whose credentials appear to be well recognized by Reagan's foreign-policy advisers, the US has every right to control the fate of the nations of the Central American area. This 'right', he claims, is based on two fundamental principles:

(a) Central America bears geographical proximity to the United States, and historically it has long been regarded as falling within our sphere of influence. As such, we have long exercised the role great powers have traditionally exercised over small states which fall within their respective sphere of influence. We have regularly played a determining role in making and unmaking governments, and we have defined what we have considered to be the acceptable behaviour of governments.

and

(b) In Central America our pride is engaged.... If we do not apply policy of a resurgent America to prevent the coming to power of radical regimes in Central America, we have even less reason to do so in other areas....

In short, Tucker succinctly summarizes the Reagan administration's abandonment of any pretence at 'Wilsonian Ideals' or 'Human Rights' in favour of the pursuit of 'Resurgent America'. Though there are occasional offstage noises by minor officials that perhaps such an open reassertion of power is embarrassingly explicit and in need of some sugar-coating, there is no doubt that Tucker correctly reflects the mood of the hawks in the administration. The primary test case for this political group is Central America where, it is thought, the shame of the Vietnam war can be exorcized, the compliance of the Western allies can be tested (only France and Mexico have publicly dissented on Nicaragua), and a useful contrast can be made with the soft-bellied period of the Carter years. As Black has argued, 'The sclerotic American far right selected Central

America—above all rapid victory in El Salvador—as a test case for re-affirming international will and Pax Americana' (Black, forthcoming). One of Reagan's officials likewise claimed that an assertion of raw military power in the area was a signal to the electorate and to the USSR that the US 'will take the necessary steps to keep the peace anywhere in the world' (*Guardian Weekly* 8 March 1981).

This odd notion of 'keeping the peace' includes trebling military aid to the bankrupt regime in El Salvador to $66m in 1981–82 and authorizing $19m for covert action against the Sandinistas in Nicaragua in November 1981. The US has also engineered border incursions into Nicaragua from neighbouring territories and has, once again, tightened up the trade and financial embargo with Cuba (*International Herald Tribune* 21 April 1982). Even the small island of Grenada whose limited experiment in partici-patory democracy might have been tolerated by another imperial power, or at another time, has not escaped the wrath of Washington. As Prime Minister Bishop plaintively complained in a published letter to Reagan, the US has 'cut off our traditional aid possibilities both regionally and inter-nationally with a view to strangling our fledgling economy and to sub-verting the political, economic and social process which we have instituted' (*Caribbean Contact* March 1982). Bishop also had good reason to express concern about the mercenaries being trained in the US for deployment against the regional enemies of the US. In fact, it is perhaps less likely that outside intervention in Grenada would succeed: the fact that it is an island protects Grenada against any obvious incursions from neighbouring territories, and American allies in the region (particularly Barbados and Trinidad) are disinclined to adopt too obviously a reactionary position. No such inhibitions apparently affect the USA's rather wilful ally, Israel, who have been selling arms to El Salvador and Nicaragua, which, so a news-paper surmises, 'Congress and public opinion in the US prevents Washington itself from supplying' (*Financial Times* 3 February 1982).

Conclusion

When we use the overworked word 'crisis' to describe the current situation in the Caribbean, we do so not simply as a form of journalistic licence, but in at least three specific senses. There is, we argue, a manifest crisis at the level of the state. In its baldest contrast, the choice facing the peoples of the Caribbean is that between socialist and capitalist paths to develop-ment. But within the former category, only the Cuban state has so far been able to record a measure of lasting success in combining redistributive principles with demands for popular participation. However, the Cuban experiment, despite lasting for over two decades, must remain isolated unless it can effect some unity of purpose with the two other revolutionary states in the area, Nicaragua and Grenada.

Within the other states surveyed, there are large divergences and con-trasts. Some smaller islands have been unable to shake off the heritage of mercantile, colonial or metropolitan control. In the case of the French Antilles, the terrain of culture and identity has, in consequence, become the battleground for self-assertion. Other states have embarked on a policy of dependent semi-industrialization, sometimes concealed behind a socialist rhetoric, sometimes in a more open alliance with foreign capital. Yet none of the capitalist states in the region has escaped the internal crises born of massive unemployment, poor housing, health and educational services, political instability and dependence on an ailing world economy. Some seek to prop up their discredited regimes by military alliances and injections of capital from Washington and the aid agencies, but this solution can act only as a temporary palliative, rather than a permanent cure.

It is perhaps overstretching the term 'crisis' to say that the progressive forces in the region are experiencing a crisis in how to analyse and combat the conditions of underdevelopment. Yet there is certainly a good deal of confusion and uncertainty in evolving the strategies, tactics and ideologies appropriate to a socialist transformation. Can there be a possibility of 'socialism in one country', especially if the countries concerned are small, weak, isolated and located close to Uncle Sam's looming shadow? Is it possible to combine with progressive elements of the national bourgeoisie, even assuming that this class has developed some corporate identity and strength? And will not a tactical alliance with such an ally lead to a more permanent co-optation and ultimately betrayal of mass demands as a number of our contributors have argued? On the other hand, will an alliance of revolutionary intellectuals, workers and displaced peasants hold together long enough to capture the state apparatus and attempt the task of socialist reconstruction from the bottom up? Are the class organs of such an alliance—the trade unions, youth movements and socialist and communist parties—able to effect something more than an *étatist* or bureaucratic solution once they have achieved power?

Finally, there is a rapidly escalating crisis directly linked to the assertion of US power in the region. Bankrupt and murderous juntas like those of El Salvador and Guatemala are granted both the physical means and diplomatic support to suppress popular movements in their countries. Elsewhere, driplets of aid and rivers of 'security assistance' are poured in to tie countries just escaping from colonial rule even more firmly to the apron strings of the State Department. And where the carrot of aid is too tentatively grasped, the stick of military intervention is raised in an ever-present threat. While a more detailed analysis of the elements that go up to make US foreign policy in the area would reveal a number of countervailing pressures, there is no doubt that the hawkish elements are sufficiently in the ascendant to threaten interventionist and sometimes wild schemes for the maintenance of US hegemony in the region. As long as open military involvement remains a serious possibility, it is difficult to predict the exact contours of mass struggle in the territories of the Caribbean basin. But despite the turn to the right in Jamaica, it is unlikely that the US will be able to contain the forces of change that surfaced in Cuba twenty years ago, have emerged in Nicaragua, Grenada and El

Salvador more recently and threaten to overwhelm the US-supported regime in Guatemala.

REFERENCES

Ambursley, F. 1982, 'Whither Grenada? an investigation into the March 13th revolution one year after', in S. Craig (ed.), *Contemporary Caribbean: a sociological reader*, vol. 2, Trinidad and Tobago, Susan Craig, pp. 425–463

Andreyev, I. 1977, *The noncapitalist way*, Moscow, Progress Publishers

Beale, H. K. 1956, *Theodore Roosevelt and the rise of America to world power*, New York, Collier Books

Beckford, G. 1972, *Persistent poverty: underdevelopment in plantation economies of the third world*, London, OUP

Beckford, G. and Witter, M. 1982, *Small island ... bitter weed: struggle and change in Jamaica*, London, Zed Press

Black, G. forthcoming, 'Central America: crisis in the backyard', *New left review Caribbean Contact* July 1980; March 1982

Castro, F. 1972, 'The Latin American communist parties and revolution', in M. Kenner and J. Petras (eds.), *Fidel Castro speaks*, London, Penguin

Chomsky, N. 1981, 'Resurgent America', *Socialist review*, vol. 11, no. 4, July–August, pp. 135–154

Davis, M. 1981, 'The rise of the new right', *New left review*, no. 128, July–August

Dunkerley, J. 1982, *The long war: dictatorship and revolution in El Salvador*, London, Junction Books

Financial Times 17 July 1979; 1 July 1981; 10 July 1981; 14 July 1981; 3 February 1982; 27 May 1982

Fitzgerald, F. 1982, 'The direction of Cuban socialism: a critique of the sovietization thesis', in S. Craig (ed.), *Contemporary Caribbean: a sociological reader*, vol. 2, Trinidad and Tobago, Susan Craig, pp. 243–274

Girvan, N., Bernal, R. and Hughes, W. 1980, 'The IMF and the third world: the case of Jamaica, 1974–1980', *Development dialogue*, vol. 2, pp. 113–155

Gonsalves, R. 1979, 'The importance of the Grenadian revolution to the eastern Caribbean', *Bulletin of Eastern Caribbean affairs*, vol. 5, no. 1, March–April, pp. 1–11

Gonsalves, R. 1981, *The non-capitalist path of development: Africa and the Caribbean*, London, One Caribbean

Gonzales, E. 1976, 'Castro and Cuba's new orthodoxy', *Problems of communism*, March–April

Gouré, L. and Weinkle, J. (eds.) 1972, 'Cuba's new dependency', *Problems of communism*, March–April

Guardian Weekly 8 March 1981

Halliday, F. and Molyneux, M. 1981, *The Ethiopian revolution*, London, New Left Books

International Herald Tribune 21 April 1982

Jacobs, W. R. and Jacobs, B. I. 1980, *Grenada: the route to revolution*, Havana, Casa de las Américas

James, W. A. 1982, 'The non-capitalist path of development and the Caribbean: A critique and an alternative', paper presented at the annual conference of the Society for Caribbean Studies, High Leigh, Hertfordshire, May 1982

Khan, J. 1979, 'De la matraque à la morale: la relance américaine dans les Caraibes', *Alternatives-Caraïbes*, vol. 1, no. pp. 29–53

Latin American Regional Reports 5 December 1980

Lenin, V. I. 1971, 'Report on the national and the colonial questions', in *Selected works in three volumes,* vol. 3, Moscow, Progress Publishers

Lenin, V. I. 1971a, 'Preliminary draft theses on the national and colonial questions', in *Selected works in three volumes,* vol. 3, Moscow, Progress Publishers

Levitt, K. and Best, L. 1978, 'Character of Caribbean economy', in G. Beckford (ed.), *Caribbean economy: dependence and backwardness,* Kingston, ISER, University of the West Indies

Löwy, M. 1981, *The politics of combined and uneven development,* London, New Left Books

Maingot, A. P. 1979, 'The difficult path to socialism in the Caribbean', in Richard R. Fagen (ed.), *Capitalism and the state in US–Latin American relations,* California, Stanford University Press

Manley, M. 1982, *Jamaica: struggle in the periphery,* London, Third World Media Ltd

Mesa-Lago, C. 1974, *Cuba in the 1970s,* Albuquerque, University of New Mexico Press

Newsweek 20 July 1981

Palmer, R. W. 1979, *Caribbean dependence on the United States economy,* New York, Praeger

Petras, J. and Laporte Jr., R. 1971, 'Total system change: a decade of revolutionary government in Cuba', in *Cultivating revolution: the United States and agrarian reform in Latin America,* New York, Random House

Sale, K. 1979, *Power shift: the rise of the southern rim and its challenge to the eastern establishment,* New York, Pantheon

Smith, M. G. 1965, *The plural society in the British West Indies,* Berkeley and Los Angeles, University of California Press

Socialist Challenge 9 July 1982

Solodovnikov, V. and Bogoslovsky, V. 1975, *Non-capitalist development,* Moscow, Progress Publishers

Taber, M. 1981, 'Introduction' in *Fidel Castro speeches: Cuba's internationalist foreign policy 1975–80,* New York, Pathfinder Press

Thomas, C. Y. 1978, 'The "non-capitalist path" as theory and practice of decolonization and socialist transformation', *Latin American perspectives,* vol. 5, no. 2, pp. 10–28

Trinidad and Tobago Review May 1979

Tucker, R. W. 1980/81, 'The purposes of American power', *Foreign Affairs,* winter, pp. 241–274

Ulyanovsky, R. 1974, *Socialism and the newly independent nations,* Moscow, Progress Publishers

Ulyanovsky, R. 1977, 'Foreword' in I. Andreyev, *The noncapitalist way,* Moscow, Progress Publishers

Weber, H. 1981, *Nicaragua: the Sandinist revolution,* London, New Left Books

Weekly Gleaner, The 11 August 1982

State Capitalism in Guyana: an Assessment of Burnham's Co-operative Socialist Republic

Clive Y. Thomas

Introduction

1953 was a watershed year in the political development of Guyana. After centuries of mass struggle, first against colonial slavery and later its modified form, the system of indentured immigrant labour, the twentieth-century national independence movement had succeeded in forcing colonial authorities to hold elections under a system of universal adult suffrage and a constitution that offered what was for that time a relatively high degree of 'internal self-government'. The previous constitution was the classic crown colony type, in that it provided for a legislature and executive made up mostly of nominated Colonial Office officials, with the 'elected' element being elected by the 3 per cent of the population which was then entitled to vote, despite an overall literacy rate of 80 per cent in the country. In the 1953 elections, the People's Progressive Party (PPP) won eighteen of the twenty-four elected seats and formed the first Marxist government to be elected to office, if not power, in the British Empire. However, within 133 days of the election and formation of the government, the Colonial Office intervened forcibly, dissolved the government and suspended the constitution.

The electoral success of the PPP had been based largely on the achievement of a broad unity among the masses of the two dominant ethnic groups: East Indians and Africans. But after the suspension of the constitution an active colonial policy of 'divide-and-rule' was pursued; and by 1955 the PPP and the mass movement it embraced was split into two main groupings. One of these was led by Cheddi Jagan, leader of the original PPP, and the other by Forbes Burnham, his deputy. In the internal struggles that followed, the latter failed in his bid to inherit the leadership of the original PPP and instead, in 1957, formed, from his faction, the People's National Congress (PNC). The split was based on both ideological and ethnic differences.

The suspension of the constitution was followed by four years of Colonial Office interim rule. When elections were held under a modified constitution in 1957, Cheddi Jagan's party won; the same thing occurred again in the 1961 elections. This forced the colonial power to resort to a well-documented manoeuvre in collaboration with the PNC, the US government and the CIA; the manoeuvre required the provocation of internal unrest and a modification of the electoral basis of the constitution (by replacing the 'first-past-the-post' electoral system with one based on proportional representation) in order to install the PNC to office with the new elections held in 1964. In May 1966 formal constitutional power was handed over to the PNC government under the leadership of Forbes Burnham.

Space does not permit any lengthy discussion of this period and the interested reader should consult Jagan (1966) and Thomas (1982) for an extended analysis. For our immediate purpose, however, certain features of the independence settlement need special emphasis because of their later significance. First, an examination of the circumstances surrounding the independence settlement arrived at between Burnham and the colonial authorities reveals that this was based on the exclusion of the masses, and in particular the PPP as the then organized expression of the masses, from any real political power. Secondly, in order to achieve this, the electoral system was undermined as the colonial power, in collusion with the PNC, resorted to the most cynical manipulation of the constitution. This is an important point, since as Thomas (1982) has stressed, in the political history of Guyana, constitutional struggles, while important in themselves, have usually reflected deeper social considerations connected with the state of the class struggle and the question of which class wielded political power in the country. When to this is added previous recourse to arbitrary interventions against the constitution as occurred in Guyana in 1928, 1953 and in the present phase in 1978, it is clear that despite the tradition of Westminister-style parliamentarianism in the English-speaking Caribbean, neither rulers nor ruled in Guyana have functioned in terms of an enduring legal framework within which the exercise of state power occurs.

Third, the events of 1953 and after, particularly as they unfolded in the context of the Cold War hysteria of this period, brought Guyana, although a British colony, more and more within the orbit of American strategic interests. In keeping with the hegemonic and hemispheric role of American imperialism at the time, the American government asserted its influence on Guyana's politics not only through the British government, but directly through crude interventions in the country's domestic affairs. This incorporation of Guyana into the orbit of American interests was no doubt influenced by the consideration that the PPP, the majority party of this period, under the leadership of Cheddi Jagan, was clearly supportive of the official pro-Moscow grouping of communist and workers' parties.

Perhaps, above all else, the independence settlement demonstrated that there was no 'smashing of the colonial state' in Guyana. The absence of a revolutionary break with the colonial state structure, however, should not be allowed to mask the fact that the post-colonial state, almost as it were on the morrow of independence, began a significant dimensional growth in three areas, namely, bureaucratization, militarization and ideologization. This development was a functional imperative of two considerations. One was, that Guyana became a new state in a capitalist world system made up of nation states. The other was that the state of internal class struggles in Guyana required that state power should play a vital role in the consolidation of a hegemonic class in the country. The under-development of the two dominant classes of our historical age (working class and bourgeoisie) in Guyana, combined with the country's highly complex and variegated class structure, in which ethnic factors play critical roles, has resulted in a certain fluidity of political power and in the particular instrumentalist role that the state is playing in class formation. In the development of capitalism in Europe and America the consolidation of economic power by the bourgeoisie preceded their acquisition of state and political power. In Guyana, as elsewhere in the capitalist periphery, the reverse is generally occurring: that is, political/state power is being used as an instrument for the consolidation of a now developing ruling class.

Co-operative socialism

In 1970, four years after independence the ruling party declared Guyana a Co-operative Socialist Republic. A number of factors prompted this particular development. To begin with, the broad mass of the population had had a very militant anti-colonial tradition. This militancy is reflected in the early maturing of relatively highly developed trade-union structures in the country. The harsh conditions of plantation labour and enclave mining and the influence of anti-colonial ideas on these were no doubt mainly responsible for the high level of class consciousness among the main sections of the work force in the sugar and bauxite industries, al-though ethnic differences (the sugar workers are mainly of Indian descent and the bauxite workers mainly of African descent) hindered the growth of cross-industry class solidarity. Second, the tradition of militant anti-colonialism and trade unionism was both product and producer of a situation in which large sections of the work force were influenced by Marxist ideas and functioned within organizations that claimed a Marxist-Leninist leadership. This is seen in the history and development of both the PPP itself and of its associated trade union (the General Agricultural Workers' Union: GAWU), the largest trade union in the country and one which has organized labour on the sugar plantations since the 1940s. The combination of these factors meant that all effective opposition to the PNC state occupied the 'left' of the political spectrum, a development strength-ened by the fact that the local 'businessman's party', the small United Force, which had entered a coalition with the PNC government in order to remove the PPP from office in 1964, had been all but absorbed into the PNC structure.

Third, the PNC's need to use the state to transform itself into a national bourgeois class meant that it had to adopt a popular socialist rhetoric if this process was to be made acceptable to the masses. It is this situation which forced the state to seek to establish its legitimacy in populist-socialist ideology, hence the Co-operative Socialist Republic.

In concrete terms, the declaration of this republic was promulgated as embracing four fundamental features of the new state. The first of these was the expansion of state property over the 'commanding heights' of the economy through a programme of nationalization. Historically, the economy of Guyana has been narrowly based on the production and sale in the world market of three primary products: sugar, rice and bauxite-alumina. Sugar and bauxite-alumina together accounted for approximately 90 per cent of export earnings and 33 per cent of GDP, and continue to be as they have been during this century the largest employers of wage labour. Both these industries were owned and controlled by foreign capital. About 90 per cent of the sugar plantation assets were owned by Booker McConnell Ltd, a world-wide Transnational Corporation (TNC) based in the UK. At the time of nationalization, the remaining 10 per cent of the plantations' assets were under the control of Jessel's Securities, a speculative financial corporation also based in the UK. Only 10 per cent of the sugar cane plant was cultivated in the peasant economy, while the two TNCs owned all the processing facilities. Bauxite-alumina production was also organized through two TNCs (Alcan of Canada, by far the largest producer, and Reynolds of the USA). Both were operated as enclave mining activities located in interior settlements. Rice was cultivated as a peasant crop and this industry grew up under the patronage of the colonial state and the estates, both of which saw it as a complement to sugar production, since it produced a basic staple, found outlets for labour in the off-seasons of the sugar crop, and did not compete significantly with sugar for agricultural land. Despite Guyana's large land area (83,000 square miles) relative to population (currently about 800,000 persons), agricultural land is in scarce supply, as a complex system of drainage and irrigation is required before the coastal strip, on which over 90 per cent of the population is settled, can be successfully cultivated.

TNC control of the Guyana economy was not confined to these two major industries. Other activities, for example, retail distribution outlets, drug manufacture, alcohol production, shipping, cable and wireless communications, foundries and small-scale ship yards, and so on, were all under strong TNC direction. After the completion of the nationalization of sugar in 1976, the government boasted that it now 'owned and controlled 80 per cent of the economy of Guyana'.

The pattern of nationalization was aptly described by Kwayana (1976) as that of the 'mortgage-finance-type'. This meant firstly, that a commercial 'repurchase' of Guyanese assets was negotiated. There is not a single instance of any TNC being dissatisfied with the terms of compensation in these nationalizations. On the contrary, as Thomas (1978) has pointed out, there is strong evidence that in the cases of the nationalization of the two sugar TNCs it was the companies that first approached the government offering their assets for sale. In both instances this was prompted by the severe financial pressures these companies were facing in the UK. Secondly, the effect of such a commercial repurchase was to turn national assets into a national foreign debt, denominated in external currency; this meant that a heavy premium was placed on all future foreign exchange earnings. Thirdly, the stipulation in these agreements that compensation payments would be made out of the 'profits' of the nationalized entities has always been a dead letter. The reason for this is simple. All these companies have continued to rely on the world market for capital financing and the implementation of any such policy would certainly have led to a drying up of these sources of finance. Thus it has been observed that despite heavy losses in some of the nationalized entities, the government has not enforced the stipulation and incurred the risk of being labelled as a 'defaulter' on these debts. Fourthly, the nationalization agreements included the usual array of new contractual obligations which the state is expected to enter at this point. These covered marketing the product overseas, the purchase of equipment and supplies required to operate the industry, management operations in the enterprises, and licences, fees and other royalties and patent payments for the utilization of technology in the industries.

The second principal feature of co-operative socialism is its incorporation of a declaration by the government that henceforth the strategy of national development would be embraced in a programme of feeding, clothing and housing the nation. This, it was claimed, substituted the 'private profit' motive with the social goal of making 'the small man a real man'. This programme was embodied in the 1972–76 development programme and was from the outset heavily propagandistic. Thus it was that the 1972–76 development programme, which was supposed to have incorporated this basic principle of economic planning, first appeared as a public document in draft form in July 1973, and has never been revised and presented as a document for public scrutiny. Moreover, as we shall see later, the actual course of production bore little relationship to the objective of 'feeding, clothing and housing the nation by 1976' which the draft proclaimed.

The third feature of co-operative socialism is that given a tri-sectoral national economic structure (private, state and co-operative), the co-operative sector should be the dominant sector. It is through co-operative ownership and control that the socialist foundations of the society are to be laid. Historically the co-operative sector in Guyana has been and remains a very minuscule part of the national economy. But even among institutions designated as co-operative and founded by the state, e.g. the Guyana National Co-operative Bank, these do not function or operate on co-operative principles. They are usually state-run and operate on ordinary commercial principles, whatever the formal co-operative ownership structure may appear to be. Many of the economically significant co-operatives formed through private initiative also operate on capitalist principles. Thus many co-operatives employ wage labour, as membership does not mean automatic enfranchisement and the owners of the co-operatives then proceed to accumulate on the basis of exploited wage labour. Because of tax concessions afforded to co-operatives many enterprises find the co-operative a convenient form for private accumulation. In addition, many co-operatives are organized with specific and limited objectives in mind, e.g. a land co-operative may be formed in order to acquire a piece of land, but after the land is acquired it is then sub-divided and exploited on an individual basis.

The fourth feature of co-operative socialism as its claim that, as part of 'socialist doctrine', the ruling party (the PNC) is 'paramount' over all other parties and over the state itself. As the government did not come to power either on the basis of free and fair elections, or as the result of a popular social revolution, this is in effect a thinly disguised proclamation of a 'dictatorship'. The policy of paramountcy was enshrined in the creation, in 1973/74, of a new government department, the Ministry of National Development and Office of the General Secretary of the PNC. As the name suggests, the PNC party office was merged into a department of the state and financed through public funds.[1] The state thereafter rapidly proceeded to make it clear that there could be no legal or constitutional change of government. The rigged elections in 1973, the postponement of elections due in 1978 and the rigged elections of 1980, are an indication of how earnestly the process of fascistization of the state developed. A truly authoritarian state (Thomas 1982) has since been entrenched in Guyana. However, before examining in the next section how this degeneration of the polity occurred, it is essential for us to make an important observation on these developments outlined here.

The features of co-operative socialism outlined above were combined with certain publicly self-advertised 'radical' foreign policy initiatives by the state: the recognition of Cuba, support for the Movimento Popular de Libertação de Angola (MPLA) in Angola, militant anti-apartheid rhetoric, support for the 'Arab cause', support for a New International Economic Order, visits to and contacts with Eastern Europe and China, and so on. When examined closely, however, many of these pronouncements can be seen to have been merely propagandistic. Thus support for the MPLA came only during the final stages of the war, the Guyana government having all along given its support to the CIA-backed group: União Nacional para a Independência Total de Angola (UNITA). Recognition of Cuba was also undertaken as part of a broad-based Caribbean initiative embracing regimes of differing outlooks united on the basis of the need to assert an independent and separate identity for the region.

However, despite such evidences of the real worth of government propagandizing in the area of foreign policy, the acts of nationalization plus socialist and other progressive rhetoric produced a number of theorists who argued about the 'radicalization' of the regime (Mars 1978; Mandle 1976, 1978). These were joined by the PPP; the same party which, after the 1973 elections, had launched a programme of 'passive resistance and civil disobedience', began in 1975 to proclaim a policy of 'critical support' for the government because of the 'radical turn' the regime was taking.

The new position held by the PPP reflected its formal adoption of the line of argument contained in the Havana Declaration of 1975, which as

Thomas (1977) has pointed out, was the acceptance by communist and workers' parties of the hemisphere of the application of the 'non-capitalist thesis' of revolutionary democracy to the region. I have developed a critique of this line of argument elsewhere, and while space does not permit the repetition of these arguments here, it is important to note two major points at this stage. One is, that the alleged radicalization of the state in Guyana was accompanied by anti-democratic measures, some of which were indicated above, for example, rigged elections designed to deny the will of the electorate. At the broader democratic level, these developments included the suppression of human rights, trade-union rights, the rule of law, and the traditional 'independence' of the judiciary, etc., in the society. It was clear, therefore, that theorists of the radicalization of the state did not see radicalization as being premised on the increased access of the working class and peasantry to the development of their own forms of democratic organization through which their power could be exercised. On the contrary, radicalization was interpreted here as consistent with the reduction of the limited access of the masses of the working people to these rights and in this view therefore, radicalization and democratic development were in real opposition. Second, the line of argument ignored the internal class struggle and the role the state must necessarily play in the consolidation of a hegemonic class in the capitalist periphery. In the periphery, the state is not only an object of class conquest, thereby constellating in its structure a dominant class, but in the complex circumstances of an underdeveloped bourgeoisie and working class it is the principal instrument for the long-run consolidation of one or other class as the dominant class. In this sense, therefore, radicalization can be measured only in terms of the possibilities opened up for working-class advance in the new state structures and a broadening of the democratic base of the society. This is a necessary, if not sufficient, condition for the consolidation of the position of the emergent working class.

As events have shown, nationalization in Guyana has aided the expansion of the state in all three of the dimensions mentioned earlier (bureaucracy, ideology and military). In so doing it has increased the capacity of the ruling PNC to assert its forms of authoritarian control over 'civil society'. This process, however, required other accompanying developments, and it is to these we turn in the next two sections.

Co-operative socialism: the production crisis

Production and reproduction in the capitalist world economy have always been accompanied by 'crises' and/or 'interruptions' in the process of accumulation. Since the mid-1970s, there has been such a continuing 'crisis/interruption' in the capitalist world economy. In the non-petroleum-producing countries on the capitalist periphery, this has been reflected in low or negative rates of growth of real output per head, increasing unemployment, inflation and acute foreign exchange and balance of payments crises. These, in turn, have exacerbated the wide-spread conditions of poverty which prevail in these societies. Guyana is no exception to this general process, but two characteristics of the society have exacerbated the process. One is the lack of 'legitimacy' of the present regime, given the basis on which it came to power and has held power. The other is that in the process of its consolidation, the regime has greatly expanded the state productive sector through nationalizations, with the state, as we noted, presently controlling over 80 per cent of the economy. Having acquired power in the way that it did the Burnham government has consistently used the state to promote a base in the system of production for the class that it represents. In pursuance of this goal, it has contributed much to the destruction of the productive capability of the traditionally dominant industries which underlines the current economic crisis facing Guyana.

In Guyana a production crisis of unprecedented dimensions has been raging since mid-1975. A decade and a half after independence there has been no noticeable diversification of the economy, as the country remains as dependent as ever on the three traditional primary commodities—rice, bauxite-alumina and sugar. In the agricultural sector, domestic food production and the livestock industry currently average only about 7 per cent of gross domestic product. At the same time manufacturing (other than the processing of rice and sugar) accounts for only 8 per cent of gross domestic product. Despite the absence of any significant diversification of the economy, physical output in the sugar and bauxite-alumina industries has seriously declined, and those industries currently produce at levels substantially below the capacity developed in them over the past fifteen years. Thus, over the period 1980–81, sugar production averaged about 285,000 tons, while the annual rated output capacity of the industry is 450,000 tons. Indeed, as far back as 1971, the industry already produced 369,000 tons. Dried bauxite production in 1980 was 1.6 million tons compared with 2.3 million tons in 1970. Calcined bauxite produced in 1980 was 602,000 tons compared with 692,000 in 1970. Alumina production in 1980 was 211,000 tons as compared with 312,000 tons in 1970. Rice production in 1980 was 160,000 tons as compared with an annual output capacity of 200,000 tons. These output levels were about 20 per cent below the targets set by the government over the period, even though, as can be inferred from the figures given here, targets were substantially below the rated capacity levels of the industries.

The collapse of the traditional producing sectors, with little or no diversification of output taking place, has been accompanied by a deterioration of the services of the various public utilities, a decline in the quality of social services available, and a considerable flight of persons from the country. All the major public services: electricity, pure water supply, public transport, postal services, telephones, and sanitation have deteriorated so much as to constitute major bottlenecks in the production process. Thus electricity 'outages' occur for several hours daily in the main production and residential areas. Public transport is so poor that workers' representatives claim that as many as four hours per day on average have to be spent on commuting to and from work. All the major social services —education, health, social welfare and housing—have also drastically deteriorated. For example, in the state health services foreign medical personnel (mainly from Cuba, India and the Philippines) account for 75 per cent of the doctors. Less than 10 per cent of health personnel are engaged in preventive medicine. In housing, the targeted production for the development plan period 1972–76 was 65,000 housing units; of these 6,000 were built. Since then, because of the collapse of the main producing sectors and declining employment and incomes, housing construction has been at a near standstill. Finally, out of a natural population increase of about 180,000 persons during the inter-censual period 1970–80, approximately one-half, or 90,000, have migrated from Guyana, principally to neighbouring countries in the Caribbean, especially Suriname, Europe and North America.

The result of the above has been a serious decline in real per capita income. Official estimates place this at 15 per cent between 1976 and 1980, but these estimates have been seriously challenged as being too low because of the price deflators used. Unemployment has also been increasing and is now officially estimated at over 40 per cent of the labour force. Between 1976 and 1981, annual rates of inflation have been well into the double digit rate. Official estimates indicate a 70 per cent rise in consumer prices between 1976 and 1980, but this also has been challenged as a serious underestimate. Declining output of the main export commodities together with the inflationary rise in import prices have created a serious balance of payments problem, with additional pressures being placed on the external account by the burden of foreign debt created through the nationalizations discussed above.

The government's initial response to the crisis was to assume it was shortlived, that is, another 'normal' downswing in the post Second World War business cycle. An effort was made to buy time through printing money and borrowing. Between 1973 and 1975 the money supply doubled and between 1975 and 1977 it grew by a further 38 per cent. But by then the problems were clearly not of the usual type, yet between the beginning of 1977 and the end of 1979 the money supply grew by 41 per cent and in 1980–81 it rose again by about 30 per cent. The public debt, which stood at G$267 million in 1970, had risen to G$673 million in 1974, and to G$1.3 billion in 1976; at the end of 1981 it was over G$3.1 billion, of which G$1.9 billion was internal and G$1.2 billion external debt. It is no surprise that this easy money policy was associated with (although it was not necessarily the principal cause of) a progressive decline in external reserves. At the end of 1975, net international reserves were approximately G$200 million, but by the end of 1977 the figure was *minus* G$100 million and at the end of 1980 *minus* G$396 million.

The easy money policy of the initial years only added fuel to the economic crisis which was worsening on the external front on account of a number of structural features, for example the world-wide inflation, the 'oil crisis', and the depression in the main capitalist centres. In the face of these developments, the government turned to the IMF for balance of payments support in 1978. The result was that in August of that year a one-year IMF standby facility of 15 million special drawing rights (SDR) was negotiated but as the expected balance of payments turnaround did not materialize, in August 1979 resort was made to a further three-year extended fund facility. However, the government was unable to meet some of the economic and financial targets set under this arrangement, and the facility was interrupted. As production continued to fall and the turnaround in the balance of payments still did not materialize, in July 1980 a new three-year extended fund facility was agreed upon. This involved a loan of 100 million SDRs, as well as a World Bank structural adjustment loan of US$23.5 million. The former was subsequently increased to 150 million SDRs, or 400 per cent of the Guyana quota of 37.5 million SDRs with the IMF.

The treatment accorded to the PNC regime by these institutions contrasted strongly with the highly publicized destabilizing attitudes which they displayed in their dealings with the Manley regime in Jamaica in the same period. Two factors would seem to account for this difference in attitude. One is, that despite the socialist rhetoric, the Burnham regime, which was installed in the Anglo–US–CIA pre-independence manoeuvre, continued to serve the fundamental interests of American capital better than Manley's 'democratic socialism'. We have noted earlier that in Guyana, opposition to the state comes from the left; in Jamaica, by contrast the main opposition to the Manley regime was the conservative Jamaica Labour Party led by Edward Seaga, the present prime minister. The second factor is that the main lines of government policy genuinely conformed to the IMF recipes for this situation: the economic crisis was seen as first and foremost a crisis of sustained external disequilibrium, and the key to the solution, in conditions where the obvious mismanagement of the state sector meant that export supply increases could not be produced in the short run, was seen as a lowering in the workers' living standards in order to reduce the levels of real consumption; given the high marginal propensity to import, this was expected to achieve a drop in foreign exchange expenditure. Even before the highly publicized resort to the IMF in 1978, i.e., from the first signs of a prolongation of the drain in foreign resources, the government had instituted massive deflationary policies. Thus the 1977 government budget cut public expenditure by 30 per cent. In addition, subsidies on a wide range of consumer items, many of which were introduced during the colonial period to ease the pressures on the poorest sections of the work force, were removed. Indirect taxes were also increased and the state sector proceeded to charge commercial prices for items it produced or handled; this meant, in effect, that they used their monopoly position to generate revenues so that cash surpluses could be achieved. Large-scale retrenchment of the work force in the state sector was instituted.

Later in 1979 this policy was to be extended into a wage freeze that denied to state employees any increase in wages including normal increments. In 1980 and 1981 wage increases of 5 per cent and 7–12 per cent respectively were allowed, but these were substantially below the inflation rate indicated earlier. Finally, expenditure on the social services was also drastically cut from the inception and has continued every year since.

However, despite these deflationary measures and extensive resort to foreign exchange rationing (first introduced by the government in 1976), the balance of payments has shown no signs of reversal. The result was that in 1981 even more massive deflationary measures were introduced and the currency devalued by 18 per cent against the US dollar. It is clear that whatever might have been its original objectives, the policy of deflation has intensified the production crisis outlined above, and continues to do so. To give a few examples, as the availability of public transport has deteriorated and electricity supplies have become grossly irregular and unreliable because of reduced spending and mismanagement of the public utilities, these have hampered production and hindered worker productivity. Workers spend so much time queuing for food or transport, or without electricity and pure water, as to be unable to sustain the required levels of effort at work. The policy of state borrowing to finance expenditures has created a serious fiscal constraint. Thus we find that in 1980 debt charges payments by the state accounted for 37 per cent of current expenditure as compared with 31 per cent for current spending on the social services and 32 per cent on personal emoluments for employees in all government departments.

The repressive escalator

The production crisis and the mismanagement of this in terms of both its internal and international dimensions have been self-reinforcing. This self-reinforcement, which has brought the economy to its present stage of collapse, is also responsible for the emergence of a built-in repressive escalator in the state in Guyana which reflects the dialectical relation between oppression as a ruling-class solution to the present crisis, and a crisis which is increasingly taking the form of popular resistance to the imposition of power as it is constellated in the present state. The economic crisis has become generalized into a social and political crisis, calling into question the very character of the state. This has been brought to issue because of both popular demands for change and the ruling regime's option to rule out all legal or constitutional means of changing the government. In this section we shall briefly outline the working of this thesis as the main point to emerge from the study of the post-colonial state and politics in Guyana.

Stage 1

The first stage of repression developed in response to the situation in which the government sought to enforce a reduction in the real wage in order to overcome the production crisis and its manifestations of declining output, sales and surpluses in the state sector, domestic inflation and foreign exchange and balance of payments crises. Nationalizations having resulted in the state being the major employer of labour, in order to fulfil its class function the state has had to intervene to alter the historically determined system of industrial relations. This has meant among other things: reducing the power of the trade unions; raising to the level of national policy the elimination of all wage payments which have as their aim the restoration of the purchasing power of the worker if the general price level increases; linking all wage increases exclusively to increases in productivity as defined by the state; and taking advantage of the state's position as common employer over a wide range of activities to insist on wage agreements across the board for all unions. This latter has also meant negotiating wages with the central trade union organization and rejecting the historical role of individual unions in the wage determination process. Justification for these measures has been couched in ideological terms, for example 'the need to replace the colonial system of wage determination by a socialist one'; 'strikes in the state sector at a time of economic crisis are treasonable and political', and so on. Here the propagandist aim has been to legitimize the use of the severest force in implementing the state policy of maximizing at all costs the rate of surpluses in the state sector. This policy, as we have noted, has been since 1978 pursued in alliance with the IMF, to which the government has turned for balance of payments support.

The principal focus of repression in stage 1 is containment of workers' rights inherited under the existing system of industrial relations. In pursuit of this the state has employed three broad strategies. The first has been to undermine the *right to work*. As the Guyana Human Rights Association (GHRA) in its 1980–81 report (1981: 39) has pointed out:

the extensive control over employment exercised by the government as a result of 80% of the economy falling within the state sector is being increasingly used as a form of political coercion. A large number of persons have been dismissed, or transferred for reasons which constitute a violation of the right to work. This trend goes back to 1978. Dismissals are not restricted to the State sector, they have occurred in the private sector also under direct pressure from government officials.

The report then proceeds to list, under article 23 of the Universal Declaration of Human Rights and articles 6, 7 and 8 of the Covenant on Social Economic and Cultural Rights, evidence in support of this allegation for the period 1978–81.

The second strategy employed has been to undermine the *right to strike* by invocation of the doctrine of the 'political strike'. This doctrine claims that any strike which the government does not 'approve' as being industrial is in effect 'political'; in these circumstances, 'no holds are barred'. By this is meant that unapproved strikes will be treated as subversive activity, that is as attempts to undermine the state, and that the state is consequently justified in using its full repressive weight to break them. This doctrine was first invoked in 1977 during a strike in the sugar industry, in the course of which military and para-military personnel were brought in to cut the sugar cane, striking workers were physically attacked, and a general campaign of terror introduced into the sugar belt. The doctrine was again invoked in 1978 and 1979 to crush industrial actions by the workers.

The third strategy of the state has been to manipulate the composition of the executives of as many trade unions as it can, in order to determine the final composition of the national Trades Union Council. This has been made possible by resort to rigged union elections and by using the state's 'muscle' as the major employer in the country to determine which union is recognized as bargaining agent. This line of attack reveals that, in a country such as Guyana where there is a noticeable absence of enforceable rights to work, the weapon which the state controls as the principal employer in the country cannot be underestimated.

Stage 2

The second stage of this process of increased repression develops as repression of the work force inexorably spreads to the repression of legality and human rights for all citizens. This progression follows because it is impossible to separate the rights of trade unions and trade unionists from the larger exercise of rights of citizens within a framework of justice. Worker repression therefore requires the setting in place of mechanisms to ensure more generalized repression. This attack on human rights is in the first instance focused on the courts, where efforts are made to 'bend' the judiciary to support the executive arm of the state. Thus in the GHRA report 1980–81 it has been observed: 'The courts have been used as an instrument of political harassment on a widespread scale. This has been made possible by the subordination of the Judiciary to the political executive in a number of ways' (GHRA 1981: 21). It then proceeds to list the following: interference in the appointment of judges; political instructions on specific issues; political interference in specific cases; the Administration of Justice Bill (explained below); the Criminal Law Bill (explained below); blank warrants signed by magistrates; and trials with a political dimension. Specifically, the GHRA report indicated that the Administration of Justice Bill was denounced as 'obnoxious' by the Guyana Bar Association because, among other features, 'it removed in the majority of cases, the right of the accused to elect to be, and to be tried by a judge and jury', and permits the Court of

Appeal to enter 'a guilty verdict even where the accused has been acquitted by jury'. The grave implications of this latter point are fully appreciated when account is taken of the interference in the appointment of judges noted above. The introduction of the Criminal Law Bill was met by a boycott of the courts staged by the Guyana Bar Association. The Organization of Commonwealth Bar Associations also condemned the Bill because of 'its infringement of the citizens' right to trial by jury', and its deliberate aim of having 'retrospective effect on pending criminal proceedings to annul decisions of Courts of Justice and to abrogate the civil liberties of the citizens of Guyana'.

As the mechanisms for more generalized repression are set in train, an important transformation in the nature of resistance becomes manifest. The continuous attack on industrial rights and the merging of industrial rights issues into human rights issues are accompanied by the sub-merging of ethnic differences among the work force and an increasing class solidarity that cuts across traditional racial boundaries. Thus the 1977, 1978 and 1979 strikes saw the bauxite and sugar workers acting in greater unison than they had ever done since 1953.

Stage 3

In the third stage the attacks on due process, legality and human rights generally become increasingly politicized and this leads to a qualitative intensification of the process of fascistization of the state. Opposition political formations organize in defence of democracy, and as claims to a popular base of the state disappear in the face of growing repression, the regime has to extend its repression to opposition political groups in order to survive. To sanction this process under some form of legality, the state is 'legally' restructured, as the existing constitution is found to be 'unworkable' for the newer forms of dictatorship. In this stage political assassination, direct repression of all popular manifestations, and a rapid growth of the security apparatuses of the state take place. These developments are propagandized with the familiar claims of 'law and order', 'the necessities of development of a poor country', and 'we cannot afford the luxuries of democracy'. The fascistization of the state is now very much on the way and from here on, the government, through state-manipulation, propaganda and force, makes it unmistakably clear that it cannot be changed by legal or constitutional means.

Evidence in support of the workings of the repressive escalator as it leads up to the constitutional restructuring of the state can be gleaned from the following:

(i)   The rigging of national elections held in 1973.

(ii)   Local government elections constitutionally due every two years since 1970 were never held.

(iii)   When national elections constitutionally fell due in 1978, they were postponed, and in their stead a national referendum was held. Under the previous constitution, only a referendum could change entrenched provisions, for example, the life of Parliament. The purpose of the referendum was to remove the referendum safeguard so that these entrenched provisions could be changed by a two-thirds majority in Parliament, which the PNC had already rigged the 1973 election in order to acquire. A Committee of Concerned Citizens (1978) who surveyed the 1978 referendum claimed that the maximum possible turnout of voters was 14.01 per cent, yet the government claimed a turnout of 71.45 per cent of the voters, with itself winning 97.7 per cent of the votes cast!

(iv)   National elections were held under a new constitution in 1980. A team of international observers sponsored by the Guyana Human Rights Association who came to Guyana during the election period to observe these denounced the elections as the 'most blatant fraud'. They went on to point out in their report (International Team of Observers 1980: 28) that:

We came to Guyana aware of the serious doubts expressed about the conduct of previous elections there, but determined to judge these elections on their own merit and hoping that we should be able to say that the result was fair. We deeply regret that, on the contrary, we were obliged to conclude, on the basis of abundant and clear evidence, that the election was rigged massively and flagrantly. Fortunately, however, the scale of the fraud made it impossible to conceal either from the Guyanese public or the outside world.

Because the new constitution which came into operation in 1980 marks the formal stage of the restructuring of the state as the process of fascistization proceeds, the nature of this restructuring as it is revealed in the provisions of the constitution requires brief mention. Under the 1980 constitution, by 'law', Burnham became executive president before elections were held, but nevertheless 'as if he had been elected thereto'. The dictatorial purposes of the constitution are revealed in the array of powers that the executive president commands. Thus:

(a)   Article 182 (1) says that the President 'shall not be personally answerable to any court for the performance of the functions of his office or for any act done in the performance of those functions, and no proceedings, whether criminal or civil, shall be instituted against him in his personal capacity in respect thereof either during his term of office or thereafter'.

(b)   In the constitution, the President is head of state, supreme executive authority and commander-in-chief. In addition he is supreme over the National Assembly, the local democratic organs, the National Congress of Local Democratic Organs and the Supreme Congress of the People, all created by the new constitution. This supremacy is embodied in his powers 'to summon, suspend or dissolve all' these so-called 'democratic' and 'supreme' organs. He also has a veto over the elected National Assembly.

(c) The President's powers also require him to appoint the chairpersons of the Elections Commission, the Public Service Commission, the Police Service Commission, the Judicial Commission and the Teachers' Commission. In addition, he has the power to appoint either a majority of the members or the whole of each commission. Furthermore, the President appoints the army chief of staff and all army commanders, the director-general of the National Service and all the deputy directors-general, the commissioner of police and his deputies, the attorney-general, the chancellor of the judiciary, the chief justice, the director of public prosecutions and literally every other important official of the state. In these circumstances, the practice noted by the GHRA in its report (GHRA 1981: 7) for: 'Burnham ..., to adopt the dress of the Chief-of-Staff of the Army (he is the only general), the Commissioner of Police, and so on' takes on a significance greater than that of a national joke.

The absolute powers conferred on Executive President Burnham under the constitution mirror the absolute powers conferred on him as 'leader' of the PNC. In that party's constitution it is stated that:

the reserve powers of the Leader are (a) If the Leader in his deliberate judgement is of the opinion that a situation of emergency has arisen in the Party, he shall have power notwithstanding any provision in these Rules, on giving written notice to the General Secretary of his opinion, to take all action that he may in his absolute discretion consider necessary to correct such a situation; *and for this purpose he may assume and exercise any or all of the powers of the Biennial Delegates' Congress, the General Council, the Central Executive Committee, any other Committee, Group, Arm, Organ or of any officer or official of the* Party. [Our emphasis] (b) If General Council, the Central Executive Committee or the Administrative Committee has not been constituted or for any reason cannot function, the Leader may exercise all or any of its powers or may authorize such members as he may deem fit to exercise its powers for the time being.

The stages of repression highlighted here should not be interpreted mechanistically. They are the products of the dialectical interaction of the main forces of repression (the state) and liberation (the workers, independent trade unions, opposition parties, democratic social groups, and so on). Because of the dialectical nature of this process, other issues have to be borne in mind when studying the state and politics during this period. In Guyana the use of state violence, political murder and open terroristic rule which characterizes the third stage of the fascistization of the state is associated with the increasing militarization of the society. A number of new military and para-military agencies, all pledged to defend the ruling party, have been created: the National Service, the People's Militia, the Pioneers, the National Guard Service and an armed Youth arm of the ruling party, the Young Socialist Movement. Danns (1978) estimated that by 1977 Guyana had a ratio of 1:35 of the population in one or other military or para-military organization. This total does not include what the GHRA in its 1980–81 report has termed the 'private strong arm groups . . . the most notorious [being] a sect known as the House of Israel, whose members are freely used by the ruling party to break up opposition meetings' (GHRA 1981: 7).

Over this period, the rapid growth in the numbers of security personnel has also been associated with an increasing orientation of the state towards 'security' matters, which is another way of saying towards the harassment and containment of the regime's political opposition. This occurrence has added to the burdens on the economy in two principal directions. Firstly, it constitutes an 'economically non-productive' utilization of the social surplus, while secondly, it increases the orientation of the state to its self-preservation above all else, with the usual consequences for public sector efficiency and productivity.

Finally, it should be noted that the process of militarization has been accompanied with the progressive politicization of the security services. This began with efforts to make the security forces act and think partisanly, in favour of the ruling party. It is for this reason that such rituals as the daily raising of the national flag are combined with the daily raising of the PNC flag in places such as National Service camps, and the attendance of security personnel (in mufti) to party rallies is enforced. The deprofessionalization of the security services which this entails, however, does not stop here. It leads one stage further into the constitution of a definite PNC 'political element' within the security services. This is somewhat akin to the development of the 'political police' within developed fascist states, and constitutes in Guyana an important stage in the transformation of state and political relations.

Historically, ruling classes have preferred the *threat* of the sanction of the force which they monopolize, rather than its routine use, as the basis of their rule. In other words, government with the 'consent' of the governed is always sought after in class societies. That is why the development of open terroristic forms of rule always signifies a particular stage of degeneracy in the political culture. In this regard Guyana offers no exception. The increased resort to terroristic rule by the regime is the dialectical opposite of increased popular resistance to the present form of state domination. But because such methods are not compatible with the long-run survival of the regime, it has sought to combine its increasing militarization with increased control of the ideological and propaganda arms of the state. The hope is always that the more successful the propaganda, the less the need to resort to physical repression, which by its nature is more obvious than other forms of repression and thus increases the chances of armed uprising by the oppressed classes and groups. In Guyana, the PNC has used all the ideological apparatuses of the state to project its legitimacy and paramountcy. The chief ideological line has been to identify the 'leader' Burnham as embodying the PNC, the PNC as embodying the state, and the state as being identical with the country as a whole, or with society at large. All anti-PNC or anti-Burnham activity is therefore projected as being anti-state or anti-national and hence subversive. This ideological stance has also been associated with calls for unity of all peoples and classes (though not of all parties) in the country in the face of the economic difficulties which have been 'thrust' on the country by developments in the world economy. For obvious reasons no local mismanagement of the economy is ever admitted as a major or contributory factor. More recently, this national consensus rhetoric has been linked with calls to produce more and to defend the country against territorial claims being made by Venezuela.

The means to put this propaganda into effect has been the nationalization of the private media, allied with administrative or other obstacles to the publishing by independent or opposition groups and their exclusion from the use of state organs to propagandize their ideas. Thus, in Guyana, the so-called 'national' radio stations and 'national' press function as PNC in the most insulting of senses. The language used, and the style of reporting, perhaps give the quickest insights into the degeneracy of the political culture that has accompanied the dictatorship. Meanwhile, the opposition is refused newsprint; as in the case of the party organ of the PPP, the *Mirror*, and a democratic church newspaper, the *Catholic Standard*, is denied the use of the state facilities to print; the organ of the Working People's Alliance (*Dayclean*) is published illegally, with two of its leading members going to prison for this reason; and the printing machinery and equipment of trade unions and other opposition groupings being frequently 'seized' by the police.

These controls of the media facilitate cover-ups of the evidence of terroristic methods of rule. Even the national Parliament cannot be heard or read through these media, thereby removing the last vestige of Parliament's usefulness to the opposition. Thus it was possible to clamp the news lid on the infamous 'crime of the century', the Jonestown murders, the murders of Teekah (a government Minister of Education) and the assassinations of Walter Rodney, Ohene Koama, Edward Dublin and Fr. Drake. As the GHRA in its 1980–81 report has pointed out (GHRA 1981: 28):

Strict political control is exerted over the content of the *Chronicle* and the state-owned radio. This is done by directive and personal intervention rather than by a formal censorship arrangement. The extent to which news is kept from the Guyanese people can be judged by the fact that an event as important as Jonestown was learnt by the Guyanese people from the BBC over 24 hours after it had happened. An instance of gross distortion is the manner in which the death of Walter Rodney was reported. For almost 12 hours the national radio carried a story to the effect that a man had been killed when a bomb which he was carrying exploded, but that the man was unrecognizable because his face had been blown off. In fact, Rodney's face was not in the slightest way disfigured and he was immediately recognizable. Distortions of events reached such proportions that in February 1980 a directive was circulated to all members of the *Chronicle* staff to the effect that 'contrived' photographs must no longer be used, and that the newspaper 'must never be seen to be lying on behalf of the government'.

A further complement to this misuse of the media has been attempts to force the participation of the public in PNC events. State employees are routinely forced to attend PNC party events at the risk of being fired. When these events are held, state facilities are commandeered and given over to the PNC free of charge to organize them. This development is, of course, common to many dictatorships, particularly in the context of a populist tradition in politics such as we have in Guyana. More threatening, however, is the stage in this phenomenon when the dictator comes to believe that the crowds are evidence of 'real' support, and that the unpopularity of the regime is merely due to the propagandizing of a few dissidents and opposition elements who should be removed. This stage of self-deception is the most dangerous, as it merges into the use of state violence and political murder. In this process the regime misjudges its own capacity for action (i.e. repression), and the extent to which this will be 'popularly' accepted. In the process of finding out its miscalculation, however, the historical evidence shows that many, many tragedies have occurred.

As the repressive escalator operates, the divorce of elementary forms of the democratic process from the state machinery rapidly proceeds and deprives the state of all its pretences to be 'building socialism'. The growth of state property is more and more clearly seen as a path of development for those in control of the state. Even in the so-called co-operative sector this is rapidly observed, as consumer and producer co-operatives alike are organized along capitalist lines, with extensive use of wage labour and accumulation by a few proceeding apace. Meanwhile, in the state sector, capitalist managerial prerogatives prevail and worker control is absent. In the absence of any alteration of the capital–labour relation, those who control the state machinery use their prerogatives to help their stratum/class (mainly through family and friends) to accumulate wealth in enterprises which they privately own. Given the colonial forms of domination that have historically prevailed, the location of the petty bourgeoisie in the system of economic reproduction in Guyana was initially somewhat tenuous. Consequently, as we have pointed out previously, the state is being used as the principal instrument to secure the material basis for the extended social reproduction of this class. As this process develops, however, the class character of the state becomes more and more obvious, and the state capitalist form which 'co-operative socialism' takes degenerates into openly authoritarian forms of rule. This development is generated both by the internal contradictions referred to here and the specific manner of Guyana's insertion into the capitalist world system. Indeed, it is the pattern of this insertion that principally explains the rapid generalization within Guyana of the present structural crisis of world capitalism.

Conclusion

The degeneration of the state capitalist model in the face of the structural crisis of world capitalism and the internal crisis in Guyana into authoritarian forms of state rule, raises one question which I would like to tackle briefly by way of conclusion, that is, the issue of the relation of political democracy to socialism. This question I have discussed in a number of other places (Thomas 1978, 1982) and the main burden of my position is that socialism cannot be built without a democratization of all social relations, including the power relations of the state. It follows, therefore, that we must bear the following in mind when assessing co-operative socialism in Guyana:

(i)   All democratic rights within the society have to be seen as the gains of mass struggles and not gifts bestowed by the former colonial masters to be taken away at the behest of their inheritors in the post-colonial situation.

(ii)   The task of socialist development, if it is being seriously pursued, has to rest on the progress of these rights in the society and on their progressive endowment with socio-economic content.

(iii)   Bread (i.e. development) cannot be traded for justice (i.e. social equality) as is commonly propagandized by the state in Guyana, for in the context of historically determined underdevelopment there can be no development to socialism that is not based on justice.

(iv)   Political democracy and socialism are therefore not counterposed as far as working-class interests are concerned. They are counterposed by the propagandists of the ruling class only in order to bolster its claims to hegemony.

The authoritarian state form that has accompanied the growth of state capitalism in Guyana is therefore the direct antithesis of socialism. This view is an old, sometimes forgotten, one, in socialist theory. As it is impossible to improve on Rosa Luxemburg's formulation of it (Looker 1974: 244–245) I shall quote an important, but frequently neglected observation of hers:

Freedom only for the supporters of the government, only for the members of party—however numerous they may be—is no freedom at all. Freedom is always and exclusively freedom for the one who thinks differently. Not because of any fanatical concept of 'justice' but because all that is instructive, wholesome and purifying in political freedom depends on this essential characteristic, and its effectiveness vanishes when 'freedom' becomes a special privilege.

She then goes on to warn (Looker 1974: 246–247):

The public life of countries with limited freedom is so poverty-stricken, so miserable, so rigid, so unfruitful, precisely because, through the exclusion of democracy, it cuts off the living sources of all spiritual riches and progress. Public control is indispensably necessary. Otherwise the exchange of experiences remains only with the closed circle of the officials of the new regime. Corruption becomes inevitable ... with the repression of political life in the land as a whole, life in the soviets must also become more and more crippled. Without general elections, without unrestricted freedom of press and assembly, without a free struggle of opinion, life dies out in every public institution, becomes a mere semblance of life, in which only the bureaucracy remains as the active element. Public life gradually falls asleep, a few dozen party leaders of inexhaustible energy and boundless experience direct and rule. Among them, in reality only a dozen outstanding heads do the leading and an elite of the working class is invited from time to time to meetings where they are to applaud the speeches of the leaders, and to approve proposed resolutions unanimously—at bottom, then, a clique affair—a dictatorship, to be sure, not the dictatorship of the proletariat, however, but only the dictatorship of a handful of politicians.

The relationship highlighted here between the democratization of the state and political relations and the building of socialism reinforces the earlier observation that was made: that in Guyana the expansion of state property has nothing to do with socialism. State property of itself does not automatically ensure the use and management of those resources by the people, which constitutes a fundamental condition of the socialist path of development. Indeed state property can, as it has happened in Guyana, produce the worst of all possible worlds. In the first instance, state property has not solved, or even seriously approached, the problems of lack of national control over the economy. Indeed, because of slow rates of growth of output, productivity and surpluses in the state sector, the society's ability to exercise control over the national economy has been further reduced and not enhanced. The most crippling manifestation of this has been the operational constraints posed by the acute foreign exchange crisis that has plagued the country. Because state property has been promoted principally to strengthen the positions of the ruling petty bourgeoisie, it has also fostered the growth of corruption, elitism and clientelism in the society. At the same time, in the absence of any real socialist intent on the part of those who control the state machinery, the work force has not been promoted into positions of effective control in these enterprises. Indeed, these state enterprises, sensitive to declining rates of profit, have sought to reduce the effectiveness of existing worker organizations. This has occurred because of the need to contain wage demands in the face of declining living standards in the country and also because of the broader intent of containing the political power of working-class organizations in the society; thereby serving the real class interests of those who control the state.

NOTE

1 It was the burning of this building in July 1979 that led to charges of arson against three members of a political grouping known as the Working

People's Alliance (WPA). This led to loud popular protest, mass demonstrations, and the transformation of the WPA into a political party in the same month. In 1980 one of the three accused, Walter Rodney, was assassinated by state agents. Later in 1981 the other two accused (Roopnarine and Omawale) were acquitted. The state has appealed against the decision.

REFERENCES

Burnham, L. F. S. 1970, 'A vision of the co-operative republic', in L. Searwar (ed.), *Cooperative republic: Guyana*, Georgetown, Guyana

Burnham, L. F. S. 1975, *Declaration of Sophia: address by Prime Minister to the special congress, 10th anniversary of the PNC government*, Georgetown, Guyana

Committee of Concerned Citizens 1978, *A report on the referendum held in Guyana, 16 July 1978*, Guyana

Danns, G. K. 1978, 'Militarization and development: an experiment in nation building', *Transition*, vol. 1, no. 1, pp. 23–44

Guyana Human Rights Association 1981, *Human rights report: January 1980-June 1981*, Georgetown, Guyana

International Team of Observers at the Elections in Guyana 1980, *Report: December 1980*, London, Parliamentary Human Rights Group, House of Commons, reprinted by the Guyana Human Rights Association, 1981

Jagan, C. 1966, *The west on trial*, Berlin, Seven Seas Publications

Kwayana, E. 1976, 'Pseudo-socialism', paper presented to seminar, University of the West Indies, Trinidad

Looker, R. (ed.) 1974, *Rosa Luxemburg: selected political writings*, New York, Grove Press

Mandle, J. 1976, 'Continuity and change in Guyanese underdevelopment', *Monthy review*, vol. 28, no. 4, pp. 37–50

Mandle, J. 1978, 'The post-colonial mode of production in Guyana', University of Guyana and Temple University, mimeo.

Mars, P. 1978, 'Co-operative socialism and marxist scientific theory', *Caribbean issues*, vol. 4, no. 2, pp. 71–106

Thomas, C. Y. 1974, *Dependence and transformation: the economics of the transition to socialism*, New York and London, Monthly Review Press

Thomas, C. Y. 1976, 'Bread and justice: the struggle for socialism in Guyana', *Monthly review*, vol. 28, no. 4, pp. 23–35

Thomas, C. Y. 1977, 'The non-capitalist path as theory and practice of decolonization and socialist transformation', *Latin American perspectives*, vol. 5, no. 2, pp. 10–28

Thomas C. Y. 1978, *Plantations, peasants and state: a study of the modes of sugar production in Guyana*, ILO Report, forthcoming as a book

Thomas, C. Y. 1981, 'From colony to state capitalism', *Transition*, issue V

Thomas, C. Y. 1982, *The rise of the authoritarian state: an essay on the state in the capitalist periphery*, forthcoming

THREE

Achievements and Contradictions of the Cuban Workers' State

Jean-Pierre Beauvais

On 1 January 1981, the Cuban revolution celebrated its twenty-second anniversary. Meeting a few days earlier in Havana, the Second Congress of the Cuban Communist Party (CCP) had focused attention on international policy: its spectacular reaffirmation of solidarity with Nicaragua, Grenada and the popular mobilization in El Salvador and Guatemala; its firm, unyielding stand in face of the growing threats which the inauguration of Ronald Reagan would bring to bear on the Cuban workers' state; its convergence with the Soviet position on the Polish crisis (Maitan 1981). This was enough to overshadow the other questions on the congress agenda. In his closing speech, addressed to a crowd of several hundred thousand in Revolution Square, Fidel Castro himself reinforced this emphasis by declaring: 'Our congress has above all been internationalist!'

And yet, a crucial part of Castro's long speech, and hence of the congress itself, was devoted to economic questions. The task had been to analyse the results of the first five-year plan (1976–80), to adopt broad outlines of the second plan (1981–85), and to draw an initial balance sheet of the 'gradual and accelerating' implementation of the new System of Economic Management and Planning, launched in 1978 on the basis of general orientations that the First CCP Congress had adopted in December 1975.

The first part of this chapter, dealing with some of the existing achievements and weaknesses of the Cuban economy, should be related to this congress balance sheet.

Still at the level of the economy, however, the Second Congress closed a crucial decade that spanned the failure to reach the 10-million tonne *zafra* (sugar harvest) in 1970, and the general application of the new 'management system' in the latter part of 1980. Between these two dates, new strategies gradually took shape with regard to the organization, planning, management and control of economic activity, and of work in particular.

In the last analysis, many of these policy decisions were an attempt to raise the dramatically low level of labour productivity; to solve perhaps the most striking of the many contradictions of the Cuban revolution— namely, the very high political consciousness and low 'economic consciousness' of the masses.

It is above all in this light that the second part of the chapter discusses some of the measures designed to relaunch the economy, taken between 1971 and 1974, as well as the main orientations of the central event in these generally decisive years: the thirteenth congress of the CTC (the Cuban Workers' Federation). The chapter goes on to examine some features of the new System of Economic Management, which systematizes and deepens the approach adopted in the early 1970s.

1980: The struggle against underdevelopment, gains and problems

The spate of figures in Fidel Castro's four-hour congress report on economic matters did not convey anything really new about the achievements and broad guidelines at the end of the first five-year plan. Essentially, they confirmed at a global level what the partial analyses and statistics of previous years already suggested to be the case.

1   *The sugar industry*, still the basic sector of the Cuban economy, recorded considerable progress: after 1972, when it reached a bottom of 4.3 million tonnes, output grew continually to 7.9 million tonnes in 1979 (see table 3.1). Major new investment (some $1,250m since 1976), together with improved co-ordination of the industry, led to higher agricultural productivity on the plantations, greater mechanization of cane-cutting, and a rise in the capacity and industrial output of the refineries.[1] Four results should be particularly stressed:

(a)   The total area of irrigated land rose from some 50,000 hectares in 1959 to 467,000 in 1980.

(b)   More rational and systematic attention was paid to cultivation practices: the area receiving nitrogenous fertilizer rose 250 per cent between 1976 and 1980, while the total consumption of such fertilizer nearly doubled.

(c)   45 per cent of cane-cutting was mechanized, mainly with machinery from Cuban industry, although this was still short of the level on which hopes were set a few years earlier.

(d)   Forty refineries were enlarged or modernized, two brought into operation for the first time, and two more placed under construction. These were the first new refineries built in Cuba for fifty years, and nearly 60 per cent of their equipment was produced in the country.

2   Despite the progress of the sugar industry, and despite its 'strategic' importance in the economy (85.9 per cent of the value of Cuban exports in 1979), *its weight within the social product* (the annual total of goods and productive services) *has continually declined* from 22 per cent in 1959 to 7.4 per cent in 1975 to 6.1 per cent, according to the latest statistics, in 1980. This is the best indication of the recent progress in agricultural diversification and, above all, industrial development.

3   The progress in *agricultural diversification* is demonstrated by the fact that while the total area devoted to sugar cane increased only slightly in the last ten years, 500,000 hectares of unploughed land, and 1,800,000

TABLE 3.1 Cuba: production, export and export price of sugar (1959–79)

Year	'000 tonnes		US cents per lb	
	Sugar production	Sugar exports	Price paid by USSR	World-market price
1959	6,039	4,951	—	2.97
1960	5,943	5,634	—	3.14
1961	6,876	6,413	4.09	2.75
1962	4,882	5,132	4.09	2.83
1963	3,833	3,520	6.11	8.34
1964	4,475	4,176	6.11	5.77
1965	6,156	5,316	6.11	2.08
1966	4,537	4,435	6.11	1.81
1967	6,236	5,683	6.11	1.92
1968	5,165	4,612	6.11	1.90
1969	4,459	4,799	6.11	3.20
1970	8,538	6,906	6.11	3.68
1971	5,925	5,511	6.11	4.50
1972	4,325	4,140	6.11	7.27
1973	5,253	4,797	12.02	9.45
1974	5,930	5,491	19.64	29.66
1975	6,315	5,744	30.40	20.37
1976	6,156	5,764	30.95	11.51
1977	6,485	6,238	35.73	8.14
1978	7,328	7,231	40.78	7.80
1979	7,992	—	—	—

Sources: Statistical yearbooks of Cuba; National Bank of Cuba, *Development and Prospects of the Cuban Economy*; CEPAL; *Statistical Bulletin* of the International Sugar Organization.

hectares[2] of natural grassland, were brought under cultivation. Output rose very considerably in the cases of rice, tubers and market-garden produce. Above all, citrus-fruit production increased 60 per cent during the first five-year plan, reaching 400,000 tonnes in 1980 and has now become a major new export area (200,000 tonnes in 1980). At the same time, the production of poultry meat and pork doubled in comparison with the 1971–75 period—from 140,000 to 290,000 tonnes in the latter case. The milk supply rose by 54 per cent, and the annual output of eggs also increased spectacularly (see table 3.2).

TABLE 3.2 Cuba: egg production (millions)

Year	
1962	175
1970	1,403
1975	1,749
1980 (est.)	over 2,100

Source: Statistical yearbooks of Cuba.

4   *Industrial growth*, with some important yearly variations, has averaged 6.25 per cent since 1961. For the last five years, the total output of basic industries (electricity, fuels, fertilizer, steel, machinery, mining) rose 5 per cent, while light industry, mainly thanks to textiles, expanded by 23 per cent. Four examples will serve to illustrate this development of industry:

(a)   Steel production, non-existent in 1959, was slightly higher than 400,000 tonnes per annum at the end of the five-year plan.

(b)   In value terms, the mechanical and electronic industries had a higher annual output than the sugar-refining industry: refrigerators, cooking stoves, radio and television sets were produced mainly in Cuba; buses were assembled on the basis of imported chassis; and equipment for the production and processing of sugar was exported in significant quantity.

(c)   Annual cement production, now some 230 kg per head of the population, is by far the highest among the so-called 'developing' countries.

(d)   The brand-new fishing industry has recently overtaken in value terms Cuba's traditional mineral product, nickel.

5   The Cuban leadership reaffirmed its preference for *collective over private consumption*—a deliberate policy ever since the early days of the revolution. In the future, however, private consumption will greatly benefit from the development of electric consumer goods and various light industries. As was shown by the Peruvian embassy crisis and the subsequent flood of departures to the United States, minority sections of the population do not accept the priority given to collective consumption. Reinforced by their awareness of this, imperialist propagandists have often used the empty shop windows as ammunition against the revolution. At certain periods, the restrictions have indeed been very severe.[3] But particularly in view of the results, it is unquestionable that the priority is accepted by the great majority of Cubans, and that it actually corresponds to their interests.

The overall results provide the best current example, anywhere in the world, of a victorious struggle against the terrible social effects of imperialist domination and economic 'underdevelopment'. Let us take the cases of education and health.

6   The extent of the achievement in *education* is apparent from table 3.3 alone.

(a)   The third great stage in the development of the educational system is well on the way to completion. The first two stages were the great literacy campaign and the 'level-six battle', which sought to ensure that the whole population, both child and adult, received a full primary education. Once that had been achieved, a 'level-nine battle' was set in motion. In two years' time, all children of school age will follow the first cycle of secondary education. At the start of the 1980–81 school

TABLE 3.3 Cuba: pupils enrolled by type of education

Type of education	School year			
	1958–59	1970–71	1975–76	1979–80
Primary				
(pre-school to level 6: 5–11 years of age)	717,400	1,664,600	1,922,400	1,672,900
Secondary	88,100	239,199	606,750	1,150,300
1st cycle (level 7–10)	63,500	171,200	382,600	690,500
2nd cycle (level 11–13)		15,500	37,700	135,300
Technical and occupational	15,600	27,899	102,750	214,600
Teacher training (primary and 1st secondary cycle)	9,000	24,600	83,700[a]	109,900[a]
Higher	21,000	35,137	89,957	146,240[b]
Special (handicapped children)	134	7,880	12,483	25,026

Notes: [a] The figures for 1975–76 and 1979–80 include students at teachers' colleges for the first secondary cycle, and qualified first-cycle teachers following an in-service course.
[b] These figures only include students enrolled in a higher-education centre coming under the ministry. They do not include students abroad, or higher-level training within the army and party or at special occupational evening courses. According to a survey published in *Granma weekly review*, 16 November 1980, all these additional categories accounted for 53,960 students in the year 1979–80.
Sources: Ministry of Education, Havana; *Statistical Yearbook of Cuba, 1976*; Report by Humberto Pérez, president of the Central Planning Council, to the second session of the People's Power Assembly, December 1977; Documents of the Second Congress of the Cuban Communist Party, December 1980.

year, 98.5 per cent of children leaving primary school went on to secondary courses: the 'level-nine battle' may already be considered won.
(b)   The whole educational system, including equipment, books, transport and very often food is free of charge from the kindergarten to university.
(c)   The government has conducted a systematic adult-education policy, which closely relates study to work and constantly strives to adapt the educational system to the requirements of economic development. In this field, however, the results still appear to be limited.
(d)   Early stress on the quantitative side (free universal education for nine years) led to neglect of the quality of most higher or specialized education. No doubt this is one reason why *the massive development of education has had little effect on labour productivity*. Unfortunately, the recent introduction of 'Marxism-Leninism' classes at every level of the educational system, following syllabuses 'imported' from the Soviet Union, is not very likely to improve the situation.

7   It is in the *health sector* that spectacular infrastructural development has been most clearly combined with experimental innovation. The Cuban public health system now has enough decentralized units, with enough resources and skilled personnel, to practise genuinely preventive medicine, free of charge. Not only does this create a different kind of relationship between doctor and patient, but the population itself, through the local structures of people's power (Beauvais 1981) is ever more involved in the organization and development of health-care centres.[4]

Tables 3.4 and 3.5 illustrate two aspects of what has been achieved: a rise in the number of consultations and the availability of preventive medicine; and a very sharp drop in mortality rates.

TABLE 3.4 Cuba: medical consultations

	1963		1973		1976	
	No.	No. per head	No.	No. per head	No.	No. per head
Total	14,575,478	2.0	39,971,851	4.4	45,011,622	4.7
Not involving hospitalization	10,223,963	1.4	24,127,533	2.6	25,650,702	2.7
Emergencies	3,650,703	0.5	10,514,281	1.1	12,254,287	1.3
Dentistry	700,812	0.1	5,330,037	0.6	7,106,633	0.7

Source: Ministry of Public Health, Havana; CEPAL Publications.

TABLE 3.5 Cuba: Mortality rates (per 1,000 inhabitants)

	1958	1974	1976	1979
General	6.3	5.6	5.5	5.4
Infant (0–1 years)	33.4	27.9	22.9	19.3
Pre-school (1–4 years)	2.7	1.2	1.0	0.9
School (5–14 years)	0.7	0.4	0.4	0.4

Sources: Ministry of Public Health, Havana; Report by Fidel Castro to the Second Congress of the Cuban Communist Party.

It should be added by way of comparison that the average density of doctors is higher in Cuba than in France (159 against 135 per 100,000 inhabitants), and that life expectancy at birth is reaching the level of the most highly developed countries (74 years for women, 71.5 for men).

All these gains, resulting from a very high rate of accumulation,[5] should not blind us to two crucial problems with which we shall now deal.

8   As table 3.6 shows, the economy is still dependent upon sugar as the main export product. This has a number of consequences.

TABLE 3.6 Cuba: structure of exports, 1980 (%)

Sugar	85.9
Mining	4.6
Tobacco	1.7
Fishing	2.8
Others	5.0

Source: State Statistics Committee, Havana.

Sugar-dependence entails dependence upon fluctuations in the world-market price—even though long-term bilateral agreements with the Soviet Union, linking the price of Cuban sugar sales to the price of Soviet oil, have mitigated this effect (see table 3.1).

Since sugar exports are a major source of *accumulation*, it is this which, in the last analysis, remains partially dependent upon world-market fluctuations. Thus the first five-year plan, drawn up at the end of 1975, had fixed an average yearly growth rate of 6 per cent for the 1976–80 period. But then the price of sugar, which had averaged 29.66 cents a pound in 1974 and reached an all-time peak of 65.18 cents in November, plummeted to 7.80 cents a pound in 1978 (see table 3.1). This reduced the financial resources available, so that the accumulation targets rapidly proved to be unattainable.

In particular, the plan had envisaged industrial investment of the order of $15,000m over the five-year period, only a third of which would come from the USSR and other Comecon countries. But the large shortfall in foreign-currency earnings from the free sugar market forced the planners to cut back sharply on investment projects.[6]

Sugar failed as a source of accumulation throughout the first years of the 1976–80 plan, its average world-market price being equivalent to 55 per cent of average world production costs (Castro, F. 1980). As a result, Cuban foreign trade showed a clear and constant decline after sugar prices began to drop in 1975. In 1978, for instance, imports from Europe, Canada and Japan were 22.1 per cent down on 1977, and this strengthened still further the dominant role of trade with Comecon countries.

Table 3.7, which should be read in conjunction with table 3.1, affords an overview of Cuba's foreign trade since 1970.

9   The structural deficit of Cuba's foreign trade is apparent from table 3.7. For although the *size* of this deficit largely varies with the selling price of sugar, its structural character cannot be explained in these terms alone. Among the other factors are a total dependence on imported energy supplies, and the effect of inflation on the price of numerous equipment goods required for the industrialization drive.

This ever-growing problem may result in a veritable bottleneck.

TABLE 3.7 Cuba: principal indicators of foreign trade
(million pesos)

	1970	1971	1972	1973	1974	1975	1976	1977	1978
Total exports	1,050	861	771	1,153	2,237	2,947	2,692	2,912	3,417
USSR	529	304	224	477	811	1,661	1,638	2,066	2,496
'Other workers' states'	248	261	197	268	472	341	452	378	410
Rest of world	273	296	350	408	954	945	602	468	511
Total imports	1,311	1,387	1,190	1,463	2,226	3,113	3,180	3,433	3,558
USSR	691	731	714	811	1,025	1,250	1,490	1,858	2,317
'Other workers' states'	226	239	200	224	328	354	374	467	516
Rest of world	394	417	276	428	873	1,509	1,316	1,108	725
Total balance	−261	−526	−419	−310	11	−166	−488	−521	−141
USSR	−162	−427	−490	−334	−214	411	148	208	179
'Other workers' states'	22	22	−3	44	144	−13	78	−89	−106
Rest of world	−121	−121	74	−20	81	−564	−714	−640	−214

Source: Statistical yearbooks of Cuba.

According to several converging estimates, Cuba's cumulative debt with non-Comecon countries now stands at $2,700m—that is, five times more than the country's yearly export revenue in convertible currencies.

10   Although Fidel Castro's 1980 report makes a brief and very hazy reference to a 3.4 per cent rise in labour productivity,[7] the level is still *extremely low* in the economy as a whole and in each sector of activity. An example from the construction industry will show the scale of the problem: a Havana block of flats, about ten storeys high, takes an average of five years to build, even though the technology is modern (with, in particular, many prefabricated elements), and even though 30 per cent more workers are employed than on an equivalent site in France.[8] Throughout the 1970s, labour productivity was a central source of concern for the Cuban leadership in its choice of economic policies. Numerous examples mentioned in the press, as well as leadership speeches and the empirical evidence of my own visits to a few workplaces, cannot fail to suggest that this is indeed a major problem.

1970–80: the decade of productivity

The failure of the 1970 campaign for a record 10-million tonne *zafra* or sugar harvest is rightly seen as an event that had decisive consequences at one moment in the history of the Cuban revolution. In 1969–70 the mass of the population and the whole of the economic apparatus were mobilized for this objective. The campaign symbolized and brought to an end the economic orientation pursued in previous years, especially since 1966. Its most evident feature was voluntarism, both in its production targets and in the means used to achieve them. Three aspects may serve to illustrate this policy.

1 In 1966 the power and functions of JUCEPLAN (the Central Planning Council) were reduced. The attempt made between 1962 and 1965 to work out a medium-term economic plan was abandoned, and in practice even annual plans were largely discarded. The work of establishing a statistical apparatus, set in motion in the preceding years, fell into total neglect. Instead, a series of 'special plans' or 'mini-plans', each relating to a very narrow sector of activity, were launched under the direct responsibility of Fidel Castro. In theory, they were to involve a very high level of centralization: the adoption of a 'mini-plan' would entail that a particular sector had priority over others in such fields as investment and the supply of fuels and raw materials, and that the planned objectives would take precedence over all other projects in the sector in question. As one 'mini-plan' succeeded another, however, it became quite common for investment funds and technical personnel to be switched between different projects already under way. In the end, a high and rising mass of half-finished, unusable or abandoned projects stood as the symbols of this experiment in 'special plans' and 'mini-plans'.

2 In spring 1968, while the 'mini-plans' were still at their height, a 'revolutionary offensive' was launched on the economic front. The aim was to nationalize the remaining private-sector pockets (actually of quite secondary importance) in industry and the services; and above all to set new records in investment and accumulation, even if consumption had to be drastically curtailed.[9] Contemporary speeches justifying this offensive stressed that Cuba was making 'rapid headway in the construction of a communist society'.

3 The policy of rapid industrialization and agricultural diversification, practised in the period up to 1964, was judged unrealistic in the context of scarce resources and imperialist economic blockade. From 1965–66 onward, a new policy sought to maximize sugar production and to use the foreign currency obtained in this way to mechanize and modernize the sector.

Within this framework, a 'Sugar Plan' was adopted for the period 1965–70. Major new investment, totalling some 4,500 million French francs of the time, was to be allocated mainly to the modernization and expansion of sugar refining, where 90 per cent of the existing plants were already more than thirty years old. By 1970 only a third of this planned investment had actually materialized, so that, for example, only 152 refineries were then in operation, as against 161 in 1959.

In these circumstances, the 10-million tonne *zafra* was a completely unrealistic end target for the 'Sugar Plan', especially as the cane-cutting and transport infrastructure suffered from the same deficiencies, and there was a dramatic shortage of skilled labour.

In retrospect, technical staff from the International Sugar Organization calculated that Cuba's infrastructure then allowed an output of 6 million tonnes. But although it did not reach the 10-million target, the 1970 *zafra* set a new record of 8.5 million tonnes (see table 3.1).

There was a heavy price to pay, which affected nearly all the sectors of the economy. In the absence of an overall plan, all the operating 'mini-plans' were subordinated to the 'Sugar Plan'. The most immediate effects were delayed investment and falling output; and in some industrial branches, the lengthy departure of much of the workforce to the voluntary cane-cutting brigades led to a major slowdown or even standstill in activity. The sugar infrastructure itself suffered from hyper-intensive utilization: whereas 152 refineries were functioning at the start of the famous *zafra*, only 115 were still in service by the time of the 1972 harvest.

The resulting chaos laid bare all the economic problems of the Cuban revolution. The leadership, and in particular Fidel Castro, did not attempt to disguise the scale of these problems, making the economy the main focus of their speeches over the next two or three years. Through consistent study of these speeches, one can see new orientations gradually emerging behind the critique of the previous period, while institutional structures emerged in numerous measures taken between 1971 and 1974 to relaunch and reorganize the economy.

The new System of Economic Management and Planning, drawn up at the end of this period and adopted in broad outline at the First Congress of the CCP, merely deepened and systematized this orientation. It had, anyway, been in place for three years.

The essential economic options were therefore made in the early years of the 1970–80 decade which was closed by the Second CCP Congress. Although the Cuban masses were at the heart of these options, they had no *real* possibility of debate through which they might *organically* participate. And yet, the key problem to be solved is the very low productivity of labour, one of whose crucial dimensions is the low 'economic consciousness' of the workers.

New orientations

Ending waste and dropping the mini-plans

Both Fidel Castro and various officials responsible for the economy have devoted many of their speeches to the inefficiency or poor utilization of investment. During his visit to Chile in November 1971, the Cuban Prime Minister said: 'Often the wish to achieve a great deal in a very short space of time has led us to concentrate numerous resources on a particular objective. The result is that, far from making the best use of these resources, we have actually squandered them' (Castro, F. 1971). Concrete examples of waste may be quoted in abundance. In the same speech, Castro looked at waste at the level of agricultural investment, particularly tractors. The 50,000 tractors imported between 1959 and 1970, he said, 'have been used for all manner of non-productive activity' such as 'transporting peasants to baseball matches, to the beach, to fiestas of every kind, or to their friends'. Tractors were entrusted to agricultural workers who knew nothing about machinery: they did not know how to use them properly, still less to keep them in repair. 'So,' he concluded, 'when the farm used to belong to a private owner, a tractor would last twenty-odd years. But since the state has become owner, a tractor no longer lasts more than two, three or at most four years.'

The inefficiency (wastage) of industrial investment was also severely attacked. Speeches referred to many nearly complete factories which could not be brought into operation because, for months or even years, they had not been able to get a machine or a part vital to the production process. A considerable quantity of expensively imported equipment goods had been rendered unusable through months of exposure to the elements on the wasteland lying around the ports. The list can easily be continued.

The crucial transport sector, key to the collection of the sugar harvest, provides many similar examples. Thus, in a document that greatly assists our understanding of this period, Osvaldo Dorticos mentions that only 134 of Cuba's 300 locomotives were in working order. The others, mostly of recent origin, had become unusable through bad maintenance over a long period of time (Dorticos 1972).

All these examples point to two broad categories of problem: the chaos, not to say disappearance, of planning in the wake of the 'mini-plans'; and the low level of 'economic consciousness' among Cuban workers. The 'mini-plan' policy was in fact rapidly discarded. JUCEPLAN formally regained its old functions and prerogatives, and with Soviet technical assistance intermediate plans were drawn up in anticipation of the first five-year plan already scheduled for 1976–80.

Low labour productivity: a return to work-norms

A survey published by *Bohemia* in May 1970, referring to 200 different-sized enterprises from various economic sectors and geographic regions of the country, revealed the extent of the productivity problem facing Cuba. It appeared that, on average, a third of the working day was wasted, and that the figure was quite often as much as a half. Two reasons were given for this: the employment of redundant workers by many enterprises; and the abandonment in 1966 of any system of individual output-norms.

Enterprise directors, and staff responsible for production and personnel matters, stressed in relation to the survey results that the lack of output-norms gave them no real way of controlling labour productivity.

In late 1970 and early 1971, a number of commissions were formed from enterprise directors, output managers, technicians, skilled workers and party members, their task being to discuss the reintroduction of a system of norms. One of the questions most frequently raised in their meetings was whether such a system conflicted with 'moral incentives'. Dominant, too, was the fear that the proposed measures constituted a major turning point. The then Minister of Labour, Jorge Risquet, refused to make a pronouncement during these debates, merely arguing that the restoration of norms was the only instrument for measuring the worker's individual effort.

The system of norms was progressively reintroduced between the second half of 1971 and the end of 1973. When the CTC trade-union federation met for its thirteenth congress, from 11 to 15 November 1973, '70 per cent of the state-employed workforce was using the norm system of work'. A report to the congress even stated that the introduction of norms had led to a 21 per cent rise in labour productivity in 1972. Apparently these results refer only to industry, since low labour productivity was still the rule in agriculture. Raul Castro gave some striking examples of this in his speech to the founding congress of the National Union of Agricultural and Stock-Farm Workers, held in September 1973. Reporting that wage costs on state farms alone greatly exceeded the value of production, he stressed the need to eliminate the sizeable proportion of surplus workers employed in these enterprises (Castro, R. 1973).

Wages policy and individual incentives

The CTC congress of November 1973 marked a real watershed in respect of wage policy. One of its main theses concerned 'the strengthening of the socialist system of distribution according to work', as opposed to 'distribution according to need'. In his closing speech, moreover, Fidel Castro sharply criticized the notions current in the 1960s: 'To pay the same wage for the same kind of work, irrespective of productive effort, is an egalitarian principle we must correct.' He went on to announce that cars would be imported and sold to technical staff, 'so that their productivity may be increased'. A few months later, in the first half of 1974, it was announced that 182 million pesos (about 600 million French francs) would be released to improve the pay of technical and managerial personnel, 'in recognition of their skills'.

Another thesis adopted by the thirteenth CTC congress dealt with the reorganization of work and wages. Pay was again tied to norms (as had partially been the case between 1963 and 1966): workers who fulfilled their quota would receive their wage in full; and those who overfulfilled it would receive correspondingly higher pay, plus a bonus equivalent to 100 per cent of the extra. At the same time, voluntary unpaid overtime was called into question. It was shown that an hour of unpaid overtime cost more than an hour of ordinary time, since labour productivity fell to a very low level under such circumstances, while the other elements in the cost of production remained the same.

The new system of 'socialist emulation' approved by the thirteenth CTC congress envisaged other types of 'material incentive' alongside the existing 'moral incentives'. The framework of 'competition' was most often of an individual, but sometimes of a collective character. Thus 'material incentives' for individuals included priority access to holiday facilities (rest homes and so on) or recreational programmes; while for group bodies, they involved the improvement or construction of social, cultural or sporting facilities attached to the enterprise. The so-called 'moral incentives' consisted of diplomas, medals and titles, such as 'national labour hero'.

Both the CTC congress resolutions and subsequent government declarations emphasized that the new individual material incentives should be tightly linked to productivity. The resolution on the distribution of electrical household goods—the 'CTC Plan', as it is still known in Cuba—is a good illustration of this linkage. Consumer durables would not be available in the retail trade, but would be allocated to particular enterprises by the Ministry of Internal Trade.[10] The list of available products was then posted up, and an elected workforce committee, or in some cases a general meeting of the workers, decided who should take priority by reference, first, to their individual merits (norm fulfilment or overfulfilment, productivity) and secondly to their needs. The same criteria were largely used in the allocation of housing.[11]

The Cuban leadership still presents the thirteenth CTC congress as a decisive event that reactivated and democratized the trade-union movement. Within the limits assigned to union activity—essentially, control over the application of social legislation—this is doubtless true. But the real importance of the congress lies in its focus on *the struggle to raise labour productivity*. For the congress resolutions have ever since underpinned policy guidelines on the organization and remuneration of work and socialist emulation.

Systematic introduction of norms, linkage of pay to output, privileges for skilled labour, 'incentives' of a basically material and individual character—these broad options form a coherent whole which, in the absence of mechanisms for democratic participation, cannot be seen as a contribution to the raising of 'economic consciousness' among the masses. It is hard to imagine a cleaner break with the 'egalitarianism' propounded during the earlier period. The resolutions adopted in support of a reduction of the money in circulation are a good illustration of this.

Reducing demand, increasing output

The purchasing power of the population grew considerably with the first great social measures taken by the revolution. In varying degrees, this rise was assisted by full employment, the assurance of a full year's wage for sugar workers, a very substantial increase in lower wages and pensions, the expansion of free social services (education, health, social security, telephones, water, and so on), and a cut in rents and the cost of many services such as electricity, gas and transport.

On the other hand, the low level of national consumer-goods production, combined with the systematic export of goods previously consumed within the country (tobacco and alcohol, for example), and above all with the fall-off in imports, effectively produced a very sharp decline in the supply of consumer goods.

A rationing system was introduced in 1962 and rapidly extended to the whole consumer-goods sector, so that the available products might be distributed on an egalitarian basis. As a general rule, however, family incomes largely exceeded what could be bought each month, and this prompted a considerable rise in the quantity of money in circulation.

According to Osvaldo Dorticos's *Analysis and Prospects of the Cuban Economy*, there was an excess of 3,478 million pesos in 1970, and the total income of the population was twice the value of goods available for purchase. Theoretically, then, the population could have lived for a year without working—a situation that inevitably led to the development of a black market. In order to reduce the quantity of money, the government opted both to reduce demand and to increase the production of goods. Some prices were raised; and a decision was taken to annul the already postponed abolition of rent, as well as a fresh rise in the lowest wage level. It was against this background that the thirteenth CTC congress called into question some of the benefits gained by workers during the preceding period: 'vanguard workers' would no longer be given 100 per cent cover for retirement and periods of incapacity, and sugar workers, who work a maximum of six months a year, would lose their entitlement to a full year's wage.

At the same time, an effort was made to ease the draconian consumer restrictions. An increase in the supply of consumer goods was indeed consistent with the new pay policy; for if there was nothing to be bought, a wages system 'tied to output and involving bonuses' would be of dubious effect upon productivity. These measures soon yielded results: the surplus of money over annual population income fell from 87 per cent in 1970 to 47 per cent in 1973.

New links with the USSR: membership of Comecon

The failure of the '10-million tonne *zafra*' led to a qualitatively new set of economic relations with the USSR. According to JUCEPLAN, Cuba's *cumulative* trade deficit with the Soviet Union stood at about $2,000 million in 1970 (Lago 1975).

In 1971 imports from the USSR rose in value by 5 per cent, while Cuban exports to the USSR fell nearly 40 per cent. In that year alone, the trade deficit was 427 million pesos (about $500m); and in 1972 it crossed the threshold of 500m pesos (about $600m). Roughly 50 per cent of Cuba's foreign trade was then being conducted with the Soviet Union (see table 3.7).

The considerable rise in the deficit was essentially due to falling sugar production in 1971, which made it impossible for Cuba to honour existing bilateral trade agreements. It should be added, however, that the price paid by the Soviet Union for Cuban sugar (6.11 cents a pound) had remained the same since the signing of a bilateral agreement in 1963. World sugar prices had fluctuated widely in the intervening period. But whereas the price agreed with the USSR had been *three times higher* than the world-market level between 1965 and 1968, it was 15 per cent lower in 1972 (see table 3.1).

Since the imports from the USSR were virtually incompressible (energy, equipment goods), the whole field of bilateral economic and commercial relations had to be renegotiated. This happened in two stages, *at a time when Cuba had no room for manoeuvre.*

First, Cuba officially joined Comecon at its twenty-sixth session, on 11 July 1972. The head of the delegation, Carlos Rafael Rodriguez, made a speech in which he undertook to provide 'the socialist camp' with a stable supply of sugar, asking in return for help in the development of the nickel industry and in the establishment of new planning methods. Speaking in reply, Alexei Kosygin stressed the need to co-ordinate Cuba's forthcoming five-year plan (1976–80) with the plans of Comecon countries. This, then, was the general framework for a process of co-ordination and integration that has continually grown stronger in the years since 1972.

The second stage in these decisive negotiations took place six months later, when Fidel Castro and Leonid Brezhnev signed five bilateral economic accords in Moscow. It was agreed that the USSR would immediately pay a higher price for Cuban sugar, and that in future a fairly complex mechanism would index this to the price of Soviet oil supplies to Cuba. The Soviet Union also promised Cuba major technical assistance to mechanize sugar-cane cutting, to develop the nickel industry, to increase the output of electricity, to modernize the oil refineries, and to reorganize planning methods (particularly through the use of computers). Repayment of the debt accumulated between 1960 and 1972 would be spread over twenty-five years, between 1986 and 2011. A further credit of 1,000 million rubles, to cover the deficit expected for 1973–75, was granted on the same conditions. A three-year trade agreement was also signed (Castro, R. 1973).

These agreements were of capital importance. Immediately, they allowed the Cuban economy to pull itself out of an extremely tight corner. In the medium to long term, they confirmed Cuba's decisive role as a sugar producer within the Comecon 'division of labour' and system of plan co-ordination. They consequently defined some of the priorities to be found in the first five-year plan as well as the second (mechanization of cane-cutting, nickel, and so on). Lastly, they ensured that the reorganization of the central planning and management structures would be accomplished with the aid of Soviet and Comecon specialists.

This was a real turning point in relations between Cuba and the Soviet Union. In the early 1960s, the blockade organized by US imperialism against the nascent workers' state had largely tied Cuba's survival to its economic relations with the USSR. The 1972 agreements not only expressed a considerable heightening of this distinctive 'dependence', but actually institutionalized it on a long-term, planned basis. They were to be the ground for a struggle against underdevelopment adapted to the framework of this relationship.

In this sense, it is no exaggeration to say that the agreements were the most decisive factor in these difficult years of economic restabilization, the backcloth to the policy options and various measures analysed above.

The systematic implementation of all these measures (output-norms, individual material incentives, new methods of management) was facilitated by the surge in world sugar prices which raised the average 1974 price to 29.66 cents a pound, seven times higher than the average level for 1971. This development, combined with the provisions in the Soviet–Cuban agreements, allowed a very high rate of accumulation to be achieved, at the same time that steps were being taken to raise personal consumption by some degree. Productivity, however, did not greatly increase after the initial post-1970 phase of reorganization.

The improvement in everyday life, much of it made possible by the favourable sugar conjuncture, increased the popularity of the new policy options to which it was causally attributed. The climate was particularly good for the new orientations to be broadened and systematized through the 'system of economic management and planning' approved by the First Congress of the CCP.

The 'System of Economic Management and Planning'

We cannot here examine the whole of this new system, involving as it does, in the words of the congress resolution, 'the totality of principles, sub-systems, methods and procedures for the organization, planning and management of economic activities'. Besides, although the general principles were adopted in December 1975, it was only in 1978 that they began to be experimentally applied to selected and representative enterprises covering a broad spectrum of productive and service activity. And it is only in the last few years that the new system may be said to have become the general practice—that is to say, after the establishment of all the new organs of economic management, and after the restructuring of the enterprise network through the introduction of 'profit' criteria in the second five-year plan now in force.

As yet, no study is available of the overall practical application of the new system, although very many articles in the daily press have taken up limited and specific points. With regard to its impact on economic activity, especially productivity, any initial assessment would have to base itself on serious data referring to the realization of the first stages of the plan.

We shall therefore confine ourselves to the essential aspect: namely, the decision to establish a planned economic system based on 'the objective economic laws operating in the stage of socialist construction', above all the law of value and 'generalized money-commodity relations' (CCP 1981). It is a system based no longer on hyper-centralized administrative directives but on relatively decentralized economic 'levers'; a system that involves a major degree of enterprise autonomy or 'economic-operational decentralization', particularly in the use of funds made available by the state.

Three initial points should be made in order to locate the significance and importance of the new system.

1   The introduction of this system has involved an upheaval in the state structures responsible for economic matters. It is enough to recall that the last five years have witnessed the creation of a State Finance Committee, a State Prices Committee, a State Committee for Material and Technical Supply, a State Norms Committee, a State Statistics Committee, and a Computer Institute.[12] At the same time, the whole banking apparatus has been substantially reorganized.

The scale of enterprise restructuring has been such that the total number of state enterprises contracted from 3,050 in 1976 to 2,420 in late 1980 (Castro, F. 1980). Their mutual relations have gradually been placed on the basis of bilateral contracts, negotiated within the framework of plan targets. A corresponding system of short-term credit has been introduced for enterprises, and a general ordinance defines their degree of autonomy in economic management. This applies equally to enterprises in the distribution sector, so that relations between factories and shops are now also becoming of a contractual character. As a result, production enterprises should be able to take more note of consumer tastes.

2   The establishment of this 'system' in Cuba is closely bound up with the institutionalization process that developed in 1976 and 1977 (Harnecker 1975: 312–313; Cuban Ministry of Justice 1979; CCP 1981: 167–185). 'People's power' assemblies at municipal, regional and national level have brought a real decentralization of economic activity concerning the region or locality. Directors of relevant enterprises are now answerable to the corresponding assembly.

3   This process is based upon a reaffirmation and further extension of output-linked norms and material (mostly individual) incentives. More generally, the whole body of decisions taken at the thirteenth CTC congress have been built into the new system.

Economic management and the law of value

After a socialist revolution in an 'underdeveloped' country like Cuba, there are real dangers in referring to the law of value as one of the objective economic laws on which the new 'system of management and planning' must be grounded.

Even if we take into account the choices made between 1971 and 1974, the determination of economic and social priorities has so far always resulted from conscious political decisions, which have had the upper hand over the law of value, particularly in the field of investment. Thus, priority has been given to full employment in both town and country, universal education, and technological advance, rather than to some principle of 'profit maximization'. This *political* choice of priorities has necessarily violated the law of value.

If this had not been the case, if investment during this period had corresponded to the law of value rather than political choices, then it would have flowed into sectors with the highest profitability in terms of world-market prices, inevitably leading to the development of a single export-crop economy. This is obviously not what the Cuban leadership has in mind, when it now argues that the persistence of the law of value in the stage of socialist construction must be one of the foundations on which the new 'system of economic management and planning' is based. Their first, positive aim is that *the law of value should no longer be ignored*, as it often was during the first ten years of the revolution. In other words, there has to be serious economic calculation of the costs of production, and hence precise knowledge of the sums allocated to priority sectors. Not to ignore the law of value is not at all the same as to make choices *as a consequence of* the law of value. Since priorities are decided beforehand according to political and social criteria, the point is rather to employ strict cost-accounting in order to avoid that waste of resources for which the masses ultimately have to pay in useless sacrifices. Such calculation is all the more necessary in Cuba, in that the economy depends on foreign trade for its crucial supplies of energy and equipment goods.

Although in this sense the Cuban leadership is right to take account of the law of value, it may prove dangerous and fraught with consequences *not to stress at the same time that the law of value must be constantly and deliberately violated in the choice of economic guidelines*. Otherwise, a certain confusion ('one of the economic laws on which the new system of management must be grounded') may lend credence to the idea that the law of value is also a major factor in regulating production and determining investment decisions.

The law of value and the autonomy of 'socialist enterprises'

In the present context of deep and still 'uncompleted' reforms, this is not an academic question: it is intimately bound up with *the real content of enterprise autonomy in decision-making.* Although the formulations in the texts remain fairly general, the limits are quite clearly laid down: the 'socialist enterprise' will be endowed with 'a relative independence which allows it to be distinguished from other basic units of the economy, and is concretely expressed in its economic-operational autonomy of management'. At the same time, 'higher bodies shall equip the enterprises with sufficient technical-material and financial resources for the fulfilment of the Plan' (CCP 1981: 199–200).

In other words, budgetary mechanisms still fully integrate enterprises into the centralized planning decisions. Yet the door seems to be left open for enterprises, at a later stage, to make their own investments out of some of the surplus product (their net surplus product). According to a number of congruent sources, this possibility has been debated and is still being debated by certain JUCEPLAN economists.

Nor is there always a clear distinction between self-investment and the use of 'decentralized funds as enterprise incentives'. These funds, 'consisting of enterprise profits after deduction of the national budget share', are allocated for: improvement of the social and cultural conditions of the workforce (collective material incentives); individual bonuses to the workers and the managerial and administrative staff, in accordance with enterprise performance; and improvement of 'the technical-productive conditions of the enterprise' (Martell 1979: 96–97).

The confusion stems from the third of these areas, which is supposed to involve a kind of sinking fund for the modernization of productive equipment. Some economists and enterprise directors, however, are tempted to see it as a potential gateway to self-investment. This brings us to one of the key problems posed by the new 'system of economic management and planning'.

Since bonuses, especially in the case of managerial staff, depend upon enterprise results, the personnel will logically tend to seek the best conditions for profit-maximization. One of these conditions is, of course, the size and efficiency of new investment. Insofar as they have a *material interest*, then, managers will seek ever more to control the scale and character of such investment, as well as the quantity, quality and price of the commodities to be produced. They will do this all the more systematically in that their powers (above all for *directors*) have expanded considerably within the new framework of enterprise autonomy. Responsible for the whole operation of the enterprise, for the organization of production, and for relations with other production units and the administrative authorities, the director only really shares his decision-making power with the workers' union delegates in relation to the allocation of bonuses and social funds.

Should the principles and mechanisms of the new system entail that the enterprise (or rather, the director) is itself systematically able to make decentralized investments out of past profits, then the consequences could not fail to be disastrous. For, insofar as an 'underdeveloped' Cuban-type economy retains a great productivity differential between various sectors or enterprises, and insofar as the number of high-productivity units remains very small, enterprise control over just part of its net surplus product is enough to bring about a rise, rather than a fall, in the development and income differential between enterprises with old and with advanced technology. Moreover, if an enterprise has significant self-investment possibilities, it (or rather, the director) will tend to meet the general scarcity of industrial goods by steering investment into the production of commodities of which the enterprise or the locality, for example, is most short.

Thus, as soon as the law of value is 'applied', sectoral or local interests may rapidly gain the upper hand, and inequalities may grow between different sectors of activity (and hence of the working class) (Germain 1964, 1965).

We repeat: things have not reached such a pass in Cuba; as the system is currently practised, the fact that enterprises have greater autonomy than before in using centrally allocated funds does not in any way affect the complete budgetary control exercised by higher bodies. Nevertheless, one cannot deny the growing 'economic-operational' autonomy of enterprises, the effective use of profit as a key plan indicator, the related introduction of material incentives for both workers and 'managers', and the heightened role of directors and their managerial staff. All these factors together generate a powerful thrust towards decentralized self-investment, while an extremely favourable terrain is provided by the fuzzy theoretical statements on the applicability of the law of value.

The 'common-sense' argument from *immediate effectiveness* must surely play a major role in deepening this trend. In a country where the hyper-centralization of the first decade is equated with economic chaos and deprivation, where decentralization is equated with the increased efficiency since the establishment of 'local people's power', also with the increased well-being that accompanied the simultaneous sugar boom, and where industrial commodities are still in very short supply, it would be hard to imagine that the idea of decentralized self-investment should not be widely popular. (And this is not to mention the enthusiasm of those layers who are assured in advance that they will profit from the change.)

Now that the new System of Management and Planning has been fully established, the technical rationalization measures having their first positive effects in 1980, the Cuban economy risks being drawn into this dangerous logic. It is true that the new system merely pursues the course of the last ten years, and that, taken in isolation, many of the measures adopted during this period may have been quite justified and beyond argument. However, a false underlying logic marks the whole experience: from the general introduction of output-norms, through the thirteenth CTC congress, to the new system of management and planning.

The basic logic is a search for solutions to the key problem of labour productivity that do not involve *genuinely organized workers' power*. Such a quest is illusory. Beyond immediate advances—the fruit of better management and planning techniques, new technological gains, and individual material incentives—it is impossible to achieve a lasting improvement in productivity without tackling the essential question: *the low 'economic consciousness' of the workers*. In a planned collectivist economy, only workers' participation in both broad economic decisions and day-to-day management can significantly raise such consciousness. The instruments are democratic planning, and self-management of the units of production and distribution.

The Cuban leadership, unlike the rulers of a 'degenerated workers' state' such as the Soviet Union or of the current regime in Poland, is not the expression of a privileged bureaucratic layer with interests antagonistic to those of the masses. In general, its decisions express both the immediate and the longer-term interests of the Cuban masses. This is the fundamental reason why it continues to enjoy considerable support, twenty-two years after the victory of the revolution.

Behind the choices of the last ten years concerning the organization of economic life, there is not a deliberate decision to increase existing privileges and thus to consolidate, at a later stage, a hitherto non-existent bureaucratic *caste*. These choices do, however, create favourable ground for such a development; indeed, they may even precipitate it, above all in conjunction with possible trends in international politics (for example, a setback for the Latin American revolution). Two main factors lie behind these policy decisions:

1   The major role of the Soviet Union in relation to the Cuban economy, together with the lack of Cuban traditions and research in economic planning and organization, have naturally, almost inevitably, led the Cuban leadership to turn to the models which the Soviet bureaucracy established in pursuit of its own interests.

2   The Cuban leadership has a 'verticalist' or 'paternalist' conception of its relationship to the masses, in which there is no real idea of workers' self-organization as the basis for the articulation of self-management and democratic planning.

The raising of the economic consciousness of the masses *necessarily* involves self-organization, workers' management and mass control. It implies free public discussion, and the possibility of open debate within the party and mass organizations.

It was essentially this alternative which the economic decisions of the 1970s were designed to parry. But in the end, when it has used up all the reserves contained in these partial choices and technical reforms, the Cuban leadership will have to settle the matter once and for all: *either* democratic self-organization of the masses, *or* confiscation of the revolution by bureaucratic layers which previous choices, and their social effects, will have helped to create.

NOTES

1 The Ministry of the Sugar Industry is responsible for co-ordinating all sugar-related activity.

2 Figures supplied by the Ministry of Agriculture. In his report to the Second CCP Congress, Fidel Castro mentioned the figure of 850,000 hectares for the years of the first five-year plan.

3 There has been a real improvement in this field since the beginning of 1980, particularly in the second half of the year.

4 These are fairly small, decentralized units.

5 With regard to the rate of accumulation in Cuba, JUCEPLAN sources indicate a rate of 'approximately 30 per cent' for the early 1970s. According to a survey by the US journalist James Higgins, the rate of accumulation of capital was 31 per cent in 1968, 33 per cent in 1970, and 28 per cent in 1971 (Lago 1975).

6 According to calculations made by the Ministry of the Sugar Industry in 1975, a one-cent variation in the price of a pound of sugar increases or diminishes earnings from the world market by $40 million.

7 Figures available on the productivity of labour are extremely imprecise, and there are even different statistics for particular periods or sectors of activity. Fidel Castro's report to the Second CCP Congress also lacks precision. The figure of 3.4 per cent seems to refer to the whole five-year period, since there is no other specific indication. In that case, it would be very low. Such an interpretation does in fact tally with the many partial data concerning sectors like the docks and the building industry.

8 There are many other examples of this kind. A brief investigation of the port of Havana, where major efforts are continually being made to raise productivity, suggests that productivity is 50 per cent below the level of the big French ports.

9 See note 7.

10 Although they are beginning to appear on the open market, at much higher prices and with no credit facilities, this is still the way in which most electrical household goods are distributed.

11 The housing crisis is one of the most acute problems facing the Cuban population. Priority in construction has been given to the social infrastructure (schools, hospitals, etc.), industry and transport. Although a massive house-building programme is planned for the coming years, the population growth and the deterioration of the existing stock is so pronounced that a satisfactory solution hardly seems possible before the end of the century. The many social consequences would be worth a separate study. But just to take the most obvious example, the fact that three generations very often occupy cramped quarters under a single roof has perpetuated the significance of the family.

12 A 'state committee' is equivalent to a fully fledged ministerial department.

REFERENCES

Beauvais, J. P. 1981, 'Cuba: extension de la révolution et défense de la bureaucratie soviétique'; 'Cuba: "pouvoir populaire" et démocratie socialiste'; 'Cuba: aquis et choix économique'; 'Cuba: déformations bureaucratique, réorganisation démocratique', Rouge, nos. 951–954, January–February

Castro, F. 1971, 'Sélection hebdomadaire', Granma, 5 December

Castro, F. 1973, 'Report to the people on the economic agreement signed with the Soviet Union', Granma weekly review, 14 January

Castro, F. 1980, 'Rapport au IIe congrès du PCC', Granma, 28 December

Castro, R. 1973, 'Palabras en la clausura del acto de constitución del sindicato nacional de trabajadores agropecuarios', *Granma*, 10 September

Cuban Communist Party (CCP) 1981, *Primer congreso del partido comunista cubano: tesis y resoluciones*, Havana

Cuban Ministry of Justice 1979, *Reglamento de las asambleas nacional, provincial y municipal*, Havana

Dorticos, O. 1972, *Economia y desarrollo*, no. 12, July–August

Germain, E. 1964, 'La loi de la valeur, l'autogestion et les investissements dans l'économie des états ouvrier', *Quatrième internationale*, no. 21, February–March

Germain, E. 1965, 'Les réformes Liberman-Trapeznikov de la gestion des enterprises soviétiques', *Quatrième internationale*, no. 24, March

Harnecker, M. 1975, *Cuba: dictature ou démocratie?*, Paris

Lago, C. M. 1974, *Cuba in the 1970s: pragmatism and institutionalisation*, Albuquerque, University of New Mexico Press

Maitan, L. 1981, 'IIe congrès du parti communiste cubain', *Inprecor*, no. 93, 20 January

Martell, R. 1979, *La empresa socialista*, Havana

FOUR

Jamaica: from Michael Manley to Edward Seaga

Fitzroy Ambursley

The landslide victory of Edward Seaga's Jamaica Labour Party (JLP) in the October 1980 general elections brought about an abrupt end to the People's National Party's (PNP) eight-year-old experiment in 'Democratic Socialism'. The fall of Michael Manley, the Socialist International's most important representative in the Third World, dealt a serious, if not fatal, blow to the gradualist strategy of social change advocated by broad sectors of the Caribbean left and endorsed in recent years by the Cuban leadership. At the same time, the restoration of the stalwartly anti-communist JLP provided the Reagan administration with an invaluable collaborator in its crusade to contain and roll back the wave of revolutionary mobilization that has swept the Caribbean and Central America since 1979. In particular it has increased the grave danger of intervention against the revolutions in Grenada and Nicaragua, both of which had enjoyed Jamaican support in their efforts to escape the noose-hold of US economic and political isolation.

The defeat of Manley has been widely compared with the overthrow of Allende, and, indeed, many of the same counter-revolutionary forces—IMF, CIA, North American mineral corporations, etc.—which conspired against Unidad Popular were also busy subverting the PNP. Yet there is an obvious and decisive difference between the Chilean and Jamaican cases: despite economic sabotage and rampant inflation, the Chilean popular classes continued to stand behind Allende, who could in the end only be toppled by one of the most bloody putsches of the twentieth century; Manley, on the other hand, was *voted out* of power by sections of the same super-exploited mass of 'sufferers' whose plight he had promised to change forever. Although in Jamaica there was an attempted coup, as well as a state of *de facto* civil war in the slums of Kingston and other towns, there is no way to deny the fact that the ultimate weakness of the PNP was its failure to unite and mobilize the small peasants, farmworkers, urban wage earners and casual labourers who comprise the overwhelming social and political majority of Jamaican society. A Marxist balance sheet of the Manley experiment, therefore, must be more than a narrative of imperialist machinations, IMF ultimatums and internal intrigues. It must also confront the huge obstacle to social revolution constituted by Jamaica's neo-colonial political system with its singular contraposition (on the right) of an oligarchic 'labour party' with a powerful trade-union base and (on the left) a bourgeois nationalist-populist party with a Fabian façade. The PNP's inability to overthrow economic dependency was centrally determined by its failure to use the favourable conjuncture of the 1970s to transform its own traditional structure and ideology.

This paper is divided into three sections. In part one, I highlight certain features of Jamaica's history, politics and socio-economic structure. Part two is devoted to an assessment of the venture in 'Democratic Socialism'. The discussion here is based upon an analysis of some of the most salient aspects of the PNP's two terms in office. Finally, in part three I have made a detailed investigation into the first fifteen months under the JLP administration, in order to explore the political prospects of the Seaga regime. My examination of the JLP in office also throws into greater relief the PNP interregnum.[1]

Background to the 1972 PNP victory

Some aspects of Jamaican society

The present political system in Jamaica emerged in the wake of the labour unrest that swept the island in 1938. Ken Post's mammoth study of this event has provided us with valuable information about the genesis of modern Jamaica (1978). Post's work is also a bold and pioneering attempt to conceptualize the Jamaican social formation through the grille of historical materialism, and is infused with rich insights into the metabolism of this island society. It completely transcends the corpus of political and sociological studies that have viewed the society primarily in terms of racial and cultural divisions, and vigorously asserts class struggle as the fundamental object of social inquiry. Indeed, one of Post's major contributions is his treatment of the question of racial consciousness. Drawing inspiration from propositions advanced by Trotsky and Lukács, he considers this to be a facet of the conservatism of the social mind of Jamaica. That is, the preoccupation with race of all classes in the society has its origins in the caste-class system of chattel slavery, under which economic and social status were closely associated with white, brown or black skin. However, while emancipation in 1834 and the demise of the old sugar estates engendered a dissolution of the caste-class system, and its replacement by new economic and political structures, it did not end the obsession with race. Part of the reason for this was the fact that the new class structure continued to bear a stark resemblance to that of the slavery days, although black and brown elements had joined the capitalist class and there were black members of the intermediate strata. Hence, consciousness of race, often coupled with religious revivalism, has served both to mediate and deflect class consciousness.

... an underdeveloped agrarian capitalist Jamaica resembled its slave-based predecessor's structure sufficiently for the old racial concerns to continue to eat into the heart and spirit of its people, at all social levels, moulding their perceptions of their lives. In this way the 'everyday' level of their consciousness was profoundly affected, and an ideology created which explained all social divisions in terms of colour (1978: 60).

It is, in effect, this ' "everyday" level of consciousness' which provides the basis for the obscurantist sociological models of the cultural pluralists and others.

A second innovation made by Post is his attempt to theorize in terms of Marxist political economy the extreme causalization of the Jamaican labour force. He argues that the hybrid relations of production in the countryside, whereby poor peasants are poised between working their own plots and selling their labour to the big estates or government bodies, has been directly beneficial to capital in that it drastically reduced the cost of wage labour, while at the same time enlarging the reserve army of labour. In order to exploit even further their highly favourable position *vis-à-vis* rural labour, employers have deliberately followed a policy of rotating work to new employees over short periods of time. Government agencies have also engaged in this practice, ostensibly to 'spread out the available work'. The net consequence has been the consolidation of a casual labour market, 'a structural condition in which the total supply of jobs and significant sectors of employment are characterized by short periods of tenure of low-paid jobs' (1978: 439). Post goes on to explain the emergence of the Jamaican phenomenon known as 'scuffling' in terms of the casual labour market. He suggests that since large sectors of the urban unemployed could not fall back on their own land, they were compelled to engage in marginal own-account work such as collecting and selling fruit, shoe cleaning, peddling sweets and cigarettes, chopping firewood and so on. As with the operation of the casual labour market itself, Post draws an interesting parallel with nineteenth-century Britain. He considers the scuffler to be part of the lower petty bourgeoisie, and opines that the existence of such a stratum, in symbiotic relationship with the working class, corresponded to the objective needs of Jamaican capitalism. This was because it provided a refuge for the temporary or permanent victims of the casual labour market (1978: 135).

In spite of the tremendous explanatory power of Post's appraisal of the casual labour problematic, it does, nevertheless, betray a certain flaw in his analysis. That is, a failure to appreciate the full dialectic of underdevelopment in Jamaica. He writes:

The dominant moment in all the contradictions which [the casual labour market] implied, the keystone of the structure's arch, were the capitalists, to [*sic*] weak to build an expansive industrial capitalism but strong enough to enforce low wages and short periods of work, the heart of the casual labour system (1978: 469–70).

Post does not seem to realize that the existence of the casual labour market and the incapacity of the Jamaican bourgeoisie are but two sides of the same coin. It is precisely the fostering and retention of pre-capitalist relations of production in the countryside, and the recourse to a systematic turnover of the labour force, which, although enabling a higher rate of surplus value to be extracted, has also impeded the development of industrial capital and a comprehensive expansion of the capitalist mode of production. For both the rural class structure and the extreme causalization of labour have served to restrict the size of the domestic market and induced the local ruling class, allied with British and American imperialism, to invest in land, trade, real estate and ganja (marijuana) instead of building up modern industry.[2]

The political background

The nationalist dimension of the 1938 events crystallized in the formation of the People's National Party under the leadership of the Oxford-trained barrister Norman Manley—the father of Michael Manley. But the workers' rebellion found its most striking expression in the meteoric rise of the Bustamante Industrial Trade Union (BITU) led by the authoritarian moneylender Alexander Bustamante. Initially the PNP hoped to enrol the support of 'Labour Leader Number One', but after a brief flirtation, Bustamante (with prompting from the Colonial Office) established the competing Jamaica Labour Party on the eve of home rule in 1944. Bustamanteism was essentially a reflection of the nascent character of the Jamaican working class, its lack of stable mass organization, and the pervasiveness of clientelism. In contrast, the early programme of the PNP reflected the interests of the urban petty bourgeoisie, middle peasants and small traders against the encroachments of the big landholding class and comprador bourgeoisie. Manley advocated the establishment of a marketing and industrial board to provide easy credit to small capitalists and middle peasants, the curtailment of large-scale capitalist agriculture and the formation of rural co-operatives. The PNP's nationalism was extremely moderate in character; proposing a two-stage framework in which universal adult suffrage and an indigenous civil service would be established before seeking full internal self-government within the British Commonwealth.

In the first general elections held under universal adult suffrage in 1944, the JLP swept to victory in a dramatic demonstration that it, rather than the PNP, was seen by the masses as representing the militant tradition of 1938. Yet ironically it was the PNP, with its fraternal ties to the British Labour Party and its blending of moderate nationalism with elements of Fabianism, that was viewed as the greater threat by the island's ruling oligarchy. Since the oligarchy's own political project, the Jamaica Democratic Party, had been completely routed in the elections, it turned toward the volatile and co-optable Bustamante as the political instrument of its interests. Despite the fact that to this day the BITU is empowered to appoint around sixteen members of the JLP executive, the labourism of the party has become a pendant to its domination by the oligarchy. In office between 1944–55 and 1962–65, Bustamante became a slavish defender of the interests of British and American imperialism. For example, during the 1949–52 period when Atlee's Labour government made proposals to nationalize the operations of Tate and Lyle, the giant sugar monopoly which dominated Jamaican agriculture, Bustamante threatened to call strikes all over the island in opposition (Beckford 1972: 141). The JLP government's provocatively conservative policies soon gave rise to a new proletarian radicalization in the form of the Trade Union Congress (TUC), representing mainly public sector workers. The TUC had close links with the PNP, and in 1959 it was transformed into a blanket union with formal ties to the party in order to mount a more effective challenge to the BITU–JLP complex. A pattern was thus established for political differences between the two parties to be automatically transformed into intense inter-union rivalries—a paramount feature of modern Jamaican politics.

The economic strategy of the JLP-oligarchy alliance was based on the model of Puerto Rico's 'Operation Bootstrap' and its open-door invitation to transnational capital to take advantage of tax holidays and cheap labour. By 1950 the great North American aluminium monopolies—Alcoa, Alcan, Kaiser and Reynolds—were investing millions of dollars in the exploitation of Jamaica's bauxite reserves, then estimated as the largest in the world. This bauxite boom together with the prevailing Cold War climate stimulated attacks by the PNP's right wing against the radical and 'anti-imperialist' leaders of the TUC. Bending to these pressures, in 1952 the PNP executive broke off relations with the TUC and expelled four of its leading members from the party. The PNP set up a new trade union, the National Workers' Union (NWU), which was sponsored by US imperialism through the bureaucracy of the United Steelworkers of America (USWA) (Harrod 1972: chapter 8). The NWU was, in fact, headed by Michael Manley, who in the capacity of island supervisor, made frequent trips to Canada and the US in order to attend USWA meetings. Henceforth, the NWU served as the industrial arm of the PNP while the TUC declined in support. In 1955 the PNP was elected to office. By this time the party had become dominated by a fraction of the industrial bourgeoisie which had emerged in the island under the impetus given to construction and manufacturing activity by the mining of bauxite. The PNP continued the JLP's open-door policy towards foreign capital. Throughout its term in office the PNP failed to develop any mass movement in favour of independence, and allowed the colonial government to dictate the pace of decolonization. By 1962 even Bustamante was in favour of independence, so that there was a consensus between the two parties.

The JLP returned to power in 1962 (the year of formal independence) and again pursued the strategy of 'industrialization by invitation'. By the mid-1960s, however, the contradictions of this dependent development began to manifest themselves. The economic boom generated by the bauxite industry had come to an end. Furthermore, the outlets for mass migration to Britain had been closed.[3] Between 1962 and 1972 unemployment increased from 13 per cent to 24 per cent, while the share of the poorest 40 per cent of the population in personal earned income declined from 7.2 per cent in 1958 to 5.4 per cent in 1968 (Girvan, Bernal and Hughes 1980: 115). This social deprivation and inequality gave rise to mass outbursts, such as the attacks on the Chinese community in August–September 1965[4] and the Black Power riots of October 1968, sparked off by the dismissal of the Guyanese Marxist historian Walter Rodney, who had been lecturing at the local university. The response of the JLP government of Hugh Shearer to this rising discontent was to ban all Black Power and socialist literature and step up repression against leftists. Social protest was also taking the form of cultural and musical expression, and this was the period of the most intense development of the reggae musical idiom. By orienting towards this general discontent, and especially to the Black Power and Ras Tafari movements which had mushroomed during this period, the PNP won the 1972 elections. Manley adopted an overtly populist appeal and deployed such well-known catch-phrases as 'Betta Mus Come' and 'Power to the People' which had been widely used in reggae lyrics. As a new hope and vigorous militancy grew in the 'sufferer' slums and forgotten mountain villages, it seemed that at last the PNP might redeem its promises and turn slogans into reality.

The social and economic structure

The rapid economic growth that took place in Jamaica during the 1950s and early 1960s led to significant transformations in the island's economy and social structure. In 1948 traditional exports—sugar, bananas and other agricultural products—accounted for 96 per cent of visible export receipts. Twenty years later their share in the value of visible exports had shrunk to 37 per cent, and, as a proportion of total export value it was only 22 per cent. The displacement of agricultural exports was effected by three main groups of new exports: bauxite-alumina, tourism and manufactures. Their respective contribution to the island's economy in 1968 is shown in table 4.1.

TABLE 4.1 Jamaica: contribution of major sectors to the value of export receipts (1968)

	%
Bauxite-alumina	29
Agricultural products	22
Tourism	19
Manufactures	8

Source: Girvan 1971: 244.

Between 1950 and 1962 the various indices of economic growth were quite spectacular. Foreign trade increased eightfold, nominal GDP grew sevenfold and per capita national income also grew by 700 per cent. In real terms GDP growth averaged 5–6 per cent per annum overall, and

3–4 per cent per capita. However, this impressive economic performance was based upon a massive inflow of foreign capital and a prodigious growth in imports for the island's productive system. Between 1953 and 1972 foreign investment financed 32 per cent of total investment. Imports of raw materials, fuels and intermediate capital goods grew far more quickly than total imports, and, during the same period, increased their share in the total of imports from 26 per cent to 36 per cent. Thus, local productive activity became increasingly dependent on a regular and uninterrupted supply of imports, at the same time as imports became increasingly dependent on external financing (Girvan *et al.* 1980: 114, 133). The strong correlation between the growth rate and the relative size of capital inflows to the island's economy is shown in table 4.2.

TABLE 4.2 Jamaica: phases in real economic growth

Years	Average real growth of GNP (%)	Capital inflows (% GNP current values)
1953–57	10.2	6.9
1958–62	3.4	2.8
1963–66	6.1	5.1

Source: Adapted from Girvan 1971: 221, table 8.2.

By far the most important and dynamic form of foreign investment was in the bauxite industry. However, the potential contribution of this sector to overall economic development was considerably underutilized. The industry was greatly undertaxed, and, because of its high foreign exchange content and overseas ownership, its payments to the Jamaican economy as a share of GNP were markedly less than its domestic value added as a share of GDP. The pivotal role played by the bauxite industry during the period of rapid growth was a corollary of the low levels of investment that characterized agriculture and manufacturing. Between 1956 and 1967 these two sectors absorbed only 26 per cent of total gross investment, about 5 per cent of GNP. Investment in real estate and by the government, whose direct effects on the economy are relatively unproductive, exceeded investment in manufacturing and in agriculture respectively during this period. The growth of the manufacturing sector, which catered primarily for the home market, basically followed the trend of the economy as a whole and displayed little capacity to become an autonomous determinant of economic growth. Its share of GDP increased by less than 3 per cent between 1953 and 1966 (Girvan 1971: 226–233). More perverse still was the inability of manufacturing, along with the bauxite and tourist industries, to provide adequate employment for the island's labour force. Thus, while the proportion of the classifiable work force engaged in agriculture did decline from 45 per cent in 1943 to about 35 per cent in the late 1960s, this decline was proportionately much smaller than the fall of the relative share of agriculture in GDP. The economic importance of the new growth sectors was not matched by a corresponding provision of employment. In fact, total unemployment, after declining in the 1950s due to emigration, had by 1968 returned to the level of the 1940s—around 24 per cent (Jefferson 1972: 285). Thus, despite a net investment rate of over 15 per cent of GDP for the period 1950 to 1967 the Jamaican economy failed to achieve self-sustained economic growth and made no real improvement in the level of unemployment. The assertion of bourgeois development economists during the 1950s, that a rate of net investment of around 10 per cent of national income was sufficient to reach the point of 'take off', showed itself to be wholly erroneous (cf. Girvan 1971: 226–227). Jamaica continued to bear all the hallmarks of an underdeveloped country; there had been no cumulative growth, no diffusion of industrialization to increasingly large sectors of the economy, no major reduction in unemployment and no increase in the autonomy of economic policy. There had also been a tendency for a significant proportion of the surplus product to be invested in less productive spheres. The extreme tenuity of the growth record was most authoritatively documented by Norman Girvan. In fact, one of his observations turned out to be an accurate prediction of what was to happen under the Manley regime.

If the two dynamic export industries [bauxite and tourism] experience either a slowing down of their rate of growth or a contraction of output, the foreign debt service problem could become a serious one for the Jamaican economy. It should be borne in mind in this connection that both the bauxite and tourist industries are geared primarily towards the US market, and are therefore highly vulnerable to changes in the level and structure of US demand (1971: 165).

The pursuit of the Puerto Rican model served to buttress the pre-existing ruling class bloc, in that the 'industrial' bourgeoisie that emerged arose out of and/or maintained an organic link with the comprador bourgeoisie and oligarchy. For example, the powerful Henriques family which started business in 1907 soon acquired substantial interests in the manufacture of paper products, glass and plastic containers. Another leading capitalist family, the Matalons, set up Industrial Commercial Developments (IDC) which became one of the largest companies on the Jamaican stock exchange. IDC's pre-eminence was based upon construction and installations, which have been one of the growth areas of the economy. However, after having established themselves in this field the Matalons soon became important landowners. The Da Costa and Delisser families underwent a similar evolution (Reid 1977). At the same time, merchant capital itself continued to play a predominant role in overall economic activity, as is indicated by the data concerning new companies registered with the Jamaican registrar-general. Between September 1957 and March 1964 a total of 1,574 companies registered with an authorized share capital of £14.7 million. The distributive trades sector formed the largest single group—36 per cent of the number and 40 per cent of the authorized share capital. Manufacturing, the second largest group, formed only 24 per cent of the authorized share capital (Girvan 1971: 226–233). In terms of contribution to GDP, distribution was surpassed by manufacturing in 1963 as the single largest industry. In 1968 the contribution of each of the two sectors was: manufacturing, 16·2 per cent; distribution, 13·6 per cent (constant prices). Finally, evidence concerning the continued hegemony of the old ruling class bloc, including the descendants of slave-owners, has been provided by Stanley Reid. His analysis showed that in 1972 some twenty-one families dominated society, accounting for 125 of the 219 directorships of corporate firms and nearly 70 per cent of the chairmen. And whereas Chinese, Lebanese, Syrians, Jews and 'Jamaican whites' held controlling interests in some of the largest companies, not one firm was in the hands of blacks, who represent around 80 per cent of the population. Out of the 219 directorships only 6 were held by blacks, and of these 2 were government appointees (1977: 24).

Along with its interlocking interests with the *ancien régime*, Jamaican industrial capital had an institutionalized relationship with metropolitan capital through joint ventures and directorships on the boards of multinational corporations. By the late 1960s more than half of all economic activity in the island was foreign-owned (see table 4.3).

TABLE 4.3   Jamaica: foreign ownership of the main economic sectors of the economy (late 1960s)

	%
Mining	100
Manufacturing	75
Financial institutions	66
Transportation	66
Communications	>50
Storage	>50
Tourism	>50
Sugar industry	40

Source: EPICA Task Force 1979: 52.

The subordination of the Jamaican bourgeoisie to North American and British capital was revealed on a number of occasions. One of the main reasons for the collapse of the West Indian Federation in 1960 was the ambition held by Jamaican industrialists of entering into a bilateral association with the United States. Canada and later the EEC were also looked upon as more interesting candidates for economic and political integration than the territories of the Caribbean basin (Payne 1980: 16–17). In 1961 the Jamaican bourgeoisie successfully agitated for the inclusion and entrenchment in the independence constitution of a clause positing property rights as fundamental, and providing that the question of the adequacy of government compensation for property was an issue that should be subject to juridical rather than political approval. L. E.

Ashenheim, the owner of the island's principal bourgeois newspaper, the *Daily Gleaner*, argued that these articles were necessary to placate the fears of foreign corporations which had invested heavily in Jamaica (Phillips 1977: 147–154).

When the PNP came into office in 1972, the chief co-ordinates of the Jamaican social structure were as follows: agro-proletariat, 5 per cent; industrial working class, 20 per cent; service workers and other proletarians, 17 per cent; salaried middle strata, 18 per cent; urban petty bourgeoisie, 17 per cent; peasantry, 22 per cent; and employers, 1 per cent (figures relate to the economically active population). In addition to these figures, account must be taken of the vast pool of unemployed and the casual labourers, some of whose members straddle one or two of the above categories (Nelson 1975).

The experiment in 'Democratic Socialism'

The PNP turns left

The first two years of the PNP government brought a general liberalization as well as a number of limited reforms. The previous ban on Marxist and Black Power literature was lifted and the policy of intimidating known leftists was discontinued. On 23 May 1972, the annual day of commemoration to the 1938 rebellion, the new government mobilized tens of thousands of people to do voluntary work such as planting trees, repairing old people's homes, starting beautification projects and laying the foundations for basic schools. The early reforms included free secondary education, a literacy campaign, a partial land reform (Project Land Lease), and the nationalization, with compensation, of the foreign-owned electricity, telephone and bus companies. The multi-class character of the PNP regime soon became evident. Most of the state institutions were placed under the control of representatives of the island's capitalist class. For example, Aaron Matalon was made chairman of the Urban Development Corporation, and three of his brothers, Eli, Moses and Mayer, were also given senior government appointments. Other capitalists promoted by Manley were Karl Hendrickson and Peter Rousseau, who, along with the Matalons, belong to the twenty-one ruling families. At the same time, some of the most prominent individuals who had led the popular opposition to Shearer were also given portfolios in the new administration. These included Paul Miller and D. K. Duncan (who had been members of the Black Power Abeng Group), Lloyd Barnett of the Jamaica Council for Human Rights, and Fay Saunders who was the ex-president of the Jamaica Teachers' Association (Abeng Group n.d.). In early 1974 *The Politics of Change* was published, Manley's blueprint for social transformation in Jamaica. In this book the PNP leader advanced a Fabian-type notion of participatory democracy ('the politics of participation') and put forward a critique of capitalism and imperialism analogous to that of

Julius Nyerere in Tanzania (cf. Nyerere 1969). In outlining his remedies for Jamaica's social and economic ills, Manley began:

I have deliberately chosen to consider the question of the psychological elements first because of the conviction that all human achievement flows from states of mind without which the more technical elements in human performance cannot develop. For Jamaica the two critical elements are to be found in the areas of confidence and attitude. Because colonialism undermined confidence, the great need now is to develop a mood of national confidence in which the people at large assume that they have both the duty and the capacity for great achievement (1974: 91–92).

Due notice was thereby given of the PNP's intention to restrict societal change to the level of the superstructure and not tackle the fundamental problems of class and imperialist domination. In a manner wholly characteristic of idealism, Manley posits the cultural revolution *ahead* of the social revolution, whereas in reality it is only the latter which can lay the material basis for a qualitative leap in the mass psychology of the oppressed. Later on in his book, Manley went on to suggest that the wearing of 'karebas' (a form of bush-jacket) by government ministers was 'part of the struggle for the freedom of dress' and helped to create a sense of national purpose (1974: 203). Symbolic gestures formed an integral part of the political philosophy of Jamaica's new prime minister.

The inflationary spiral of 1973 and the generalized recession of the world capitalist economy of 1974–75 severely dislocated Manley's reform programme. The drastic price increases in raw materials and machinery, the erratic fluctuations in imported supplies, and the sharp jump in the interest rates charged by foreign banks, all combined to curtail investment and the expansion of employment. The import bill for oil alone rocketed from J$50m* in 1973 to J$180m one year later (Maingot 1979: 278). Manley's response to this chain of events was to shift his reform programme into a higher gear. In January 1974 the PNP announced that it would re-negotiate tax agreements with the US- and Canadian-owned aluminium companies. This move was supported by Jamaica's relatively weak bourgeoisie, which had increasingly come to rely upon the state for investment funds. Then, in mid-1974 Manley officially abrogated previous agreements and imposed a novel method of taxation: a production 'levy' on all bauxite mined or processed in Jamaica. The levy was set at 7.5 per cent of the selling price of aluminium ingot, instead of the former method of computing the tax based on an artificial profit negotiated between the government and the companies. As a result, the tax rate increased 480 per cent between 1973 and 1975, while in the meantime the government began negotiations towards the purchase of majority control in the bauxite industry. The discomfiture of North American interests was increased by Jamaica's leading role in the formation of the International Bauxite Association in March 1974, a producers' organization inspired by OPEC (Keith and Girling 1978).

* US$1 = J$1.77 (1980).

In November 1974 the PNP published its 'Thirteen Principles' of 'Democratic Socialism'—a somewhat contradictory move given that during the election campaign Manley had categorically denied holding any political philosophy, claiming that the PNP did not believe in 'isms'. The principal themes of this document were 'co-operation', 'socialism as a way of life', 'the right to private property' and 'the mixed economy'. Within the party the left wing, represented by D. K. Duncan and Arnold Bertram, became more prominent. Manley emerged as a spokesman for the Third World, and Jamaica assumed a leading role in UN debates appealing for a New International Economic Order. One of the PNP's major foreign policy shifts was to develop closer ties with Jamaica's nearest neighbour, Cuba. As these links strengthened, Cuba began to provide Jamaica with technical assistance, especially in the areas of education (school construction) and fishing. Manley paid a state visit to Cuba in 1975 and Fidel Castro returned it two years later with a five-day visit to Jamaica. The PNP government also announced its support for African liberation movements, in particular the MPLA in Angola, and both Julius Nyerere and Samora Machel made official visits to the island.

The response of the US government to the new posture of the Manley regime was to make a sustained effort to destabilize the Jamaican economy. The bauxite levy itself received no adverse comment from government sources in either the US or Canada—in fact, Manley made personal visits to Secretary of State Kissinger in Washington and Prime Minister Trudeau in Ottawa just before the announcement of the tax increase (Girvan 1976: 150). However, the aluminium companies made a two-pronged counter-attack. On the one hand, they filed suit with the World Bank's International Centre for the Settlement of Investment Disputes contesting the legality of the levy, while on the other hand they began to transfer bauxite and alumina production from Jamaica to other countries. Although the recession did reduce world production, Jamaica suffered a disproportionate, overtly political cutback. While American aluminium companies doubled their bauxite imports from Guinea in 1975, they reduced their Jamaican imports by 30 per cent, for a net industry-wide decrease in US bauxite imports of 20 per cent (Keith and Girling 1978: 29). Jamaica's share of the world market for bauxite plummeted (see table 4.4). In tandem with sabotage by the aluminium companies, other multinational corporations also curtailed their investments and activities on the island. Foreign capital inflow shrank from US$254m in 1973 to US$115m in 1975, and in 1976 a net outflow was recorded (Girvan 1980: 62).

TABLE 4.4 Bauxite: world market shares (%)

	1970	1975
Jamaica	27	17
Australia	14	24
Guinea	2	23

Source: Maingot, 1979, p. 297.

It was Manley's close relationship with Cuba and support for the MPLA in Angola that invoked the wrath of the US State Department. In 1975 the US Agency for International Development (USAID) turned down Jamaica's request for a US$2.5m food grant, refusing to lend additional funds to the Manley regime until it changed its stance. One year later the American Export-Import Bank dropped Jamaica's credit rating from a top to a bottom category.[5] The US press contributed to the destabilization effort by discouraging people from visiting the island, thereby undercutting the tourist industry. The actual number of visitors from the US, a figure that had been rising steadily since the 1960s, declined by 13 per cent between 1974 and 1975, and dropped by more than 10 per cent in 1976 (Keith and Girling 1978: 30–31). Finally, the Jamaican capitalist class also joined in the anti-Manley offensive. The *Daily Gleaner* kept up a barrage of vituperation and slander against the PNP, which Fred Landis, who had been a consultant/researcher to the US Senate sub-committee on the CIA's covert action in Chile, compared with the role played by *El Mercurio* in helping to overthrow the Allende regime (cf. Press Association of Jamaica n.d.).

Despite the sabotage of the economy, the activities of the CIA (reported by Philip Agee) and a terror campaign unleashed by JLP gun-thugs, the PNP swept the December 1976 elections with a landslide vote (the PNP won forty-seven seats—56.8 per cent of the vote; the JLP thirteen seats—43.2 per cent of the vote). In particular there was a decisive shift in working-class votes towards Manley's party, with the proletarian districts of Kingston opting overwhelmingly for the PNP. Riding the wave of popular militancy, Manley was able to confront the IMF on 5 January 1977; 'We are not for sale,' he declared in rejecting a proposed loan package with too many reactionary strings attached. Then a second reform programme was announced: higher taxes were imposed on the rich, Barclay's Bank was nationalized (with compensation), restrictions were placed on foreign exchange, new trade links established with the workers' states and a State Trading Corporation (STC) set up to regulate foreign trade. The bourgeoisie responded with more production cutbacks and layoffs, while the social and economic situation on the island reached crisis proportions. The PNP had reached the Rubicon of retreat or social revolution.

Manley retreats

In the event, at the end of April 1977 Manley chose to back down and accept on draconian terms a standby loan of US$74m to ease the balance of payments situation. In spite of his electoral mandate from Jamaica's poor to press ahead against the imperialists and native oligarchy, Manley led the PNP in a demoralizing retreat which alienated much of his popular support. The IMF credit line was explicitly conditional on the institution of a programme of anti-working-class measures, including a wage freeze, a near 40 per cent devaluation of the Jamaican dollar and a drastic cutback in public spending. The agreement with the IMF was followed by a shift to the right within the party which was symbolized by the resignation of D. K. Duncan as general secretary and the appointment, the following year, of the conservative Eric Bell as Minister of Finance. At the same time, there was a growing rapprochement with the new Carter administration in Washington and a thaw in the relationship with the aluminium companies, whose financial assistance was canvassed to help meet IMF performance criteria. The contradictions of the PNP regime became increasingly apparent as Manley continued to make 'anti-imperialist' speeches at international forums, while at home he presided over a massive reduction in working-class living standards.

The new situation in the Caribbean opened up in 1979 by the revolutions in Grenada and Nicaragua and reflected at the Sixth Summit Conference of the Non-aligned Movement held in Havana caused the Carter administration to reassess its attitude towards the PNP. As for Manley, his eye was by now firmly fixed on the forthcoming general elections. A demagogic shift back to the left seemed imperative. In September 1979 the PNP conference received a delegation from the People's Revolutionary Government of Grenada and renamed D. K. Duncan as general secretary of the party. In March 1980 Manley broke off relations with the IMF and grandiosely announced the beginning of an 'Alternative Self-Reliant Economic Path'. As a consequence Eric Bell resigned as Minister of Finance and was replaced by a figure on the left of the party, Hugh Small. However, the recomposition of the government was too cosmetic, and the turn to the left too late, to recapture the popular support squandered over the previous two years by the PNP's capitulation to the IMF. The erosion of PNP support was staggering, as the October 1980 election gave the JLP the largest margin of victory in Jamaican history: fifty-two seats (58.7 per cent of the vote) versus the PNP's paltry eight seats (41.2 per cent of the vote). The US State Department had by this time made clear where its support lay, and this was confirmed by spokesman John Tratner, who commented: 'We welcome this further demonstration of democracy in this hemisphere' (*Caribbean Contact* November 1980).

The balance sheet

The record of eight years of 'Democratic Socialism' speaks for itself. Real income fell by 25 per cent, while the cost of living rose 320 per cent. In 1980 net foreign exchange reserves stood at minus J$900m—a fall of 1,014 per cent. Real investment fell by 65 per cent. Unemployment went as high as 31 per cent in October 1979, although by the time of the elections it had been reduced to around 27 per cent—an increase of 2 per cent for the period as a whole. The foreign debt left by the PNP was J$3,147m—a 47 per cent increase (*Jamaica Weekly Gleaner* (JWG), 29 October 1980; *The Weekly Gleaner* (TWG), 16 December 1981). During the period 1973 to 1980 GDP plummeted by an amazing 18.3 per cent (TWG 30 September 1981) and the JLP inherited an economy in which the factories were running at only 30 per cent of capacity (*Financial Times* (FT),

5 November 1980). The bauxite levy, it is true, did result in a substantial increase in government revenue, rising from J$24.51m in 1973 to J$185m in 1977. However, the counter-offensive mounted by the multinational companies pulled most of its teeth. In November 1979 the PNP, desperately concerned about Jamaica's declining share of world production, conceded the corporations a 0.5 per cent reduction in the levy rate and introduced a new formula linking tax decreases to increases in production (Keith and Girling 1978: 21; FT 15 October 1980).

The PNP's attempts at land reform were scarcely more successful than their efforts to control bauxite production. Historically, the Jamaican countryside has been dominated by a few giant plantations and a small number of large landholdings. Thus in 1968, 0.15 per cent of all holdings monopolized 43 per cent of arable land, while 78 per cent of holdings were pathetic minifundia of five acres or less covering only 15 per cent of the land area. The PNP's Project Land Lease was essentially a strategy designed to persuade the big landowners to make some of their idle land available to poor peasants. When in 1975 young people in the parishes of Portland and Westmoreland took the PNP's rhetoric against the 'big man' seriously and organized land seizures, they were roundly condemned by Manley. In late 1978 the PNP Minister of Agriculture, Belinfanti, helped to crush a similar movement of land occupation. Official government data show the lamentable record of the PNP's agrarian policies. The ten Food Farms set up to reduce imports and provide employment yielded poorly and by January 1976 had lost nearly J$3.5m—the scheme had to be abandoned (Grant 1977: 47–61). As for Project Land Lease itself, statistics show that the scheme was most successful in Portland, Manchester and St James where the land is mountainous and/or lacking in irrigation. Out of 112,654 acres acquired up to August 1978 only 63,309 were arable. Big landowners found it easy to circumvent the programme. Out of 128,731 acres adjudged idle by the August 1978 Land Development and Utilization Commission report, only 61,086 were still considered idle after representation from the landowners. Of this figure only some 28,700 acres could in fact have been acquired, since the remainder were covered by 'development plans' which the owners submitted if they did not wish their estates to be taken over (Harriot 1979: 48–57). At a cost of millions of dollars Project Land Lease hardly made a dent in the island's lopsided agrarian structure, and settled only a small proportion of the poor peasants who required land. In addition, despite a firm commitment by the PNP to make agricultural production a priority area, the Jamaican sugar industry was also left in a parlous state. The 1980 sugar crop at 242,000 tonnes was the worst for thirty years and the accumulated debt of the industry was US$67m (FT 10 September 1980, 14 January 1982).

The extent to which the Manley regime was successful in its endeavour to 'create a sense of national purpose' is revealed in the following statistics. In 1978 Jamaica trained 4,286 persons in managerial, administrative and technical skills. In the same year the island lost to migration some 2,705 persons employed in these categories, resulting in a situation in which unfilled vacancies in key areas of the economy averaged over 30 per cent (TWG 26 August 1981). Another index of the 'brain drain', which reflected the disaffection of the middle class with the PNP government, was the number of Chinese who left Jamaica. In the pre-1972 period, there were approximately 78,000 persons in the country who were considered Chinese (regardless of the fact that they may have been mixed). By the time of the 1980 elections there were only about 20,000 of them left (TWG 26 August 1981).

Along with its dismal economic performance, the Manley regime did little to break from the pattern of party political patronage and was in the end a victim of this very system. Political patronage and the corresponding political violence have been basic features of the Jamaican body politic since universal adult suffrage was introduced in 1944. The large pool of unemployed workers and the extreme causalization of labour provided the social framework for 'patron–client' structures to emerge. It was common knowledge that under both JLP and PNP regimes the distribution of tickets for seasonal farm work in the US proceeded along political lines. An official PNP document of 1959 went so far as to declare openly that the duty of the good party member was to 'see that PNP people get work.... out of every ten, make it six PNP and four JLP' (Munroe 1972: 93). The Manley regime continued this tradition with great zeal. The Impact Programme, the Food Farms, Project Land Lease and even the Brigadista Programme which sent Jamaicans for technical training to Cuba, were used for purposes of patronage (cf. Harriot 1979; Jacobs n.d.; Race Today 1980). An example of PNP victimization emerged in the Rema Commission of Enquiry Report, set up to inquire into the eviction of JLP supporters from the housing development project at Rema in Kingston. The report not only substantiated complaints of intimidation of JLP supporters, but also pointed out that the Minister of Housing, Anthony Spaulding, was assisted by hired gunmen in his re-organization of the community (Caribbean Contact January 1979).

It is in light of the PNP's clientalism and use of armed thugs that one has to view the violent confrontation that took place during the 1976 and 1980 general elections between PNP and JLP supporters. US destabilization and assistance to the JLP, while undoubtedly adding a new dimension to the conflict, essentially exploited a pre-existing antagonism based on partisanship and not class struggle. This explains fundamentally why the various confrontations with US imperialism never developed the revolutionary dynamic witnessed in other such situations—most notably in Chile under the Allende regime. Lacey's conclusion with regard to political violence in Jamaica during the 1960s could equally be applied to the Manley era: the violence was 'functional to the political system and was not dysfunctional or in opposition to it' (1977: 161). The JLP was able to regain the support of the working class and popular layers—albeit on a platform of anti-communism—not only by exploiting the economic disaster occasioned by 'Democratic Socialism', but also by offering an alternative to PNP victimization. Indeed, by the time of the October 1980 elections the PNP's resources for political patronage could not match those of the imperialist-financed opposition.

The bitter struggle between Jamaica's two main political parties also reflected an intra-bourgeois dissonance. The PNP was quite selective in its policies against the 'big man'. Manufacturers and commercial enterprises that were close to the party found it easier to obtain import licences from the trade administrator. Pro-PNP capitalists like the Matalons loomed large in a number of government projects,[6] and one of the central demands that Seaga put forward throughout was for the appointment of a contractor general to monitor the award of all government contracts. The JLP was also able to point to instances of corruption of PNP appointees and government progammes. In June 1978 the chairman of the Bank of Jamaica was forced to resign after it was discovered that he was simultaneously the director of two companies that were clients of the bank. In the same year half-a-million dollars from the fund of the Pioneer Corps (a youth training programme) could not be accounted for and some thirty centres which were included in the project's accounts were found to be non-existent. Prior to this, Ted Ogilve, who was the permanent secretary in the Ministry of Works, had been shot dead after investigations into certain government schemes which were suspected of involving serious corruption (*Caribbean Contact* August 1978; June 1979). Finally, Dexter Rose, who was the head of the State Trading Corporation, was found to be receiving 'kickbacks' from certain companies, but was able to escape from the island after having been detained by the security forces.

The headlong decline of economic activity in Jamaica led to a spectacular growth in the illegal ganja (marijuana) trade. In testimony on 30 March 1981 before a joint meeting of the House Inter-American Affairs and Judiciary Committees, Drug Enforcement Administration Director Peter Bensinger said Jamaica was the most rapidly growing supplier of marijuana to the United States, probably surpassing Mexico as the number two source. According to reports contained in both *Newsweek* and *Time* magazines, the ganja trade between Jamaica and the US is now worth over US$1 billion a year (*Newsweek* 8 Feburary 1981; *Time* 8 June 1981; Williams 1981). This represents quite an increase over the estimate of US$146m made by the Drug Enforcement Administration in 1974 (Lacey 1977: 159). In 1979 and 1980 information surfaced concerning the complicity of the island's security forces in illegal shipments of ganja from Tinson Pen, St Andrew. However, the PNP government paid scant attention to the matter. An explanation for this has been provided by Alan Gabbidon:

The short answer is that law and order had broken down. The security forces were fully occupied in preventing civil war. Ganja had become the alternative to the IMF, and both the business establishment and the government saw the ganja trade as vital to their survival.

As the election approached the information to me is that both parties were relying more and more heavily on the ganja trade to provide election funds, foreign exchange to buy election equipment, and on illegal flights to bring that equipment into the island (yes, guns included). One side was doing this to preserve socialism and the other to save the country from Communism. The ganja men were doing it to get rich. It was ganja's finest hour (Gabbidon 1981).

The Workers' Party of Jamaica

The prospects for class struggle in Jamaica under the Manley regime were also hampered by the strategy adopted by the Workers' Party of Jamaica (WPJ), the largest working-class political formation on the island, led by Trevor Munroe. Founded in 1974 by former Black Power advocates who refused to be co-opted by Manley, the Workers' Liberation League (as it was then called) initially projected a quite plausible analysis of the Manley regime. The PNP was characterized as 'liberal bourgeois' and the WLL adopted the slogan: 'The Working Class Must Rule'. However, at the end of the summer of 1976 a review of the official line took place, and the party subsequently adopted a stance of 'critical support' towards the Manley government (cf. Miller 1976). Influenced by the positions of the international communist movement, and in particular the Havana Declaration (cf. chapter 1 of this volume), the WPJ began to place more emphasis on the progressive character of Manley's ties with Cuba and the USSR than on the rightward turn of the PNP's domestic policies. During the 1976 elections, the party supported the declaration of a state of emergency. After the capitulation to the IMF the WPJ organized a campaign against the Fund without ever mentioning the PNP by name or criticizing its role. Despite its sheer opportunism, the slogan popularized by the JLP in this period, 'IMF = Is Manley Fault', uncomfortably drew attention to the WPJ's evasion. Ultimately the unhappy result of the party's line was to be their 'critical support' for the government's repression of mass protest. During the so-called 'gas demonstrations' of January 1979 (a mass protest movement provoked by a government increase in the price of gasolene) WPJ cadres joined PNP henchmen and the police in physically breaking up the movement. The JLP, on the other hand, was able to exploit this popular discontent for its own ends since the WPJ's orientation ruled out any confrontation with the Manley regime. As Cecil Nelson, the party's leading theoretician explained: 'Any opposition by a left, not strong enough to lead this opposition, is going to end up in the strengthening of reaction' (1979). When Manley made his tactical shift to the left shortly before the 1980 elections, the WPJ immediately abandoned plans to stand their own candidates and devoted all their energies to supporting the PNP. In retrospect, it would seem that Trevor Munroe had it right in 1974, when, in response to calls for an alliance with the PNP, he wrote:

This call, far from hastening revolutionary social and political change, amounts to strengthening the national bourgeoisie, dragging out and prolonging the agony of the people. It is a call to give up revolution and take the path of reform, since any alliance with the bourgeoisie can only be on the basis of the bourgeoisie, the basis of reform (Munroe 1974: 15).

The PNP and populism

The 'Democratic Socialism' of the Manley regime should be viewed as a belated experiment in bourgeois nationalist-populism. For despite Manley's position as vice-president of the Socialist International and his personal adherence to certain tenets of Fabian socialism, the PNP cannot be described as an authentic social-democratic party as has been argued by Petras (1980) and Post (1980). Whereas social democracy is essentially a product of the labour bureaucracy, the PNP does not have such an 'organic' relationship to the working class. The NWU was set up by the PNP to suppress the militant and radical leadership of the TUC and to consolidate bourgeois hegemony over the Jamaican labour movement. Under the Manley regime the NWU participated in the system of political patronage, acting as the distributor of work to PNP supporters. A study has, in fact, shown that in Jamaica there is a strong correlation between the party in power and the subsequent growth of its trade-union adjunct (Gonsalves 1977: 93).

The moderate nationalism of the early PNP and the tortoise-like pace of Jamaican decolonization was not only a reflection of Norman Manley's intoxication with English jurisprudence, but also corresponded to a very real problematic—the low level of national consciousness in Jamaica. This was not just a Jamaican phenomenon but a characteristic feature of the English-speaking Caribbean, where the long years of chattel slavery and colonial rule served to retard and deflect national awareness. In contrast to the situation in India and Africa, where nationalism pervaded the body politic, the emergent states of the Commonwealth Caribbean were often headed by trade-union leaders who had organized the labour struggles of the 1930s and 1950s (Grantley Adams in Barbados, Eric Gairy in Grenada, Vere Bird in Antigua and Bustamante in Jamaica). Hence, class consciousness, often adulterated and mediated through racial and religious expressions, has held greater currency than nationalism in these 'exploitation societies'.[7] Bustamante's election slogan in 1944, 'self-government means slavery', encapsulated this paradoxical and somewhat schizophrenic relationship between underdeveloped nationalism and its labourist surrogate.

However, the 'anti-imperialism' of the younger Manley represented an attempt at national assertion in a world context in which the objective bases of the bourgeois nationalist-populism of the classical type (led by such figures as Nehru in India and Peron in Argentina) have been substantially reduced. The shifts that have taken place in the world capitalist economy over the last thirty years have given rise to a pattern of industrialization in the Third World which has both increased the dependence of these countries on the advanced capitalist centres, while enlarging the industrial proletariat.[8] The timidity of the Manley regime *vis-à-vis* American imperialism and the IMF was to a large extent a reflection of the configuration of the bourgeois layers associated with the PNP. Local industrial capital hardly played an autonomous role in the process of capital accumulation and was structurally linked to the *ancien régime* as well as foreign capital. The bauxite industry, it must be remembered, was the one major industry in which national capital had not been incorporated as a junior partner. However, the ultimate result of the confrontation over bauxite was to unleash a chain reaction that undermined all sectors of the local bourgeoisie. Similarly, the PNP's attempt to place restrictions on imports had repercussions way beyond the parameters of merchant capital. The rightward evolution of the PNP from mid-1977 until the beginning of 1980 was an indication of the limit to which national capital was prepared to venture against imperialism (something which the theory of 'the patriotic anti-imperialist national bourgeoisie' upheld by the WPJ was unable to explain). Correlatively, the final 'left turn' of Manley in 1980 was not only too little and too late, but presupposed for its success a dynamic of working-class self-organization and consciousness that was incompatible with the PNP's class composition and evolved ideology.

The populism of the Manley regime proved so effective for a period because it struck certain chords in the popular consciousness of the Jamaican masses. In particular, it exploited popular reaction to the continuing dominance of the island by non-black oligarchs. Despite the structural changes that had taken place in the Jamaican economy the traditional class structure and its associated racial hierarchy had remained intact. Manley's deployment of populism was in continuity with the mode of appeal of earlier Jamaican mass leaders—Paul Bogle during the Morant Bay rebellion of 1865, Robert Love in the 1890s, Alexander Bedward in the 1920s, and Marcus Garvey and Busta-mante in the 1930s. While Manley did not, in fact, adopt an explicitly racial discourse, he did try to place himself within this tradition, and his government was the first in the island's history to legitimize the cultural and social predispositions of the black masses. Along with the overtures towards Black Power and Rastafarianism, Manley made frequent recourse to 'Jamaican patois', identified himself with the African liberation movements and launched invectives against the 'big man'. Manley also manipulated religion to his own advantage and in the 1972 general elections adopted the epithet 'Joshua'. 'Democratic Socialism', then, was but the final ingredient in this populist *mélange*, serving to enhance Manley's stature in the international community, but not fundamentally transforming the class basis or ideology of the PNP. However, the PNP could claim no monopoly of populist politics, whose specifically Jamaican idiom had been pioneered by the JLP under Busta-mante. The demise of the PNP government in the October 1980 elections in Jamaica provides an indication of the growing inadequacy of nationalist-populism as a form of bourgeois rule in the Third World today and the scope that exists for a reactionary appropriation of its appeals. (For a more extended discussion of the Manley period see James 1981, forthcoming (a), forthcoming (b).)

The prospects for Jamaica under Seaga

Shifts among the masses

The return to office of the JLP can be looked upon as a sort of pragmatic move by the Jamaican oppressed to avert economic catastrophe and the adventurism of 'Democratic Socialism'. For while it is true, and highly germane to point out, that the JLP managed to build a fairly extensive mass movement based upon anti-communism and physical attacks on Cuban doctors and technicians, there has not been a widespread acceptance of the JLP's political philosophy. This is borne out by a number of opinion polls conducted since the election by Carl Stone. For example, the poll carried out by Stone in November 1981 found that a large majority of the people interviewed held the opinion that if the PNP had stayed in office the situation in the country would have been worse than it had been under the new JLP administration. Significantly, this view was shared by one out of every six PNP supporters. Stone also found that despite the widespread feeling that the PNP was more 'people-oriented' than the JLP and was more concerned about the interests of the poor, deep doubt existed about the PNP's competence to run the country efficiently. The JLP, on the other hand, had an image of supporting the rich, but many interviewees had confidence that the JLP had a good understanding of economic matters and was the better of the two parties when it came to running the affairs of state and managing the economy. Much of this belief in the greater managerial capability of the JLP over the PNP was based on favourable opinions of the technocratic ability of Edward Seaga (TWG 30 December 1981). This last finding is quite pertinent since in a poll conducted by Stone during the 1976 elections, Manley was considered to be three times as popular as Seaga, whose anti-communist crusade and revanchism met with little public sympathy. By the time of the 1980 elections, however, Manley's globe-trotting and oratory in support of the New International Economic Order was increasingly seen as a diversion from the concrete problems facing Jamaican society. Conversely, Seaga's excursions abroad served to enhance his reputation as something of a financial wizard in that his principal destinations were Miami and Washington, where he colluded with government officials, prominent businessmen and representatives of international lending agencies. Probably the most important, and controversial, of the JLP leader's sojourns in the US was in June 1980, when he met Walter Robichek of the Latin American and Caribbean division of the IMF.

This meeting caused quite a scandal in Jamaica because, coming shortly after the PNP scission with the Fund, it clearly constituted interference in the political process of the island. Furthermore, the JLP election manifesto, which was published a few months later, included figures about the foreign exchange gap which could only have been arrived at as the result of discussions between Seaga and the Fund. The promise to obtain the foreign exchange to meet the deficit was a major plank in the platform of the opposition party (FT 29 October 1980).

The US connection

Seaga's early collaboration with the IMF was to pay substantial dividends when he came into office. In April 1981 it was announced that the Fund was lend Jamaica US$698m over a three-year period. The most significant aspect of the deal was the leniency of the conditions imposed on the Seaga regime, compared to the way that the PNP government's requests for support were treated. Above all, there was no insistence on a devaluation of the Jamaican dollar and no demand for the introduction of wage and price controls—as had been the case under Manley. Nor were the restrictions on domestic public sector borrowing made to apply to the private sector, while the ceiling on government borrowing abroad excluded loans to refinance existing debts. The signing of the loan agreement with the IMF opened the way to further inflows of financial support for Jamaica's battered economy. Some US$400m in loans was provided by the Caribbean Group for Co-operation in Economic Development, a multilateral lending agency which is supported by the US, Canada, Britain and West Germany (FT 15 September 1981). The significance of all this has been summarized by Payne:

[Seaga's] experience with the Fund, following that of Manley, provides yet more evidence of the direct political role of the IMF in defending the interests of the Western capitalist system.

The whole episode also offers a textbook illustration of how a loan from the IMF can put the stamp of financial respectability on a country which had effectively been frozen out of the international money markets since the Manley government's 'break' with the Fund (1981: 436).

Part of the reason for the favourable treatment given to Seaga by the IMF was the fact that he had managed to establish a close relationship with the Reagan administration in Washington. Seaga was the first foreign head of state to be invited to the White House by the new American president. The visit took place in January 1981 and resulted in the formation of a Jamaican–American Business Investment Committee, designed to channel new investors in Jamaica's direction. The Committee is led by prominent bourgeois figures: on the American side, David Rockefeller, the former chairman of the Chase Manhattan Bank, and, on the Jamaican side, Carlton Alexander, the chief executive of the Grace Kennedy group, one of Jamaica's largest private companies. The presidents and chairmen of some twenty-two major US companies have joined the ranks of the new body and its creation was followed by the establishment of joint business committees with Venezuela, Canada, Britain and West Germany. Another outcome of the talks in Washington was the momentum generated in support of Seaga's concept of a 'Mini-Marshall Aid Plan' for the Caribbean. This idea was first mooted by Seaga at the Fourth Conference of the Caribbean–Central American Action (CCAA) held in Miami in November 1980, where he called upon the US government to formulate a 'Caribbean policy' and provide financial assistance for the creation of new anti-communist alliance in the region (JWG 3 December 1980). The concept was discussed again at a summit held in Nassau in July 1981, at which the US Secretary of State and the Foreign Ministers of Canada, Mexico and Venezuela tried to hammer out a common approach to the provision of development aid to the Caribbean. The Nassau meeting revealed the basic elements of Washington's strategy in the Caribbean. The Reagan administration emphasized that it conceived a development programme more in terms of trade and investment than massive increases in aid. The plea that had been made by a number of Caribbean governments for a commitment to increase aid from US$1 billion to around US$3 billion a year fell upon deaf ears. Furthermore, the US specifically sought to exclude Nicaragua, Grenada and Cuba from the four-nation aid plan, because of their alleged association with 'Soviet expansionism' in the region. However, this proposal was rejected by Mexico, who received the backing of Venezuela and Canada, and this and other differences among the prospective donor countries resulted in a failure to agree on any concrete initiatives. The tightfisted and ideological nature of US diplomacy in the region was again in evidence at the Fifth Conference of the CCAA held in Miami in November 1981. During the parley William Brock, Reagan's chief trade representative, cautioned that 'any economic formula would not lie in some grand American design but, instead, in well-planned, significant cooperative action' (TWG 16 December 1981). Following the conference Brock made a proposal in Kingston concerning the creation of a one-way free trade area between the Caribbean basin and the US market place. This suggestion was immediately hailed by Seaga and the *Daily Gleaner*, although by late 1981 no details had yet emerged (TWG 9 December 1981).

If not the region as a whole, then at least the JLP government has received some tangible benefits from what has now come to be known as the Caribbean Basin Initiative. In 1981 Jamaica received US$40m from USAID and a loan agreement for US$38m has been signed for 1982 (TWG 6 January 1982). The US Senate has ratified a new taxation treaty between Jamaica and the United States, which gives the island 'most favoured' treatment as in the case of Canada and Mexico. The treaty enables Jamaica to tax certain US corporations which would otherwise have been taxed in the US. American individuals will also be subjected to the new law and the treaty should result in a certain improvement in government revenue. Another clause in the act will provide a stimulus to Jamaica's tourist industry. Companies and organizations holding conferences in the island will be able to write off expenses against their tax liability in the US, and this will attract more business conventions to Jamaica (TWG 6 January 1982; FT 13 August 1981). The Thatcher government in Britain has followed Washington's lead in bestowing honours on the JLP government. In July 1981 it was announced that Seaga had been appointed to the Privy Council, a privilege that has been reserved for only the most loyal servants of British imperialism in Jamaica (such as Bustamante and Shearer). Two months later the Export Credit Guarantee Department decided to restore insurance cover to British exports to the island, which had been terminated during the last year of the Manley administration (TWG 8 July 1981; 8 September 1981).

This special consideration which has been lavished upon Jamaica has provoked an outcry from political leaders in the other territories of the Commonwealth Caribbean. One Caribbean government official is reported to have screamed: 'What do we have to do? Elect a Manley or a Fidel Castro first, then throw him out in order to get help?' (TWG 30 December 1981). Disquiet has also been expressed about Reagan's declared aim of reducing bilateral and multilateral aid flows to the region and promote, in their place, injections of private foreign capital. This has led to tensions in the tacit alliance against communism which had crystallized among the Caricom states, in the wake of events in Grenada and Nicaragua. Even the countries that share Seaga's anti-communist fervour have become suspicious of the exclusivity of the rapport between Kingston and Washington. In many ways this development shows a certain lack of far-sightedness on the part of the Reagan administration. As Carl Stone has observed:

Such a trend will defeat US intentions which saw Seaga as being potentially as influential as Manley was in the region. The jealousy over US–Jamaica aid and special assistance and Jamaica's inability to convincingly or militantly champion the cause of the poorer Eastern Caribbean states for more aid will mean a decline in Jamaican influence in the region and a considerable growth of Trinidadian regional political influence. If Chambers continues the Eric Williams tradition of foreign policy that development will not mean greater US Caribbean influence....

... Jamaica's standing and influence in the region could well become a casualty of Reagan's miscalculations about how to build support among Caribbean states (1981).

As we have intimated above, the fraction of capital most closely associated with the JLP has often displayed a proclivity towards turning Jamaica into an overseas province of the US, and has thus been totally unmoved by the accusations of its Commonwealth allies. The *Daily Gleaner*, which faithfully reflects the views of this interest group, dealt with the question in the following cavalier manner:

Without chauvinism we would recommend that the Eastern Caribbean study, and possibly copy, the details of Jamaica's strategy as they unfold. For it must be remembered that there can only be one bellwether in the flock (TWG, 30 December 1981).

The economic front

Consistent with his stated goals of 'freeing up the market' and returning Jamaica to the Puerto Rican model, Seaga has set about the task of clearing out the institutional debris of 'Democratic Socialism'. A Divestment Committee has been set up to sell off the various public enterprises established during the Manley era. A dry dock company, a dairy processing plant, a paper factory, two agricultural enterprises, an airline catering service and the island's second daily newspaper, the *Daily News*, have already been advertised, and the committee is at various stages of negotiation with potential buyers. The National Hotels and Properties Company, which managed a number of the hotels taken over by the PNP (as the only means of keeping them operational), has been instructed to offer several of its properties for lease and possible sale (*West Indian World* 7 August 1981). The JLP government has lifted nearly all the restrictions which Manley had placed on the granting of import licences, and in September 1981 Seaga reported that there had been a 50 per cent increase in the number of licences issued during the first year of JLP rule. In addition, the State Trading Corporation has been scrapped and replaced by a new body, the Jamaica Commodity Trading Company. The new company is headed by David Henriques, of the twenty-one families, and the reason given for its establishment was that of 'corporate efficiency and central management control'. Finally, the Sugar Workers' Co-operatives set up by the PNP in 1976 have also been discarded, due to bankruptcy. In November 1981 the accumulated debts of the twenty-seven co-operatives stood at J$82.6m and their supply of sugar cane to the factories had fallen from 1 million tonnes in 1976 to 630,000 tonnes that year (TWG 30 September 1981; 7 October 1981; 11 November 1981).

Seaga's ability to secure new inflows of foreign capital has given a certain stimulus to local economic activity. Shortly after the agreement with the IMF several banks on the island agreed to refinance US$103m of the debts owed to them, and granted a new loan of US$70m. Reports published by the Central Bank of Jamaica and the IMF in mid-1981 indicated that there had been significant growth in the construction sector, non-government services, the distributive trades, manufacturing, agriculture and fisheries. Total exports increased by 9 per cent in the first six months of 1981, and receipts from tourism rose by 10 per cent up to July and 15.5 per cent in August, over the same period the year before (FT 15 September 1981). This picture was confirmed by the Economic and Social Survey published by the government planning department. The survey also covered the period January to June 1981, and its projection of a 1 per cent increase in GDP for the year has been subsequently confirmed (TWG 30 September 1981; FT 22 January 1982). There has thus been a reversal of the downward trend in GDP witnessed since 1973. Jamaica has passed all three of the quarterly performance targets set by the IMF so far which has enabled the government to continue drawing from the US$698m loan. Finally, there has been a marked improvement in the local investment climate. In September 1981 Seaga disclosed that Jamaica National Investment Promotions Ltd, the body set up to facilitate all private investment in the island, had received 408 'serious' investment proposals totalling more than J$1 billion in capital investment. Of these proposals some 244 were said to be foreign, representing J$676m in capital investment, and the remaining 164 were local representing J$433m (TWG 9 September 1981). One month later Craig Nalen, president of the US Overseas Private Investment Corporation (OPIC) and leader of a 24-man business mission that visited Jamaica in November, stated that OPIC had received applications from businessmen to the tune of US$520m for investment in Jamaica (TWG 19 November 1981).

Seaga's achievements so far in taking Jamaica out of the tailspin left by the Manley administration do not, of course, demonstrate the superiority of a pro-capitalist and pro-imperialist orientation over that of a socialist option, since, as we have submitted, the political enterprise of the PNP had little to do with socialism. What Seaga's successes do provide an indication of, is in fact the utopian character of 'Democratic Socialism'. For the 'halfwayism' of the Manley regime, to use the jargon of the WPJ comrades, took no account of the fact that a capitalist economy can only be regulated and can only prosper in conformity with the logic of capital; i.e. production for profit. The PNP government had nothing in its political arsenal to counter the flight of capital, investment strikes, economic sabotage and financial conspiracies, which were the inevitable consequence of a reformist and anti-imperialist posture, given: the level of foreign capital in the island, the organic relationship between the local bourgeoisie and overseas capital and the strategic importance which US imperialism has traditionally accorded to the Caribbean basin. Manley could only have secured the acquiescence of local and metropolitan capital to the extent that *either* (i) his policies had such a tremendous resonance among the Jamaican oppressed that no concerted campaign to remove him could have met with success (this was partially the case up until 1977), *or* (ii) no viable alternative bourgeois political formation existed with which to replace him (as is the case in Guyana where the main opposition parties are even more anathema to the interests of native and foreign capital than is the demagogic Burnham regime). Certainly neither of these two conditions can be said to have been satisfied at the time of the 1980 elections.

The jubilation with which the JLP's electoral triumph was greeted in ruling class circles in Jamaica and abroad, and the subsequent flow of financial rewards and privileges, were a celebration of the fact that the shift from left to right was effected through the existing political institutions. The editorial printed in the *Financial Times* was wholly typical of international capital's response:

The first and perhaps the most important deduction to be made [from the election result] is that, despite the worst forebodings of the prophets of doom, the island, like much of the rest of the Commonwealth Caribbean, is a functioning pluralistic democracy. The people's will, as expressed in the ballot box, is still paramount. Jamaica is therefore an example to other countries of the region, from Cuba in the north to Guyana in the south, where effective democracy is nonexistent or gravely ailing (FT 4 November 1980).

The 'democratic' aspect of the transfer of power was applauded by bourgeois commentators for two main reasons. First of all, because the social and political costs of the operation were thereby kept at a minimum; although the Reagan administration would probably not have had any 'moral' objections to a military coup. However, even more important than that was the fact that the electoral débâcle of 'Democratic Socialism' has had a far more potent effect in reinforcing the disaffection and cynicism of the Jamaican masses towards an authentic socialist solution. The various remittances to the JLP have therefore evinced a certain tributary character and it is this factor which places the biggest question mark over the long-term strategy of the Seaga regime. For there are no objective (i.e., economic) reasons for the present love affair with the Reagan administration, and as time goes on there is inevitably going to be a cooling in the relationship as other and more pressing candidates emerge also seeking special assistance to 'halt the spread of communism'. Furthermore, it is already clear that even the current inflows are not going to be sufficient to 'mek money jingle in yu pocket' as the JLP promised during the elections. For despite the modest overall improvement of the island's economy, two crucial sectors—bauxite and sugar—remain severely depressed with somewhat precarious long-term prospects. The onset of the current capitalist world recession has led to a steep reduction in the mining and refining capacities of all the aluminium companies operating in Jamaica. Total exports of bauxite and alumina during 1981 have been officially estimated at 11.5m tonnes, a fall of just under 500,000 tonnes from the year before. However, with the cutbacks in production which have already been announced this figure is expected to fall to 9.15m tonnes in 1982, which will have a drastic effect on government revenue. This anticipated decline of 2m tonnes would have been even greater but for the decision of the Reagan administration to purchase 1.6m tonnes of Jamaican bauxite for the US national defence stockpile (FT 9 December 1981; 20 January 1982; TWG 2 December 1981; 9 December 1981). This further act of support by Washington fits in with a US government commitment to beef up the defence stockpile. Jamaica has in fact been singled out as a potential candidate for a new barter programme. Such a scheme was widely used in the 1950s and 1960s when the US swapped agricultural commodities for strategic minerals. The idea of reinstituting the programme has been floated by the National Security Council, the Department of Interior and several congressmen, anxious to unload some of the nation's vast farm surplus and at the same time replenish the stockpile without massive capital investment. It has been proposed that Jamaican bauxite be traded for agricultural products (FT 18 November 1981).

The most ominous aspect about the present reduction in Jamaican bauxite production is that apart from being a response to the capitalist business cycle, it also presages a downgrading of Jamaican bauxite in the long-term strategy of the North American mineral companies. The reaction of these companies to the advent of a sustained overcapacity in the aluminium industry (which in 1981 was estimated at around 3m tonnes worth £2 billion), has been to promote big expansion schemes in those parts of the world where they believe it is possible to secure new sources of cheap energy—the vital ingredient for the smelting of alumina into aluminium metal. This was explained by William Renner, president of Alcoa, in a speech given during a visit to Jamaica in March 1981. Renner stated that the island was no longer a priority area for investment by his company. The new capital that Alcoa had available was being reserved for energy-rich nations, in particular Australia with ample coal deposits, and Brazil where there is a massive hydro-electric power potential. He also made it quite clear that the bauxite levy had been an important factor in the shift of Alcoa's interest away from Jamaica. In a meeting with Seaga earlier in the year, the aluminium companies had pressed for a further reduction of the index from 7 per cent to around 5 per cent. The government said in the meeting that it would consider a reduction at a later date, and instead proposed to the companies massive increases in bauxite mining and refining. Seaga's proposals were rejected by the companies (FT 18 March 1981; 22 July 1981; 28 October 1981).

The Jamaican sugar industry is also in the doldrums. Output in 1981 was 200,000 tonnes, a fall of 45,000 tonnes from the disastrous harvest of 1980. This was after a pre-crop harvest was set at 300,000 tonnes and had the embarrassing result that after meeting the 125,000 tonnes quota to Britain under the Lomé Convention, the domestic market of 115,000 tonnes had to be supplied with imports from the US. The accumulated losses of the industry now stand at US$112m (FT 14 January 1982). It is Jamaica's deficiency in energy resources that remains the Achilles' heel of the island's economy. Imported oil provides 99 per cent of all energy needs, and in 1980 Jamaica paid US$418m for its oil imports, leaving only US$274.6m from its total foreign earnings. The JLP government has launched a drilling programme in a desperate attempt to find oil. The project is being funded by loans of US$23m from the Inter-American Development Bank and US$7m each from the World Bank and USAID. However, there is no more than cautious optimism about striking oil. Raymond Wright, the director of exploration for the Petroleum Company of Jamaica, has said that the chances of finding a commercially worthwhile deposit were about 1 in 25. Seaga, who is also the Minister of Mining, put the chances of success at 'only about 2 per cent'. The Jamaican government is also giving active consideration to the use of coal-fired rather than oil-fired processes in the refining of bauxite. However, like oil the coal would have to be imported (FT 9 December 1981).

It is patently obvious that Seaga's pursuit of the Puerto Rican model is going to meet with even less success than it did during the 1950s and early 1960s. For the high rates of growth registered at that time were directly related to the general upswing of the world capitalist economy as a whole. The widely accepted prognosis of a lengthy period of extremely sluggish growth for world capitalism makes a repeat performance of the 1950s and 1960s quite unrealistic, particularly since, as we have just indicated, Jamaica has not been accorded any pride of place in the redeployment of world capital which is now under way. Furthermore, the medium-term and global consequences of Reaganism will also be inimical to sustained economic growth, in that the policy of high interest rates and reduced contributions to the World Bank, IMF and other international lending agencies will more than cancel out the various concessions that have been made so far. A presentiment of just how inadequate the open-door strategy to foreign capital is going to be was given in Seaga's disclosure about the 408 investment proposals. He said that the projects had a combined employment potential of some 25,000, which is quite a drop in the ocean when one considers that there are 263,000 people officially registered out of work in the island.

Political prospects

One of Seaga's first political moves on taking office was to expel the Cuban ambassador, Ulises Estrada. This action was quite expected, since much of the JLP's anti-communist agitation was centred around the ambassador and Seaga had made an election pledge to have him removed. However, this did not put an end to the campaign against communism. Revelations about Cuban and Russian subversion have continued to appear in the *Daily Gleaner*, and finally led to a complete diplomatic break with Havana in October 1981. According to Seaga this decision was taken because the Cuban authorities refused to hand over criminals wanted by the Jamaican police. However, the impulsiveness of the move would tend to lend greater credence to the Cuban version of events: 'the move was carried out by Seaga but was decreed in Washington'. The continued hysteria about 'communist subversion' is somewhat disturbing because not only did Manley religiously accept the electoral *fait accompli* but he has also moved to terminate all collaboration between the PNP and the WPJ. He claims that it was this relationship that sealed the fate of his party at the elections (Munroe 1981). Furthermore, it is as clear as daylight that the Soviet Union does not have any grand design on the island, and that the Castro government consistently advocated support for the PNP and not social revolution. In fact, a story published in the *Daily Gleaner* and based on information provided by Alexi Leshtchou, who was the second secretary in the Soviet embassy in Kingston and defected to the West in July 1980, contradicts all the claims about Soviet expansionism in the region. According to the story, Manley requested substantial economic assistance from the Soviet Union during the visit he made to Moscow in April 1979. However, the Soviet leadership was extremely cool towards the idea of financial aid and instead spent the time giving political lectures to the Jamaican leader on how to build 'socialism'. Speaking on behalf of the Soviet government Kosygin explained:

... according to Soviet revolutionary experience a change to socialism could not be done quickly; it required planning. Mr Kosygin said that Lenin had criticized leftist extremists in the Soviet Union, and that he Kosygin did not think a quick break with the US and traditional partners was reasonable or wise. Mr Kosygin is reported to have commented on Allende's experience in Chile and the mistakes Allende had made as well as the importance of Cuba as an example of the step-by-step development. While he understood the need for Jamaica to get rid of what he referred to as the US yoke, and the need for a good life for the Jamaican people, he felt that a prudent approach to revolutionary changes was the best approach (TWG 30 December 1981).

Hardly the counsel of a man conspiring to turn Jamaica into a Soviet satellite! The *leitmotiv* of anti-communism, and the arrest and intimidation of members of the WPJ, must therefore be seen as part of a strategy designed to secure continued revenues from Washington and prepare the ground for a right-wing authoritarian state. Contrary to the assertions of bourgeois commentators in the West, the 1980 electoral triumph of the JLP did not represent a victory of parliamentary democracy. Nor did it signify the vitality of bourgeois democratic institutions in Jamaica. For what was most evident about the JLP's success was their recourse to *extra-parliamentary* methods, of which the party's ability to bring on to the streets sections of the police and army was the most decisive. Moreover, the ability of the society to again withstand the fratricide involved in the last two elections must be severely cast in doubt. For its part, the Reagan administration has made an unequivocal statement to the US Congress to maintain the Seaga government in office (TWG 16 December 1981). Washington has already prepared itself for the future battles in El Salvador, Guatemala and Honduras, and would be loathe to tolerate any more 'experiments' in a country it considers already 'liberated' from the scourge of communism. All this serves to suggest that the JLP victory heralds the extinction of bourgeois democracy in Jamaica, rather than its renaissance.

The decision taken by the Jamaican bauxite workers in January 1982 to undertake strike action over pay shows that the political will of the

Jamaican masses has not been broken by the outcome of the 1980 elections. For not only did Seaga and the *Daily Gleaner* wage a concerted campaign to impress upon the bauxite workers the need to make sacrifices in the national interest, and warn that industrial action could jeopardize the bauxite agreement with the US, but the action in the bauxite industry has been only the latest in a series of strikes which have involved workers in the water industry, the docks, the railways, electricity and public transport. The JLP's message of economic austerity has met a cool response and is increasingly putting strains on the relationship between the party and the BITU. Given the prospects for the island's economy and the trajectory of the regime as a whole, what seems to be on the agenda is a break-up in the traditional relationship between the party and the working class. It would be nice to think that such a development will automatically give rise to a new proletarian radicalization. Unfortunately the growth of class consciousness is a far more complicated matter than that. Nevertheless, when the Jamaican masses do make another lurch to the left it will not be under the banner of 'Democratic Socialism'. Bourgeois nationalist-populism has had its day in Jamaica.

NOTES

1 Parts one and two draw heavily from an earlier paper (Ambursley 1981). I am grateful to the editors of *New left review* for their permission to use some of the material here.

2 For a fuller discussion of Post's work on Jamaica see the excellent study by Cohen (1982).

3 The great exodus to Britain between 1950 and 1964 has been followed since by a new wave of mass emigration to the United States and, to a lesser extent, Canada (cf. Koslofsky 1981).

4 A large proportion of the grocery shops and other commercial enterprises in Jamaica are owned by Chinese, who, as a result, have frequently been targets of social discontent. See Lacey (1977: 85–87).

5 Kissinger reportedly told Manley that US aid would be forthcoming if Jamaica declined to support the MPLA and broke off relations with Cuba (Keith and Girling 1978: 31).

6 Mayer Matalon was placed in charge of the Capital Development Fund, which was set up by the PNP to handle the additional revenues from the bauxite levy. The bulk of the fund's budget was channelled into the construction industry to finance companies owned by Matalon and other capitalists close to the PNP.

7 This notion has been advanced by Knight (1978) to explain the weakness of the nationalist movement in those Caribbean territories that did not experience substantial European settlement.

8 This theme is developed at length in the excellent study by Manuel Aguilar Mora (1980). It is based on an analysis first developed by Ernest Mandel (1976).

REFERENCES

Abeng Group n.d., *Joshua, Aaron, Moses, Eli: two months of selling out Jamaica*, Kingston, Jamaica

Ambursley, F. 1981, 'Jamaica: the demise of "democratic socialism"', *New left review*, no. 128, pp. 76–87

Beckford, G. L. 1972, *Persistent poverty*, London, OUP

Caribbean Contact various dates 1979–81

Cohen, R. 1982, 'Althusser meets Anancy: structuralism and popular protest in Ken Post's history of Jamaica', *The sociological review*, vol. 30, no. 2, new series, May, pp. 345–57

Epica Task Force 1979, *Jamaica: Caribbean challenge*, Washington

Financial Times (FT) various dates 1979–to date

Gabbidon, A. 1981, 'Probe Tinson Pen as ganja centre', *The Weekly Gleaner*, 9 September

Girvan, N. 1971, *Foreign capital and economic underdevelopment in Jamaica*, Kingston, Jamaica, ISER

Girvan, N. 1976, *Corporate imperialism: conflict and expropriation*, New York, Monthly Review Press

Girvan, N. 1980, 'Swallowing the IMF medicine in the 'seventies', *Development dialogue*, no. 2, pp. 55–74

Girvan, N., Bernal, R. and Hughes, W. 1980, 'The IMF and the third world: the case of Jamaica, 1974–80', *Development dialogue*, no. 2, pp. 113–155

Gonsalves, R. 1977, 'The trade union movement in Jamaica: its growth and some resultant problems', in C. Stone and A. Brown (eds.), *Essays on power and change in Jamaica*, Kingston, Jamaica, Jamaica Publishing House

Grant, A. 1977, 'The land reform programme of democratic socialism', *Socialism* (theoretical organ of the Workers' Party of Jamaica), vol. 4, no. 4, pp. 47–61

Harriot, T. 1979, 'The IMF and the struggle for land', *Socialism*, vol. 6, no. 2, pp. 48–57

Harrod, J. 1972, *Trade union foreign policy*, London, Macmillan

Jacobs, W. R. n.d., 'Patterns of political corruption—a comparative study of Grenada, Jamaica and Trinidad and Tobago', mimeo.

Jamaica Weekly Gleaner (JWG) various dates 1979–80

James, W. A. 1981, 'The state, class and dependent capitalism in Jamaica', Paper delivered at the annual conference of the Society for Caribbean Studies, Hoddesdon, Hertfordshire, May 26–28

James, W. A. forthcoming (a), 'The IMF and "Democratic Socialism" in Jamaica', London, Latin American Bureau

James, W. A. forthcoming (b), *Love is all I bring: a critical analysis of "Democratic Socialism" in Jamaica, 1972–80*, London

Jefferson, O. 1972, *The post-war economic development of Jamaica*, Kingston, Jamaica, ISER

Keith, S. and Girling, R. 1978, 'Caribbean conflict: Jamaica and the US', *Nacla*, vol. 12, no. 3, pp. 3–36

Knight, F. 1978, *The Caribbean: the genesis of a fragmented nationalism*, New York, OUP

Koslofsky, J. 1981, 'Going foreign—causes of Jamaican migration', *Nacla*, vol. 15, no. 1, pp. 2–31

Lacey, T. 1977, *Violence and politics in Jamaica, 1960–70*, Manchester, Manchester UP

Maingot, A. P. 1979, 'The difficult path to socialism in the English-speaking Caribbean', in R. R. Fagen (ed.), *Capitalism and the state in US–Latin American relations*, Stanford, California, Stanford UP, pp. 254–301

Mandel, E. 1976, 'Imperialism and national bourgeoisie in Latin America', *International* (theoretical organ of the International Marxist Group, London), vol. 3, no. 1, pp. 23–27

Manley, M. 1974, *The politics of change: a Jamaican testament*, London, André Deutsch

Miller, C. 1976, 'A Review of our political line', *Socialism*, vol. 3, nos. 8 and 9, pp. 2–41

Mora, M. A. 1980, 'Populisme et révolution permanente', *Quatrième internationale*, ser. 3, no. 1, pp. 15–34

Munroe, T. 1972, *The politics of constitutional decolonization: Jamaica, 1944–62*, Kingston, Jamaica, ISER

Munroe, T. 1974, 'The new political situation in Jamaica', *Socialism*, vol. 1, no. 6, pp. 3–18

Munroe, T. 1981, 'Jamaica in turmoil', *Marxism today*, vol. 25, no. 5, pp. 23–26

Nelson, C. 1975, 'Class structure in Jamaica', *The black liberator*, vol. 2, no. 3, pp. 217–226

Nelson, C. 1979, 'The present political situation', *Socialism*, vol. 6, no. 3, p. 21

Newsweek 8 February 1981

Nyerere, J. 1969, *Freedom and socialism*, Dar es Salaam, OUP

Payne, A. J. 1980, *The politics of the Caribbean community, 1961–79: regional integration amongst new states*, Manchester, Manchester UP

Payne, A. J. 1981, 'Seaga's Jamaica after one year', *World today*, vol. 37, no. 11, pp. 434–440

Petras, J. 1980, 'Social democracy in Latin America', *Nacla*, vol. 14, no. 1, January–February, pp. 36–39

Phillips, P. 1977, 'The business sector and Jamaican foreign relations: a study of national capitalist orientations to third world relations', *Social and economic studies*, vol. 26, no. 2, pp. 146–168

Post, K. 1978, *Arise ye starvelings: the Jamaican labour rebellion of 1938 and its aftermath*, The Hague, Boston and London, Martinus Nijhoff

Post, K. 1980, 'Capitalism and social democracy in Jamaica', *Caraïbisch forum*, vol. 1, no. 1, pp. 3–17

Press Association of Jamaica, n.d., *Psychological warfare in the media: the case of Jamaica*, Kingston, Jamaica

Race Today 1980, 'The Jamaican elections: betta nevah come', Editorial, vol. 12, no. 2

Reid, S. 1977, 'An introductory approach to the concentration of power in the Jamaican corporate economy and notes on its origin', in C. Stone and A. Brown (eds.), *Essays on power and change in Jamaica*, Kingston, Jamaica, Jamaica Publishing House

Stone, C. 1981, 'Reagan and the Caribbean', *The Weekly Gleaner*, 23 December

Time 8 June 1981

Weekly Gleaner, The various dates 1981–to date

West Indian World 7 August 1981

Williams, L. 1981, 'Ganja: a billion dollar operation', *The Weekly Gleaner*, 15 July

FIVE

Nicaragua: the Sandinist Revolution

Henri Weber

The victory of the Sandinist revolution on 19 July 1979 broke the long chain of defeats suffered by the workers' movement in Latin America since 1965. It is a living refutation of the two leitmotifs of the imperialist ideological offensive: that it is impossible to defeat a military dictatorship which employs all the coercive instruments of the modern state for the practice of mass terror; and that every socialist revolution always ends in totalitarian dictatorship.

By combining armed struggle, political mass action and a broad alliance policy, the Frente Sandinista de Liberación National (FSLN) wore down one of the fiercest and best-armed dictatorships in the region. Nor has Sandinist Nicaragua become that 'tropical gulag' predicted by the pro-Somoza lobby in the US Congress. It is, indeed, a *revolutionary democracy*: its legitimacy is derived from an insurrectional general strike rather than elections; but power is limited by juridical theory and practice. There is real pluralism of the press, parties and trade unions. There have been real strikes, street demonstrations and national rallies of political parties. Human and civil rights are respected more than in most countries of the American continent.

Where is the Sandinist revolution going? Towards bourgeois restoration? Towards 'people's democracy'? Or towards a democratic socialism that avoids both neo-imperialist backsliding and bureaucratic degeneration? The question is of great importance not only for the revolution in Latin America, but also for the international revolutionary workers' movement. We shall try to provide an answer, stressing at the outset our sympathetic attitude to the FSLN and our unconditional solidarity with the Sandinist revolution against the imperialist counter-offensive. Sympathy and solidarity, however, do not exclude but actually imply the right to criticism.

'Implacable in struggle, generous in victory': the FSLN strictly adhered to this traditional Sandinist motto. The white terror that marked the final years of the dictatorship (50,000 dead, 2 per cent of the population) did not give way to red terror. The death penalty was abolished. The 7,500 captured Somozist guardsmen, including the worst torturers, had the right to a normal trial and faced a maximum of thirty years' imprisonment. Such 'generosity' was extended even more to the anti-Somoza bourgeoisie, whose property and political rights were preserved in spite of its manoeuvres to save the state apparatus of the old regime.

Decree no. 3 of the government of national reconstruction nationalized only the finance system, the fishing industry and industrial or agricultural businesses owned by the Somoza clan. In other words, the private sector was left 80 per cent of agricultural production (Nicaragua's main foreign-currency earner), 75 per cent of industrial production and 45 per cent of 'services'.[1]

The employers are strongly organized by branch of industry, and their national federation—the Consejo Superior de la Empresa Privada (COSEP)—deals directly with the FSLN. The bourgeois opposition paper *La Prensa* remains a powerful rival to its left-wing splinter, *Nuevo Diario*, and the official FSLN daily, *Barricada*. COSEP and Catholic radio-stations compete with the state service, although the new regime does have a television monopoly. At first, the bourgeois parties even had a majority on the Council of State. But the FSLN eventually won control in April 1980 by expanding its size from thirty-three to forty-seven—an action that triggered the first serious political crisis of the new regime. Alfonso Robelo, leader of the 'Nicaraguan Democratic Party' immediately resigned from the government of national reconstruction, followed a few days later by Violeta Chamorro, widow of the bourgeois anti-Somoza leader who was assassinated in 1978. Replacements were soon found, however, after talks between COSEP and the FSLN.

During this period, the FSLN's 'generosity' towards its real enemies and false allies aroused some fears, both in Nicaragua and elsewhere, that the Sandinists were giving in to the disastrous Stalinist line of 'revolution by stages', with the risk of losing control to the counter-revolution. Events have shown that there was never any real justification for these fears.

'Giving space to win time'

The Sandinist revolution benefited from unusually favourable conditions. It triumphed before the seizure of the American hostages in Tehran and the entry of Soviet troops into Kabul, at a time when US public opinion, still reeling from the Vietnam débâcle, paid little heed to the war-hungry brigade. For the first time, the Organization of American States (OAS) had spoken out strongly against US intervention; and Panama, Costa Rica, Venezuela and Mexico were even prepared to offer support to the new regime in Managua.

Within Nicaragua itself, the megalomanic, paranoid rule of Somoza had whittled his social base down to his own clan, large sectors of the bourgeoisie being alienated by the systematic use of the state apparatus for private accumulation. The last straw was the brazen diversion of international aid received after the 1972 Managua earthquake.

Faced with mounting hostility and isolation, Somoza showed his ingenuity in sabotaging every alternative proposed by the liberal bourgeoisie and the US Embassy. Right up to the last minute, his strategy was to confront bourgeois opponents with an apocalyptic choice: 'I or the Sandino-communists!' In 1978 he instigated the murder of his most dangerous challenger, *La Prensa* director Pedro Joaquín Chamorro. Naturally, such catastrophist politics played into the hands of the FSLN.

Founded in 1960 under the impact of Castro's victory in Cuba, the Sandinist National Liberation Front more than once found itself on the brink of annihilation. After the 1975 'hammer and anvil' operation, launched by the National Guard with the assistance of American, Vietnamese and Central American Defence Council (CONDECA)[2] 'advisers', only a few dozen survivors remained, and even they were split into three tendencies. Yet by 22 August 1978, Comandante Eden Pastora was able to carry out the finest hostage-taking operation in the history of terrorism, capturing the National Palace and all the deputies present in the building. In the end, a total of 600 dignitaries were exchanged for FSLN prisoners and $500,000. Although the Front still had only 200 fighters in 1977,[3] the rapid disintegration of the regime was working in its favour. For the existence of a revolutionary alternative did not allow the dictatorship to exploit the failure of compromise solutions put forward by the bourgeoisie and imperialism. The Sandinist guerrilla struggle, supported by the semi-legal political action of the mass organizations, sharpened the crisis of the dictatorship and helped to radicalize both the popular masses and the FSLN itself. Under bourgeois leadership between 1974 and 1978, the anti-Somoza movement gradually passed under FSLN hegemony. After the Estelli insurrection of September 1978 and the 40 per cent devaluation of the cordoba in April 1978,[4] the Sandinist leadership finally issued a call for an 'insurrectional general strike' on 4 June 1979. So successful was their action that, to nearly everyone's surprise, the National Guard collapsed within the space of forty-five days. The Somozist state vanished into thin air, while the Urucuyo episode, the last attempt by Washington and the Nicaraguan bourgeoisie to impose a sharing of power, ended in farce. When the *comandantes* triumphally entered Managua on 19 July, the Somozists were in flight, the 'liberal bourgeoisie' was keeping a low profile, and the FSLN alone enjoyed immense authority and prestige. It could easily have pushed through a 'maximum programme': wholesale nationalization, renunciation of the huge foreign debt contracted for Somoza's war needs, and assumption of all power. But it steered well clear of all such measures.

A very special kind of NEP[5]

'I am too weak to make any concessions,' said de Gaulle in 1945. 'We are too strong to do without compromise,' the Sandinist leaders must have said to themselves on the evening of their victory.

In effect, they spoke in these terms to the Nicaraguan bourgeoisie: 'We have not forgotten your recent manoeuvring, but we shall say no more about it; for we need your technical skills as entrepreneurs, managers and administrators, as well as the confidence you inspire in Western financiers. Help us to lift the country out of ruin—we shall give you the means in cheap and plentiful credits, labour discipline, and moderation on the wage front. In return, we shall ensure respect for your property and your participation in high office.' Having no other solution, the Nicaraguan bourgeoisie accepted with all the more alacrity.

The FSLN leaders thus proposed a revival in government of the alliance formed in opposition to the dictatorship. As in the earlier struggle, however, they were not inclined to compromise on essentials: the alliance —and this is what differentiated it from Stalinist front politics—was grounded both on conflict and on Sandinist hegemony. The FSLN leadership had no illusion about the deep-seated conflict between their own socialist perspective and the goals of the Nicaraguan bourgeoisie.

The bourgeoisie wanted both to rid itself of the Somoza mafia, and to preserve a social and economic system in which two-thirds of Nicaraguans lived in abject poverty. Sooner or later, this antagonism had to break into open conflict. It was a conflictual alliance, then, since the two protagonists were bearers of radically different social projects which they would eventually seek to impose on each other. It was a temporary 'marriage of reason' full of mental reservations. In the eyes of the Sandinistas, the hegemony the FSLN enjoyed within the alliance put it in a good position to win this close-fought contest. For the collapse of the Somozist dictatorship had left the FSLN masters of the state apparatus, particularly of its coercive apparatuses; and the nationalization of foreign trade and credit, together with the development of workers' control, gave it a certain control over economic acitivity. Besides, the FSLN's authority in the mass organizations allowed it to have recourse to popular mobilization at any moment, while the structures of hegemony would be continually reinforced in the years to come.

Thus alliance politics, so monstrous in the eyes of dogmatists who graft the 'October model' on to every situation, had the tactical justification that it gave the FSLN a breathing space to consolidate its positions before a new leap forward. But it also had a strategic justification. In rejecting all voluntarism, the FSLN sought to determine the rhythm of revolution according to the real level of consciousness of the broad masses, and not only of the most radicalized sections. For these broad masses remembered the active role played by the oppositional bourgeoisie in the struggle against the dictatorship; and in the hour of victory, they did not see that there was now an irreducible conflict of interests between the bourgeoisie and the people. *One key function of the FSLN alliance policy was precisely to enable the working masses to grasp this conflict through their own experience of the bourgeoisie's attitude in the transitional phase; and to make this possible without endangering the process of transition itself.*

If this political approach is understood and accepted by the most advanced sections of the proletariat—if, that is, it does not divide the all-important forces of the working class—then it makes possible the broadest alliance with the urban and rural petty bourgeoisie. The big bourgeoisie may thus be isolated, divided and demoralized, and the inevitable *faux frais* of revolution may be kept to a minimum. But only, if it is understood and accepted. For, like any genuine policy of alliance, the FSLN approach involved real and major concessions to the bourgeois ally, which could repel the most radical sections of the popular masses.

The bold FSLN strategy carried the risk that the bourgeoisie would prepare the conditions for a victorious counter-offensive or, in the case of defeat, for an easy reconversion abroad; and that a deeply divided popular movement would lose its combativity. Still, the Sandinistas' sense of optimism was shared by Fidel Castro. 'The key thing in a people's revolution,' he said in Havana on 26 July 1980, 'is to have the people and the guns on your side. What happened in Chile cannot recur in Nicaragua in any form. Since the people has the power, since it has the weapons, the Revolution is guaranteed and will follow its course as a function of the objective conditions in the country' (*Barricada* 28 July, 1980).

A 'generally positive' balance sheet

When the Sandinistas assumed power, they found a grand total of $3.5 million in the bank and a foreign debt of $1,600 million—the highest per capita in the whole of Latin America. In 1979 the servicing of this debt (repayments and interest charges) alone amounted to more than $600 million, the entire value of annual exports. The government of national reconstruction secured a two-year moratorium, rescheduled the whole debt burden, and received an additional $750 million in the form of gifts and long-term loans ($122 million from the United States). This massive inflow of capital gave a spur to economic reconstruction. For although businessmen refused to invest their own capital, they agreed to take up the government's insistent offer of very cheap credits (between 7 and 8 per cent interest).

In 1979 800,000 hectares of land were sown, nearly as much as in the 'pre-war' period. The harvest was reported to be good for cotton, sugar, coffee and 'basic cereals'. The only real black spot was the live-stock sector, where more than 500,000 animals, out of a total of 2.5 million, disappeared through smuggling and internal slaughtering. This led, in turn, to a marked drop in milk production.

The situation is more uneven in industry, which accounts for 24 per cent of gross domestic product. The upturn has been strong in foodstuffs, leather and pelts, and clothing; hesitant in textiles and construction; and almost non-existent in chemicals and agro-chemicals, the real bastions of the private sector. Two trends point to the fact that the industrial bourgeoisie has little enthusiasm for industrial recovery: the decline in manufacturing exports to the Central American Common Market, and the sharp drop in imports of equipment goods (down 41 and 81 per cent over the first quarter of 1978 and 1979 respectively). The bourgeoisie has generally adopted a wait-and-see attitude, using bank loans for investment and showing no excess of zeal. Will it now reinvest its profits or export them by relying on every book-keeping device (under-invoicing, over-invoicing) and the foreign-currency black market?

In order to stimulate the productive ardour of business chiefs, the FSLN prepared a series of laws to nationalize idlers or saboteurs. The second agrarian reform law, made public by Comandante Daniel Ortega on 19 July 1980, authorized the nationalization of uncultivated latifundia; and heads of economic units were placed under an obligation to match their 1981 investments with credits received during 1980. Investment policy is continually strengthening the public sector in production, distribution and exchange—a trend which, though perhaps encouraging businessmen to produce, also prompts them to draw up discreet reconversion programmes for more favourable times.

The harshest aspect of this 'historic compromise' was the government's social policy. 'The country is in a state of collapse,' it seemed to be saying to the workers. 'Instead of demanding wage rises, you should be rolling up your sleeves! In return, we promise to develop social provisions, to reduce unemployment, and to keep prices stable for subsistence goods.' The promises have been partly kept. But as a Frente Obrero trade unionist put it: 'although the workers are prepared to make sacrifices, they would like to be sure that they are working for the collective, and not so that the bosses can have a nest-egg in Costa Rica or Miami.' This is why calls for austerity sound a lot better in the public sector than in private enterprises. Besides, wages are too low in view of the inflation of the last four years: 1,500 cordobas a month for an industrial worker, 20 to 27 cordobas a day for an agricultural worker. Unemployment has been reduced, but it still affects more than 30 per cent of the population. The rate of inflation is higher than the 22 per cent envisaged by the Reconstruction Plan.[6] People can't manage, and so they make demands and go on strike, even if this causes trouble for the 'Front'.

The bourgeoisie in a vice

The Nicaraguan bourgeoisie has certainly adopted a wait-and-see approach, but this does not mean that it is resigned or inactive. The 'COSEP gentlemen', as the Sandinistas call them, are still full of hope. They know they can count on their counterparts in Latin America and the 'free world'; and Western aid is not at all free of strings. Sixty per cent of the US contribution, for example, is earmarked exclusively for the private sector. The church hierarchy is already showing the cloven hoof, and Mgr Obando, archbishop of Managua, has just claimed that General Pedro Altamirano, the right-hand man of Augusto Cesar Sandino, was no more than a 'common criminal'.

The Nicaraguan bourgeoisie is counting on a rapid exhaustion of the FSLN regime. The few Sandinist cadres, lacking in technical experience, face the thankless task of rebuilding a country in ruins. Their productivist austerity policy, at times rather roughly implemented, does not win them only friends; and their popularity may crumble as quickly as it appeared. Although the FSLN is quite homogeneous at the top, its rapid growth has been won at the price of considerable heterogeneity at the base. Against a background of economic chaos and social tension, therefore, the organization may divide and throw up a faction interested in alliance with the liberal bourgeoisie. After all, the 26 July Movement produced such divisions on the morrow of the Cuban revolution, although the aggressive policy of the United States did not allow these to be profitably exploited.

In waiting for these hopes to be fulfilled, the organizations of the bourgeoisie are waging their battle on three fronts: they oppose any extension of the nationalized sector, they demand strict respect for public rights and freedoms, and they call for a schedule of free elections (municipal in 1981, legislative in 1982, presidential in 1983).

To paraphrase the late Chairman Mao, the FSLN did not wish for a trial of strength, but nor was it afraid of the prospect. In fact, the Sandinists used the cease-fire period of conflictual alliance with the bourgeoisie to consolidate their positions in the state and society: the guerrilla columns have become a modern army and police force; the economic and administrative apparatus has been significantly developed; and the FSLN has secured an absolute majority on the Council of State. At the same time, the Sandinistas have built up a whole system of mass organizations: the Asociacion de Trabajadores del Campo (ATC), the Central Sandinista de Trabajadores (CST), and the Comités de Defensa Sandinista (CDS), which are an extension of the 'civil defence committees' that played a logistic role in the struggle against the dictatorship. Finally, the ever-present People's Militia organizes the armed people in the factories, haciendas and *barrios*.

One of the tasks of these organizations is to assure popular control over production and local community life. The ATCs, for example, report on land that has been left fallow, on any suspicious reduction in the area under cultivation, on failure to use fertilizers or pesticides, and on excessive slaughtering of livestock. The labour unions alert the planning authorities at the first sign of 'decapitalization'.[7]

The Nicaraguan bourgeoisie knows that it is caught between the state apparatus and the popular movement, and *for the moment* it has no inclination to force a trial of strength. Thus COSEP did not follow Robelo in April 1980, when he embarked upon a confrontationist course by calling on his supporters to resign from the government. Indeed, COSEP negotiated a renewal of the alliance and put new men into vacant posts. However, if the strategy of tying down the revolution proves unsuccessful, the Nicaraguan bourgeoisie and its powerful ally to the north will not hesitate to use violence. Already armed bands are operating in the north of the country, and thousands of former National Guardsmen are waiting across the border.

The goal of hegemony

The national literacy campaign is a perfect example of FSLN tactics in the present phase of the revolution—100,000 volunteer students and schoolchildren were sent to the countryside in an effort to eradicate illiteracy, which affected one of every two Nicaraguans. Their mission was to teach the *campesinos* how to read, write and count, to give lessons in the history of Nicaragua, including recent history, and to help the agricultural workers to organize unions and militias. But they were also to learn for themselves how two-thirds of the active population could be reduced to a sub-human existence in a rich and fertile land.

For six months, these 100,000 young people shared the lives of 'the wretched of the earth'. Most of them, FSLN leaders believe, will be permanently marked by the experience, and will know how to approach political problems 'starting from the class interests of rural proletarians'. Conversely, the schoolchildren's arrival *en masse* to teach and serve them did more than any material benefit to convince the peasants that something fundamental had changed 'at the top', that power belonged to them and no longer to the *señores*.

This fine exercise in hegemony, blessed by the World Council of Churches and three-quarters financed out of international aid, would have a more or less permanent sequel. A network of Sandinist People's Education Committees, embracing graduates of the crusade, was formed in the workplaces and local communities to consolidate the gains and encourage ongoing adult education.

If there is to be an exacerbation of class struggle in Nicaragua, then, the FSLN would appear to be in a position to carry the day. The danger of a Mexican or Bolivian-type repression seems limited. But what of the other threat to socialist revolution, particularly in an underdeveloped country: the danger of bureaucratic degeneration? Here there is greater cause for concern. Not only do such objective factors as the new Cold War and the hardening of bourgeois attitudes tend towards an authoritarian shrinkage of power, but the majority of FSLN cadres are oblivious of the bureaucratic danger.

Popular and bourgeois democracy

Nicaragua does not, to be sure, resemble the bureaucratized societies of 'actually existing socialism', where civil and political rights are mere ornaments in the constitution. There is a real pluralism of the press, parties and trade unions; *habeas corpus*, the freedom of worship and the right to strike and demonstrate are genuinely respected. As in other parts of the world, these rights and freedoms are subject to regulation and sometimes draconian restriction (*Barricada* 24 August 1980).[8] But Nicaragua is a very long way from Cambodia, and even from Hungary.

What gives rise to concern, and to fears of a Cuban-type development, are a series of all too familiar theories and practices. The FSLN has given a two-point answer to the calls of the bourgeois opposition for early elections. 'Before general elections are held,' it is most commonly said, 'the basic conditions for an honest electoral verdict must exist: national reconstruction, literacy, civic education of the people. And given the legacy of Somozism and war, these goals will probably not be achieved before 1985. Until then, the legitimacy of the regime will remain revolutionary in character. The people voted in June–July 1979 by means of an insurrectional general strike, and the resulting Junta of National Reconstruction may legitimately carry out its mandate for one legislative term. Early general elections would be a caricature of democracy: they would not institute popular sovereignty, but allow the old chieftains to manipulate universal suffrage.'

The arguments in support of the second point are much less persuasive, focusing as they do not on the objective conditions for the free exercise of suffrage rights, but on the 'type of democracy' to be established in Nicaragua. This, it is said, should be 'real' and not 'formal', 'popular' and not 'bourgeois', 'direct' and not 'parliamentary'. The daily polemic between *La Prensa* and *Barricada* spells out what lies behind these oppositions.

The 'popular democracy' whose advent the FSLN invokes is opposed to 'bourgeois democracy' in three respects. Firstly, the content of government is to serve the exploited and not the exploiters. Thus, *Barricada* contrasts the content of democracy to its 'form', its essence to its appearance. The 'essence' is its class content, the formal aspect is elections. After all, have we not seen electoral farces in every dictatorship in Latin America?

Secondly, this 'democracy for the people' is also claimed to be 'democracy by the people'. Unlike bourgeois democracy, which everywhere organizes the delegation of power to professional politicians, Sandinist democracy is supposed to be 'direct'. Unfortunately, however, the Sandinist leaders are not here referring to the Athenian Agora, the Paris Commune, or the soviets of the Russian Revolution. By 'direct democracy' they mean mass participation in power—through unelected, unrecallable and unmandated 'representatives'! Examples are the Council of State, which includes 'representatives' from the trade unions and popular organizations; and the *cabildos abiertos*—big local meetings at which members of the Council of State explain government policy and take note of suggestions.

Thirdly, the role of elections is not the same. In the Sandinist view of democracy, their function is not to organize party rivalry for political power, but 'to select the best among the good', to call on the people to 'appoint its own vanguard'. 'The elections to which we refer,' declared Minister of Defence Humberto Ortega on 23 August 1980, at the closing of the literacy campaign, 'are very different from those demanded by the conservatives and liberals. . . . Keep it firmly in mind that these elections are to consolidate revolutionary power, not to place it at stake.

For power is in the hands of the people, through its vanguard, the FSLN.' Visible here is the Cuban model of 'people's power', not the best aspect of the Castroist experience.

The Cuban model of the organization of power

For the moment, and one hopes this will be true for a long time to come, the Cuban 'model' is contradicted by genuine political pluralism and real respect for democratic rights and freedoms. There are numerous signs, however, that such a model underlies the thinking of many Sandinist officials, if not of the entire leadership.

On the pretext of opposing the bourgeois-liberal campaign for *early* elections, the Sandinist press deprecates elections in general as the customary stratagem oligarchs employ in assuming power. The revolution, according to this view, has better things to do than squander its funds and energy on a popular consultation whose result is known in advance. Thus, on the day after the solemn commemoration of 19 July, *Barricada* carried a full-page slogan: '500,000 demonstrators—the people have voted!' Such an attitude does not smoothe the way for elections at the base, within the mass organizations and local communities. Indeed, it serves to legitimate practices of co-optation and appointment from above.

When someone opposes the FSLN, they are quickly denounced as a Somozist or CIA agent. Such labels are currently applied not only to the bourgeois opposition, but also to workers' organizations: the CNT (Christian-Social trade unions), the Central de Accion y Unidad Sindical (CAUS), the Consejo de Unificación Sindical (CUS), Frente Obrero and the Partido Comunista Nicaragüense (PCN).[9] Yet the fact that these unions and parties—with the exception of the pro-Albanian FO, the least suspicious of them all—have retained their place on the Council of State suggests that the FSLN itself does not believe such accusations.

This denunciatory approach, which tends to stigmatize all opposition and deny its legitimacy, is characteristic of single-party regimes, not of a revolutionary democracy. It points to a conception of 'the dictatorship of the proletariat' as the dictatorship of a vanguard party in which other political formations are doomed to the role of innocuous ornaments.

There is a strong influence of Comintern traditions in the 'vanguard party's' view of its relations with the masses and the mass organizations. The 'vanguard' quality is conceived as an essence. By single-handedly leading the people to victory, the FSLN is said to have proven that it is 'the indisputable vanguard of Nicaraguans', the expression of a people alive to its historic interests. As such, the FSLN knows better than the workers themselves where their true interests lie and how they can be attained. It may therefore substitute itself for the people, if the latter ever yield to demagogy or lassitude.

No consideration seems to have been given to the possibility that 'the undisputed people's vanguard' might one day succumb to 'the professional dangers of power' and, like other 'undisputed vanguards' before it, give rise to an oppressive bureaucratic caste. Highly significant in this respect is the FSLN attitude to the mass organizations, particularly the trade unions. It does seek to build them up—less as genuinely autonomous bodies, however, than as transmission belts through which the vanguard party and the state can structure and mobilize the masses. The FSLN has no problem controlling the mass organizations of its own creation: the CDSs, the ATCs, the people's militia, and so on. But it is a different story with the long-established labour unions, which have cadres and a mass base historically constituted through the elemental class struggle under the dictatorship. Their autonomy was reaffirmed in the series of (sometimes demagogic) strikes and protest movements of autumn 1979 and winter 1980.[10]

Such autonomy is all the more vexing for the Sandinistas in that their productivist austerity policy leaves the field open not only to demagogues, but also to union militants who simply wish to maintain the workers' purchasing power. The FSLN has therefore been applying all kinds of pressure to impose the unification of the trade-union movement under its own leadership.

The methods have varied a great deal according to the period and concrete situation, and there is every sign that a debate is taking place among the Sandinist leaders. For the moment, the supporters of a strong-arm solution, involving FSLN appointment of 'reliable cadres' to the key union posts, seem to have lost out to those who favour voluntary integration of as many traditional structures as possible into a single union movement, even if a price has to be paid in terms of the union's programme and the relative autonomy of its leading personnel. However, the fact that it is generally old Partida Socialista Nicaragüense (PSN) (pro-Moscow Communist) cadres who are entrusted with 'animating' the mass organizations, particularly the CST, is hardly a reassuring sign for the future.

Another worrying feature is the attitude of the Sandinist regime towards legality. With a majority in the government and the Council of State, the FSLN is passing a number of vaguely worded laws which pose a danger to revolutionary democracy. Thus, article 4, paragraph C, of the Maintenance of Public Order Act opens the way to the arbitrary use of power to control the press. Of course, some degree of control is necessary, and no press in the world is entirely free of regulation. Absolute freedom of expression in Nicaragua would mean absolute freedom for the bourgeoisie to slander the Sandinist regime and foment panic by spreading false rumours. However, the deliberately vague wording of this law effectively leaves FSLN good will as the only guarantee of the freedom of expression.

The Sandinist leaders also show a rather lax attitude towards their own laws. It is far from the case that all 'suspects' appear before a magistrate within twenty-four hours of their arrest, as is required by the Nicaraguan *habeas corpus*, the *ley d'Amparo*. The FSLN explains this by referring to the shortage of policemen and efficient magistrates. On 30 June 1980, for example, the Sandinist police launced a 'cleaning-up operation' in the Managua *barrios* to ensure that the 19 July festivities would take place without incident. Several hundred suspects were picked up—nearly a thousand according to *La Prensa*—half of whom were set free the next day. But the others were held without charge in the Zona Franca after the initial period of arrest had expired, most of them being released in groups of fifty to sixty throughout the month of July.

An even more significant episode in this respect was the repression of the Frente Obrero leadership. Arrested in November 1979, they spent a fortnight in prison before their formal indictment in a magistrate's court. General secretary Isidoro Tellez was charged under article 4, paragraph C, alongside directors of the organization's paper, although he was not a member of the editorial board. After a trial in which defence witnesses were never allowed to take the stand, the FO leaders were sentenced to two years of 'public works' with no explicit mention of incarceration. Yet they were confined in Chipote prison, and the commutation of the sentence to a fine,. although allowed by law, was denied them. Four months later, the FSLN leadership simply set the court's decision aside and had them released. When *La Prensa* waxed ironic and the judiciary expressed its indignation, the government proceeded to adopt an amnesty decree!

This whole episode is instructive in more than one sense. It shows that the FSLN is loathe to use repression and tries to end it as quickly as possible. But it also reveals a very free-and-easy attitude to the law, and a propensity to arbitrary rule which, however good-natured today, may easily assume a quite different character if harsher conditions prevail.

The dynamics of democratization and bureaucratization

The development of the Nicaraguan revolution does not, of course, essentially depend upon the Sandinists' idea about democracy. First and foremost, it will hinge on the relationship of class forces at the international, regional and national levels—on such un-theoretical questions as the strategy of the Reagan administration, the outcome of the civil wars in El Salvador and Guatemala, and the development of the counter-revolution in Nicaragua itself. However, close attention to the objective circumstances of the Sandinist regime should not lead us into fatalism. The FSLN's conception of workers' democracy and the transition to socialism, as well as the practices informed by it, will play a far from negligible role.

A clear awareness of the dangers of bureaucratic degeneration that threaten proletarian revolution, particularly in a backward country, would help to avert any measures that could usher in an all-powerful bureaucracy—or, at least, such measures would then be taken in full knowledge of the risks, temporarily and with a multitude of safeguards. Conversely, as the Bolshevik experience demonstrates, any under-estimation of this peril greatly assists the crystallization of bureaucratic deformations into a rigidly authoritarian system.

The lack of foreknowledge in this respect of the first Marxist revolutionaries who conquered power is comprehensible—anarchist and Social Democratic warnings lacking credibility at the time.[11] A similar lack of preparation or awareness half a century later, when the ravages of bureaucratic despotism have been revealed in their full scope, is another matter.

It is regrettable that the Sandinistas draw on the Comintern arsenal for many of their arguments against the liberal-democratic offensive of the bourgeoisie, rather than the incomparably more solid weapon of a real process of socialist democratization, lengthy though it would have to be in Nicaragua. The task is not to produce a carbon copy of the institutions of the Swiss Confederation, nor immediately to establish a pyramid of workers' councils. A developed socialist democracy cannot be directly installed in a backward, war-ruined and largely illiterate country. (While the national campaign has reduced the illiteracy rate from 55 to 14 per cent, the general cultural level in Nicaragua is still very low.) It can only be the fruit of a long process of building and extending democracy—a process all the longer and more difficult in that the revolutionary regime must reckon with enemies both internal and external. Only demagogues or idealists would dare blame the FSLN for restricting democracy in the phase of national reconstruction and consolidation of the new regime. It may be legitimately criticized, however, for presenting such restrictions as other than regrettable and temporary limitations on socialist democracy imposed by historical circumstance. Making a virtue of necessity, the FSLN quite wrongly presents them as a higher form of democracy.

If Nicaragua is to embark upon a process of long-term democratization rather than bureaucratization, then a number of provisions are required from the very outset. The more numerous and coherent these pro-visions, the better chance the revolution will have of following a democratic course. It is the good, though perhaps shortlived, fortune of Nicaragua that the conditions under which victory was achieved favour such pro-visions.

The measures needed to check an authoritarian dynamic flow, in fact, from two of the greatest political problems posed by the transition to socialism.

First, how is it possible to limit the formidable power of a 'bureaucratically deformed workers' state' (Lenin)? How can the working people, the citizens, be protected against a power which, ruling in their name, does so through the mediation of a more or less independent bureaucratic apparatus endowed with interests of its own? Secondly, how can the often yawning gap be bridged between the myth of workers' power and the reality of uncontrolled bureaucratic rule?

The Marxism of the Comintern, of the first four congresses of the Third International, did not confront these questions. Later, they were to obsess the left opposition to Stalinism, Leon Trotsky in particular, though its answers were not always convincing.

The solution to the first problem must involve a juridical and judicial limitation of state power. Once the emergency period of open war has given way to civil peace, the revolutionary regime cannot be that 'rule based directly on force and unrestricted by laws' which Lenin wrongly gave as the definition of the dictatorship of the proletariat (Lenin 1970: 13). No one should be above socialist legality, not even the *comandantes* of the revolution. Moreover, state power should be applicable only to a clearly demarcated sphere, excluding science, literature and the arts, for example.

Counter-powers should exist to limit the state power. As a matter of fact, one of the most original features of the Sandinist revolution is the real pluralism of political parties, the only condition being respect for revolutionary legality, renunciation of armed subversion. There is also a real pluralism of the press and other media, even though strict regulations prevent the freedom of expression from working in favour of those with the material resources to aquire powerful means of imparting information. Unification of the trade-union movement is not in itself a blow against pluralism. Indeed, a single powerful labour federation, provided it is really democratic and independent of the state, is an incomparably more effective counterweight than nine more or less representative unions.

The answer to the second question depends on the relationship of those in power to their mass base. It is, of course, perfectly possible to advocate a system in which the leaders are responsible to the led without at the same time pleading for bourgeois parliamentary democracy in Nicaragua. Besides, a growing section of the real power-holders in a Western 'liberal democracy' (the economic apparatus, the civil service) are themselves sheltered from popular control. Universal suffrage is conceived in such a way as to ensure maximum autonomy of the elected from the electors for their entire term of office. The president of the French Republic, for example, is little short of an elected monarch. Half the citizens of the United States, when asked to choose between a Democrat and a Republican, are so little interested that they do not bother to cast a vote.

The real danger in Nicaragua is that a system will develop in which the holders of power are independent of their base and responsible only to their own hierarchy. That system has a well-known logic: it begins by discarding independent minds and massively promoting time-serving mediocrities; it then leads to negligence and arrogance on the part of officials, and to mass disaffection, cynicism and passive resistance; finally, it crystallizes into the domination of a privileged caste, which has an interest in reproducing the system long after the disappearance of the objective conditions that first gave rise to it.

A leadership is most responsible to the rank and file not in geo-graphically defined constituencies that cease to exist that day after the ballot, but within the framework of real workplace and neighbourhood collectives. The rooting of suffrage rights in collectives that exist both before and after the vote—a characteristic feature of socialist democracy —allows the rights of control, mandate and recall to be genuinely exercised. Thus, in Nicaragua a council democracy may gradually take shape on the basis of the Sandinist Defence Committees, the factory and hacienda committees, and so on, provided that these committees really have the capacity, even under strict regulation, to influence decisions and to appoint, control and recall leaders.

Democracy can and should first assert itself where it runs the least risk of manipulation by reactionary forces: in the FSLN, the workers' and peasants' unions, the defence committees, and, through them, the municipal councils and production units. It would be wrong to pretend that nothing is being done in this direction—one has only to think of the genuine efforts to stimulate management and workers' control in certain enterprises. However, their significance for an authentic workers' democracy is still limited by their unsystematic, uncentralized character.

The FSLN: an anti-Angkor

Will the Sandinist revolution produce yet one more variant of bureau-cratic rule? Will the monolithic dictatorship of the 'vanguard party' replace the pluralism and democratic freedoms currently in force? A number of factors give hope that this will not happen.

First of all, there is the character of the Sandinist leadership itself, born out of the 1979 fusion between three violently opposed tendencies, that has taught them the value of pluralist practice. If they were able skilfully to combine rural guerrilla warfare, an insurrectional general strike and a classic war of position, this was because the FSLN integrated different experiences and orientations that had initially been seen as mutually exclusive. The new leadership has so far shown a great capacity to understand and correct its mistakes, clearly preferring to rule by 'consensus' than by 'coercion'.

The Sandinistas can also benefit from the Cuban experience, pondering its lessons, both positive and negative, at a time when the Castroist leader-ship is modifying its own economic policy. The view in Havana now seems to be that the blanket nationalizations of 1968 were a gross error, and that an underdeveloped economy stands to gain from an extensive private sector, provided that the revolutionaries retain a firm grasp on the reins of power.

It is not clear why the FSLN leaders should repeat, in the economic or any other field, precisely those errors which their prestigious fore-runners are in the process of correcting. It is therefore possible to hope that pluralism and relative respect for democratic freedoms will be preserved and gradually extended as the conditions for a socialist democracy develop. It should never be forgotten, however, that the future of workers' democracy and socialism in Nicaragua ultimately depends on factors over which, all niceties aside, the Sandinistas unfortunately have little control. A ruthless onslaught by the counter-revolution would lead to a hardening of the FSLN, the progressive militarization of society, and perhaps eventually the introduction of the 'Cuban model', for which certain ideological presuppositions are already in place. All this only underlines the importance of the international solidarity movement. Aid for the Sandinist revolution today will help to safeguard the chances for the birth of a democratic socialist state in Central America.

Postscript

Patrick Camiller

Although the situation in Nicaragua has not changed in any fundamental respect since the above article was written in September 1980, a number of factors have assumed increasing weight.

Internationally the Reagan administration, continuing the course of Carter's last year in office, has dropped the human rights rhetoric and returned to the traditional profile of US imperialism in Central America. Its warships are now permanently stationed off the coasts of Nicaragua; its paymasters have earmarked hundreds of millions of dollars to bolster the armed forces of the Central American oligarchies for both internal and external operations; its ideologists strive hard to equate popular liberation movements with 'totalitarian communism'; and its civil servants are working overtime in ever more bungled attempts to reveal the hand of 'Managua–Havana–Moscow' behind every struggle against military oppression. In the climate following the Falklands/Malvinas conflict, however, it seems unlikely that Washington will feel able to stage a direct military intervention. The Honduran regime, already engaged in 'joint operations' in El Salvador, supports the 5,000-strong anti-FSLN forces who carry out ever more extensive raids across its border with Nicaragua. In July 1982 alone, some 200 are reported to have entered Zelaya Province, killing as many as forty Sandinist soldiers in several days of fierce fighting. The aim of Tegucigalpa seems not so much to provoke an all-out war as to exert a destabilizing pressure on the FSLN and to disrupt key sectors of the Nicaraguan economy. For although the Honduras air force may hold local air superiority, the 30,000-strong Sandinist army and the dense network of people's militias are a formidable barrier to any invading force.

On Nicaragua's southern border, a threat of a somewhat different nature has been taking shape. In April 1982 the legendary FSLN 'Commander Zero', Eden Pastora, publicly denounced the Sandinist regime as a 'totalitarian tyranny' and, rejecting any alliance with the *somocistas*, began to organize a new guerrilla movement from base camps in Costa Rica. Pastora's defection, expressing that strand of the anti-oligarchic movement which seeks to keep it within the bounds of bourgeois nationalism, more or less coincided with the open espousal of socialist ideology by the Sandinist mass organizations. Pastora's forces do not pose a serious military threat to the FSLN; but if he establishes an alliance with Alfonso Robelo, the self-exiled leader of the Nicaraguan Democratic Movement, the anti-Sandinist opposition may acquire a coherence and central focus it quite visibly lacked throughout 1981.

The Nicaraguan bourgeoisie cannot, of course, openly identify with any of the regime's military opponents, and so it has continued its wait-and-see approach while resisting as far as possible the extension of state control over the economy. Since no important political leaders are left inside the country to centralize anti-FSLN mobilizations, the ultra-reactionary archbishop of Managua, Mgr Miguel Obando Bravo, would doubtless be called upon to lead a final crusade against 'Sandino-communism' if the conditions are ever judged ripe.

The atmosphere of almost wartime mobilization, reflected in the official designation of 1982 as the Year of National Unity against Aggression, has further heightened popular support for the regime and swollen the ranks of the Sandinist mass organizations. At the same time, it has evidently not favoured the electoral principle either in those mass organizations or in the polity as a whole. At the beginning of 1982 an intense debate took place around a draft law to legalize the country's twelve political organizations. The bourgeois parties generally opposed the new law on the grounds that it required them to participate in the FSLN-controlled Council of State. But in the event, the whole issue disappeared into the state of emergency that was decreed in March 1982 after a major cross-border raid from Honduras and has continued, with periodic renewals, ever since.

Considerable strains have also appeared in the relationship between the FSLN and the COSEP employers' federation. Thus, three leading members of COSEP were jailed for three months in November 1981 for issuing a public attack on the government; and employers' circles are full of complaints about the lack of labour discipline and the uncertain prospects for the private sector. Still, the Sandinist leadership shows no sign of ending its quest for co-operation with private capital. A number of new incentives began to be introduced in February 1982 and were quite favourably received by COSEP representatives. The government suspended the right to strike in September 1981 in an effort to raise flagging productivity, even going so far as to close down the Fabritex textile factory in Managua that had been severely affected by CAUS-organized disputes. New legislation on foreign investment is due to appear in autumn 1982, and COSEP leaders are impatiently waiting to see what it will reveal about the FSLN's long-term policy towards the private sector.

Whereas no major changes in industrial ownership have taken place since 1979, a new National Agrarian Reform Council embarked on a programme in July 1981 to redistribute 3.28 million hectares of land, most of it owned by absentee proprietors or intentionally left uncultivated. By July 1982 only some 171,000 hectares of arable land had been expropriated, but FSLN leader Jaime Wheelock stated that the programme would be accelerated in the course of the following year. Agricultural production figures for 1981 point to a fairly sharp turn away from export commodities such as coffee and cotton (down 9 and 12 per cent respectively on 1980) towards food crops intended for domestic consumption (rice up 89 per cent, beans 45 per cent). However, government targets for 1982 project a modest revival of the traditional foreign-currency earners.

As in other underdeveloped countries, the foreign-trade balance has become a major worry in the context of world capitalist recession and mounting debt charges. Apart from Somoza's debt legacy, the Nicaraguan economy registered a $400 million trade deficit in 1980 alone. The government was able to cover this by negotiating surprisingly favourable loans from Mexico, the EEC countries and international organizations, but debt payments in 1981 already amounted to nearly two-thirds of total export revenue. A drastic curtailment of imported consumer goods has been carried through, the overwhelming burden falling on middle-class 'luxury' consumption. But the main structural problem is still the reluctance of private capital to engage in sizeable investment projects. Indeed, the real value of private-sector investment in 1981 was even lower than in 1980, capital formation dropping to a mere 3 per cent of GNP. State resources have been further squeezed by expansion of the armed forces and the $200 million losses (largely in agricultural infrastructure) resulting from the disastrous floods of May 1982.

Three years after the July revolution, the Sandinist leadership still faces a knot of problems for its original strategy of transition to socialism—political, economic and social problems that admit of no easy solution. Whatever the military options it may be considering, Washington has a clear interest in imposing such a great burden upon Nicaragua that it will cease to exert an attractive power over the other peoples of Central and South America. It is to be hoped that the FSLN leadership, while meeting the exigencies of national defence and economic reconstruction, will have the capacity not only to withstand the open pressure of its enemies but also to avoid the many traps laid in the path of revolutionaries.

NOTES

1 The contribution to GDP in 1980 for the main sectors of the economy was as follows: agro-pastoral sector, 20 per cent public, 80 per cent private; industry, 25 per cent public, 75 per cent private; construction, 70 per cent public, 30 per cent private; mining, 95 per cent public, 5 per cent private; services, 55 per cent public, 45 per cent private; trade, 30 per cent public, 70 per cent private; transport and communications, 60 per cent public, 40 per cent private. The overall contribution

of the public sector to gross domestic product rose from 15 per cent in 1977 to 41 per cent in 1980. It then accounted for 20 per cent of the active population and 82 per cent of investment, controlling all credit and receiving 40 per cent of the total credit allocation (Programa de reactivación 1980).

Large and medium-sized property dominated the agro-pastoral sector: 1.5 per cent covered 41.2 per cent of the total agricultural area (latifundia); 20.3 per cent occupied 41.1 per cent of the land (medium-size properties); and the remaining 78.2 per cent of landowners had to make do with 14.7 per cent (minifundia).

The large and medium landowners use modern technology and are oriented to the world market. Smallholders produce chiefly beans, maize and rice for internal consumption, relying on inferior equipment that helps to keep labour productivity at a very low level. Nicaragua's foreign-currency earnings therefore depend mainly upon the willingness of big and medium farmers to sow and harvest their land.

Similarly, although the state has a strong presence in animal slaughtering (60 per cent), textiles (40 per cent) and building materials, it is very weak in the key industrial sectors, chemicals and agro-chemicals, which account for most of the country's industrial exports to the Central American Common Market and receive a number of important 'economic inducements'.

2   CONDECA then comprised Honduras, El Salvador, Guatemala and Nicaragua.

3   See the excellent study by Pisani (1980).

4   In September 1980 the Nicaraguan cordoba was worth 10 US cents at the official rate of exchange, and 17 on the black market.

5   New Economic Policy, pursued by the Bolsheviks during the 1920s.

6   The rate of inflation was 6 per cent for the first quarter of 1980.

7   Thus in the southern town of Carazo, the CST at Plastenic factory noticed a continual decline in exports and a complete halt in investment, despite a 5 million cordoba loan from the Development Bank. The workers suspected their boss, René Lacayo Debayle, of economic sabotage and appealed to the courts to prevent the transfer of machinery. An inquiry found that Lacayo had been gradually converting his Carazo factory into a sub-contracting firm for another Plastenic factory in Costa Rica. The Carazo works were expropriated on 7 August 1980, and their former owner is currently seeking to recover them through the courts.

8   For his part, the FSLN secretary for propaganda and political education put the matter as follows: 'The aim of the elections will not be to decide who holds power in Nicaragua. That question has been settled by history, and the people continually ratifies its decision. Elections in our country, at the various levels announced, will take place in order to confirm the people's authority, the representativeness of people's power.'

9   See El Trabajador (organ of the Sandinist CST), no. 4, an issue devoted to the theme: 'CAUS—Agency of the CIA'.

10 In January 1980 the traditional building workers' union SCAAS, which the Ministry of Labour refused to recognize as a rival to the CST, called a strike in the construction industry. After a few mass demonstrations and stormy sessions with the FSLN leadership, SCAAS was finally accepted as the single building workers' union. In the textile industry, a strike was launched in February 1980 by the Communist-led Committee of Trade Union Action and Unification (CAUS), centred on the giant Fabritex company. Strikes also broke out in the health sector, the sugar refineries, the cement factories and the timber industry, on the initiative of the Christian-Social Workers' Federation of Nicaragua (CNT) and ex-Maoist Frente Obrero.

11 It cannot be recalled too often, however, that the danger of bureaucratic degeneration was also indicated by a Marxist revolutionary above all suspicion: the great Rosa Luxemburg. See, in particular, her pamphlet (Luxemburg 1961).

REFERENCES

Lenin, V. I. 1970, *The proletarian revolution and the renegade Kautsky*, Moscow, Progress Publishers

Luxemburg, R. 1961, *The Russian revolution*, Michigan, University of Michigan, Ann Arbor

Pisani, F. 1980, *Les Muchachos*, Paris, Maspero

Programa de reactivación económica en beneficio del pueblo 1980, Managua

SIX

Class Structure and Socialist Strategy in El Salvador

James Dunkerley

The case of El Salvador is very distinct from the others considered in this book in that the country is immersed in a particularly barbarous civil war. Under such conditions, when according to commonly held social and logistical precedents the only possibility of victory for the domestic ruling class and imperialism lies in a slaughter approximating to genocide, and when both the level of US military assistance and the considerable political importance it places upon success constitute the central challenge to the wave of anti-imperialist mobilization in Central America and the Caribbean, it is clear that attention is focused on military matters. In El Salvador the question of the armed struggle or the 'peaceful road' has long been superseded. As a result the victory of the forces of the Frente Farabundo Martí para la Liberación Nacional (FMLN) over the US-backed military dictatorship is of paramount importance. Without it, all discussion of a socialist strategy for El Salvador falls by the wayside. This remains as true in the face of the offensive launched by the pseudo-democratic regime of Magaña, as it did under the Duarte government, and the 'reformist' junta of colonels and 'independent' bureaucrats before him. It goes without saying that whatever pro-imperialist apparatus replaces Magaña will present the same acute challenge in the military field. Yet, we should be equally clear that the extremely advanced stage of the conflict with the regime does not signify that the transition to socialism is either unproblematic or substantially resolved bar the final question of taking state power.

Although this might appear self-evident, it is often the source of much disagreement. This is largely because the various political formations which are grouped together in a national liberation movement do not possess a uniform political outloook, reflecting the very nature of such movements, which, despite claims about their singularity, often conform to type in their incorporation of diffuse social and political forces. Of course, each movement, by virtue of having a predominantly national orientation, is determined by a multiplicity of specifically national factors that are conducive to a perspective that views it as *sui generis* and tends to subordinate the class struggle. Supporters of national liberation struggles have in turn displayed a tendency to give uncritical support to these multi-classist conceptions. A recent and forceful example of this genre is George Black's book (1981) on Nicaragua, which demonstrates that such a position need by no means derive from unreconstructed nationalism or liberalism, but coheres equally well with a reformism that admits to a class analysis and employs its terms, yet stipulates that the oppressed nation is embroiled in a conflict between two fundamentally static and *natural* blocs: the anti-popular-dictatorial-imperialist and the popular-democratic-progressive. This is, in essence, a defence of the popular front. Of course, in the everyday struggle anti-imperialist movements often take on this form, and nowhere is this more true than in El Salvador. But, for the proponents of the popular front, all political debate is relegated to the question of attaining state power and the ensuing problematic of how the state apparatus is to be run in an efficient and effective manner by the popular forces. The class character of the new revolutionary power is overlooked because of the preoccupation with its outward appearance (popular and democratic) and the call for 'national' unity in the face of imperialist reaction.

Before moving to trace the trajectory of this current in El Salvador it should be noted that, while such a *démarche* can at times take on a fiercely radical form, it often conduces an attack upon the independence of the working class and decomposes into a bulwark against socialism. Nevertheless, in almost all cases it is constructed around a set of objectives which are by no means alien to socialist aims, but rather integral to them. As outlined by Michael Löwy in his recent highly suggestive book, these objectives may be designated as constituting the tasks of the bourgeois democratic revolution: (i) a solution to the agrarian question through the abolition of pre-capitalist modes of exploitation, (ii) 'the unification of the nation and its economic emancipation from foreign domination', and (iii) the establishment of 'a secular democratic republic based on democratic freedoms' (1981: 161). In themselves, these objectives are not a source of contention. It is how they are to be realized and if it is viable to fight for them alone that is the crucial question. Löwy demonstrates with theoretical skill and abundant material that only in those states where an extensive anti-capitalist mobilization and expropriation of the bourgeoisie have taken place (China, Yugoslavia, Cuba, Vietnam are discussed in particular), have these popular and democratic tasks been realized to any significant degree. As is evident from the examples, they have been far from fully met, but in each case more emphatically so than in those countries where, by one means or another, mass mobilization did not go beyond certain democratic demands and lead to the overthrow of capitalism.

It is, then, apparent that the relationship between the struggle for bourgeois democratic demands and the struggle for socialism in the capitalist periphery is highly problematic, for although the latter encompasses the former, there is no natural slippage between the two. History has given us no example of a popular democratic regime becoming a socialist one without a process of rupture and conflict, nor any case of a national liberation movement that has held back from the abolition of capitalist property relations and not subsequently capitulated before imperialist pressure, with the progressive erosion of democratic gains which that entails. Today this problematic is most evident in Nicaragua, for which Henri Weber holds out an optimistic analysis that the process underway is precisely a transformation towards socialism (1981, see also chapter 5 of this book). Weber's attention is directed towards the experiments in democracy of the Frente Sandinista de Liberación Nacional (FSLN) and the extent to which it has gone in carrying out its bourgeois democratic programme. Löwy shares this position, perceiving the possibility of the Sandinistas following a course not dissimilar from that taken by Castro as a result of confronting the exigencies of realizing democratic tasks in a neo-colonial state. However, neither author dwells for long on the countervailing tendencies aside from that of external imperialist pressure for an unrestrained counter-revolution. This is not just a dangerous omission but betokens erroneous analysis. The popular and democratic aspirations of the FSLN provide no guarantee that it will lead an unqualified offensive against capitalism; although it is to be hoped that they will. Still less do they provide it with a resistance to creeping bureaucratism or, more acutely in the present crisis, a commitment to a real internationalism predicated on the understanding that the Nicaraguan revolution will either fall decisively or ossify if it does not develop into the Central American revolution and supersede the limits of national liberation. Nicaragua is not an island like Cuba, and the geo-political realities of Central America today coupled with the vigorous counter-offensive mounted by Washington pose a grave danger to the very existence of the Sandinista regime.

At present, as Weber in fact implies, the FSLN government is, in the parlance of Poulantzas (1974), an 'exceptional regime', authentically petty bourgeois in its Jacobinism, populism and *dirigisme*, anti-capitalist in spirit, but under the pressure of the native bourgeoisie and the international banks on the one hand, and the workers and poor peasants on the other, forever oscillating between the two, and, up until now, continuing to guarantee capitalist property relations. While Black demonstrates his 'Sandinismo' by making a positive virtue of this, Weber and Löwy tend to view it as a moment in a process. For Weber the break with capitalism will develop largely as a result of the FSLN's own volition. For Löwy the implication is, in line with his general thesis, that the Sandinistas may well adopt a 'permanentist' line through to socialism because they show every sign of being unconscious Trotskyists. This is not the place to develop this debate, but elements of it have been raised for the very good reason that the FSLN has produced a model that is now adhered to by most of the national liberation movements in Central America, and most explicitly so by the Frente Democrático Revolucionario (FDR) in El Salvador. As has been suggested, the model is far from remarkable or indigenous to Nicaragua, although the particularly acute fissure inside the bourgeoisie, caused by the monopoly of one family over the state apparatus, undoubtedly gave it added impetus there. In essence the model is based upon the establishment of a cross-class alliance for the consummation of a popular democratic programme combined with an implied stagist strategy towards the achievement of socialism. These two elements are clearly mutually dependent and have an established lineage in the official communist movement from the 'Theses on the Situation in China' of Stalin and Bukharin, through Mao's bloc of four classes to the contemporary metropolitan variant of Eurocommunism. This patrimony is, of course, distinct from but also interacts with the variegated reformist and stagist projects ranging from Cardenas in Mexico to Boumedienne in Algeria.

In this chapter, I shall consider these two broad aspects in relation to El Salvador, first through an examination of the strategy of the local Communist Party, the Partido Comunista de El Salvador (PCS), and then in terms of the development of the national liberation movement, headed politically by the FDR and militarily by the FMLN. In outlining this process, the survey touches on the Salvadorean class structure in order to demonstrate the severity of the present crisis in social as well as political terms, and also the fact that, as in most neo-colonial states, the alternative to the popular front cannot be a purist united front of the proletariat for the simple reason that the industrial working class is so small that this would exclude the vast majority of the masses. The final comments pursue the argument that the critical factor in the struggle against imperialism is not unity *per se*, but the political leadership of a united front. From a Marxist perspective, this question can only be satisfactorily resolved if the proletariat is not simply a member of such a front but occupies the leading role, or, as Lenin put it, imposes its hegemony through a programme which incorporates all the democratic demands advanced by the bourgeois and petty bourgeois opposition, but seeks their implementation through the abolition of capitalism and not its rectification.

The PCS and the Salvadorean ruling class

In a far more acute manner than was evident in Nicaragua, the principal Salvadorean guerrilla organizations—the Fuerzas Populares de Liberación (FPL), the Fuerzas Armadas de Resistencia Nacional (FARN), and the Ejército Revolucionario del Pueblo (ERP)—were either born out of, or developed through, sustained critiques of the policies and activities of the PCS. These critiques were not homogeneous. They were founded upon discrete and substantive points of disagreement, centred largely around the question of the armed struggle and the characterization of social classes in El Salvador. In 1970, these issues led to a split in the PCS, the first major rupture experienced by the party since its foundation in 1930. Over the ensuing five-year period the guerrilla groups acquired their present physiognomy, and between 1975 to 1979 the mass popular organizations to which they had become linked and did much to develop—the Bloque Popular Revolucionario

(BPR) linked to the FPL, the Frente de Acción Popular Unificada (FAPU) linked to the FARN, and the Ligas Populares—28 de Febrero (LP-28) linked to the ERP—took these debates to the much wider circles of workers and peasants that adhered to them. The principal target of their polemics was the unremarkable thesis of the PCS, that the major task facing revolutionaries was the formation of a mass anti-fascist front with the bourgeois opposition, in order to advance through peaceful and parliamentary means the bourgeois democratic revolution. This was to be spearheaded by the so-called national bourgeoisie and would enable the working class to develop in both size and consciousness under a regime of modernizing capitalism and democratic liberties. Despite the criticisms levelled against it by the increasingly popular guerrilla organizations, the PCS clung to this line. As late as May 1979, the party claimed at its Seventh Congress that the support which it had given to the reformist electoral opposition bloc, Unión Nacional Opositora (UNO), 'voiced the democratic aspirations and structural changes required by the great majority of people, grouped them behind it, and forced a polarization in the electoral confrontation....' The basis for this was spelled out unequivocally: 'the bourgeois democratic path to solving the political crisis has today to be an inseparable part of substantial socio-economic reforms' (PCS, 1979a: 2). This was after two elections (1972 and 1977) in which the reformist and bourgeois parties in UNO—the social democratic Movimiento Nacional Revolucionario (MNR), the Partido Demócrata Cristiana (PDC) and the legal front of the PCS, the Unión Demócrata Nacionalista (UDN)—had been flagrantly denied victory by fraud and open repression. It was, moreover, a period during which all civil liberties had been suppressed by legislation directly modelled on the national security doctrines developed by the 'organic' dictatorships of the Southern Cone. The newly mobilized peasantry and working class were suffering from a repression of unprecedented scale, with torture, 'disappearance' and death a commonplace in the struggle between the guerrillas and the mass plebeian fronts on the one hand and the military dictatorship on the other. Furthermore, the restatement of the policy of the bourgeois democratic path (note: 'path' itself and not elements thereof) came precisely at the moment when the FSLN was launching its final offensive against Somoza! Nine days before the massacre on 9 May 1979 of twenty-five militants of the BPR, which was to be the first image of the Salvadorean crisis to hit the television screens of North America and Europe, PCS militants distributed a May Day leaflet that saluted the 'legitimate democratic aspirations' of the people and called for a 'just society', but made no mention of the armed struggle which was raging. Aptly enough, the document which contained the major theses of the Seventh Congress referred to the 1932 revolution in just two lines about 'the defeat' (PCS 1979: 21). This represented quite a lacuna in that the revolution, which was bred of the wholesale collapse of the coffee industry and whose motive force was the peasant masses of the western departments, was inspired by the left oppositionist Farabundo Martí; a founding member of the PCS. The 1932 revolution is the most important point of reference in Salvadorean history and is acknowledged as such by the overwhelming majority of the left. The PCS document could only be seen as an attempt to suppress the memory of this heroic but unsuccessful popular uprising. Even FAPU, linked to FARN, which after an initial disastrous experiment with guerrilla *foquismo* in the early 1970s was rapidly returning to a strategy of détente with the small bourgeois parties and sectors of the military, denounced the PCS line as reformist and revisionist. The FPL and BPR made notably harsher assessments. Yet this strategy, which had led the PCS to support the Salvadorean oligarchy's invasion of Honduras in 1969 and would shortly lead it to take cabinet places in the junta established by the colonels in October 1979, was at least consistent. It found its ultimate rationale in the belief—never substantiated by critical analysis—that there existed in El Salvador an independent industrially based national bourgeoisie which could displace the pro-imperialist big land-holding class. Although this position is rejected by all the other forces on the left it bears deeper consideration, if only because since April 1980 and the establishment of the FDR these forces are now grouped alongside reformist bourgeois elements in support of a political programme, which can without much difficulty be read as a variant of the PCS line.

There is some irony in the fact that it is precisely the omnipotence of the landed oligarchy, which for the last five decades has been the principal enemy of the PCS, that demonstrates the non-existence of an authentic national bourgeoisie in El Salvador. The landed bourgeoisie is not, as is often asserted, composed of only 14 families but some 250, grouped around 40 central clans who control 80 per cent of coffee production; the mainstay of the country's economy (53 per cent of all exports and 10 per cent of GDP). The modern Salvadorean state was constructed around the sale of coffee on the world market, and the landed bourgeoisie has, since its establishment in the last quarter of the nineteenth century, been intimately connected to international capital through this nexus. Yet its consolidation, first in the alienation of communal lands in the 1880s and then in the displacement of small farmers in the crises of the 1920s and 1930s, never gave rise to direct foreign investment in coffee production. This remained firmly in the hands of the oligarchy which emerged as a fusion of the traditional republican elite based upon indigo cultivation and a stratum of immigrant entrepreneurs from Europe.

The 1932 rebellion failed to dislodge the landed oligarchy or compel any significant alteration in its policy. In contrast to the major states of South America, no move was made to institute an inflationary expansion or increase the infrastructure and economic activity of the state bolstered by a Bonapartist populism. The only major alteration derived from the exigencies of suppressing the rebellion in a rapid and all-encompassing pogrom in the countryside. Direct administration of the country was passed to the military. Over the ensuing decades a number of minor reforms were introduced, such as yellow (i.e. state-controlled) trade unions in place of the outright prohibition of workers' organizations, elections controlled by fraud instead of self-proclaimed dictatorship, selective tariffs to cushion artisanal workshops, and marginal increases in public spending to finance peripheral social projects. But at no stage did these modifications lead to a removal of the landlords' veto over economic policy or constitute a challenge to their ultimate control of the state, the autonomy of which is best described as minimal rather than relative. An indication of this domination in the political sphere is the high level of stability experienced by the various client military regimes.

The landed bourgeoisie suffered no incursion into its power base on the land. This is clear from the fact that in 1971, by which time the unit size of farm holdings had been markedly reduced in line with the requirements of commercial management and as a safeguard against reform, 463 properties accounted for 43 per cent of all cultivated land and units of over 200 hectares accounted for 34 per cent. While 72,000 hectares were in the possession of six families of the oligarchy, 42,000 were worked (but not necessarily owned) by 305,000 peasant families (Downing 1978; Jung 1980; Menjívar 1977; Ruíz 1976). Placing emphasis on the distinction between the relations of production as a whole and the specific forms of exploitation, we can say that up until the 1950s an essentially pre-capitalist mode of exploitation existed between the big landlords and the labour force. Although in times of planting and harvesting a substantial temporary waged labour force was employed, permanent workers were employed either on the basis of sharecropping or, more usually, in *colonato*, under which subsistence plots were leased in return for labour rent. However, from the mid-1950s onwards the need to expand plantation land came progressively into conflict with the subsistence requirements of a population of over 3 million people occupying a mere 8,000 square miles of largely mountainous territory. The ecological limits of the prevailing labour relation were met and a diminution in labour rent took place in combination with an increase in money rent and wage labour. The other effects of this will be considered in a moment. What should be made plain here is that the growing preponderance of capitalist relations in agriculture did not lead to the replacement of a backward latifundista elite by a new agro-industrial sector, which could be identified as a modernizing capitalist class. These changes took place within the existing pattern of ownership and corresponded to the necessity of extending to the labour force the nexus of capitalism that had prevailed for nearly a century between the landlords themselves and between the landed bourgeoisie and international capital. However, these transformations do help to explain why a number of secondary contradictions have, over the last twenty years, appeared within the oligarchy, as one faction, composed primarily but not exclusively of the largest landlords, shifted a portion of its capital into processing and marketing as well as other manufacturing interests. This faction, headed by the De Sola clan and the Miraflor group of companies which it owns (the largest exporters but only the twenty-fifth largest cultivators of coffee), expanded its links with foreign capital, and sought to accelerate the growth of the manufacturing sector on the basis of a combination of external investment and surplus coffee capital. Although there was no major dislocation of the political unity of the landed bourgeoisie, and certain large clans which had substantial industrial interests (Hill, Dueñas, Regaldo) continued to lead the most entrenched and ultramontane elements of the oligarchy, there was a certain disaggregation of its political compact. This can be traced in the activities of the De Solas, who in 1978 joined with the US State Department to discuss with the Christian Democrats the possibility of replacing the military regime, and, in October 1979 broke with their peers in the oligarchy in backing the colonels' junta. However, the fact that the De Solas acted largely on their own and were closely allied with the US in its endeavour to consolidate a Christian Democrat regime backed by the military, completely undermines the view that they might open a democratic breach. In January 1980 the PCS itself implicitly accepted this fact by ending its participation in government with the colonels and the De Solas.

There still remains the apparently anomalous fact that after Guatemala, El Salvador is Central America's most industrialized state, with the manufacturing sector advancing remarkably quickly under the Central American Common Market (CACM) during the 1960s. Between 1959 and 1969 industrial investment rose from 1.6 per cent of total investment to 43.7 per cent, with manufacturing industry accounting for 20 per cent of GDP. Between 1964 and 1967 growth in the manufacturing sector averaged 11 per cent a year while that in agriculture was virtually stagnant at 1.2 per cent (Bravo 1980: 31; Menjívar 1977: 30). To explain fully why this process was not only shortlived (less than a decade, with industrial growth slipping to 5.7 per cent in 1972–75 and fixed capital formation falling by 5 per cent in the last five years of the 1960s) but also incapable of transforming the country's entire economic structure, would require an extensive discussion of, *inter alia*, the internal contradictions of import substitution, the Alliance for Progress, and the whole enterprise of industrial development in 'dependent' capitalist states, issues which do not concern us centrally in this discussion. The most important point to emphasize is that while this failure to 'take off' on a new agro-industrial base may be explained in the short term by a number of discrete causes, it was structurally determined by the enclave nature of the new industrial sector. This was particularly true of the early efforts at import substitution which proved unprofitable and established very few forward linkages. It became even more marked as major transnationals moved in to capitalize (literally) on low labour costs, an advantageous tariff regime, and the remarkably good communications network possessed by El Salvador. Between 1959 and 1969 foreign companies repatriated 120 million colones* against a total investment of
* 2.5 colones = US$1 (1960s).

179 million. Employment grew by only 2.2 per cent against an increase in production of over 8 per cent, while value added in the production process remained the lowest in the continent at between 17 and 20 per cent—which is not surprising given the fact that in 1968 Salvadorean raw materials comprised a meagre 39 per cent of those used in manufacturing (Menjívar 1977: 30, 34). This is a familiar picture. It demonstrates the dependent and parasitic nature of manufacturing industry in the capitalist periphery. But in El Salvador this did not simply result from an incursion by foreign capital that operated parallel to rural capital. The agro-exporting bourgeoisie was fully drawn into and played a large part in directing this process, with the thirty-nine largest agricultural enterprises controlling 66 per cent of the capital in the country's 1,500 biggest industrial companies (Domenech 1977). This stranglehold was confirmed by the oligarchy's control over the local finance market, with the thirteen largest clans all possessing major banking interests and the four most powerful domestic banks being wholly controlled by landed capital.

The illustrations may be multiplied but the picture remains the same. Neither shifts in the internal configuration of the landed bourgeoisie nor the swift wave of industrialization markedly altered the character or significantly reduced the power of the dominant bloc. There was no substantial dispute within the ruling class nor any challenge to it along the lines, for example, of Argentina, where a nascent industrial bourgeoisie entered into a tactical alliance with the reformist-led working class via Peronist Bonapartism, to obtain control of the state apparatus and appropriate capital. In Argentina the accumulation of industrial capital was effected through tariff manipulation and the rechannelling of the organic accumulation based on differential rent in the countryside into the manufacturing sector. The social base for such an exercise has simply not existed in El Salvador. In this context it should be borne in mind that the direct control of the state apparatus by the military and the influence of the imperialist metropolis (itself always subject to secondary contradictions) have altered the terms of this landed domination to the most minimal extent. The extraordinarily cautious agrarian reform proposals of 1971 and 1976, which both the army and the US supported, were stopped in their tracks by oligarchic resistance. The 1980 reform measure is somewhat distinct insofar as it was set up along the lines of the Vietnamese 'Land to the Tiller' programme (a US-sponsored counter-insurgency scheme which organized peasants into strategic hamlets and gave them the right of freehold on small plots of land) and was specifically designed for implementation in the midst of a civil war. The reform caused a certain amount of consternation among the landed bourgeoisie, for while only 9 per cent of coffee production was affected, a large number of cattle ranches and sugar estates were expropriated. Although it is true that some of these enterprises were returned through sweetheart deals with the powerful 'Devolution Committee', an illegal body set up by the armed forces to investigate claims by owners that their land should be returned to them, some of the land was redistributed to the peasantry (Wheaton 1980; Simon and Stephens 1981). Although the reform was brought to a precipitate halt within three months of its introduction, it has remained an important source of discontent among the oligarchy, and gave rise to a number of threats of a military coup against the Duarte regime. Oligarchic recalcitrance prevented the full implementation of the land reform and thus impeded the consolidation of a base for the new regime among small and medium farmers. Under such circumstances it has proved impossible to replace the oligarchy with a bourgeois stratum based upon either primitive accumulation through military corruption (following the Guatemalan example) or demand-orientated redistribution. However, recognition of this fact does not signify that there was a full entente between the Duarte regime and the landed bourgeoisie, and neither does it justify the notion that the government was moving to the right after an initial reformist phase. It is the form rather than the degree of reaction that distinguished the junta from the oligarchy, a difference that still allowed for substantial conflict within the dominant bloc. Nevertheless, and this is not the place for extended speculation, it is clear that this secondary contradiction did not result from a challenge on the part of a fledgling national bourgeoisie, sufficiently independent from the metropolis to launch its own political project and establish a democratic regime.

Structure of the masses

As has been argued, the capacity of the landed bourgeoisie to defend and deepen its domination in the post-war era was not a simple case of stasis and retrenchment, but the result of a dynamic process in which the relations of production were overhauled. Hence, while the physiognomy of the dominant bloc has undergone little alteration, the terms of its exploitation of the labour force have changed considerably. This is particularly evident in the agricultural sector, which employs 60 per cent of the economically active population. The two central developments here have been the proletarianization of the peasantry and the accelerated alienation of subsistence plots. The scale of landlessness is the most striking, rising from a residual figure of 12 per cent of the rural population in 1961 to 29 per cent in 1971 and 41 per cent in 1975 (Burbach and Flynn 1980: 147). Estimates for 1980 put the figure at around 65 per cent. Directly connected with this has been the progressive subdivision of subsistence holdings. Between 1961 and 1971 the number of farms of less than 10 hectares rose from 207,000 to 314,000, and for farms of less than one hectare the increase was from 70,000 to 132,000 (Downing 1978: 46). The number of families who possessed no land at all rose by 82,000 (Jung 1980: 6). Thus, the ideal middle peasant projected by the Alliance for Progress as the most secure guardian of possessive individualism barely exists in El Salvador. Moreover, at the same time as landlessness was becoming endemic and the rural labour force growing by around 30,000 a year as a result of very high population growth, there was a marked lack of expansion in opportunities for wage labour. If we take the statistics for temporary wage labour as the most accurate reflection of employment patterns we can see that developments mirrored very closely the alienation of peasant landholdings. Between 1961 and 1971 the number of temporary wage labourers fell by 1.3 per cent, with the proportion of those who possessed land falling by 3 per cent and those without land rising by 14 per cent (Downing 1978: 40). In 1975 the level of permanent unemployment in the countryside was estimated at around 45 per cent, with underemployment fluctuating between 65 and 80 per cent (Menendez 1980: 14).

From all this it can be seen that the social crisis in El Salvador revolves around a profound dislocation of the peasantry from the land in terms of both traditional usufruct through labour rent and opportunities for wage labour. The great mass of rural labourers are therefore neither classic 'peasants' nor 'lumpen', but unemployed rural proletarians for whom guaranteed wages and employment are as critical as the demand for land. This has been evident in political terms since the sharp upturn in rural mobilization in 1973–74 which saw the formation of the radical workers' union Federación Católica de Campesinos Salvadoreños –Unión de Trabajadores del Campo (FECCAS–UTC), the guiding force of the BPR. This broke forty years of relative quiescence imposed by the outlawing of rural unions and the reactionary campaigns of the National Guard and the mass right-wing vigilante organization ORDEN (Organización Democrática Nacionalista). ORDEN owes its sheer size (upwards of 50,000 members) to the deepening impoverishment that enabled the incorporation of peasants into an informal state apparatus, on the basis of petty privilege and guarantees against repression. This has had the result of situating the civil war deep inside the rural population and taking conflict into every village, in a manner quite distinct from that in Nicaragua where the rural population played a much less central role. It is difficult to explain the existence of ORDEN in terms of a conflict between a middle and poor peasantry or around the battle for land. It corresponds much more closely to a harsh clientalist obligation necessitated by the very radicalism and organizational strength of the BPR in the countryside.

The precise characterization of the urban masses, who now constitute over a third of the population and comprise the fastest growing sector, also presents a number of difficulties. There are two main features here: the growth of the industrial proletariat during the 'boom' of the 1960s and the massive expansion in the number of migrant dwellers in the shanty towns or *tugurios*. The latter greatly outweigh the former because the industrial growth of the last two decades proved palpably incapable of providing employment for the droves of peasants displaced from the land. Over the last twenty-five years the population of the capital has risen fivefold and the department of San Salvador now contains over a fifth of the total population, with a density of 843 people per square mile against a national average of 170. This phenomenon took on an added importance following the war with Honduras in 1969, when inter-oligarchic rivalry, spurred on by El Salvador's considerable trading advantages within the CACM, resulted in the closing off of the Salvadorean bourgeoisie's critical safety valve of emigration to the neighbouring state. In 1968–70 some 300,000 migrants returned to the country as refugees, the bulk settling in the capital despite prohibition. A considerable number of these refugees were not *émigré* peasants but workers who had been fired from the fruit plantations of United Brands and Standard Fruit in Honduras, and therefore brought back with them an experience of proletarian organization. This gave a greater edge to their discontent which was fuelled by the government's failure to provide the social amenities which had been promised to them on their return. This was a significant event, but still represented only a moment in a process that became increasingly central to the configuration of the class struggle in El Salvador. From the mid-1960s onwards then, the capital and its environs were flooded by a sprawling mass of rural migrants, unemployed workers and impoverished petty bourgeois engaged in casual work in the marginal economy or that pellucid category, the 'service sector'. The sheer size, structural importance and relative youth of this mass combined to give it a radicalism in the 1970s that flies in the face of most of the political connotations associated with the term 'lumpen'. A certain sensitivity is required here, for we must distinguish this sector from the industrial working class in terms of the structural conditions of the workplace and the labour process, which are, in the final analysis, the central determinants of the revolutionary character of the proletariat. Nonetheless, the *tugurios* have become the site of an acute class struggle that integrates the industrial experience of many of their inhabitants with resistance to the specific conditions and forms of exploitation prevalent in the ghettos. The result has been a militancy that has superseded localism and become a direct challenge to the state, in the form of demands for employment, social amenities and democratic rights. The natural symbiosis of many slum-dwellers with the countryside, and their radicalization both there and in the dislocating process of migration to the town, have given this move-ment both added impetus and critical links with the dispossessed peasantry. This is, of course, by no means an exception in Central America; however it has taken on a particularly acute form in El Salvador and became one of the central axes around which the plebeian fronts were formed.

Compared to the proletariats of the advanced capitalist countries the industrial working class in El Salvador is very small. In 1975 it com-prised only 27 per cent of all those economically active in the urban sec-tor and 43 per cent of all urban wage earners (Jung 1980: 6). How-ever, compared to other neo-colonial states, and especially Central America, the working class has grown rapidly and is quite substantial. In 1960 it numbered 60,000, and by 1975, when the peak of industrialization had passed, it was at least 150,000 strong and centred predominantly on San Salvador. This greatly enhanced its cohesion. Of course, this figure is dwarfed by the million-odd rural proletarians, some 600,000 of whom receive an intermittent wage of some kind. Nevertheless it is significant in and of itself since it is this sector of the labour force which is uniquely qualified to take the leadership of the revolutionary movement. The question to be posed of all working classes is less their size but their relationship to the masses as a whole with regard to political authority. If we stall at the former we are left with an insuperable sociological reductionism as objectively 'regressive for revolutionary politics in the capitalist periphery as the strategy of alliance with 'national bourgeoisies'. It is no spurious parenthesis to note that this central motif of Marxism-Leninism was in part derived from the experience of the Russian proletariat, similarly circumscribed by the peasantry and rapidly enlarged by externally financed industrial growth. This factor is equally germane insofar as it demonstrates the speciousness of the argument, according to which the working class in the neo-colonial countries is structurally separated from the impoverished rural masses and *déclassé* layers (because of their relative advantages in terms of pay and employment) and fundamentally unrevolutionary in nature.

It was only in the late 1960s that significant elements of the Salvadorean proletariat manifested signs of emerging from the terrible legacy of 1932 and breaking with the economism of the reformist organizations and the tight control of the yellow trade unions controlled by the military. One notable feature of this process, which incorporated a notable antipathy towards the PCS, was that it occurred in tandem with the upturn in radicalism of the rural proletariat. As radical factions or spin-offs from the old union structures affiliated to the BPR, FAPU or the LP-28, they became the principal points of reference for industrial workers in struggle as well as the organizational terrain for co-operation with the rural and marginalized sectors. The plebeian fronts thus contain the germ of the worker–peasant alliance, which quite palpably has to be the principal axis of the revolutionary movement in El Salvador. Again, this took place in a manner that was largely absent in Nicaragua. It accounts for the relative paucity of sectoral divisions in El Salvador that might otherwise have impeded mass mobilization in the last five years of the 1970s.

The question of the non-existence of an authentic national bourgeoisie in El Salvador has a highly important additional aspect which we shall now consider. This absence is determined by the nature of the relationship between the domestic oligarchy and international capital, a relationship that has the direct effect of enhancing the relative exploitation and lack of prospects of the native petty bourgeoisie, professional middle class and small entrepreneurs to a far greater degree than occurs in the metropolitan states. While these sectors exist in substantial numbers and derive their well-being from the exploitation of the masses, they are themselves, by virtue of the plunder of the 'underdeveloped' capitalist nation as a whole, the victims of oppression by imperialism. Thus, although it is a phenomenon of a distinctly transient character, they may and often do support anti-imperialist movements at determinate moments precisely to better their own condition. This was certainly the case in Nicaragua, it may also be clearly perceived in Peronism, in the early stages of the Mexican, Iranian and Cuban revolutions, and in the Bolivian revolution of 1952. There is no intrinsic contradiction between the popular democratic character of the national liberation movement and the interests of these forces, and in this sense the task of national liberation not only can, but positively must go beyond the worker–peasant alliance to incorporate the impoverished middle sectors. However, as the case of Nicaragua shows, they should not be confused with the opposition bourgeoisie which in political extremis will take the same line. Moreover, once such a broad alliance is established the critical question becomes whether these forces, which are seeking to ameliorate the terms of their relationship with imperialism, or those forces which need to sever that relationship, gain control of the front. It is precisely this contradiction, and the fact that it still remains unresolved, that is at the heart of the indeterminate nature of the Nicaraguan revolution and has now come to occupy a central place in the Salvadorean national liberation front.

The anti-imperialist front

In schematic terms one might say that the formation of the FDR took place in two phases. First of all there was the unification of the guerrilla forces and the radical plebeian fronts, and in the second stage this unified mass movement allied itself with the parties of the reformist and bourgeois opposition (as defined by ideology rather than social base). The emergence of the FDR was a more complex and crisis-ridden process than the corresponding consolidation of the Nicaraguan opposition to Somoza, which took place through the reunification of the three tendencies of the FSLN. In El Salvador there was a greater antagonism between the guerrilla groups than between the FSLN tendencies, and one of the main reasons for the fact that this endured for so long was that the differences between the groups had been translated into the popular organizations, where they took on a predominantly political as opposed to a military character. The BPR was born in 1975 out of a sharp conflict within FAPU, which had been established the previous year. The BPR accused FAPU of being reformist and petty bourgeois for its strategy of alliance with the parties of UNO and dissident sectors of the military. As an alternative to this the BPR and its armed detachment, the FPL, advanced a line of class independence and the 'guerra popular prolongada', modelled largely on the Vietnamese experience and designed to deepen political mobilization through immersion in the masses over years of struggle. In broad political terms the

BPR's critique of FAPU corresponded to that made of the Terceristas by the Proletario and Guerra Popular Prolongada (GPP) factions of the FSLN. FAPU responded to this by accusing the BPR–FPL of adventurism and terrorism, but, interestingly, it failed to draw out an even greater pitfall of the 'guerra prolongada' strategy. That is its tendency to orientate the struggle away from the working class and towards the peasantry, and the fact that Salvadorean topography is not suitable for such a campaign. As a consequence the strategy is particularly conducive to high levels of attrition and thus gives rise to a quick loss of morale. Over the last two years the limitations of the strategies pursued by both the BPR and FAPU have become apparent. After the mismanagement of the general strikes of June and August 1980 and the partial failure of the general offensive of January 1981, the BPR's line played a major role in shifting the terrain of confrontation away from the towns and towards the countryside. This took place in a politically and militarily lopsided manner that has been marked by a noticeable reflux in the radicalism of the working class. FAPU's line has been characterized by a certain inconsistency. Nine months after the creation of the Coordinadora Revolucionaria de Masas (CRM) by the left in January 1980, FAPU broke from it for a brief but critical period during which they threw their resources behind the coup attempt made by the dissident junta member, Colonel Majano. The failure of this, and the prospect of becoming marginalized, led the organization rapidly back into the fold. At the same time its guerrilla affiliate, FARN, rejoined the new combined military command, the Dirección Revolucionaria Unificada (DRU), which in October 1980 was transformed into the FMLN.

The disagreements over strategy between the BPR–FPL and the FAPU–FARN may be partly explained by the different origins of the two revolutionary movements. After its split with the PCS in 1970 the FPL made a studious critique of guevarism in their adoption of the Vietnamese road. At the same time the BPR amassed a considerable following in the countryside. The FAPU–FARN orientation can be more closely understood by the fact that the organization originated from radicalized Christian Democratic elements and not the PCS. Thus the FAPU–FARN inherited part of the petty bourgeois urban following of the Christian Democratic Party. After a disastrous experience with guevarism it elaborated a self-criticism that placed exaggerated importance upon the necessity of defending the masses from repression by securing partial gains through negotiation, and removing the 'fascists' from government by whatever means. To some extent these differences still persist at the time of writing (March 1982) but originally they were less acute than those which obtained between both these organizations and the LP-28–ERP. The ERP pursued a thoroughly *foquista* strategy (based on the form of guerrilla warfare popularized by writer Regis Debray), which caused it to take a far more erratic course than the rest of the left. The ERP concentrated its forces in the eastern department of Morazán to the exclusion of operations in much of the rest of the country. While it subsequently registered some of the most substantial victories for the left in 1980 and 1981, it proved extremely difficult for it to expand its operations beyond Morazán and the neighbouring department of La Unión. The LP-28, formed in 1977 and making a nominal break with *foquismo*, steered an even more unpredictable course under its largely student leadership. This reached a peak of confusion during September and October 1979 with the crisis and eventual overthrow of the Romero dictatorship by the colonels. Shortly before the coup of 15 October the reformist parties of UNO, which by then had ceased to exist as viable political organizations, had combined with a number of important affiliated unions as well as FAPU's largest union member, FENASTRAS, to form a tactical front known as the Foro Popular. The Foro was designed to counter the so-called ultimatism of the mass organizations by offering an acceptable link to dissident officers, and a means by which to secure a civilian reformist representation in any new regime. The LP-28 reversed its early radicalism by joining the Foro when even FAPU, which nominally stood to its right, had desisted from formal approval. The LP-28 supported the Foro's nomination of ministers in the new junta and all its overtures to the colonels before and immediately after the coup. However, on the day after the coup the ERP launched an attempted insurrection in which it suffered high losses. In the ensuing disarray, which in effect split the two wings of the organization, the ERP was forced to align itself much more closely to the graduated strategy of the other guerrilla organizations. Meanwhile the LP-28 joined with FAPU and the BPR in breaking from the Foro and embarking upon a campaign of popular mobilization for the implementation of the democratic policies espoused by the junta.

The consolidation of the Salvadorean revolutionary front was therefore an extended process fraught with imbalances. As an effective fighting force it could not be relied upon until the autumn of 1980, nine months after the establishment of the CRM and the provisional agreement on a unified guerrilla command. The basis of this unity was laid most firmly in the period of October to December 1979, the period of the 'first junta' of the colonels and their allies from the Foro. Over this period the left concentrated upon mobilization around concrete economic and democratic demands in the face of an ever-accelerating repression that soon outstripped that of the Romero regime. It was the experience of this campaign, orientated towards minimal demands on which there was absolute agreement, and the unambiguous response of the military, that forged the unity. Of equal importance, however, in the ultimate configuration of the national liberation front was the increasing disenchantment and eventual 'changing of sides' of the majority of the bourgeois and reformist parties that made up the Foro (MNR, UDN, PDC). These forces had enthusiastically welcomed the coup and taken cabinet places in the new junta, but over the following three months suffered severe political damage and internal crises as it was made obvious on a daily basis that the military were neither willing nor capable of putting an end to repression, introducing democratic reforms or implementing the structural economic changes that had been promised in October. In the face of a deep polarization the tiny reformist centre came under extreme pressure, and eventually, in December 1979, split from the regime. Having suffered a categorical defeat in the electoral arena they had now lost major political capital by allying themselves with the military. Total demise seemed imminent. While the rump of the Christian Democrats, under the leadership of José Napoleón Duarte, confirmed their alliance with the officers, the bulk of the supporters of the October coup embarked upon the unavoidable trajectory away from imperialism and towards the left. In March 1980 they formed the Frente Democrático Salvadoreño (FDS) as a shortlived preamble to joining with the CRM a month later to form the FDR.

Given the character of the crisis and the structure of Salvadorean society this was not an unnatural path to take. Yet this period was not simply characterized by a growing awareness on the part of the revolutionaries on the one hand and the new recruits to the CRM on the other. It was a time of particularly acute class conflict in which a thousand people lost their lives. The PCS and the reformists continued for a number of months to attach themselves if not to the specifically repressive activity of the military then certainly to the belief that substantial reformist elements existed within the armed forces who would repudiate violence, that US backing was both acceptable and efficacious, and that the revolutionary left was 'adventurist' and even 'subversive'. Undoubtedly lessons were learnt, particularly by the PCS which stood on the verge of complete auto-destruction. But political forces cannot be properly compared to individuals; they do not change views overnight and cannot be assumed to have reconstructed themselves through perceiving tactical errors. The fundamental change that occurred over this period was the realization by the PCS and the other parties of the Foro that in order to consummate the democratic revolution conflict with the imperialist metropolis was inevitable. They had been dislocated from the client military bloc and forced into the arms of the national liberation movement. But in this process they only came to accept the necessity of armed struggle: no other fundamental allegiances or policies were disowned. In this respect it can be seen that they are now attempting to realize in the FDR those aims that they previously sought to achieve in the junta. Instead of relying upon the formal repressive apparatus they are now dependent upon the armed might of the masses under the organizational leadership of the revolutionary left—a far from optimum situation from their point of view but immeasurably better than total eclipse.

The political basis of the FDR lies in the Programmatic Platform devised not by the bourgeois reformists but by the CRM itself, of which the PCS was a founding member. The platform reflects a number of important alterations in the strategy of the left that can be traced directly to the influence of the Nicaraguan revolution. In these changes it was the FPL–BPR that made the most substantial concessions. The document makes no mention whatsoever of socialism or capitalism but refers to 'the existing state powers' and a 'new society', terms eminently acceptable to the ex-members of UNO and the Foro. The platform's orientation is, as might be expected from this semantic bias, towards the implementation of structural reforms in which the targets are imperialism not capitalism, dictatorship not bourgeois government, the oligarchy and not the bourgeoisie as a whole. There is to be a sweeping agrarian reform based on the expropriation of the landed bourgeoisie (the precise character of which being undefined) but guarantees for medium and small farmers. The army is to be reconstructed, with honest elements from the existing officer corps being allowed to serve alongside the ex-guerrillas. The new popular democratic government is to rest on a 'broad political and social base, formed above all by the working class, the peasantry, the advanced middle layers' united with all those who support the programme among 'the medium-sized industrialists, merchants, artisans and farmers (small and medium-sized coffee planters and those involved in other areas of agriculture or cattle-raising)'. The new government will carry out extensive nationalizations of public utilities and greatly expand social and welfare programmes.

Other clauses of the Platform assert self-determination and independence from the US and call for the introduction and unconditional defence of broad democratic liberties. On the criteria presented by Löwy (1981) the Platform is a most eloquent programme for a bourgeois democratic revolution despite the fact that the means for realizing many of its objectives are articulated less in classic bourgeois democratic terms, than the incorporation of these into the reformist designs of state capitalism. Apart from certain sections on the military question and the phrasing of independence from the US, there is little that departs from the policies of the reformist parties in the 1970s. Fundamentally, it is the means by which the Platform is to be implemented—the armed struggle—that is different. The degree to which the Platform represents a retreat from the positions of the revolutionary left may be gained from the fact that Salvador Cayetano Carpio, a longstanding leader of the FPL and presently a commander of the FMLN, found in it the basis upon which to ally himself in April 1980 with such men as Guillermo Ungo (leader of the MNR and a member of the junta until January 1980) and Rubén Zamora (an ex-member of the PDC and Minister of the Presidency in the October 1980 junta), whom he had attacked four months earlier as being 'in close alliance with the US State Department' (Tricontinental Society 1980: 30). In February 1982 Cayetano could opine that 'we don't believe that this broad program has anything to do with Socialism or a Socialist government' (*International Herald Tribune* 11 February 1982). The same interpretation was put forward by Zamora himself when he stated that the FDR wanted a democratic government with a mixed economy, in which foreign investment would have an important role to play, and that close links with the US were imperative since without them it would be impossible for a small state to survive in Latin America (*Newsweek* 9 March 1981; 15 February 1982). It would be innocent in the extreme to imagine that a good portion of statements such as these are not consciously directed at the metropolis as a diplomatic manoeuvre designed to maximize the advantages of the increasingly substantial fissure inside the imperialist bloc. On the other hand, it would be ingenuous and fallacious to maintain that they are nothing more than this. While it is still apparent that Zamora and Cayetano adhere to different political beliefs, they have manifestly reached agreement upon a strategy in the short and medium term, and that strategy is unequivocally stagist from a revolutionary perspective. The Nicaraguan model has been fully embraced. Yet El Salvador is distinct from Nicaragua in a number of important ways which will necessarily alter the terms of such a strategy and may also militate for its more rapid supersession. First of all, as has been shown, El Salvador possesses no opposition bourgeoisie of any resource and certainly no forces comparable to those grouped around the Banco de America and the Banco Nicaragüense in Nicaragua. These forces were deeply alienated by the Somoza clan's monopoly of the state apparatus and this caused a split inside the dominant class, which not only facilitated a remarkably unified campaign against the Somozas themselves but also resulted in the survival of important capitalist sectors after the revolution. Secondly, the Salvadorean military apparatus is, despite its profound commitment to fighting the civil war, different from the Nicaraguan National Guard insofar as it is not absolutely dependent in an institutional sense upon the existing regime. Without the Somozas, the National Guard was nothing; it was a thoroughly praetorian force that defended a social system through its loyalty to the Somozas. The very fact that this meant attacking other capitalist groups as well as the masses on behalf of the dynasty reduced its potential autonomy to virtually nothing. This situation has not yet been reached in El Salvador, and while it would appear extremely unlikely, it is not absolutely impossible that under the aggregate pressure of guerrilla successes some portion of the army might suffer a total collapse of morale and agitate for a negotiated solution. Thirdly, as a result of the historically greater profile of the PCS in El Salvador than the forces of Stalinism in Nicaragua, the revolutionary left and the general tenets of Marxism are more influential than in Nicaragua. Moreover, social democracy has had a longer history and its popularity is liable to be more tentative than in Nicaragua, especially in terms of co-opting important sections of the left. While the left may achieve a *modus vivendi* with the MNR around the question of democratic liberties, the Salvadorean revolutionaries are demonstrably less 'innocent' in political terms than the Terceristas of the FSLN. This likelihood is also strengthened by the fact that the Salvadorean left has for an appreciable period of time been immersed in the masses and established strong popular organizations aside from their armed units. This is again somewhat different from the Nicaraguan case where the FSLN was, until the final victory, dedicated to predominantly military tasks and organization, and, notwithstanding the efforts of the Proletario and GPP factions, had only a marginalized presence among the masses. This fact, combined with a decade of trenchant opposition to the reformist policies of UNO (for which there was no corresponding force in Nicaragua), suggests that after a national liberation war that has already lasted two years and entered every pore of Salvadorean society, it will be extremely hard to brake popular mobilization. Any form of 'popular democratic' government which may arise out of the armed struggle will be acutely vulnerable to consolidated pressure from the masses and the left to deepen its revolutionary measures towards a complete break with capitalism.

This is, of course, pure conjecture. In his analysis of the situation in Nicaragua Weber has concrete facts on which to work (1981). However, while his comments display a correct optimism and preoccupation with the question of socialist democracy, they tend to site all impediments to this process in the external threat of US imperialism. As has already been suggested, this ignores the central question of the character of the FSLN's leadership, which still remains undefined. But it also passes over the relatively new and somewhat complex phenomenon of the role of European capital and particularly international social democracy. (For an analysis of this, cf. Castillo 1981.) It might be objected that in view of the clear disaggregation of the metropolitan strategy for Central America, to identify the current policy of the Socialist International as a threat is pure maximalism and flies in the face of realpolitik, which requires a flexible tactical stance in the face of Reagan's belligerence. In fact, the diplomatic campaign being waged by the European reformists is a double-edged sword. On the one hand it allows the national liberation movements a modicum of diplomatic space, while on the other hand it constitutes an unremitting pressure for them to suppress mass mobilization and capitulate to the lowest common denominator of the struggle for democracy. Nevertheless, it is undeniable that the broad strategy of European capital is distinct from that of the US and its closest allies (Latin American client states, Israel and Britain). The experiences of, *inter alia*, Algeria, Egypt, Iraq and Zimbabwe—examples with which the European powers are closely familiar—show that the absence of a strong national bourgeoisie (either as a result of a determinate historical development or because of annihilation through war) need by no means obstruct the reconstitution of capitalist relations of production after 'national liberation'. Moreover, this is often most efficiently achieved through the expansion of the state sector and extensive nationalization to provide the means for the regeneration of a native capitalist class. The correlate of this is, of necessity, a progressive limiting of mass mobilization and the erosion of working-class autonomy. In the early stages this is often articulated through evoking the exigencies of defending the liberation struggle and capitalizing on the popularity of its leading forces. Later on this is liable to acquire a more coercive character. Such a schema, which is certainly not alien to some of the policies espoused by either the FSLN or the FDR, and by this token becomes all the more invidious, is, for international social democracy, a very welcome alternative to the US scenario of genocide. In this sense European capital has counterposed to the designs of Washington in El Salvador a mobile strategy in which the revolutionaries are contained not through outright military defeat but through a popular front in which it is outmanoeuvred on its own terrain. It is worth noting that while a strong basis for this strategy exists in the political limitations of the national liberation movement in the capitalist periphery, it is no less a 'last chance' option than the US method of aligning itself with politically bankrupt dictatorships. It is reliant upon the rapid reconstruction of important elements of the capitalist state after they have, in all probability, been destroyed, and it lacks a mediator in a strong native bourgeoisie.

Historically the popular front has been the product of a crisis, albeit in very different circumstances. What is shared between Kerensky and Mitterand or Cárdenas and Blum is not a precise political form but a unity in response to pressure that impels the bourgeoisie to accept and even offer an alliance with workers' parties in government. This may take many forms; it is possible to perceive the essential characteristics of the popular front existing within a single party: the Kuomintang in China, Peron's Justicialista movement, the Mexican PRI. Equally, its traditional terms can be reversed, with the initiative coming not from the bourgeoisie but from the workers' movement itself, for example in Angola and Mozambique, where the Soviet bureaucracy has patronized such an *entente*. The properties of being in government, such as the FSLN, are very different from those of being immersed in a bitter civil war, such as the FDR–FMLN, but this difference does not touch on the key characteristic of the popular front: that by virtue of the incorporation of the organizations and parties of the masses it possesses a ready-made prestige and credibility among the oppressed, who in the initial stages will view it as their own. In Nicaragua this process has already developed to the extent that the principal representatives of the bourgeoisie in the first post-liberation junta (Robelo and Chamorro) were displaced at a relatively early stage and thereby lost much popularity. In El Salvador the bourgeois elements are linked to the mass organizations in a much tighter organizational structure, within the FDR. Although these forces do not represent an authentic opposition bourgeoisie and have no independent authority over the FMLN, they are far more closely identified with it than was the Nicaraguan bourgeoisie with the FSLN. This, then, presents us with a problem which is in some senses analagous to that addressed by Lenin when he argued against calling for the immediate overthrow of the Kerensky regime in the spring of 1917, in favour of a Bolshevik campaign for the education of the working class until it had reached the conclusion that its interests were no longer being served by the government. Thus, in view of the substantial possibilities of a tactical alliance based on agreement over a democratic programme, the need to win the great majority of the intrinsically unstable middle sectors, and the existing popularity of the FDR as well as the FMLN, it would be manifestly absurd to call for the expulsion of the bourgeois forces from the anti-imperialist front. However, this places a premium on demonstrating the impossibility of attaining formal bourgeois democratic freedoms in El Salvador as long as it remains a capitalist state, and at the same time showing the parallel relationship between these freedoms and the achievement of socialism. They are an integral part of the struggle for socialism because along with the principal economic tasks of the bourgeois democratic revolution they can no longer be introduced in the neo-colonial states under the socio-economic system from which they have historically been derived. In El Salvador today obfuscation with regard to this question runs particularly deep because of the omnipotence of the oligarchy. Fifty years of dictatorship and a century of economic dominance have not unnaturally resulted in an elision between an anti-oligarchic programme, which the FDR currently espouses, and an anti-capitalist programme, which significant sectors of the revolutionary left have at least temporarily discarded for the sake of unity in the FDR. A socialist strategy for El Salvador can only be consolidated by incorporating the former into the lattter and fighting for independence within the FDR to do precisely this. To wait upon events to reveal the inherent contradictions in the FDR's programme is insufficient and could concede the leadership of the masses at a crucial time. This is the challenge facing the Salvadorean revolutionaries, and it will undoubtedly continue to be a source of debate and conflict. For socialists it must be addressed hand in hand with the struggle to defeat the forces of dictatorship and imperialism not just in El Salvador but in the whole of Central America and the Caribbean.

NOTES

1 I would like to thank Jenny Pearce for reading and criticizing a draft of this essay. Much of the discussion here is developed at greater length in my book, *The long war: dictatorship and revolution in El Salvador*, 1982.

REFERENCES

Armstrong, R. 1982, *El Salvador fights: military dictatorship and people's war, 1979–1981*, London, Pluto Press

Black, G. 1981, *Triumph of the people: the Sandinista revolution in Nicaragua*, London, Zed Press

Bravo, O. 1980, *Modernización, industrialización y política en América Central: El Salvador, Guatemala y Honduras*, Occasional Paper, Stockholm, Institute of Latin American Studies

Burbach, R. and Flynn, P. 1980, *Agribusiness in the Americas*, New York, Monthly Review Press

Castillo, D. 1981, 'Presencia de empresas transnacionales y partidos políticos europeos en Centroamérica', in Latin America Bureau, *The EEC and Latin America: preliminary seminar, London, 20 and 21 March 1981*, London, pp. 8–20

Domenech, M. 1977, 'The basis of power and wealth in El Salvador', mimeo., San Salvador

Downing, T. J. 1978, *Agricultural modernization in El Salvador, Central America*, Occasional Paper no. 32, University of Cambridge, Centre for Latin American Studies

Dunkerley, J. 1982, *The long war: dictatorship and revolution in El Salvador*, London, Junction Books

International Herald Tribune 11 February 1982

Jung, H. 1980, 'Class struggles in El Salvador', *New left review*, no. 122

Löwy, M. 1981, *The politics of combined and uneven development*, London, New Left Books

Menendez, M. 1980, *El Salvador: una auténtica guerra civil*, San José, EDUCA

Menjívar, R. 1977, *Crisis de desarrollismo: caso El Salvador*, San José, EDUCA

Newsweek 9 March 1981; 15 February 1982

Partido Comunista de El Salvador 1979, *Fundamentos y perspectivas*, San Salvador

Partido Comunista de El Salvador 1979a, *El PCS celebró su séptimo congreso*, San Salvador

Poulantzas, N. 1974, *Fascism and dictatorship*, London, New Left Books

Ruíz, S. 1976, 'La modernización agrícola en El Salvador', *Estudios Centroamericanos*, vol. 31, no. 330

Simon, L. R. and Stephens, J. C. Jnr. 1981, *El Salvador land reform 1980–1981*, Boston, OXFAM

Tricontinental Society 1980, *El Salvador. The development of the people's struggle*, London

Weber, H. 1981, *The Sandinist revolution*, London, New Left Books

Wheaton, P. 1980, *Agrarian reform in El Salvador: a program of rural pacification*, Washington, EPICA Task Force

SEVEN

Guadeloupe-Martinique: a System of Colonial Domination in Crisis

Philippe Alain Blérald

The constituent elements of the economic and social formations of Guadeloupe and Martinique are logically situated within the framework of the accumulation of capital on an international level. The forms of French penetration of the Antilles are a response to the division of labour between the metropolis and its colonies, a relationship governed solely by mercantilist criteria which historically found expression in the development of a slave system of production for the world market. In socio-political and ideological-cultural terms, this colonial process brought about a predominantly aristocratic and racially segregated society.

At a later stage, under the control of the French metropolis, the Antillian formations began the transition to capitalism. Their insertion into the colonial relationship, one dictated by imperial protectionism, was accompanied by an increase in their dependence and further subordination to the French state. As far as power relations were concerned, the transition to capitalism shared the same features of the assimilationist dynamic of the class struggle. This gradually modelled colonial society along the lines of the form of representative democracy found in the metropolis and led to Guadeloupe and Martinique being given the status of 'departments' of France in 1946.

Contemporary Antillian society is basically the product of this historical movement (whereby forms of social production are articulated with forms of the state) of two phases. First, the creation of a system of merchant slave accumulation with its corresponding segregationist political-cultural order. Second, the passage to a system of capitalist accumulation and its assimilationist politico-cultural order. From slavery to capitalism, from segregation to assimilation; this, in my opinion, is what characterized the evolving form of the colonial process in Guadeloupe and Martinique.

The domination of the Antilles by international capitalism, the introduction into the islands of slave labour, then capitalist relations of forced labour, together with the contradictory functioning of the relationships of colonial oppression, all played a part in the setting up of the original superstructure. From this point of view, the development of a capitalist mode of production meant the substitution of one form of society for another. The first comprised a pre-capitalist political society in which the private coercion inherent in the reproduction of slavery imposed restrictions on state action. Its substitute is a capitalist civil society in which the main political and ideological levers of class power are organically contained within the state. Private interests are thereby subject to public regulation in the interests of the global reproduction of the system. With respect to the transformation of the class struggle induced by the rapid expansion of the capitalist mode of production, ideological-cultural oppression shifts from its original position of repressive dominance towards a position that adopts persuasive, consensual forms, integrating the exploited and dominated masses into a system that legitimates the submission of the Antillian state to France. The transition to capitalism as a dominant system of social production marks the leap of a society without hegemony to a society where class domination is built on hegemony, in this case the values and norms of republican assimilationism. It is also the case that colonial capitalism and assimilationism mutually reinforce one another as they develop.

The recent evolution of the Antillian formations—of which I shall simply outline the main features—proceeds naturally from the accentuation of earlier tendencies, namely the extension of capitalist relations of domination and the reinforcement of assimilationist mechanisms as a particular colonial mode of bourgeois hegemony. But the essential point, in my opinion, lies in the ruptures both at the objective and subjective levels, which disturb the typical socio-economic and ideological-cultural balances of the previous period. From 1946 to the present day, one outstanding development strikes the observer: Martinique and Guadeloupe's entry into a latent and creeping crisis. This crisis derives both from a change to established forms of capital accumulation and from a growing questioning of the assimilationist path.

The crisis of capital accumulation

It should be emphasized that I am concerned first with the question of a structural crisis in the whole system of accumulation derived both from external and internal conditions of reproduction and from the valorization of capital.

Historically, one of the institutional conditions that permitted the super-exploitation by capital in the colonial process of circulation and production was the recourse (since the 1920s) by the French state to an imperialist regulation of the economy which both protected and shared out the markets. Now, the internationalization of capital and France's membership of the European Economic Community entail a redefinition of Guadeloupe and Martinique's mode of articulation into the global system of production. The wider processes of the internationalization of capital as a hierarchical and contradictory world system have been usefully described in three sources (Palloix 1975; Leucate 1975; Foulon 1975). In contrast to the earlier period, the state's regulatory policies aim to propel the Antillian economy into the game of international competition in return for structural adaptations. The export markets of the Antilles, which were sheltered in the past, are today gradually being opened in one form or another to the goods of competitor countries: be they members of the EEC or third countries. While within the EEC a free trade zone operates (Rye 1970), elsewhere, through the Yaounde, Lomé I and Lomé II Conventions, preferential agreements are reached between the EEC and the ACP, a group of countries composed mainly of the former colonies and neo-colonies of the European metropole largely in Africa, the Caribbean and the Pacific (Meynaud and Prejean 1962; Tennessee 1964; Florent 1966; Andic 1969; Chambre de Commerce et d'Industrie de la Martinique 1975, 1976, n.d.; PUG 1979). Evidence of the growing lack of structural competitiveness can be seen in the ever diminishing share of the main Martinican and Guadeloupan exports (sugar, rum, pineapples, bananas) in supplying French and European markets, a tendency amply attested to in numerous official governmental publications. These are the manifest signs of a crisis of the realization of capital.

At the same time, departmentalization, by its very social dynamic, aggravates the functional distortions of an economy that remains structurally open. Not that departmentalization produces an automatic resemblance to metropolitan social practices. Rather, it is more accurate to say that it is due to the demands of the trade unions and the actions of the Antillian labouring masses that successive governments have been compelled to introduce management practices characteristic of advanced capitalist countries. These include the adoption of a minimum legal wage; the indexation of the wage, at least nominally, to changes in the cost of living; the effective reduction in the length of the working week for the majority of wage earners; the introduction of popular education which favours the mobility of the labour force and correspondingly reduces the oligarchy's control over it; a partial (and still discriminatory) extension of legislation concerning pension rights, family allowances, and so on. The difficulties in extending French social welfare policy to the Antilles are described by various authors (Ouasenga 1971; Service des Affaires Administratives 1976; Clouet 1980; Lerychard and Taylor 1980). Although clearly providing a lower social wage than in France (which, because of the process of assimilation is the point of comparison) the current system of welfare benefits has to be funded by contributions by the employers, contributions sufficiently high to increase substantially the cost of hiring workers by the capitalists. Thus the mechanism of over-exploitation finds itself institutionally blocked, as is the extraction of absolute surplus value, which depended previously on the constant impoverishment of whole sections of the Antillian proletariat and semi-proletariat. The ability of employers to extract absolute surplus value is increasingly made more difficult as the trajectory of trade-union struggles is to bring Antillian welfare standards up to the level of the metropole. This leads to a decrease in the rate of exploitation and the level of profit in the branches of production that hitherto provided the engines of capital accumulation in the Antilles. The crisis which derives from the increased returns to labour finds its particular expression in the decline of traditional export activities. In this sense, as a result of the changes in the conditions of extracting surplus value, there is a crisis in the valorization of capital.

If one adds to the picture the considerable technological backwardness which built up during centuries of mercantile then industrial protectionism, it is easy to understand how Guadeloupe and Martinique find themselves incapable of meeting the stiff competition provided by countries where wage rates are incomparably lower and levels of productivity considerably higher. The structural crisis is of such a scale that the state searches in vain to juggle and restructure its financial and accompanying social policies. Contrary to Poncet's application of the notion of state monopoly capital to the Antilles, I would therefore argue that the state administers the crisis, but does not in itself create it (Poncet 1974). The means that the state assigns to itself to manage the crisis is the institution of a system of intensive capital accumulation resting, among other things, on the extraction of relative surplus value.

The process of restructuring is both a product of, and a solution to, the crisis. The state is involved in encouraging the restructuring and re-orienting of the economy through a system of subsidies, grants and tax reliefs. The effectiveness of the various financial incentives to support the accumulation process is assessed in two official reports (Julienne 1978; Comité Economique et Sociale, Martinique 1980). In this respect, it is worth noting that public funds are used to help finance the cost to private capital of shutting down those enterprises that are thought to be uncompetitive internationally. It comes as something of a revelation to learn that the different 'plans for stimulation' or 'modernization', not to mention 'land reform', are, in practice, a process of increasing concentration, accompanied by a sudden drop in the level of exports in most of the productive sectors (Lerychard and Taylor 1980: 222; Crusol 1980). The international crisis beginning in 1974, together with the consequent budgetary constraints, has forced the state into a greater selectivity in its support for industrial investment (Le Pors 1977; Cartelier 1977: 147). The object is no longer to rescue 'lame ducks' (essentially members of the oligarchy) on the pretext of saving employees, but to press for the expansion of those sectors and commercial enterprises that meet the criteria of international competitiveness. In the future the state clearly will have to broaden and deepen the process of restructuring in the Antilles.

The new specialisms adopted in the Antilles (tourism, out-of-season market gardening destined for the European market, international subcontracting, and so on) serve only to repeat the mistake of adopting a process of industrialization that reproduces present conditions and worsens the effects of the economy's external dependence. Thus Martin shows that, despite this reorientation, there is a net increase in the Antilles' dependence on external sources of food (Martin 1975). It is also important to grasp that the restructuring brought about by the contradictory development of capitalism has effects on the class structure and class relations. On the one hand, the extension of relations of capitalist domination imply the gradual absorption and elimination of small-scale independent market production (peasants, sea-fishermen, artisans, small businessmen, and so on). The restructuring equally signals the development of new proletarian and wage-earning strata: employees in the big mercantile firms, in various banks and administrative services. Thus, the development of a strong tertiary sector results as much from the directed investment by capital into spheres of activity linked principally to the sphere of circulation and to the sale of goods (essentially imported), as from the collapse of the sectors involved in direct production. Despite its location in the service sector, the overwhelming numerical strength of the Antillian proletariat is a major force in the urban areas.

On the other hand, at the opposite end of the spectrum, the modification of the structure of capital stemming from the operation of disinvestment in the traditional sectors and of reinvestment in more lucrative activities (hotels, big business, credit institutions, and so on) leads to the break-up of the traditional oligarchy and the recomposition of the bloc of dominant classes. Such a description of class relations ignores, however, the importance of departmentalization itself, which undeniably permits the development of a coloured bourgeoisie. This class is able to take advantage of those spaces that are not monopolized by the white creole minority and the French firms. This development apart, it seems far more important that two contradictory projects for capital actually confront each other in Guadeloupe and Martinique. Within the context of the structural crisis, a 'confused' strategy that favours the establishment of import-substituting industries has emerged. This policy of semi-industrialization runs headlong into the obstacles provided by the dominant position of monopoly transport companies (CGTM, CGM, Air France). Above all, such a strategy must confront the interests of the comprador bourgeoisie who respond by systematically resorting to massive imports and dumping, in order to nip in the bud any chance of an autonomous section of capital developing its own capacity to accumulate, and therefore to escape its control. Paul Dijoud, who, while Secretary of State for the Overseas Departments, confided in an interview with *Le Monde* his intention to 'get rid of abusive practices', was only able to illustrate his remark through reference to the importers:

The whole import sector is one of my main concerns because attempts to create local industries in the past have always succumbed to the full force of the importing circles who immediately put competitive products onto the market at dumping prices, thereby ruining all the initiatives that are being undertaken. Because of this, there is a real need for a policy that resolutely protects local initiatives (Dijoud 1979).

In recent years, 'the modernizing option' appears to have received the support of the 'Giscardiens' in the government who have favoured it in a number of ways. For example, they have:

(a) attacked the subsidies given to import–export houses;
(b) sought to liberalize the control over sea and air links in order to reduce the cost of imports;
(c) attempted to cut the wage bill, initially by trying to eliminate the 40 per cent wage subsidy given to civil servants. This large subsidy derived from the old 'colonial supplement' which, under pressure from increasing union demands in the early 1950s (a five-day strike in January 1948, thirty-three days in March–April 1950 and finally two months from 15 May to 15 July 1953), was extended, without restriction, to cover local Guadeloupan and Martinican bureaucrats. The announcement of its withdrawal in the name of social justice, but in reality to reduce salary bills and therefore to favour investment (one of the several proposals made by the group of experts around Mr Julienne), raised enough mobilization during the last three months of 1979 to force the authorities to postpone their plan with the promise of a review (*Information Caraïbe* 1979; Rollat 1979);
(d) refashioned the way in which public funds are allocated in order to gear them to productive investment (Jeunes Chambres Economiques 1974; Julienne 1978);
(e) provided encouragement for the creation of a wider Antilles–Guyana region with a view to promoting integration and the widening of local markets;
(f) accepted the Regional Councils' use of the *octroi de mer* (a tax collected on imports which is used to finance council budgets) as a tariff for protecting local products assigned to replace imports. The Jeunes Chambres Economiques of the Antilles argued in favour of retaining the *octroi de mer* on the grounds that: 'This neo-protectionism would guarantee products to the local market that, because of economic difficulties associated with the development process, are less competitive in their launching phase' (Jeunes Chambres Economiques 1974; Conférence Interrégionale 1979).

Irrespective of the strategies just described (a drastic cut in wage payments and a policy of import substitution sustained by massive transfers of technology), I would maintain that the bourgeoisie as a whole (in all its fractions) can only maintain its dominance in the Antilles if it can rely on reinforcement from the French state. Such an increase in dependence on the state is not exempt from contradictions. If the industrial wing of the Antillian bourgeoisie wishes to control customs' policy beyond simple manipulation of the *octroi de mer* tariffs, then a step must be taken at least towards decentralization, if not autonomy. On the other hand, attempts by the labouring masses to raise their living standards call for the consolidation of the repressive and persuasive apparatuses (a lesson learnt from the colonial French state) so that popular pressure can be contained within the boundaries of the system of social and political reproduction.

On its own, the state seems incapable of providing the rival fractions of the bourgeoisie with a sense of direction in the restructuring process to which it is committed. Rival sources of 'parallel power' proliferate—junior economic chambers, chambers of commerce and industry, clubs of various kinds, public and private development bodies, etc.—from which the different clans of the dominant class formulate the plans, and sometimes the alternatives, of what will take place. These bodies, which have been very active of late, are the instigators of numerous initiatives: the employers' 'White Book', the campaigns for 'Local Consumption', the reduction of freight, and so on. All these plans surface in colloquia mounted by the various fractions.

Through the technological changes they induce, rational policies aimed primarily at increasing the productivity of labour and the profitability of investment can only serve to stimulate the development of a level of structural unemployment of a degree and likely permanence that cannot fail but cause concern. Indeed, a survey carried out in 1970 established that in Guadeloupe only one active person in three escapes total or partial unemployment (Mendes-France 1971: 5). In Martinique, the results of surveys taken in 1971 and 1972 show that around 60 per cent of the active population is affected by unemployment and under-employment (INSEE 1972). Confronted by what nowadays constitutes the No. 1 social problem of Guadeloupe and Martinique, the state has, since the beginning of the 1960s, been driven into encouraging the international mobility of the West Indian labour force. Emigration to France 'in a continuous stream' constitutes practically the only means of bringing down unemployment (Anselin 1979). The disturbing expansion of the migratory flood has not yet managed to bring down the rate of unemployment. Similarly, it has shown iself incapable of preventing the 'marginalization' of rising numbers of the West Indian population. I follow Quijano in taking marginalization to mean long-lasting if not permanent exclusion from the sphere of proletarian wage labour, i.e. from people who have nothing other to live on but their labour power (Quijano 1971). The state's system of regulating the labour market, which in the Antilles is presented under the ideological label of an 'employment policy', has therefore entered into a state of crisis. This is so grave that those responsible for government have finally ended up by publicly recognizing that for a long time now there have been no prospects for young West Indians other than emigration to France. The issues at stake are being increasingly recognized by anti-colonial trade union and political organizations, which are beginning to mobilize around the slogan 'live and work in the country'.

In the medium term, a vigorous revival of capital accumulation will merely sharpen social tensions. All the more so since the state's redistribution policy favours concentrating income in the hands of officials in the overseas departments who, as we have mentioned, benefit from a 40 per cent salary rise, christened the *prime de vie chère*. Thus, around 1970, the salaries of these officials, who formed about 15 per cent of the working population of overseas departments, were equivalent to 50 per cent of those of all wage earners and more than 25 per cent of total domestic resources (Mendes-France 1971: 1). This tendency was to continue, for in 1976, in Martinique, civil servants representing close to 25 per cent of the working population collected 55 per cent of the total wage packet (INSEE 1976: 10). The result has been a kind of 'third claim' apart from those asserted by marginalized labour and the bourgeoisie. This claim has made a powerful contribution towards accelerating the rhythm at which durable consumer goods are imported. As was previously noted, in contrast to the earlier period, the great majority of working people have actually reached a level whereby, apart from ostentatious gadgets, they are emulating bourgeois and petit bourgeois consumption habits. This is true at least in the elementary durable consumer goods which have become commonplace, largely because of the standardization of norms brought about by the intensive mode of capital accumulation. As a result, the process of social reproduction is based more and more on the integration of market relationships, a phenomenological expression of the growing hold in the Antilles of the fetishism of money. The French state plays on this aspect. It constantly evokes 'the standard of living' in order both to legitimate its policy and its presence in the Antilles. Nevertheless, the huge disparities of income are becoming more and more difficult to mask, or to present as the 'after-effects of a bygone colonialism'. Far from being alleviated, those disparities are being reproduced. An estimate of income distribution was produced by R. Jouhandet-Bernadat (1964). Again, in the more recent Julienne Report (1978), it is shown that although the income per capita of the overseas departments is considerably less than in France, the income differentials are incomparably higher in these countries. The General Inspectorate of Finances, on the strength of income tax returns which are likely to undervalue inequalities, observed that the proportion of taxpayers declaring more than 400,000 francs per year of the total of people taxed, is three to seven times higher than in an average of fourteen French departments.

Policies of regulation and the growing mediation of the state in processes of accumulation and reproduction have resulted in an increase in public spending which contrasts with the productive sector's limited role in redistributing income. In that they take over the role traditionally played by exports, public transfers are seen by some analysts as providing the future motor for the economic growth of Guadeloupe and Martinique (Albertini 1965; Yang-Ting 1968; Mendes-France 1971; Crusol 1977). One thing is certain, the rise in public expenditure attests to a partial disconnection between the distributive function and the process of accumulation, a mode of regulation increasingly characteristic of contemporary capitalism (Lorenzi et al. 1980). This characteristic fits in with a growing tendency for the state to take charge of a not insignificant fraction of the cost of the upkeep and reproduction of the labour force. In Guadeloupe the posts reserved for 'educational and cultural action' and 'social action' represented 57 per cent and 23 per cent of the state's budgetary expenses in 1975, compared to 27 per cent and 10 per cent in 1950. In Martinique, from 1950 to 1975, the proportion of the state budget allocated to 'educational and cultural action' rose from 43 per cent to 50 per cent and for 'social action' from 11 per cent to 24 per cent (Lerychard and Taylor 1980: 47, 47a). These figures explain why, in the context of disarticulated economies, the development of public transfers offset the effects of a commercial deficit. The positive correlation between the growth of public transfers and the level of commercial deficit has been pertinently underlined by Mendes-France (1971). Thus, as the crisis deepens and unemployment is accentuated, incomes deriving from the redistributive action of the state take an increasing share from general social welfare as less and less return derives from the indirect benefits of work. It goes without saying that the French state's willingness to manage social expenditure is related to its need for legitimation. The articulation between capital accumulation and social expenditure often produces conflict (O'Connor 1973; Negri 1977: 375–423). In this respect, social assistance and political clientelism agree, as it were, to balance their electoral appeal so that within the system of popular representation, the double image of the state as manager (the Guardian of Competence) and provider (the Guardian of Generosity), can be upheld. The budgetary restrictions imposed on governments by the international crisis do, however, impose limits on the degree to which the state can get out of the structural crisis of the wider system of accumulation by simply increasing public expenditure. It is more important to change the logic of the development scheme. Will major and imperative transformations in Antillian societies be helped by the election of the Mitterand government in France? Time will tell.

The crisis of assimilationist hegemony

The second form of crisis that I am concerned with is the undermining of the assimilationist ideological-cultural system of oppression.

The massive schooling programme, about which the French state authorities in the Antilles are so fond of congratulating themselves, is clearly showing its limitations. During the 1950s and 1960s a relatively high level of social mobility maintained the illusion that the educational system was being democratized. The increase in social mobility was predicated on the recomposition of the classes, but was essentially confined to the development of large petit bourgeois strata linked to the functions of both the state apparatus and private bureaucracies. Now it is longer possible to maintain the illusion: rather, through its actual expansion, the academic and para-academic institution reproduces the social inequalities inherent in capitalist class relations. Certain branches of the educational apparatus, such as the technical training colleges, are accused of 'working for export', thereby implying that the educational system in Guadeloupe and Martinique is operated as a form of state management of the labour force of an imperialist kind. A special form of selectivity results from the fact that in the Antilles the school remains the privileged place of a process of acculturation that tends to cut young people off from their geo-historical conditioning (Devoue 1977). Today, the function of assimilationist acculturation is denounced with virulence by a growing number of teachers, pupils, parents and students, not to speak of the action of anti-colonial organizations (SNI–PEGC Colloquium 1980). Consequently, one understands why table 7.1 shows that the 'waste', the 'failures' or, if one prefers it, the school 'dropouts' in the Antilles reach proportions unheard of in France.

TABLE 7.1 France and Martinique: educational background of young population seeking employment (%)

	France	Martinique
Without qualifications	27.2	63.7
Having reached first stage towards CAP, BEPC, BAC	41.6	24.3
Second stage begun, but not achieved	7.8	3.3
Higher studies begun, but not achieved	7.8	2.7
Standard degree	7.8	1.0

Source: Lerychard and Taylor 1980: 87.

The schooling crisis also comes from a lack of motivation on the part of young people for whom, under generally depressed conditions, any prospect of socio-cultural expression is strictly limited.

Certainly, since 1946, the efficiency of the process of assimilationism for oppression has been considerably increased by the introduction of ultra-modern means of communication into semi-literate societies. According to an inquiry carried out in 1976, 96 per cent of the population of Martinique owned a radio and 69 per cent a television set, the researchers even estimating that the poor and illiterate strata could have been under-represented (ICAR 1977a). Certainly it is the case that audio-visual media exercise a primary role in conditioning public opinion in Guadeloupe and Martinique. The newspaper *France-Antilles*, which belongs to the HERSANT group and whose reputation for idiocy and manipulation seems totally justified, remains the only daily in Guadeloupe and Martinique. As for local radio and television networks, literally appropriated by established power cliques which are as partisan as they are sycophantic, these have systematically banned authentic West Indian cultural forms and held up to ridicule the right to political expression of the various anti-colonial currents (Humblot 1976). Despite these forms of media control, assimilationist norms no longer carry the consensual support of the Antillian people.

In fact, the maturing of the socio-economic crisis and the international political conjuncture where the dominant theme was helping national liberation struggles had enabled the Antillian anti-colonial movement to reach a national turning point at the end of the 1950s. Starting by questioning departmentalization, decried as the institutional mask behind which the perpetuation of colonialism was concealed, this movement has taken a political stance that breaks the prejudiced consensus establishing that the Antilles forever belong to France. The first notes of dissent were sounded, among others by A. Cesaire (Cesaire 1961; *Esprit* 1962). This revision of the assimilationist programme has, for a start, unleashed the claim for popular autonomy, i.e. for a transfer of skills which, within the unitarian framework of the French Republic, enables the people of Guadeloupe and Martinique to affirm their political personality. The signs of change take various forms. The Guadeloupan and Martinican sections of the Parti Communiste Français (PCF) have, for example, changed themselves into the PCG and PCM and adopted the slogan of autonomy (Girard 1979: 156–159; Faruggia 1979; de Lepine 1979). Another characteristic of the new period is that the Antillian workers' movement, which tends to develop itself on a national basis, has broken loose, little by little, from its organizational moorings with French union and political forces. The Parti Progressiste de la Martinique of Aimé Cesaire, which was launched in March 1958, at first fought for a 'Martinican region in a French federal structure'. Later at its Third Congress in 1967, the PPM opted for the autonomist demand (William 1979). In August 1972, the Convention of Morne-Rouge (Martinique) was held, which established a common platform for an assembly of autonomist forces from the four overseas departments and from the *émigré* community in France. This convention was reactivated by a meeting in Sainte-Anne (Guadeloupe) in September 1977. The objective of the convention's programme remains the transformation of the overseas departments into autonomous territorial communities within the framework of the French Republic, just as is theoretically authorized in article 72 of the constitution of 1958. This stipulates: 'The territorial communities of the Republic are communes, departments and overseas territories. Any other territorial community is created by law' (Anon 1979: 440).

Then, at the end of the 1960s, pro-independence currents developed: Marxist, nationalist and populist. Unfortunately no comprehensive study of the extreme left in the Antilles exists and we can ignore the numerous documents which are either too narrow or polemical. As to the short essay by R. D. E. Burton (1978), besides being inevitably superficial, it appears to us to proceed, as its title indicates, from a poor appreciation of actual political relationships at stake between the different components of the anti-colonial camp. The principal confrontation is, for the moment, situated between supporters of assimilation and supporters of autonomy. The pro-independence group, although not negligible, does not yet constitute a major focus for Antillian political life.

Whatever its exact composition, an anti-colonial movement is being organized in Guadeloupe and Martinique with a national focus that rejects the assimilationist perspective and whose apparent social base— the exploited and oppressed masses—demands a position that, to a greater or lesser degree, is opposed to the capitalist system. Clearly, as the guarantor of capitalist interests and of the French presence in the Caribbean, it is the colonial state that in varying degrees challenges the new anti-colonialist dynamic, for fear that it will be articulated into aspirations of popular emancipation. Neither selective nor intensive repression have been enough to check this dynamic. The arbitrary use of colonial power can be shown in two examples. An ordinance of October 1960 attributing to the prefects of the overseas departments the power to transfer officials who are troublesome or likely to disturb 'public order', which was used against anti-colonialist militants, was repealed only a few years ago. Second, the popular riots in December 1959 in Martinique and in May 1967 in Guadeloupe were violently crushed in the name of state security.

In our view, however, France's power in the Antilles rests less in its arsenal of repression and in its capacity to intimidate the popular masses, impressive as these may be, than in the possibility of continuing to take advantage of the electoral successes of the assimilationist camp. For in Guadeloupe and Martinique, each electoral consultation is systematically transformed by the supporters of the departmental *status quo* into a plebiscite supporting the continuing attachment to France. But what gives force to the French presence in the Antilles today, i.e. its legitimation by popular suffrage, risks becoming the Achilles' heel of tomorrow. By hysterically dramatizing the dangers of the separatist adventure, the assimilationist right wing sentences itself to winning all the elections. And this all the more so since France, by subscribing to the San Francisco Charter, incurs the risk of openly appearing as a colonial power, maintaining its domination in the Antilles against the wishes of the local populations. The San Francisco Charter, we can recall, was signed on 26 June 1945 to create the International Organization of the United Nations. It calls upon colonial powers to progressively devolve greater autonomy to the territories which they administer.

Given the unanimous condemnation of colonialism by world public opinion, the contemporary system of international relations forces the French state into constantly trying to broaden the process of her legitimation, ceaselessly reactivating the mechanisms of ideological oppression which extract political consent from the Antillian majority. This requirement of political reality is one of which P. Dijoud is well aware. In his interview with *Le Monde* he stated: 'The populations of the overseas departments are freely French. They come to decisions through free consultations, the democratic character of which has never been contested [*sic*!]' (Dijoud 1979).

On the cultural level, the French state's margin of manoeuvrability is reduced in the face of the developing crisis and the rise of a separate 'sense of identity'. By sense of identity is meant the awareness that Guadeloupe and Martinique belong to a culturally specific area: the Caribbean. This, in our opinion, is the domain in which transformation has been most rapid and most spectacular. Certainly, for over a decade, political action has been provided by mass cultural action in the process of the anti-assimilationist struggle. And it is because of this that one is able to maintain that counter-acculturation practices have passed from a spontaneous and informal to a conscious and organized phase. This raising of the question of assimilationism to the level of a 'politics of culture' is observable in all spheres and at all moments of Antillian everyday life.

Certainly the Municipal Offices of Culture in Point-à-Pitre and Basse-Terre and the Municipal Service for Cultural Action in Fort-de-France— structures created by anti-colonial town councils—occupy an important place in the devices used to resist assimilationist oppression (Humblot 1981). But apart from these centralized structures, the business of awakening feelings of identity through cultural means derives from numerous other channels and manifests itself in activities as diverse as music, dance, cinema, written literature, and so on. The appearance of popular news magazines (like *Le Naïf* and *Sport Plus* in Martinique and *Jougwa* in Guadeloupe), of theoretical journals (like *CARE*, *Mofwaz* and *Espace créole*) are just some examples of a much wider literature produced by anti-colonial political parties and pressure groups. Such publications sustain reflection and debate on subjects as hotly topical as the role of sport or of a creole language in the Antillian societies of today and tomorrow. For example, *Espace créole* defined its vocation in its first issue as follows: 'If one admits that language constitutes the womb of all discourse (ideological, scientific, pedagogic, political, strategic, etc.), it would be advisable to put an end to the monopoly French enjoys in the operational field that defines the search for the authenticity of the Creolophone people' (GEREC 1976).

The cultural sphere undoubtedly constitutes the place where reaction to the assimilationist imposition is revealed in the most vital way. The circle of those rejecting Western assimilationist values grows larger and larger and has spread to the masses. It is no longer confined to the circle of Antillian intellectuals who in the 1920s and 1930s preached Negritude and Authenticity. In relation to the growing marginalization of large fringes of youth, populism—a primitive and disguised form of national sentiment—develops as a predominant expression in the questioning of the assimilationist cultural order. The cultural sphere is most certainly the terrain where the crisis in the relations of oppression is most marked. Even the most seasoned assimilationists are, at this point, in fear of defeat on the cultural battleground. Thus V. Sable, the firmly ensconsed right-wing departmentalist member for the south of Martinique, told *Paris-Match*: 'If one is not careful, those who are pressing for autonomy and independence may trample on the political plan through winning the cultural battle in Martinique.' On the other side of the political fence, *Justice*, the organ of the PCM, maintained that 'The present crisis does not derive from a conflict of races but from a disturbed collective psychology, from a really agonizing struggle of the Martinican soul' (*Justice* 1980). In order to circumvent the rapidly maturing feelings of separate identity, the government has attempted to initiate a policy of 'controlled' assimilation. This is less all-embracing in that it permits the expression of a specifically local character, but nonetheless within the framework of French culture. In the Inter-France 'One o'clock Journal' on 26 October 1979, Paul Dijoud, the then Secretary of State of the Overseas Departments and Territories acknowledged that it was erroneous to have wanted to have introduced all the characteristics of French society into the Antilles. He spoke of giving their identity back to them. More concretely, Dijoud spoke of his desire to 'restore' the inter-regional specificity of the Antilles and Guyana along the lines of a 'Creole French Cultural Plan'. That the 'plan' was clearly motivated by a desire to recover lost ground was explained by Dijoud himself: 'The Government considers that for too long it has left the monopoly of thinking about the cultural problem to its most staunch enemies. We are therefore resolutely engaged in thought, which must lead to action and which in turn enables us to respond quickly to the aspirations of young people from the overseas departments' (Reneville 1979). The object is to set at loggerheads those feelings that fall short of national consciousness with those that constitute a total political project intended to emancipate totally Martinican and Guadeloupan societies.

It is important to grasp that, although still embryonic in its formation, national consciousness is sufficiently strong to disrupt the working of institutions that see Guadeloupans and Martinicans as individual citizens of the French Republic. These institutions function to prevent people having to restore historically specific tasks, particularly with respect to issues of development. In this respect it is instructive to note that the shrewdest departmentalists have, during their period of office, asked for a large measure of administrative decentralization (Valere 1968). In fact, it is precisely the opposite route that has been followed, though under the pretext of achieving the process of decentralization. The result has been the intensification of institutional centralization under the aegis of the French state in the person of important Parisian officials (Birnbaum 1977). Thus the wishes of the general councils, even on the rare occasions when they conform to popular demands, are never taken into consideration. This is demonstrated by the growing feelings of impotence expressed by the local assemblies—the general, regional, economic and social councils. The municipal councils, for their part, became more and more the instruments for the management of social welfare, a task under the control of the government and its local representatives—the prefects, sub-prefects, etc. Equally, the senators and deputies who are meant to act as national representatives are faced with the overriding power of the ministers in Paris. In support of this trend, the ultra departmentalists even envisaged the abolition of the post of Secretary of State for the Overseas Departments in order to enhance the role of the technical Minister and the Minister of the Interior. ICAR considers that the services of the Ministry of Overseas Departments and Territories will be progressively taken over by the Ministry of the Interior. Thus, a General Director of the Overseas Departments and Territories has been created in the Ministry of the Interior (ICAR 1977b, 1977c).

At a purely ideological level, the myth of Gaullism has for more than a decade been able to relay its insistent call directed to Antillian popular sensibilities by exalting in the virtues of a nourishing and generous France. Since being restored to its expressly technocratic course, however, the process of legitimation has had to rely on what might usefully be termed 'food blackmail'. The pro-French lobby, whom de Baleine (1980) accurately described as 'dancers of France', are cynically told that separatism is divorce without alimony. Adherence to France is, on the other hand, represented in official speeches, as the condition *sine qua non* both of economic, social and cultural progress and of rapid strides in the direction of political democracy. The main ideological line of official political discourse during the previous French regime was summarized by V. Giscard d'Estaing himself on his last visit to Guadeloupe and Martinique: 'Economic and social departmentalization is indeed the way to progress' (Giscard d'Estaing 1980).

The presentation of departmentalization as economic and social emancipation flies in the face of the hard reality is best summed up in the phrase 'the development of underdevelopment' in Guadeloupe and Martinique. The crisis of the system of accumulation opens out the national question in that there is a causal relationship between the economic and social situation on the one hand and the status of the islands on the other. As the Editorial of *L'Etincelle*, the PCG weekly, noted (4 April 1981): 'The great mass of Guadeloupans must be made to realize that no stable development base will be assured before the Guadeloupan people are freely and clearly brought into determining their own political status.' To this end the Guadeloupan communists 'will demonstrate the justice and topicality of the demand for democratic and popular autonomy, a step on the road towards a socialist independence'. In the same light, the contrast between the increasing regulation of unemployment by emigration and the growing arrival of metropolitan officials has engendered the formulation of a thesis of 'genocide by substitution'. This thesis was summarized by A. Tiquant (a member of the PPM Political Bureau and Secretary of Foreign Affairs) as follows:

Another very important aspect is what we call GENOCIDE BY SUBSTITUTION. Since no impetus is given to a truly local economy, more than 50 per cent of the active population is unemployed. The metropolis encourages emigration to Europe and this means that our young population is diminishing. Each year 5,000 Martinicans leave for Europe. At the same time, the French and other Europeans come and settle on the island. In two senses, emigration gives rise to population substitution. More and more Europeans and fewer and fewer Martinicans. Those amongst us who are fighting for national liberation have engaged in a war against time. The more years that pass, the fewer young people and workers will remain in our island, and it is they who harbour the germs of the possibilities of liberation (*Progressiste* 1981).

This substitution process also has met with some favour in some sections of the Antillian population.

The programme of the Mitterand regime envisages organizing real decentralization through regionalization. This should permit, for example, a practical possibility of planning development, the responsibility for and control of which will rest with the local authorities (Defferre *et al.* 1979; Defferre 1981). Will it prevent the crisis deriving from the colonial relationship itself? Here I have presented the socio-economic, ideological-cultural and institutional dimensions of that relationship, all of which are bound up in the crisis of legitimacy of the French state in the Antilles. It is in that area that the crisis of the coming period is located.

REFERENCES

Albertini, J.-M. 1965, 'La fausse croissance', *Economie et humanisme*, no. 163

Andic, F. M. 1969, 'La Caraïbe face à la Communauté Economique Européenne: le cas des Antilles néerlandaises, de Surinam, des Antilles françaises et de la Guyane française', *Les cahiers du CERAG*, no. 15, 1st quarter

Anon 1979, *Les constitutions de la France depuis 1789*, Paris, Garnier-Flammarion

Anselin, A. 1979, *L'émigration antillaise en France: du bantoustan au ghetto*, Paris, Anthropos

Birnbaum, P. 1977, *Les sommets de l'état: essai sur l'élite du pouvoir en France*, Paris, Seuil 'Politique'

Burton, R. D. E. 1978, 'Assimilation or independence? Prospects for Martinique', *Centre for developing area studies*, Occasional Monograph Series no. 13, Montreal, McGill University

Bye, M. 1970, *Problèmes économiques européens*, Paris, Cujas

Cartelier, L. 1977, 'Planification-politique industrielle et état capitaliste', in *ACSES Sur l'état*, Brussels, Contradictions

Cesaire, A. 1961, 'Crise dans les DOM ou crise de la départementalisation', *Présence Africaine*, no. 36

Chambre de Commerce et d'Industrie de la Martinique 1975, 'L'Europe et nous', *Promotion*, no. 1, June, pp. 7–18

Chambre de Commerce et d'Industrie de la Martinique 1976, 'Lomé et nous', *Promotion*, no. 8, August, pp. 7–22

Chambre de Commerce et d'Industrie de la Martinique n.d., 'Martinique: région d'Europe ou ACP', *Promotion*, pp. 7–21

Clouet, J. E. 1980, 'Action sociale et développement dans les départements d'outre-mer', *Les cahiers du CERAG*, no. 38, October

Comité Economique et Sociale, Martinique, 1980, *Guide des aides au développement économique mises en place par la région Martinique*, Fort-de-France, May

Conférence Interrégionale 1979, *Orientations pour le développement économique des Antilles et de la Guyane: vingt points d'appui*, Guadeloupe, Jarry S. A.

Crusol, J. 1977, 'Les déséquilibres de la croissance excentrée en économie de plantation insulaire: le cas des Antilles françaises', *Revue d'economie politique*, no. 1, January–February, pp. 1–32

Crusol, J. 1980, *Economies insulaires de la Caraïbe*, Paris, Ed. Caribéennes

de Baleine, P. 1980, *Les danseuses de la France*, Paris, Plon

Defferre, G. et al. 1979, *Proposition de loi pour les départements d'outre-mer*, J. O. document no. 1232, 28 June

Defferre, G. 1981, *Projet de loi relatif aux droits et libertés des communes, des départements et des régions*, 16 July, mimeo

de Lepine, E. 1979, 'Le parti communiste et le mouvement ouvrier à la Martinique de 1945 à nos jours', *Historial antillais*, vol. 6, pp. 181–295

Devoue, E. 1977, *Education et développement aux Antilles françaises*, Ph.D., Bordeaux I, Etat Sciences Economiques

Dijoud, P. 1979, *Le Monde*, 18 September, p. 10

Esprit 1962, 'Les Antilles avant qu'il ne soit trop tard', special number

Faruggia, L. 1979, 'Luttes politiques et ouvrières en Guadeloupe de 1946 à 1978', *Historial antillais*, vol. 6, pp. 136–180

Florent, H. 1966, 'Marché comun et colonialisme', *Action*, no. 11–12, 3rd and 4th quarter

Foulon, A. 1975, 'Firmes multinationales et internationalisation du capital', *Critiques de l'economie politiques*, no. 19, January–March

GEREC 1976, 'En guise de presentation', *Espace créole*

Girard, R. 1979, *Pour un sursaut guadeloupéen*, Paris, L'Harmattan

Giscard d'Estaing, V. 1980, *France-Antilles*, 31 December

Humblot, C. 1976, 'La télévision dans les DOM: Guadeloupe stranglé', *Le Monde*, 18 January, pp. 1, 11

Humblot, C. 1981, 'Le Cmac et le Sermac complémentaires ou en guerre?', *Le Monde*, 20 August, p. 9

ICAR 1977a, no. 160, 14 March

ICAR 1977b, no. 161, 20 March

ICAR 1977c, no. 170, 22 May

Information Caraïbe 1979, Pointe-à-Pitre, ICAR

INSEE 1972, *L'emploi en Martinique: résultats des enquêtes de 1971 et 1972*, Martinique

INSEE 1976, *Les agents des services publiques: recensement de mai 1976*, Service Interrégional Antilles-Guyane, Martinique, INSEE, Etudes et Documents no. 3

Jeunes Chambres Economiques de la Martinique et de la Guadeloupe 1974, *Idées-forces pour promouvoir le développement des Antilles-Guyane*, Ed. Caraïbes

Jouhandet-Bernadat, R. 1964, 'Notes sur les revenus en Martinique', *Caribbean studies*, vol. 4, no. 3, October, pp. 14–32

Julienne, M. 1978, *Rapport du groupe d'étude interministériel sur le régime des aides en viguéur dans les Departements d'Outre-Mer*, March

Justice 10 January 1980

Le Pors, A. 1977, *Les 'béquilles' du capital: transferts état-industrie*, Paris, Seuil

Lerychard, F. and Taylor, R. 1980, *Contribution à l'étude des dépenses publiques aux Antilles françaises*, Paris X-Nanterre, Sciences Economiques, Ph.D.

Leucate, C. 1975, 'Internationalisation du capital et impérialism', *Critiques de l'economie politiques*, no. 19, January–March

Lorenzi, J. H. et al. 1980, *La crise du XX° siècle*, Paris, Economica

Martin, J. C. 1975, 'Commerce extérieur et production agricole et alimentaire dans les départements d'outre-mer', *Cahiers des statistiques agricoles*, no. 22, May–June, pp. 1–24

Mendes-France, B. 1971, *Note sur la situation économique des DOM au terme du 5° plan et sur le rôle des dépenses publiques*, roneo., INSEE, December

Meynaud, J. P. and Prejean, A. 1962, 'Marché commun et néo-colonialisme', *Economie et politique*, no. 100, November–December

Negri, A. 1977, 'Sur quelques tendances de la théorie communiste de l'état la plus récente: revue critique', in ACSES, *Sur l'état*, Brussels, Contradictions

O'Connor, J. 1973, *The fiscal crisis of the state*, London, St Martin Press

Ouasenga, L. 1971, *Sécurité sociale et aide sociale aux Antilles*, Fort-de-France, CERAG

Palloix, C. 1975, *L'internationalisation du capital: eléments critiques*, Paris, Maspero

Poncet, E. 1974, 'Martinique, Guadeloupe, Réunion: le pillage', *Economie et politique*, no. 240, July, pp. 55–74

Progressiste 25 March 1981, p. 9

PUG 1979, 'Le désaccord sur la CEE et la Convention de Lomé parmi les organisations et la gauche française', *La France et le tiers-monde*, Paris, PUG, pp. 248–252

Quijano, A. 1971, 'Pôle marginal de l'économie et main-d'oeuvre marginalisée', in A. Abdel-Malek (ed.), *Sociologie de l'impérialisme*, Paris, Anthropos

Reneville, F. 1979, 'Les Gaulois ne sont plus leurs ancêtres', *Le Monde*, 21 December, p. 10

Rollat, A. 1979, *Le Monde*, 21 December, pp. 7, 9

Service des Affaires Administratives, Financières et Sociales du Secrétariat d'Etat aux Départements et Territoires d'Outre-Mer 1976, *La politique sociale dans les départements d'outre-mer*, August

SNI-PEGC Colloquium 1980, 'Quelle école pour demain', 19, 20, 21 December 1979, Supplement to *L'école libératrice*, Fort-de-France, no. 1, September

Tennessee, J. 1964, 'La CEE et le tiers-monde', *Documentation française* (Articles and Documents), no. 01522, 21 April

Valere, L.-L. 1968, *Condition du développement des DOM: la décentralisation administrative observations et propositions*, Fort-de-France, Lib. Relouzat

William, J.-C. 1979, 'Naissance et évolution du parti progressiste martiniquais', *Historial antillais*, vol. 6, pp. 296–318

Yang-Ting, M. 1968, *Vrai ou faux développement dans les DOM?*, Fort-de-France, Lib. Relouzat, 2nd edn

Class Formation and Class Struggle in Suriname: the Background and Development of the Coup d'État

Sandew Hira

On 25 February 1980 the new wind blowing in the Caribbean reached a former Dutch colony in South America. But unlike in Grenada and Nicaragua, in Suriname the political climate was such that the new wind blew from the right. The purpose of this chapter is to analyse the background and development of this coup d'état which ousted the comprador government led by Prime Minister Arron. The chapter is divided into three sections. The first section contains an analysis of the development of the class structure in Suriname, the second deals with the political climate during the period immediately preceding the coup, while the last provides an evaluation of the political situation during the first post-coup year.

The development of the class structure

The Second World War marked a qualitative change in the class structure of Suriname. In the first half of the twentieth century the colonial economy was based on the production of sugar and coffee. From 1922 onwards, the production of bauxite, the raw material of aluminium, became increasingly important. The pre-war society, however, was predominantly an agricultural one in which the large plantations of the nineteenth century had given way to peasant farming—partly for subsistence and partly for local and foreign markets. The urban areas, especially the capital Paramaribo, were populated with merchants employed in local and foreign trade, state employees, small capitalists exploiting a few wage workers and some businessmen working on their own account.

The Second World War created an enormous increase in the demand for aluminium and, consequently, for bauxite. In its search for new bauxite reserves, the aircraft industry made large investments in Suriname. A massive import of capital was accompanied by the stationing of a large and highly paid American army unit to protect the interests of the Aluminium Company of America (Alcoa). This stimulated the growth of local markets, especially in food, which, in turn, were further encouraged by the decline in foreign trade (due to the war) and the introduction of a general conscription which removed thousands of young peasants from their former isolation. The war brought about an economic upswing in the colonial economy which was to last until 1945. The period of economic stagnation that followed continued until the beginning of the era of development aid.

Four years after the end of the war the first development plan, the so-called Welfare Fund, began to be implemented. This was followed by one ten-year and two five-year plans. These plans, which were drawn up by Dutch scientists, largely served the interests of Dutch capital. In 1972 a new plan was drawn up by a joint commission of Surinamese and Dutch scientists. The first development plans, especially the Welfare Fund and the ten-year plan, had two definite aims.

The first aim was the transformation of small-scale peasant farming into large-scale mechanized agriculture, producing mainly for foreign markets. With the help of development aid, the Stichting Machinale Landbouw (Foundation for Mechanized Agriculture, SML) was set up to modernize Surinamese agriculture. The SML introduced a new variety of rice which required new means of production. Aeroplanes were used to sow the crops, while the reaping and drying of paddy were taken over by modern combines and drying machines. The SML acquired a large tract of land in the district of Nickerie in the west of Suriname which was used for cultivating rice. Within ten years the SML had become the most important rice producer in the country. When other farmers changed over to producing rice for export, it rapidly became by far the most important agricultural product.

The second aim of development aid was to facilitate the search for, and production of, raw materials for imperialist firms. The construction of a material infrastructure (roads, bridges, airstrips, and other means of communication such as a telephone and telegraph system) was financed by development funds. Development aid also provided a financial infrastructure by facilitating the foundation and expansion of credit institutions such as banks and insurance companies. Intensive research has gone into establishing the existence of valuable raw materials and the cost of their exploitation. As one government report put it, 'Suriname is one of the very few developing countries in which so much research has been done that our knowledge of the production potential of the country is now very extensive' (Suriname Government 1975: 21). However, government policy was not restricted to creating a material and financial infrastructure to facilitate the search for raw materials. It also tried to attract foreign investment by keeping interest rates low, by providing tax incentives (tax holidays, low import duties on capital equipment) and by offering a stable political climate. This policy was successful to the extent that it did attract foreign investments, although the most important of these were in the bauxite sector.

From the mid-1960s, development planning shifted its focus from the mining of bauxite to the processing of this raw material. A huge alumina plant near the flood-control dam in the Suriname River provided the site for Suralco, a subsidiary of Alcoa, to process the exploited bauxite. A constant stream of foreign investments, the growth of a material and financial infrastructure, an expanding internal market and the accumulation of local capital, all contributed towards the expansion of local industries. Manufacturing began to account for an increasing share in the gross domestic product. The most recent development plan, which officially began in 1975, the year of independence, continues to stress the importance of processing bauxite in Suriname. A hydro-electric station with a capacity three times the size of the one in the Suriname River was planned to be built in the Corantyn River on the border of former British Guyana. Although economic development over the last three decades has provided the potential for the growth of local industry, the plan contains no systematic drive to stimulate it.

Development planning since the Second World War has benefited foreign capital. According to a government source:

A large part of the vital sectors of the Surinamese economy, including mining, banking, insurance, business and a substantial part of manufacturing is controlled by *foreign firms*. The large foreign companies are generating 40 to 50 per cent of the total domestic product, are directly providing employment for 14 to 15 per cent of the labour force and account for 90 to 95 per cent of the export value. About 45 to 50 per cent of total annual profits which amount to between Sf80 and 85 million, until recently went to the government in the form of tax payments. These incomes were considerably increased in 1975 through the newly introduced bauxite levy. Apart from this, net factor payments (transfer of profits) led to an outflow of capital to abroad of a magnitude of Sf75 to 100 million, which makes the national product 15 per cent lower than the domestic product (Surinaams-Nederlandse Commissie 1975: 1–8).

The activities of foreign investors in Suriname have left the country in a poor and desolate state. Wealth produced in the former Dutch colony is transferred to the West through mechanisms of unequal exchange, profit transfers and salaries of expensive Western experts and advisers in development planning and technical assistance. Between 1954 and 1975 Suriname received a net sum of Sf298 million in development aid. During the same period, profits to the tune of Sf806 million were transferred out of the country by imperialist firms. Between 1971 and 1976 the salaries of foreign advisers and experts amounted to 7 per cent of the total expenditure of the current account of the balance of payments, and in 1976 alone these payments amounted to Sf54 million. One calculation of the outflow of wealth from Suriname through unequal exchange shows that in trade with Holland during 1963–74, the country lost Nf316 million to its 'motherland' (Doest 1977).

On the other side of the coin is the growing impoverishment of workers and peasants. Although the peasantry had never been a particularly homogeneous sector, the introduction of the SML rice variety created intense competition between peasants producing for the market. Small farmers ran into debt in trying to catch up with the process of mechanization and many were ruined through being forced to sell their lands in order to pay off their debts. As a result, many small farmers have left agriculture altogether: one of the causes of the large migration from the rural areas to the city of Paramaribo and Nieuw Nickerie. The stream of migrants began in the mid-1960s and now about half of the population lives in or near Paramaribo. The populations of outer districts have decreased except in the case of Nickerie where there has been an increase in the district population. But even in this district the only city, Nieuw Nickerie, has experienced remarkable growth.

Rising unemployment, concentrated especially in the urban areas, is yet another outcome of post-war development policies. Several factors have contributed towards this rise. The expulsion of labour from the agricultural sector, which was mentioned above, is one. Another is the migration of Indians and Maroons from the interior as, in the search for raw materials, foreign capital penetrates the area and destroys their traditional ways of life. The introduction of wage labour by the companies exploiting the forests and mines or building facilities for the production of bauxite and wood, the use of money in a society that was accustomed to producing for its own consumption, the improvement of the road system and other links with the city, and the government's policy of forced migration, have all played a part in the disintegration of traditional societies. Forced migration began to be implemented on a large scale between 1964 and 1966. Thousands of Maroons were forced to leave their villages when the hydro-electric station was built in the Suriname River. Although they were offered alternative housing in the so-called 'trans-migration villages', the houses in these villages were set out in rows and as such were totally unsuitable for the Maroon way of life. Consequently, many Maroons left for the city. Since 1975 the Indians and Maroons in the west of Suriname have been similarly afflicted through the building of a railway to link the bauxite fields in the Bakhuys mountains in the south-west of Suriname with a harbour in Apoera: an old Indian village has now been totally erased from the map of the area. The resulting drift towards the city is thus an important factor in the rise in unemployment as is the age structure of the population. Over half the population is under nineteen years of age, which means that there is an ever-growing supply of labour: a supply further increased over the last decade by the need for women to seek work outside the home in order to survive.

The most important factor, however, lies in the structure of the Surinamese economy. With the government's economic policy geared towards serving the interests of foreign capital, it was not surprising that development planning primarily benefited the imperialists and that the greater part of the development fund was used to attract foreign investment. But these investments did not create employment for the job-seeking masses, for they were confined to those interests concerned with the extraction of bauxite and with rice production. Because the Surinamese economy was integrally tied up with the capitalist world economy and because the imperialists were producing for a highly competitive world market, there was little option but to adopt the cost-effective labour-saving production techniques that do not provide much employment.

The economic development policies that have been implemented over the last few decades have had consequences other than rising unemployment. Mounting inflation, increasing disparities in the distribution of incomes, a suicidal dependence on imperialist support and a greater unevenness in regional development can also be traced to the same source. Even more important, perhaps, are the social consequences of post-war economic development.

Before 1940 the class structure of the Dutch colony was characterized by a very weak, almost non-existent, creole (blacks of African descent) working class concentrated mainly in the mining sector, which was not the most important industry at the time. Agriculture was very much more important in the colonial economy and most export commodities were produced by small farmers, usually of East Indian or Indonesian descent. Although in some districts, such as Coronie, creole peasants became important small producers, the petty bourgeoisie consisted mainly of Asians. These farmers were mercilessly exploited by the class of white and coloured merchants which controlled foreign and local trade and which had close links with the imperialist bourgeoisie. The colonial state apparatus was designed primarily to serve this bloc of classes. The urban petty bourgeoisie was relatively weak and consisted mainly of artisans in handicrafts, lawyers, doctors and so on who were usually white or coloured, although some blacks had also managed to work their way up into this class.

After the war, the class structure underwent deep and far-reaching transformations. The rapid development of capitalism led to a mammoth increase in the size of the working class, and in the rural areas agriculture became organized along capitalist lines. The resulting differentiation of the peasantry reflected new ways of integrating agricultural production into the capitalist world economy. Mechanization produced a new layer of dispossessed farmers in the countryside, who either formed the ranks of the rural proletariat by becoming wage labourers on the agricultural estates of the large landowners, or who moved away to the city to become members of the lumpen proletariat. Some, of course, were able to work as wage labourers while still managing to cultivate their own small plots of land. The working class has been further increased by the migrations from the interior to Paramaribo of Indians and Maroons who have settled in slums on the outskirts of the capital. In the meanwhile, with the help of government policy, the penetration of capital into the Surinamese jungle had been creating a labour market in the interior and it was not long before the Indians and Maroons had become enmeshed in capitalist relations of production. Yet another source of working-class recruitment lay in the lowest strata of the urban petty bourgeoisie being thrown out of their class and reduced to abject poverty by stiff competition between independent producers in the city which the development of capitalism had brought to post-war Suriname. The total agricultural work force decreased from 26,900 in 1960 to 15,260 in 1976, and in 1974 more than 75 per cent of all small peasant farmers had to supplement their incomes from outside the agricultural sector in order to maintain their living standards (de Graaf 1974: 72; Klink and Nagel 1976: 65).

Thus, the proletariat is a heterogeneous class composed of a number of different overlapping strata. The highest-paid and best-organized workers are found in sectors with the most advanced capitalist development, namely mining and processing. For example, in 1974 the average annual wage in the mining and processing industry concentrated in and around Paramaribo reached Sf10,000 (*Jaarplan* 1978: 151). The lowest strata, the lumpen proletariat, are those prostitutes, petty thieves, shoeshiners, beggars, people selling fruit or other foods at the side of the road, and so on who, unable to sell their labour power, engage in marginal activities in order to survive. The strength and characteristics of the different layers are determined largely by the extent of capitalist development. For example, in the banking and insurance sector of the economy (after bauxite mining and processing the most developed sector in the Surinamese economy) workers on average earned Sf8,300 in 1974 (*Jaarplan* 1978), almost as much as their colleagues in the bauxite industry. On the other hand, workers in the civil service—a notorious reservoir of hidden unemployment—and in the construction industry are among the worst-paid wage labourers. Only very recently has the position of workers in the construction industry begun to improve and this is very clearly connected with attempts to reorganize the construction sector along capitalist lines: small builders giving way to large, more efficient competitors who can offer high wages to attract skilled workers. This does not necessarily mean that wages always rise as capitalist relations of production develop, for obviously wage levels depend on the cost of labour power. But in the transition from petty bourgeois to capitalist relations of production, the labour force becomes more highly skilled to meet the demands of the more developed productive forces and thus the cost of labour power correspondingly increases.

To understand the true nature of the coup d'état fully, it is perhaps even more important to look at the transformations within the ruling classes. The post-1940 wave of investments has gone hand in hand with the establishment of a class of local representatives of foreign firms: the comprador bourgeoisie. Members of the comprador bourgeoisie own no means of production and their incomes are neither primarily nor directly dependent on the exploitation of wage labour. Their function is essentially to render services to their foreign masters—they are the imperialists' errand boys—and it is this function alone that provides the material base for their existence and, along with their dependence on the goodwill of their foreign bosses, distinguishes them from the national bourgeoisie. The material base of the national bourgeoisie, the class of local capitalists, lies in its possession of the means of production and in its ability to exploit labour power to operate this means of production. Whereas members of the comprador class are mere slaves to the imperialists, local capitalists are independent *in principle* from imperialism. This independence *can*, however, lead to conflict with the imperialists. Since the national bourgeoisie has its own independent base for capital accumulation and is concerned essentially with extending this base, by so doing the interests of this class may well clash with the imperialists' aim to transfer the wealth produced in Suriname to North America and Europe.

Economically, the comprador bourgeoisie emerged from the massive import of capital after the Second World War. But sociologically, it is an offshoot of the process of differentiation within the urban and rural petty bourgeoisie. Even during the Second World War, the petty bourgeoisie was mobilizing against the colonial authorities and pressing for the introduction of local autonomy. Eventually the colonialists agreed to co-operate with members of the petty bourgeoisie in an attempt to prevent the radicalization of the masses. In 1948 institutional reforms, including the introduction of universal suffrage, enabled the petty bourgeoisie to participate in the administration of the country for the first time, although, of course, such important matters as defence remained under imperialist control. Shortly after the war political parties were formed, mainly along racial lines, in an attempt to gain some control over the state apparatus. The Nationale Partij Suriname (National Party of Suriname, NPS), established by the coloured urban petite bourgeoisie, had a large following among Protestant creoles. Catholic creoles tended to join the Progressieve Surinaamse Volkspartij (Progressive People's Party of Suriname, PSV) which was also formed by members of the coloured petty bourgeoisie. The Verenigde Hindoestaanse Partij (United Hindustani Party, VHP) was supported by the East Indian peasants, while the Kaum Tani Persuatan Indonesia (Indonesian Peasants' Party, KTPI) built up a large following among Javanese peasants. Not unnaturally, the urban petite bourgeoisie provided the first reservoir from which representatives of foreign companies were recruited in Suriname. The imperialists had little difficulty integrating the upper echelons of this class into the new social relations that came into existence. Considering the importance of the role of the state in transforming the Surinamese economic structure, it was inevitable that the imperialists would soon affiliate themselves with the petty bourgeois parties in Parliament and in the administration in order to consolidate their position in the economy. Foreign capital became deeply involved in the mechanization of agricultural production, in the clearing and reclamation of land, and in the general transformation of agricultural production. In this process, the imperialists were successful in recruiting an important sector of the rural petty bourgeoisie as the representatives of foreign capital and in integrating them into new relations of production. The comprador bourgeoisie is also, in part, recruited from the old merchant class. Since foreign trade has grown considerably since 1945, there has been a marked increase in the number of local agents employed by foreign companies that trade with Suriname.

Although the national bourgeoisie is equally as much the product of post-war transformations, the real base for this class's expansion has only emerged since the mid-1960s. The proletarianization of large sectors of the population has stimulated the growth of an internal market and this has enabled some small capitalists to expand their firms. The sociological and economic origins of this class can be traced back to the growth of the comprador bourgeoisie and to the process of differentiation of the petty bourgeoisie. By the mid-1960s, the comprador class had grown to a point at which a qualitative change occurred: a certain section of this class had accumulated sufficient capital to start a business, or to buy shares in an existing one. And thus they began to constitute an independent base for capital accumulation. Although, of course, strong links exist between the imperialists and this section of the national bourgeoisie—they are often the common shareholders of local enterprises—it is not unusual for this sector to join hands with other sectors that have emerged as offshoots of the process of differentiation of the urban petty bourgeoisie. The small businessman who eventually succeeds in climbing up to the ranks of the big capitalist is an illustration of this point. A small entrepreneur who began a shoe business fifteen years ago with a few workers is now employing fifty to one hundred people. The national bourgeoisie is still small, but it is growing.

Differentiation of the petty bourgeoisie has also contributed towards the emergence of a class of large landowners. Some middle farmers and traders involved in buying up paddy have acquired large tracts of land by successfully pressurizing small farmers into selling their plots. But since most of the land was originally state-owned, the government has also been in a strong position to influence its distribution. Thus, land has been acquired by not only the existing large landowners, but also by members of the comprador bourgeoisie who have usually been in control of the state apparatus, at least that part of it concerned with land distribution. In this way, strong links have been established between the big landowners and the comprador bourgeoisie.

New economic developments have not only brought about radical changes in the class structure, but have also completely altered the whole system of race relations. Broadly speaking, before the war there was an amalgam of race and class relations, i.e. race relations corresponded with the class structure. The proletariat in and around the cities was composed of blacks, as was the lowest stratum of the petty bourgeoisie. Higher strata of the urban petty bourgeoisie consisted of coloured people. As a general rule, it could be observed that the lighter the colour of the skin, the higher the position in the class structure. Whites were at the top of the social pyramid: the colonial elite and the merchant class were white, or lightly coloured. Peasants were usually of Indonesian or East Indian extraction, except in the Coronie district where they were mainly black. Not only did the different racial groups belong to different classes, they also lived in different regions. The Indonesians were concentrated mainly in the Commewijne district, the East Indians in Nickerie and

Saramacca, the blacks in and around the urban areas and in the Coronie, Para and Brokopondo districts. Other districts, such as Marowijne, were barely integrated into the money economy.

After the war, communications between districts improved considerably and internal migration reduced the regional isolation of the different racial groups. The differentiation of the peasantry, the disintegration of traditional societies in the interior and the spreading of capitalist relations of production all over the country, have produced a situation in which the working class is no longer composed of one racial group. The same applies to the comprador bourgeoisie whose multi-racial character strongly reflects its sociological background. It should perhaps be noted that the white colonialists have now withdrawn from the public political arena in order to work more effectively behind the scenes. The development of capitalism in Suriname has produced a national bourgeoisie which, due to its sociological genesis, also has a multi-racial character.

Before the war, racial tensions were concentrated in relations between the whites on the one hand and blacks, coloureds and Asians on the other. The whites and their light-coloured allies were the oppressors of the blacks, Asians and dark-coloured people. The relationship of antagonism between the two groups had a clear material base in the economic and class structure of the society. The development of race relations since the war can be described in two phases. During the first phase, between 1940/45 and about 1975, the dark-coloured creoles organized themselves against the whites and the light-coloured creoles. At the same time, creoles were denouncing the East Indians as 'servants of the whites who were trying to take over the economy to oppress the blacks'. The East Indians, on the other hand, depicted the blacks as 'lazy thieves who only want to rape Indian women'. The Javanese were regarded as 'unreliable traitors' by both groups. Bourgeois academics tried to explain the racial tensions after the war in terms of traits inherent in the psychological nature of each racial group, as something natural. In the field of politics especially, bourgeois social scientists (e.g. Dew 1978) saw the issue of race as central to most conflicts and discussions. But from the beginning of the 1970s the race issue had begun to loose its grip on the political scene and was being replaced by the concept of national unity and by the struggle against 'strange ideologies', notably communism. Bourgeois social scientists are unable to provide a consistent explanation for these developments. Obviously, recent developments cannot be accounted for in terms of traditional enmity between different racial groups: certainly an event as important as the coup d'état of 25 February 1980 can hardly be explained in terms of racial struggle. Instead it was seen as a social revolution against the 'old order', and bourgeois social scientists began to abandon their pluralist theories. Marxism, however, is seen to offer a sound material analysis of the development of racial politics in Suriname.

The coincidence between race and class did not break down in a mechanical and linear way. The white colonial elite did not immediately change into a multi-racial comprador bourgeoisie. The black working class was not transformed overnight into a multi-racial class. Capitalism developed in an unequal way. The process of the differentiation of the peasantry took off earlier in the Nickerie district, while other districts lagged behind. The same applied to internal migration. Moreover, while the coincidence between race and class no longer holds in Paramaribo, in a district like Marowijne or Para the parallel still exists and this has an effect on the consciousness and ideology of the masses. In Saramacca, for example, creole wage labourers reproach East Indian peasants for being greedy, while East Indians curse creoles for being lazy and irresponsible. These reproofs are, however, rooted in real relationships between peasants and wage labourers. The peasants do appear greedy, for as independent producers of commodities they are forced by competition to be 'greedy', or in other words, they are forced to be efficient or economically rational. Wage labourers do not have to carry the same responsibilities. These ideas persist because areas still exist in which there is a coincidence between race and class. But the above-mentioned factors cannot explain the *increase* in racial tension after the war and, especially, the emergence of political parties organized along racial lines. To explain these, it will be necessary to examine the nature of the comprador bourgeoisie in Suriname.

The comprador bourgeoisie is not a homogeneous class. Its growth is characterized by struggles between competing fractions for larger and larger slices of the cakes received from the imperialist bosses. There is a direct relationship between the size of the slice and services rendered to the imperialist firm. Here, the fraction that controls the state apparatus can procure more advantages for foreign capital than can fractions that do not exercise this form of control. The very survival of the comprador class hinges around what benefits it can arrange for the imperialists. The various fractions compete with one another in their attempts to secure a stronger hold over the state apparatus and it is here that the issue of race comes into play. By depicting a social struggle as a racial struggle, the comprador tries to consolidate his own position within his ethnic group and at the same time builds up a stronghold from which to confront the other fractions in the political struggle for control over the state apparatus. Racial mobilization, therefore, is totally tied up with the material existence of the comprador class, which brings us to an essential difference between the comprador bourgeoisie and the national bourgeoisie in Suriname. Local capitalists do not have a primary material interest in maintaining or in promoting racial tensions. On a board of directors, for example, it may well be harmful to do that. It is more in the interests of the national bourgeoisie to preach class harmony, i.e. harmony between creole and Asian workers and their capitalist employers. The ideology of the national bourgeoisie consequently stresses the need for national harmony: the issue of race is reserved for tactical use in the event of an upswing in the class struggle. The class that acted as the driving force behind the coup d'état used nationalist ideology to justify and legitimate its support for the coup. By analysing the political climate on the eve of the coup, we can learn a lot about the real nature of the military take-over in Suriname.

The political climate of a coup d'état

The economic, social and political contradictions that post-war capitalist development brought to Suriname (Hira 1979; 1980) have been accentuated by the world economic crisis and by the change in the political face of the Caribbean as a result of the Nicaraguan and Grenadian revolutions. Capitalist development in Suriname has sharpened class contradictions: the poor are getting poorer while the rich are getting richer. The 1974 economic crisis in the world aluminium industry has hit the economy very hard. The poor peasants and the working class have had to carry the burden as mounting inflation and unemployment have gone hand in hand with wage cuts and growing emigration. But the new development aid package which began operating in 1975 has staved off some of the worst economic effects of the world crisis. On 25 November 1980 Suriname gained independence and an economic plan for the 1980s was agreed upon. The plan provided for the building of a huge hydro-electric station in the west of Suriname, for an alumina and aluminium plant and for a city on the site of the present Indian village of Apoera. The plan revolved around the mining and processing of the enormous bauxite reserves in the Bakhuys mountains in the south-west of the country. The new development programme would cost approximately 6 million Dutch guilders, of which approximately 2.7 million would be contributed by the Dutch government. Independence and the large capital fund made available by the Dutch led to rising expectations on the part of the masses that things were going to get better. In 1975 emigration came to a virtual halt, but by 1978 the stream of Surinamese to Holland was again assuming enormous proportions. Mass emigration had a two-fold significance: it deprived industry of all forms of labour, skilled and unskilled, and it exercised an upward pressure on wages. As regards un-skilled or semi-skilled labour, this pressure could be relieved through the import of cheap labour from Guyana and Haiti—an estimated 20,000 Guyanese are now in Suriname, while half of the 400,000 Surinamese are in Holland—but highly skilled workers could not as easily be replaced. Local capitalist firms suffered more from this situation than rich imperialists who had more reserves and were better placed than the local capitalists to offer high wages to skilled personnel. Despite repeated requests from the national bourgeoisie to implement an active policy to encourage the return migration of skilled labourers from the Surinamese immigrant communities in Holland, the comprador government of Prime Minister Arron did nothing to set this in motion. The government's failure in this respect was at the source of a heated controversy between the Arron government and the local capitalists, whose campaign was conducted in public mainly through the Chamber of Commerce and Trade and through the Society for Surinamese Trade and Industry.

Mass emigration, which began at the beginning of the 1970s and peaked at the end of 1973, was an expression of a crisis of confidence in the bourgeois economic and political system. In 1973 the VHP/Progressieve Nationale Partij (Progressive National Party, PNP) comprador coalition government headed by Jules Sedney fell under the impact of a general strike, but no substantial gains were made by the workers. Then a coalition of comprador parties and the bourgeois nationalist Partij Nationalistische Republiek (Party for a Nationalist Republic, PNR) came to power in the 1973 elections. The only substantial reforms that were initiated at this time were the installation of the Centrale Inkoop Suriname (Central Purchasing Agency of Suriname, CIS) and the proclamation of independence. The CIS was a government agency set up to compete with existing import firms rather than as an import controlling institution. It tried to curtail the influence of importers by selling imported goods at cheaper prices through operating a system of state subsidies. Not surprisingly, the policy met stiff resistance from importers who organized a campaign against the Minister for Economic Affairs, a lawyer and leader of the PNR, by refusing to import goods that were also imported by the CIS. Since state subsidies were exceedingly limited, the CIS were unable to meet the demand for imported commodities, mainly basic goods, and the scarcity that followed provided a further stimulus to emigration. At the beginning of 1975, when it was announced that independence would be declared on 25 November, emigration reached a peak with 6–7,000 Surinamese leaving the country each month. People feared that after that date they would not be able to enter Holland freely, despite an agreement between the Dutch and Surinamese governments that unrestricted entry to Holland would be allowed for another five years.

The struggle for independence was for the most part led by Bruma's PNR, although the NPS leader, Henk Arron, became prime minister of the coalition government. A comprador fraction headed by VHP leader Jaggernath Lachmon tenaciously resisted the move towards independence and at one time many people feared that a racial war would break out. On the eve of independence, however, Lachmon changed his tune and declared his support for it, but by then some tens of thousands had already left the country. For the first year after independence an atmosphere of enthusiasm and national unity prevailed, but it was not long before emigration had again climbed up to levels reached before 1975. There could be no clearer expression of the disillusionment of the masses in the economic and political system.

The basis of the political system in Suriname before the coup was that of a parliamentary democracy. One of the functions of a parliamentary democracy is to create and maintain the illusion that the oppressed classes have as much influence over the administration of the country as the ruling classes. The idea of a formal equality between classes is the essence of bourgeois democracy. In the eyes of the law every citizen is free to stand for election to parliamentary or administrative posts: every citizen can exercise the same influence over the decision-making process. But in reality the situation is quite different. The ruling classes control the press, the radio and television networks, the printing offices. They have infinitely more resources with which to influence public opinion than workers or working-class organizations could possibly muster. Members of the comprador, foreign and local bourgeoisie spend large sums of money on supporting the election candidates of their choice. Workers and small farmers do not command these resources. Once members of parliament are elected and the government installed, workers and peasants have no means of influencing the political process other than through non-parliamentary means such as strikes, mass demonstrations, and the like. Capitalists, however, have direct access to government officials and members of parliament through business relationships and informal contacts. The capitalists use these channels—sometimes with a little help from the bribery fund—to promote their own interests within the state apparatus. Parliamentary democracy thus serves to conceal the real relations in capitalist society: the implacability of the class contradictions, the fundamental inequality of the relationship between capitalist and worker, between oppressor and oppressed, and the need to contain class contradictions through the use of the state apparatus.

During periods of relative stability, the masses are not usually aware of the nature of the relations underlying a bourgeois democracy. But during a period of social and economic crisis, when the masses put forward demands for change, the true character of the ruling political system is revealed. This was particularly evident after 1976, when it became apparent that the bourgeois democracy was in crisis, and especially so at the height of the crisis in 1979. Members of parliament were repeatedly involved in corruption scandals and even a minister was convicted for receiving bribes from landowners who were trying to acquire extra land from the government. A new land distribution project, which was set up in 1976 to provide extra land for about 11,500 small farmers, ended up by giving all the land to fourteen large landowners. The Minister of Agriculture, who was deeply involved in this scandal, was also eventually arrested and tried in another corruption case. The masses began to view members of parliament and the government as a gang of crooks. Frequent trips abroad at the expense of the state and constant squabbles among themselves from the comfort of their armchairs in the Houses of Parliament earned this hallowed institution the nicknames of *Vereniging Ons Plezier* (the Society for our Pleasure)—an allusion to the trips abroad—and *circus stupido*. The degeneration of the bourgeois democracy culminated in 1979 in the so-called Koorndijk Affair. The ruling coalition led by Henk Arron, the Nationale Partij Kombinatie (National Combination of Parties, NPK), had a one-vote majority (20 out of 39 seats) in parliament. The death of Mr Zalmijn, a member for the NPK, provoked a crisis in the Houses of Parliament, for the NPK had thereby lost its majority. A new MP would have to be appointed to replace Mr Zalmijn, but the opposition refused to agree to the appointment of Mr Koorndijk as the new NPK member of parliament. By boycotting the appropriate meeting, the opposition were able to deny the NPK a quorum and thereby prevented Mr Koorndijk from being installed as an MP. Arron then declared that the NPK could appoint a new MP without a quorum, but the opposition and some important sectors of the ruling class vigorously opposed this manoeuvre and demanded new elections. The crisis was resolved only three months later when an agreement was reached between the NPK and the opposition which stipulated that elections would be held in March 1980 and that the opposition would no longer oppose the appointment of Mr Koorndijk. This compromise could not, however, prevent the welling up among the masses of a growing resistance to the Arron government.

Mass resistance to the NPK government began to build up in 1978 over a whole range of issues. Indians and Maroons from the interior joined forces to struggle for recognition of their rights over land in the interior from which they had been expelled by the imperialists in co-operation with the government. The Indians and Maroons organized rallies and drew up petitions in an effort to gain support for their struggle which culminated in a march from Albina to Paramaribo (a three-day walk) to demonstrate their determination to fight till the end. In the village of Apoera, Indian children joined the campaign to save their land by standing in the way of bulldozers that had been sent into the interior to fell the trees. Ultimately the bulldozers won and the children had to make way for imperialism. In 1979 several youth organizations arranged demonstrations and rallies in support of lowering the age at which people were entitled to vote from twenty-one to eighteen years. Before the coup, women were not legally allowed to act in commercial and juridical cases without their husband's permission: they could not even buy a refrigerator without his signature. Prior to 1978, protests against this system, called *handelingsonbekwaamheid*, were voiced through articles in the newspapers, but in 1979 demonstrations were being organized and demands made for a complete re-evaluation of the whole system. In the same year, workers employed in the public sector and organized in the Centrale van Lands-dienaren Organisaties (Federation of Unions of Public Servants, CLO) called for wage increases to compensate for rising prices—between 1972 and the third quarter of 1979 prices rose by 111 per cent, while wages in the public sector rose by only 63 per cent (*De Ware tijd* 1980). An agreement was eventually reached between the government and the CLO, but when it became apparent that Arron did not intend to honour the agreement, the CLO went on strike but lost the fight through their own bureaucratic incompetence. The NPK did not move an inch. In the meanwhile resistance from other sectors of the population was beginning to build up against the government. In Paramaribo, recurrent water shortages sparked off a series of rallies organized by neighbourhood committees demanding that the cause of the problem—a drop in pressure in the water circulation system—be corrected. The poorest sections of the population suffered most from this situation, since wealthier strata could buy an apparatus to suck water from the water circulation system through a pump. Protests against water shortages were particularly rife during 1979.

Arron and his government also succeeded in alienating the churches and retired workers. The Comité Christelijke Kerken (Committee of Christian Churches, CCK) had repeatedly issued communiqués harshly criticizing the government for favouring the rich and oppressing the poor. In the churches, there is a growing tendency towards adopting socialist positions, which is particularly apparent among a group in the Roman Catholic Church which organized a demonstration against the government in July 1979. Even the retired workers have taken to the streets under the banner of the Union for Retired People to protest against the government's refusal to raise their old-age pensions. But it was the struggle in the Surinaamse Krijgsmacht (Surinamese Army, SKM) that was particularly instrumental in bringing about the coup.

On 25 November 1975 the old colonial army was replaced by the SKM. Shortly after independence, the 1,000-strong army (of which 200 were non-commissioned officers) began to complain of corruption, wage differences and an unreasonable level of discipline being imposed on them by the army leadership. Non-commissioned officers were at the centre of this resistance. They resented the nepotism and favouritism so blatantly displayed by the army command. The head of the SKM, Colonel Elstak, was more interested in the little pleasures of life than in organizing an efficient army on which the bourgeoisie could rely in the event of mass resistance. The second area of resentment in the SKM, the wages policy, arose because soldiers in compulsory service earned less than their professional colleagues, even though they were carrying out the same duties. Feelings of resentment grew even stronger when the applications for professional status of some fifty-five soldiers in compulsory service were turned down by the army command. The sense of grievance over wages was also sharpened by the maintenance of a compensation subsidy for military personnel from the colonial army who transferred to the SKM. The compensation subsidy meant that non-commissioned officers who had served in the colonial army were getting very much more money than their professional counterparts. This situation arose because, in an attempt to encourage military cadres from the colonial army to join the SKM, the Dutch government had agreed to make up the discrepancy between the salaries of the old and the new army. Finally, the third area of resentment in the SKM arose over relations between the army command and the lower military cadres who were severely punished for the slightest offence. Non-commissioned officers began to take serious steps towards changing this situation in 1977, when the union of non-commissioned officers was formed. The union organized meetings in the barracks to discuss these issues, it brought out into the open the accusations against the army command, and it demanded recognition as the legitimate organization of the non-commissioned officers. Elstak, who refused to enter into any kind of dialogue with the representatives of the union, immediately arrested its leaders. About one hundred non-commissioned officers then took part in a sit-down demonstration in front of the Houses of Parliament and demanded the release of their union leaders. Throughout 1979 and up to 25 February 1980, a dynamic enveloped the country which eventually led to the coup d'état. To understand this dynamic, it is necessary to take into account the context in which the struggle for recognition of the military union took place.

It has already been pointed out that the oppressed classes in Suriname were beginning to mobilize against the comprador government in the early 1970s. But the workers and peasants were now in a better position to fight the ruling class than they had been in 1973 when the government fell under the impact of a general strike. The political situation in the Caribbean had been completely altered by the Nicaraguan and Grenadian revolutions, which not only inspired other Caribbean islands to continue their struggle against oppression and degradation and show that it is possible to end imperialist rule, but also, and this is important, they put the imperialists on the defensive. At the national level also the situation in Suriname in 1979 was politically quite different from that in 1973. Particularly noticeable in this respect was the rapid, though uneven, growth of left-wing organizations. The Maoists, in accordance with the theory of the three worlds, allied themselves with Arron's comprador government after the 1977 elections in a bid to halt 'Soviet expansionism'. After the coup they dissolved their organization and joined the NPS. The subsequent turn towards Arron led to a split in the party and the formation of a splinter group to work towards building a 'true' revolutionary party, along the lines of Albania's Enver Hoxha. Other left-wing groups, particularly the Progressieve Arbeiders en Landbouwers Unie (Progressive Workers' and Peasants' Union, PALU) and the Volkspartij (People's Party, VP), also increased their forces. PALU, a petty bourgeois formation of technocrats who once proclaimed the virtues of workers' self-management, cannot easily be located within the international workers' movement. PALU saw themselves as a typically Surinamese group with the technical know-how to reorganize Surinamese society without the working class having to mobilize to overthrow the capitalist system. In the 1977 elections, rather than stand with a bloc of united working-class parties, PALU proposed forming an alliance with the VP. As it turned out, an agreement with the VP was reached in only one district, Coronie.

The VP is the largest and fastest-growing organization on the left. Although its leaders are schooled in Stalinism, they do not clearly identify themselves as followers of the Moscow line and have been attempting to build up a multi-class party by creating a following among workers and small farmers as well as among the national bourgeoisie. The VP weekly, *Pipel* (People), has frequently criticized the Arron government but has never taken the lead in the struggle against the comprador bourgeoisie. To have done this would have brought the party into conflict with all the sectors of the ruling classes, including the national bourgeoisie. Although *Pipel* was sympathetic to the struggle of the masses, it did not exactly tell its readers how to go about furthering it. The VP's programme was aimed partly at improving the parliamentary system by replacing corrupt MPs with more honest ones from the VP and partly at satisfying the demands of the national bourgeoisie to reorganize the economy in order to expand local industry. The growing influence of PALU and the VP can be seen as an expression of the oppressed people's discontentment with the old political parties and of their wish for a change. In a situation of mounting class tension, the leadership of these parties may well have taken more extreme positions than they themselves might have wished. Nevertheless, despite the lack of any clear and consistent leadership in 1979, which made it easier for the ruling class to impose its will on the people, the masses could at least be reassured of a growing left-wing tendency that might be pressed to take up their struggle in the future.

In-fighting between the various factions of the ruling class was yet another factor that set the scene for the dispute between the non-commissioned officers' union and the SKM. The emerging national bourgeoisie became more and more dissatisfied with the comprador government. Local capitalists (and their organizations such as the Chamber of Commerce and the Society for Surinamese Trade and Industry) repeatedly complained about the NPK's lack of co-operation and about its failure to implement the necessary measures for expanding local industry. But Arron did absolutely nothing to stop the steady stream of emigration out of the country, or to encourage skilled workers from the immigrant community in Holland to return to Suriname. Proposals to set up a centre for the promotion of local industry and exports which could undertake research in this field and work out concrete suggestions for the expansion of local capital, were totally ignored. No steps were taken to curb the import of competitive goods. Corruption within the state apparatus was so rife that local entrepreneurs could no longer compete with the better-off foreigners in bribing government officials. As a result, most state contracts for implementing development plans were given to imperialist firms. The few capitalists who did succeed in getting government orders, frequently had to wait months to receive their payments, for more often than not the coffers of the treasury were empty.

Because the national bourgeoisie had no single political party through which to express their interests, they had very little political power. But of all the political parties, the PNR perhaps came closest to ful-filling this function. The PNR was an offshoot of the black nationalist cultural group founded in the 1950s, Wi Egi Sani (Our Own Business), which had struggled to dignify the creole culture and language. The PNR was formed by a group of Wi Egi Sani leaders at the end of the 1960s to fight for independence. The party attracted a large following in the Centrale-47, an important trade-union federation of forty-seven unions which, under the direction of PNR leader Fred Derby, organizes workers in the mining sector. The party participated in the first NPK government, which was formed after the 1973 elections, but it was not long before differences began to develop within the PNR. A group of trade-union leaders within the party were being pressurized by their rank and file members to resist the economic and social policies of the NPK government, whereas another wing, led by Minister of Economic Affairs Eddy Bruma, was more interested in the question of independence and in import controls. People began to see Bruma as the main person responsible for the worsening economic and social situation and in 1977 the PNR was dismissed from the NPK. This did not, however, lessen tensions in the PNR. The Bruma wing favoured moving closer to the local capitalists, whereas the trade unionists around Fred Derby wanted to move closer to existing left-wing groups. In January 1980 the two factions split and the Bruma wing of the PNR announced its intention to fight the next election in an alliance with the comprador parties as the VHP. But meanwhile the struggle within the army was coming to a head.

Discussions among non-commissioned officers, soldiers and other lower-ranking members of the military had led to the foundation of the Bond van Militair Kader (Union of Military Cadres, Bomika). During December 1979 and January 1980, Bomika made repeated public protestations against conditions in the SKM. A demand that Bomika be recognized as a legitimate union was openly presented to both the government and the army leadership, but Arron and Colonel Elstak refused even to listen to the complaints. On 25 January 1980 the union sent a telegram to the government demanding the resignations of certain army leaders, especially those of Colonel Elstak and of his aide-de-camp, Lt. Col. R. Essed. The telegram accused Elstak and Essed of provoking 'the committing of acts directed against the government on the eve of the elections' (which were to be held on 27 March). The government wrote a sharp letter to individual union leaders asking them to explain what the telegram meant, but the union leaders refused to answer on the grounds that the letter should have been directed to the union: an act designed to force the government into recognizing the union's status as a union. The government reacted by replacing the guard of the Memre Boekoe barracks with military policemen who barricaded the barracks and prevented about 150 military men from entering the Memre Boekoe. The Bomika members then stormed the entrance, occupied the barracks and were promptly locked up. The barracks were then surrounded by military policemen who were later reinforced by police forces from the capital. By the time the rebels were ordered to leave the area or be shot, the non-commissioned officers had disarmed themselves, thus demonstrating their willingness to work towards a peaceful solution. But when it became clear that the police did indeed intend to shoot at any demonstrators still in the barracks, the union leaders decided to leave the area and along with some 200 Bomika men set up camp in the George Streepy football stadium. The general outcome of the demonstration was that the union leaders were charged with mutiny, three of whom,

Sital, Neede and Abrahams, were court-martialled. Others went underground. All Bomika members were threatened with a dishonourable discharge from the army: some were chased and assaulted by the police. Two alternative courses of action now seemed possible. The first course of action was that proposed by the VP to whom some of the union leaders had gone for advice. The advice given was to wait for the elections, for if the VP came to Parliament they would fight for recognition of the right to form a union in the army. Meanwhile, Bomika members were being beaten up by the police and their leaders were being held in prison. It became quite clear that this was not in fact a real solution to the harsh repression of the Arron government.

Suggestions for the second course of action came from bourgeois elements, especially from the union's official advisers in the PNR–Bruma camp, who foresaw great dangers for the system of capitalism as a whole. The struggle within the SKM had led Bomika to think about the functions of an army in a neo-colonialist society. They subsequently published a memorandum explaining the need to transform the SKM from a repressive institution into a so-called 'development army' involved in the social and economic development of the country. Although ideas were not always clear-cut, there was no doubt about the direction in which thinking about the issue was moving. The 'workers and peasants in uniform' had been in a dilemma over whether or not to obey orders to shoot at possible mass demonstrators. Youth organizations and trade unions had backed Bomika's demand for recognition as a union and the wives of soldiers and of non-commissioned officers had organized women's groups in support of the Bomika struggle. They had also collected food and money and provided hiding places for the persecuted union leaders. Thousands gathered to follow the trials of Sital, Neede and Abrahams. The Bomika affair had begun to act as a catalyst in the class struggle and other sectors started to link their own struggles to it. One example here was the CLO's claim for higher wages to offset inflation. Many saw the struggle for union rights in the army as a struggle against the Arron government, and other groups (women's organizations, trade unions, youth groups, neighbourhood action committees) began to discuss the policies of the Arron government in relation to their own demands. If the courts had convicted the union leaders or if Bomika had failed to gain recognition as a union, the situation could well have become exceedingly uncomfortable for the ruling classes as a whole, for whom a long-standing plan to oust the NPK government was fast becoming a matter of life or death. In the absence of any revolutionary alternative, the Bomika leaders co-operated with bourgeois elements to implement a coup d'état to overthrow Arron.

There had been talk about a coup among local capitalists since 1976 when, following an inquiry into the climate for the investment of foreign capital, the Dutch employers' association's monthly, the *Financieel Ekonomisch Magazine*, reported that bourgeois circles were discussing a change in the form of government 'more appropriate to South American traditions' (20 May 1976). The coup that eventually succeeded on 25 February 1980 had been planned since late 1978. Bouterse, the then commander of the group leading the coup and now head of the army, explains in an autobiographical interview (Slagveer n.d.: 30–36) how plans for the coup were made in co-operation with the Central Intelligence Agency of Suriname and some unnamed political figures, probably leaders of the Bruma wing of the PNR given the central role it played immediately before and after the coup. Although Bouterse himself had not been involved in the union struggle, without the support of Bomika the coup would certainly have failed. Only when it had become apparent that in the absence of a revolutionary alternative the coup would receive the support of the Bomika left, were plans eventually put into operation. Thus, in the name of mutinous soldiers and non-commissioned officers, the military seized power on 25 February 1980.

An evaluation

The coup took place in a climate in which the bourgeoisie, who had taken the initiative for this action, had no option but to accept the presence of a powerful Bomika wing—and moreover a wing that would undoubtedly prove hostile to bourgeois leadership—within the newly formed National Military Council (NMC). But because the NMC had emerged as the result of a deal between the union leaders and the men who, for over a year, had been preparing and organizing the coup, Bomika control within it was only partial. The NMC began by imposing a curfew, banning political meetings and censoring the press. These measures were enforced to prevent independent initiatives being taken by the masses. That the Bomika wing agreed to these measures at all is an illustration of how heterogeneous a group it was and how unclear its political thinking about how best to struggle against imperialism and oppression.

For the first six months after the coup, the political stage was dominated by more or less open conflict between the bourgeois and the Bomika wings of the NMC. The Bomika wing wanted to include large numbers of leading members of left-wing groups in the new government, whereas the bourgeois element strongly opposed any such proposal. Eventually Eddy Bruma, who was put in charge of forming the government, decided to include one member from the VP and none from PALU. Three ministers as well as the Prime Minister were, however, chosen from the Bruma wing of the PNR. The President, Johan Ferrier, remained in his post. The union wing had lost its first fight. It tried to seek support from the left-wing organizations, but PALU was reluctant to get involved. The situation then became very unclear and a factional quarrel broke out in the VP over this issue. The leadership around Lie Paw Sam wanted to tread a cautious path between supporting the NMC and preventing them from taking over the party apparatus. A minority around the Naarendorp brothers wanted to give total support to the NMC. In May 1980 the minority split from the VP to form the Revolutionaire Volkspartij (Revolutionary People's Party, RVP). In the meanwhile, the union wing had formed an advisory council made up of leaders from the VP, PALU, the Derby wing of the PNR and a rather unimportant person named Henk Herrenberg, a trade-union leader and founder of the so-called Socialist Party of Suriname, whose marginal role on the political scene had been closer to that of a clown than of a serious politician. Although Lie Paw Sam was replaced on the advisory council by a member of the RVP after the split in the VP, the advisory council was still unable to help the union wing defeat the bourgeois current. In every major conflict they ended up as the losers. Apart from losing the battle over which politicians should be selected to form the government, their proposals to implement a radical land-reform policy, in which land would be distributed to small farmers, were totally ignored by the government. Other promises of social and economic improvements for the poorest sectors of the society and of a progressive and anti-imperialist foreign policy, also could not be fulfilled.

Backed by the bourgeois element in the NMC, the government firmly withstood left-wing pressure from the unionists, who now turned to the working class for support by organizing the so-called people's committees in the villages and districts within the capital. The way in which these committees were organized, and the contempt with which they were generally regarded, partially explains why the unionists were losing ground to the bourgeoisie. The Bomika wing was too afraid to support independent initiatives from the masses or to take a firm stand over ending the ban on political meetings—only meetings at which both wings of the NMR were represented were allowed—or over lifting the curfew which was still being retained as a security measure against counter-revolutionaries. The curfew was and still is seen, not as an effective deterrent against reactionaries, but as an inconvenient, repressive and intimidating piece of legislation for which violators are severely punished. The left-wing position was further undermined by the censorship of the press being directed against the left, with the censor's bureau firmly under bourgeois control.

But perhaps the most important reason why the trade unionists were failing was because they did not form a cohesive, homogeneous group within the NMC with a clear idea of who to fight and how. At the time of the coup, at least five of the nine NMC members were known to have VP sympathies. But because they did not form a homogeneous bloc, within six months the bourgeois element had succeeded in driving a wedge between them by offering army promotions to the more wavering of the VP sympathizers. The head of the army, Sergeant Bouterse, had himself promoted to the rank of major. Another NMC member, Sergeant Horb, was made a captain, while Sergeant Abrahams, a known union sympathizer, was promoted to the head of the military police. Even though the remaining three—Sergeants Badrissein Sital, Chas Mijnals and Stanley Joeman—stayed and acted together as a group, they lacked a clear programme for the masses in the fight against oppression. But despite their weakening position in the state apparatus and in the army, the union wing still constituted a danger for the bourgeoisie. Sital, Mijnals and Joeman were not completely amenable to the control of the government or of the army leadership. They tended to act independently of both these state organs. As long as they were members of the NMC, they were entitled to put pressure on government and army leaders to take action to reform the society. And when they themselves felt they had the power to institute certain reforms, they did so independently of the government and army leadership. At the beginning of July, for example, they were instrumental in organizing a mass demonstration against imperialism. During a visit by Jan de Koning, the Dutch Minister of Development Aid who had come to discuss the government's programme and ways in which Holland could help implement it, 20,000 Surinamese gathered in Independence Square to protest against de Koning's refusal even to discuss the question of the value indexation of development aid to Suriname. Because of inflation this aid had been losing its value and the Surinamese bourgeoisie were pressing for its indexation in an attempt to get a larger share of the surplus value appropriated by imperialism. Because this would have cost the Dutch government an additional 700 million Dutch guilders in aid, the Dutch minister categorically refused even to put the subject on the agenda of the meeting between the two governments. When the trade-union wing began to organize the demonstration, the bourgeoisie were faced with the choice of joining the demonstration or banning it as a political meeting.

Two months earlier, the union wing had wanted to organize a mass meeting in the Theater Bellevue over the so-called Ormskirk affair. Ormskirk, a former officer in the colonial army who had been trying to organize a counter-revolutionary coup against the non-commissioned officers who were in power, was beaten to death after his arrest. The NMC and the government stated at the time that he had been killed in a fight between the army and 300 mercenaries whom Ormskirk had led, but this story which was clearly untrue was withdrawn when the army were unable to present even one mercenary to the press. The government and army did, however, take advantage of this incident to increase repression by extending the curfew and censoring mail. Anyway, both the army and the Bouterse government had categorically refused to allow the meeting to take place, the former under threats of armed confrontation and the latter on the grounds that it was a political meeting which had the aim of forming a unity movement of the left. The union wing had in fact announced that information about the Ormskirk affair had revealed the need to organize such a movement. The meeting was cancelled, but in July the bourgeoisie took a different stand. This time they joined the meeting, but only after they had been reassured that it could be converted into a demonstration in support of the government and against imperialism. In this way the government would be able to strengthen its position *vis-à-vis* the NMR and at the same time exert pressure on the imperialists to make some concessions to the Surinamese bourgeoisie. The July meeting had demonstrated the presence of anti-imperialist sentiments among the masses and their will to struggle against oppression. It had also encouraged the trade-union wing to push for the adoption of more radical anti-imperialist measures, such as the nationalization of certain important firms and the redistribution of land in favour of the small farmer. After a visit to Nicaragua in July 1979 where Sital met and talked to Fidel Castro, Maurice Bishop and leaders of the FSLN, the trade-union wing tried to push the bourgeoisie into taking a stauncher stand against imperialism, for example, by giving diplomatic recognition to the Polisario Front. But here lay the danger for the bourgeoisie. Although the trade-union wing had been organizing the masses in a bureaucratic way, these mobilizations had been teaching the Sital faction more and more about the nature of the government that would not make concessions to the masses and about the limitations of its power. Moreover, the mobilizations could encourage independent initiatives from the masses which neither the trade-union wing nor the bourgeoisie would be able to control. For these reasons, the bourgeoisie wanted to eliminate the trade-union wing of the NMC and on 13 August 1980 Sital, Mijnals and Joeman, along with their advisers from the RVP, were arrested on a charge of organizing a counter-coup. They were brought before the courts and sentenced to periods of imprisonment ranging from six months to two and a half years. Not long afterwards the prisoners were released in an attempt to stave off a growing dissatisfaction in the army and among the people. Members of the Sital faction had come to be regarded as martyrs, both by the trade-union wing and by some sectors of the population, especially the youth.

The move against the Sital faction did not, however, lead to any definite stabilization of bourgeois rule. In fact the differences within the ruling class became even more accentuated. On the one hand, after the July demonstration, a fraction of the national bourgeoisie around Prime Minister Chin A Sen (backed by Eddy Bruma) wanted to work more closely with imperialism in solving the country's economic and political problems and to this end he withdrew the demand for value indexation which was still in the government's programme. On the other hand, another fraction led by ex-minister André Haakmat wanted to take a tougher stand against imperialism. By December, the struggle between the two fractions had led to the sacking of Haakmat as a minister, but the fight was not over. The Haakmat fraction continued to work towards strengthening its base in the army in preparation for a future return to government. But this inter-fractional fighting within the bourgeoisie was not the only destabilizing factor. The Bomika struggle had made it difficult for the bourgeoisie to use the army as an instrument of overt repression. The army could be used against individuals and small isolated groups, but if it were used to repress strikes or to break up large demonstrations, there was an even chance that the old Bomika fighters would rise up against the army leadership. For example, despite army intervention to end the Surinam Airways strike for higher wages in November 1980 and despite a government decree forbidding strike action, protests from the trade unions and from within the army forced the government to withdraw its decree. But by filling the army with lumpen elements and by buying off the leaders of the trade-union wing, the bourgeoisie has attempted to curb the danger of a left opposition within the army. Sometimes uneasy compromises have had to be made to achieve these aims, the release of the Sital faction being one case in point. Here, the bourgeoisie agreed verbally to support a policy of socialist development if the Sital faction agreed to co-operate in maintaining the state of emergency that had been proclaimed on 13 August 1980. The ban on political meetings, the censorship of the press and the curfew were enforced on this occasion. A final factor contributing towards the unstable political situation in Suriname can be traced to the very nature of the coup itself. Although the coup was directed against the old comprador bourgeoisie, its organizers failed to mobilize the masses. Thus, in order to obtain support from the masses, the bourgeoisie has had to make concessions to them, especially to those demands that have been supported with mass action. But the world economic crisis of capitalism has left no room for concessions. It is this contradiction, this tension between the need to make concessions to the masses and the inability to do so which has had such a destabilizing effect on the political situation in Suriname.

Although it cannot be denied that the masses were deeply intimidated by the coup, they were not defeated for long. The organizations of the masses (trade unions, women's groups, youth organizations, and so on) have been kept intact and it is only a matter of time before a new confrontation between the classes breaks out. Its outcome will depend largely on the ability of the working class to build up and arm a revolutionary party to lead the working class and its allies in the struggle against imperialism and capitalism.

REFERENCES

de Graaf, L. E. 1974, *Cijferreeksen tbv de Meerjaren Plankommissie*, manuscript, August

Dew, E. 1978, *The difficult flowering of Suriname: ethnicity and politics in a plural society*, The Hague, Mouton

De Ware tijd 2 May 1980

Doest, E. 1977, 'De ontwikkeling van de handel tussen Nederland en Suriname in de periode 1963 tot en met 1974', *Economische voorlichting Suriname*, May, pp.1–6

Financieel Ekonomisch Magazine 2 May 1980

Hira, S. 1979, 'Haalt Suriname 1985', *IROS*, September, pp. 3–17

Hira, S. 1980, 'Imperialisme, akkumulatie en klassenstrijd in Suriname', *Caraïbisch forum*, vol. 1, no. 2, pp. 56–74

Jaarplan 1978, Paramaribo

Klink, A. M. and Nagel, J. J. A. 1976, 'Agricultural credit to small farmers in Surinam', *De Surinaamse landbouw*, no. 2/3

Slagveer, J. n.d., *In de nacht van de revolutie*, The Hague

Suriname Government 1975, 'De mobilisatie van het eigene', Appendix 1, *Programma voor de sociaal-ekonomische ontwikkeling van Suriname*, Paramaribo, p. 21

Surinaams-Nederlandse Commissie 1975, 'Rapport van de Surinaams-Nederlandse Commissie van deskundigen' (Programma voor de sociaal-ekonomische ontwikkeling van Suriname), Paramaribo, pp. 1-8

NINE

Grenada: the New Jewel Revolution

Fitzroy Ambursley

Introduction

The revolutionary overthrow of the dictatorial regime of Eric Matthew Gairy in Grenada on 13 March 1979 represented the highest level of class struggle attained in the English-speaking Caribbean since the tumultuous slave uprisings of the seventeenth and eighteenth centuries. The armed seizure of power led by the New Jewel Movement (NJM) headed by Maurice Bishop was enthusiastically supported by the population at large, and has since given rise to the mushrooming of popular institutions. In three years the Bishop regime has registered significant advances over Gairyism in the areas of employment, social welfare benefits for the working class, education and mass participation in the political process. Because of the new government's defiant attitude towards US domination of the Caribbean, Grenada has become the target of a counter-revolutionary offensive mounted by the Reagan administration. This offensive has as its objective the economic and political destabilization of the Bishop regime and its excommunication from the neo-colonial fraternity of Anglophone Caribbean states. However, a Marxist analysis of the New Jewel Revolution must centre on the dynamics of class struggle inside Grenada, and the transformations that are taking place on the decisive terrain of property relations. (The introductory chapter of this book contains a discussion of the regional dimension of the revolution.) Such an investigation will show that the 13 March events have provided us with another example of what Löwy (1981) has termed an 'interrupted popular revolution'.

My analysis of the NJM in office is focused upon two principal considerations. First, the extent to which the NJM has departed from the more radical aspects of its 1973 manifesto. And second, that in spite of the advances over Gairyism, the hegemony of the bloc of dominant classes has not been contested by the Bishop regime.

The political and socio-economic background

Anatomy of Gairyism

The objective conditions that gave rise to the 13 March insurrection can to a large extent be explained by the singularity of Gairyism, the most despotic and wanton form of oligarchic rule to have emerged in the English-speaking Caribbean. Gairyism was in essence a species of Bonapartism.[1] In 1950 Gairy established the first trade union of agricultural estate workers in Grenada's history, the Grenada Mental and Manual Workers' Union (GMMWU), and led it in general strikes in 1951 and 1952. However, having risen to power on the wave of this proletarian awakening he rapidly shifted his political allegiance to a minority fraction of the big property-owning class. This was the group of black estate owners that had recently emerged in the island. To the extent that he defended the interests of this clique he served the ruling class as a whole, in that their exploitation of the working class and peasantry remained intact. It is this factor more than any other that demonstrates the speciousness of the cultural pluralist analysis of Gairyism which has been put forward by M. G. Smith (1965). For the characterization of Gairy as the representative of the 'folk' (the black masses) embroiled in a conflict with the 'elite' (the white estate owners) fails to explain why significant numbers of the 'elite' played important roles in successive Gairy administrations. Neither does it take into account the penetration of the 'elite' by black estate owners. Finally, such a methodology cannot elucidate why members of the 'folk' should undertake an armed insurrection against 'their' representative, and in this act receive the support of leading individuals from the 'elite'. Similarly, Singham's (1968) depiction of Gairy as a charismatic 'hero' with a magnetic appeal to the 'crowd' simply begs the question as to why his electoral support fluctuated so dramatically between 1951 and 1967 (he lost two Legislative Council elections) and why he subsequently had to engage in election rigging and repression to maintain his rule. And again, Singham's model provides us with no clue as to why the 'crowd' should want to overthrow 'their hero' and then dance in the street in celebration (!). These developments can only be understood if the historical and ideological affinity which Gairy maintained with the rural poor is placed in a context of class struggle. Gairy served the interests of the oligarchy, albeit inappropriately, and it was for this reason that he lost the support of the Grenadian oppressed.

The Bonapartist nature of the Gairy regime had its origins in the racial and cultural prejudice which the big property owners held towards him— the sort of attitudes which have been documented by Smith (1965). However, the narrow base of support which he enjoyed among the ruling class increasingly came to reflect a general dissatisfaction with Gairyism felt by broad sectors of the oligarchy. The basis of this disaffection was the colossal impediment to economic activity which Gairy's style of government engendered. As will be seen, corruption and personal government became a serious disincentive to the Grenadian capitalist class and it is this factor which explains the insurrectionary role played by the bourgeoisie in 1973–74 (it was the prime instigator of a mass protest movement which developed in opposition to independence under Gairy)[2] and the jubilation with which it greeted the 13 March revolutionary overturn.

The Grenadian economy and class structure under Gairy

The basic feature of the Grenadian economy under Gairy was its heavy dependence upon three agricultural products—cocoa, nutmegs and bananas—for the bulk of its export earnings. However, these earnings were insufficient to cover the growing costs of imports which provided a large proportion of the island's food requirements and virtually all the manufactured goods, raw materials and fuel used in the island. This gave rise to a persistent and growing balance of trade deficit on visible earnings which was balanced by inflows from the tourist industry, established in the early 1960s, and remittances from Grenadians resident abroad. Added to this structural dependence upon primary production for export and tourism, was the high per capita cost of government which a population size of around 100,000 persons entailed. Studies conducted at the time of the West Indian Federation (1958–61) showed that the political integration of Grenada with the neighbouring islands would not produce any spectacular savings in government expenditure, even in the cost of administration, and still less in the major recurrent expenditures of education, medical and public health service, agriculture and public works. In order for Grenada to get the same standard of social amenities as larger countries with an equivalent per capita income, she would have to divert a higher proportion of national income to government. This explains why, in spite of relatively high tax rates, Grenada had difficulty managing without grant-in-aid from the British government, and why the standard of services in relation to per capita expenditure was not much better (O'Loughlin 1968: 183–184).

Another result of small size was an extremely low efficiency of capital utilization in Grenada. A World Bank study published in 1976 suggested an 'incremental capital output ratio' (ICOR is an index used by conventional economists to measure the ratio of net investment to change in output) of 6: a very high figure for an economy such as the Grenadian (*Current economic position* 1976). However, the high ICOR was only partly due to diseconomies of scale and the high overhead costs of investment in infrastructure that could be spread over a small population. It was also a reflection of government policy and the unproductive utilization of investment funds, factors which will be examined shortly.

Table 9.1 shows the modest changes that took place in the structure of the Grenadian economy during the 1960s and 1970s. In the first place it highlights the continued importance of export agriculture whose contribution to GDP fluctuated marginally at around 33 per cent. The manufacturing sector remained stagnant, never having contributed more than 4 per cent to GDP. The favourable performance made by the construction sector in 1960 was the result of the initial impetus given by the tourist industry in the form of hotel building. The progressive diminution of this sector provides a graphic illustration of the inability of tourism to sustain this activity. However, the tourist industry did have a sustained impact on the services sector whose contribution to

TABLE 9.1 Grenada: sectoral origin of gross domestic product at current prices (1960–78) (EC$ m)

	1960		1965		1970		1975		1976		1977		1978	
	Value	%	Value	%	Value	%	Value	%	Value	%	Value	%	Value	%
Agriculture, fisheries and forestry	9.45	33.3	13.4	38.8	14.54	23.7	32.7	38.8	33.8	35.0	36.7	33.2	39.0	32.2
Mining and quarrying	—	—	—	—	—	—	0.1	—	0.1	—	0.1	—	0.1	0.1
Manufacturing	0.67	2.4	1.2	3.2	2.32	3.8	2.4	2.8	2.6	2.7	3.1	2.8	3.2	2.7
Electricity and water	—	—	—	—	—	—	1.7	2.0	2.0	2.1	2.1	1.9	2.2	1.8
Construction	4.34	15.3	3.07	8.9	8.91	14.5	2.1	2.5	2.5	2.6	3.0	2.7	3.6	2.5
Wholesale and retail trade	7.84[a]	27.6	4.37[a]	12.7	9.998[a]	16.3	9.8	11.6	11.2	11.5	16.3	14.7	16.7	13.8
Transport and communications	—	—	1.17[b]	3.4	3.43	5.6	4.7	5.6	5.4	5.6	8.1	7.3	8.2	6.8
Hotels and restaurants	—	—	1.05	3.0	1.8	2.9	2.4	2.8	2.6	2.7	3.7	3.3	4.7	3.9
Government services	3.95	13.9	4.65	13.5	11.76	19.2	14.3	16.9	21.3	22.0	20.5	18.3	26.3	21.9
General services	—	—	—	—	—	—	14.4	17.0	15.3	15.8	17.3	15.6	17.3	14.3
Dwellings	2.13	7.5	2.547	7.4	4.218	6.9	—	—	—	—	—	—	—	—
Finance	—	—	1.473	4.3	2.112[c]	3.4	—	—	—	—	—	—	—	—
Services and profession	—	—	1.68	4.8	2.196	3.6	—	—	—	—	—	—	—	—
Total	28.37	100.0	34.54	100.0	61.27	99.9	84.6	100.0	96.8	100.0	110.9	100.0	120.7	100.0

Notes: — [a] Includes services and transportation; [b] Does not include communication; [c] Includes insurance.
Source: Small farming 1980: 19.

GDP remained constant between 14 and 16 per cent. Wholesale and retail trade persisted as one of the most important sectors of economic activity, a corollary of the high import content of the economy and the preponderant role played by merchant capital. Finally, the growing importance of government services is also depicted.

Subsequent to the attainment of full independence under Gairy in 1974 the Grenadian economy went into reverse gear. It has been estimated that the disturbances of 1973–74 brought about a catastrophic 33 per cent fall in GNP between 1972 and 1974. A World Bank study published in 1979 pointed out that real per capita income was below the level it had been at the beginning of the decade (*Current economic position* 1979). An indication of the retrogression is provided in table 9.2. Of course, the enduring depression of the Grenadian economy was not solely due to Gairyism. It was caused by the obstacle to productive economic activity which is engendered by the relations of production in the island, and the particularly retrograde inflection which Gairy's style of rule put upon these relations. A consideration of agricultural production will make this point clearer. As has been intimated above, the Grenadian countryside was dominated by the big landholding class, some of whose members were the direct descendants of slave-owners. In 1972 farms under 5 acres accounted for 88.7 per cent of total land-holdings but comprised only 45 per cent of the total cultivable acreage.

TABLE 9.2 Grenada: real gross domestic product 1970–77 (selected years) EC$m (1970 prices)

	1970	1974	1975	1976	1977 (est.)
Real GDP	60	34	36	30	28

Source: Adapted from *Trinidad and Tobago Review* 1979: 6.

At the same time farms of 100 acres or more, which constituted 0.5 per cent of total landholdings, made up 49.2 per cent of the cultivable acreage (Jacobs and Jacobs 1980: 143). These figures understated the resources at the disposal of the oligarchy since they do not reveal the fact that the best land in the country was monopolized by the land barons while the peasantry was forced to eke out an existence on the infertile slopes of Grenada's mountainous terrain. The Grenadian peasantry comprised, to a large extent, semi-subsistence proprietors who owned their own land and employed wage labour on a modest and intermittent level. This seems to have mitigated the impoverishment of the rural inhabitants and given a marked element of stability to the society as a whole. For despite the significant decline in agricultural employment which took place during the 1960s and 1970s, the rate of urbanization remained low. Between 1960 and 1970, the net annual rate of rural–urban migration was only 0.6 per cent. Furthermore, data compiled on the age distribution of farm employment in 1975 found that a large proportion of the island's youth were still found to be living and working in the agricultural sector (*Small farming* 1980: 10). Thus Grenada was somewhat out of line with most other Caribbean territories where a mass exodus from the countryside had swelled the environs of the chief urban centres and given rise to an acute social crisis.

Nevertheless, the Grenadian peasant did experience many of the problems that faced his Caribbean counterpart. Firstly, there was the widespread incidence of parcelling and subdivision of holdings. This was largely a consequence of the system of joint inheritance (cf. Brierley 1974: 91) and the importance which is attached to gaining land in a former slave society. Holdings in the 0.4–6 hectare category comprised on average 2.38 fragments (*Small farming* 1980: 25). Excessive fragmentation of holdings impeded agricultural production in a number of ways. These included the high degree of land wastage caused by the superfluous number of footpaths and fences, the added costs incurred from the time and expenses involved in shifting inputs from one plot to another, the increased burden of supervision, the problems involved in developing adequate drainage and irrigation systems, the difficulties of applying advanced farming techniques and technological and chemical inputs, and the added risks of praedial larceny in a society of rural deprivation.

Secondly, though the Grenadian peasant traditionally provided a considerable proportion of the island's agricultural produce—63 per cent of nutmegs, 30 per cent of bananas, 50 per cent of cocoa, 85 per cent of food and vegetable crops, 93 per cent of sugar cane—he or she faced considerable problems in obtaining credit to develop operations. The Grenada Agricultural and Industrial Corporation disbursed an insignificant number of loans to small farmers and the organization soon became a major casualty of government corruption. The requirements of the foreign-owned commercial banks—Barclay's International, Bank of Nova Scotia, Canadian Imperial Bank of Commerce and Royal Bank of Canada—were such that the majority of the small farm population were unable to utilize their facilities. The constraints upon the peasant were further exacerbated by the domination of the internal marketing system by a few large trading firms whose interests lay in food importation. The absence of guaranteed markets for domestic agricultural produce made the peasant dependent upon export crops, for which there existed stable marketing organizations. Finally, the Grenadian peasant received an increasingly smaller share of the actual receipts from export agriculture. Brizan (n.d.: 10) has calculated that whereas in 1970 nutmeg growers received about 87 per cent of the total receipts, this figure dropped to 60 per cent in 1977. He has also estimated that in 1969 and 1976, 89.5¢ and 91.0¢ per dollar accrued to millers and manufacturers respectively.

The big estates in Grenada were owned mainly by oligarchs who had some historical connection with the island. There was never any large multinational corporation operating vast acreages as in many of the other Caribbean islands. However, many of the estate owners were absentee landlords who held substantial interests outside the island. As a result of this, and also the low levels of land tax, a considerable proportion of these estates remained idle. On the basis of the 1961 census statistics, Ferguson found that over half the area in farms over 500 acres was left uncultivated (1974: 96). This was in spite of the land shortage and land hunger that prevailed among the peasantry (cf. Thomas *et al.* 1968: 66). The bit estates were also characterized by low levels of technology and the use of cheap labour. A *Financial Times* survey conducted in 1971 concluded:

... the planting elite is not noted for its progressive ideas: estates are still run on primitive lines and the average plantation worker is a sullen individual whose job is a social stigma. A change in the system could well do some good. (FT 25 August 1971).

The oligarchy's control over society was effected principally through its domination of the three main agricultural marketing organizations— the Grenada Co-operative Nutmeg Association, the Grenada Banana Co-operative Association and the Grenada Cocoa Industry Board. These were statutory bodies that had exclusive powers to buy the entire crop they represented, market it and, after deducting an operating commission, pay producers according to their output. The participation of the peasantry in the associations was minimal. The associations made very little contribution to the development of export agriculture and served to buttress the economic and political interests of the oligarchy. For example, it was not until 1966, nearly twenty years after its formation, that the board of directors of the Nutmeg Association made its first financial contribution to research into nutmeg production. As the associations were perceived by Gairy to be a threat to his rule he disbanded the three elected boards in 1969 and 1971 and replaced them with nominated members of his choosing. He also introduced a bill to prohibit the Nutmeg Association from transferring its funds to Barbados, which was the oligarchy's response to Gairy's encroachments. At around the same time Gairy invoked the further wrath of the big landowners by promulgating a land settlement scheme, 'Land for the Landless'. Under this programme the government acquired around twenty-seven of the smaller and less fertile estates in the island. Landowners sold their estates to the government because of fear of takeover, increasing labour costs and the difficulties in getting labour to work on the land. However, the net effect of the policy was to reduce the amount of land in productive use. Among the reasons for this was the fact that some of the land acquired was non-productive; and of those lands that were actually distributed most were sold in very small lots, in some instances to previous tenants and squatters. In some cases the lands had no clear boundaries or titles, thus making both payment and development quite difficult. By withholding compensation to those landowners he disliked Gairy used the scheme as a political weapon. It also served as a basis for patronage. The overall effect of Gairy's caprices was to reduce drastically the confidence of the remaining estate owners in agricultural production. Since these owners held decisive economic and ideological influence over society as a whole the consequences were quite pervasive.

Gairy's land reform programme was facilitated by the progressive shift away from agricultural production in favour of tourism, which significant numbers of the oligarchy had embarked upon since the early 1960s. By 1971 the Grenadian capitalist class owned ten of the fifteen principal hotels that had been established in the island and played an important role in services, such as yachting. However, the largest hotels and the best resorts were in the hands of foreign capital (FT 25 August 1971). The Grenadian tourist industry was a very high-class operation, and most of the hotels were small and exhibited a high ratio of staff to guests. The industry was also characterized by a significant amount of excess capacity. In 1977 bed occupancies averaged 26.5 per cent and room occupancies about 45 per cent; the latter rose to a high-season figure of 75–80 per cent and fell to a low-season figure of 20–25 per cent (*Current economic position* 1979: 16). The overwhelming majority of visitors to Grenada were cruise-ship passengers who spend much less money than stay-over visitors. The economic impact of tourism was also constrained by the high leakage of visitor expenditure into imports, which in 1976 was put as high as 50 per cent (*Demographic and economic trends* 1976: 62). Thus tourism further increased the high import content of the economy. In addition, the tourist industry led to a substantial growth of real estate. A large number of foreigners built holiday and retirement homes in some of the most congenial parts of the island and this gave rise to a dramatic increase in land prices and speculation. A substantial proportion of good agricultural land either shifted to, or was reserved for, private residential development. The effects of Gairyism on the tourist industry was equally devastating. The 1973–74 unrest and the image projected of Gairy as a ruthless despot caused a dislocation of the industry from which it did not recover until 1978.

The acute inertia and dependence of the Grenadian economy was to a significant degree fostered by the preponderant role played by the comprador bourgeoisie. The pre-eminence of this class was cemented by the lending policies pursued by the foreign-owned commercial banks operating in the island. In 1977 bank loans made available to the distributive trades sector amounted to over EC$15 million. At the same time loans to agriculture, manufacturing and tourism totalled EC$6 million, EC$2 million and EC$4 million respectively (*Grenada statistical abstract* 1979).

The Grenadian bloc of dominant classes, then, was basically a fusion of the oligarchy and the comprador bourgeoisie and had significant interests in tourism and real estate. It was also tied to imperialism by its comprador activities. The three largest companies in the island— Jonas Browne and Hubbard (Grenada) Ltd, Geo. F. Huggins and Co. (Grenada) Ltd and W. E. Julien and Co. Ltd—were listed as engaging in almost identical operations. These included the retailing and distribution of building materials, food, household appliances and motor vehicles, acting as agents for multinational insurance agencies and shipping lines, and serving as tour operators for the tourist industry. L. C. Rahmdanny and Sons provides the best example of a merchant house that also had substantial interests in land (Grenada Chamber n.d.).

Turning to the other end of the social structure, the Grenadian proletariat was composed of the semi-proletarian masses of the countryside who combined own-account work with wage labour on the estates, urban public sector workers and those employed in the services sector. The relatively small scale of Grenadian estate production and the considerable dearth of manufacturing enterprises gave rise to a particularly atomized labour movement. A survey completed in 1977 identified 120 manufacturing units, of which more than half were cottage industries with fewer than five employees. The largest manufacturing employer was the brewery with seventy-six permanent jobs, although the largest concentration of workers (apart from the estates) was to be found on the docks (*Current economic position* 1979: 19). As is the case throughout the Caribbean, the proletarian stratum in Grenada evinced a high degree of fluidity. An unemployment rate of 50 per cent under Gairy gave this phenomenon an added dimension.

To conclude this section on the Grenadian economy and class structure under Gairy it is necessary to consider the specificities of Grenada's insertion into the capitalist world market. The attainment of independence brought about an important switch in the sources of financial assistance made available to the Grenadian government and capitalist class. Direct assistance from Britain was supplanted by the lending agencies of the EEC, UN, IMF and the Caribbean Community (Caricom). Under Caricom, and its predecessor Carifta, a notable modification in Grenada's external trade relations took place with imports from Trinidad and Tobago, the most dynamic economy in the grouping, growing to occupy 24 per cent of total imports in 1979. The corresponding figure for the UK, Grenada's biggest trade partner, was only 1 per cent higher at 25 per cent. While the imports from Trinidad and Tobago were made up mainly of oil and petroleum products, a substantial proportion consisted of manufactured goods. However, under the Caricom Rules of Origin the total amount of 'local value added' in the production of these goods need not have exceeded 50 per cent, and due to the operation of the Basic Materials List (a list of raw materials not produced in the region but which were conferred 'local origin' status in order to protect light manufacturing industries) would have been a far smaller proportion of this. Thus Grenada's growing trade with Caricom served merely to mediate the island's dependence upon the imperialist metropolis. Moreover, the most important institution in Caricom specifically devised to promote the economic development of Grenada and the other Less Developed Countries, the Caribbean Development Bank (CDB) adopted a somewhat complicated and bureaucratic list of procedures which made it difficult for Grenada to gain access to its resources (Payne 1980:

40–44). And of course, the level of corruption under Gairy did little to expedite matters. In 1977 the CDB refused to lend Gairy's government any money under the Small Industry Credit Scheme due to 'inadequate managing and accounting practices' (*Current economic position* 1979: 20). In the same year, foreign governments and international agencies pledged EC$21.8 million to Grenada, only EC$2.8 million of which was actually taken up due to inefficiency and malpractices. Because of the failure to pay constitutional levies, Grenada was, in the last year under Gairy, on the verge of losing its vote and participation in bodies such as the UN, UNESCO, WHO and the University of the West Indies (Coard 1979). It should again be pointed out that because of the lack of domestic savings, combined with an abnormally high level of public sector consumption and taxation, the great bulk of capital spending in Grenada came from these regional and international sources. The drying up of these funds therefore signalled the termination of what little economic development had taken place.

The revolution

The NJM and the 13 March revolution

The NJM came into being in March 1973 under the impact of the Black Power movement in the US and the armed liberation struggles in southern Africa and after some ten years of home rule in the larger English-speaking Caribbean territories had served to highlight the contradictions of formal independence. The early politics of the NJM was shaped by the context in which it was formed, as was portrayed in the party's 1973 manifesto. This document was fundamentally a radical petty bourgeois democratic programme whose principal themes were 'genuine independence', 'self-reliance', 'anti-Gairyism', and 'anti-imperialism'. At the level of the economy the manifesto was somewhat utopian in that it proposed a series of anti-capitalist and anti-imperialist measures, without considering either the class dynamics which might be unleashed by such policies nor the effects which they might have in terms of the programme as a whole. Thus it advocated the 'complete nationalization of all foreign-owned hotels as well as foreign-owned housing settlements', while at the same time, oblivious to the possibility of dislocation, it envisaged an immediate and massive expansion of the tourist industry. Similarly, the proposal that 'a National Importing Board should be set up to import all goods into the island' displayed little appreciation of the struggle this might entail with the comprador bourgeoisie—a struggle that would not only have deleterious consequences for tourism but would also engulf the whole society, given the hegemony exerted by this class. With regard to the question of agrarian reform the document was decidedly reformist. It advocated negotiations with estate owners to set up co-operative farms and called for the provision of cheap credit and technical equipment to poor peasants. The manifesto also laid great stress on the procurement of funds from regional and international agencies which, it was argued, would look upon Grenada in a more favourable light once the trauma of Gairyism had been anaesthetized:

It is worth noting that in a recent report by Sir Arthur Lewis, the President of the Caribbean Development Bank, he pointed out that some $ million [sic] were awaiting Grenada and a few other islands. The money is available but cannot be touched because of the corruption and lack of planning existing in these islands (Manifesto n.d.: 7).

It was at the level of political institutions that the most far-reaching proposals were made. The manifesto called for the establishment of a provisional government which would be made up of 'representatives of workers and unions, farmers, police, civil servants, nurses, teachers, businessmen and students'. The task of this interim administration was to set up 'people's assemblies' which would send delegates to a National Assembly. The National Assembly would constitute the 'government of the land', and the system of 'people's assemblies', it was maintained, would 'end the deep division and victimization of the people found under the party system' and 'involve all the people in decision-making all the time' (Manifesto n.d.: 9). This conception of popular power had its origins in the writings of C. L. R. James who had an important influence upon Caribbean radicals during this period. The principal thesis that James advanced with regard to this question was to suggest that the vanguard party had been superseded by historical events and that the proletariat could, acting through workers' councils, spontaneously transform society (cf. James 1969; Gomes 1978).

The imprecision of the early NJM concerning the question of class and foreign domination was reflected in the role it played during the events of 1973–74. It formed a de facto political alliance with the bourgeois opposition, restricted its agitation to a campaign to remove Gairy and at no stage sought to transform the crisis into a proletarian offensive against the dominant class as a whole (cf. Jacobs and Jacobs 1980: chapter 4; Dabreo 1979: chapters 3 and 4). After the upheavals the organization developed close ties with the official communist movement in the Commonwealth Caribbean (the Workers' Party of Jamaica and the People's Progressive Party in Guyana) and the Castro leadership, and these ties and other events led to an evolution of the NJM's politics away from Black Power and Jamesianism. It began to function as a vanguard party and its connections with the bourgeois opposition were increasingly explained in orthodox Stalinist terms, invoking the necessity for a broad alliance against 'neo-fascism'. During the 1976 general elections the party entered into a political bloc—the People's Alliance—with the two anti-Gairy bourgeois parties. These were the Grenada National Party (GNP) and the United People's Party (UPP). The NJM formed the largest component of the Alliance and captured three of the six seats won by it in the elections. This gave the party greater access to national and international platforms from which to conduct the struggle against Gairy. At the same time it succeeded in widening its base of support beyond the circle of urban intellectuals, students and disaffected youth to which it was initially confined. Against a background of sustained anti-government ferment, NJM members won executive positions in a number of urban trade unions—the Commercial and Industrial Workers' Union, the Civil Service Association, the Grenada Union of Teachers and the Bank and General Workers' Union. In the countryside party activists undermined Gairy's GMMWU. As the NJM made further headway among the island's youth and working class the GNP and UPP vacillated in their opposition to the regime. They capitulated to Gairy's red-baiting of the NJM and the People's Alliance in practice became a dead letter. In any event, these organizations played no role whatsoever in the 13 March insurrection which was carried out by some forty combatants of the NJM.

The NJM and the transition to socialism

The 1973 manifesto made no mention of the word 'socialism'. Since the revolution, the NJM's views on this matter have become clearer. In an interview published in the theoretical journal of the official communist movement, *World Marxist Review*, Bishop explained:

We see this revolution as being in the national democratic stage. We are an anti-imperialist party and government and we believe that the process we are involved in at this time is an anti-imperialist, national democratic socialist orientated stage of development (Bishop and Carrera 1982: 84).

This notion of 'socialist orientation', which has also been designated the 'non-capitalist path of development', has been put forward by several NJM leaders (Coard n.d.; Strachan 1979) and is expounded at great length in the 'official' account of the revolution written by Jacobs and Jacobs (1980). An exposition and refutation of this theory has already been made in the introductory chapter to this book. What concerns me here is to demonstrate that far from creating the objective conditions for an ultimate transition to socialism, as the theory asserts, NJM policies are basically designed to modernize and restore rationality to the dependent capitalist system. And in so doing they are deepening the island's subordination to those classes and institutions whose interests are antithetical to the cause of socialism.

Class character of the Bishop regime

The political regime born of the 13 March overturn is to a certain extent consistent with the proposals outlined in the 1973 manifesto. The People's Revolutionary Government (PRG), which commands all legislative and executive powers, is composed of individuals from a variety of occupational backgrounds. Of course, most of these persons are members of the NJM and carry out its policy. However, at least two members of the government can be said to be members of the bourgeoisie both in terms of their class background and the objective role they are playing in the political process. Lynden Rahmdanny, who is the director of the family company mentioned above and is a former president of the Chamber of Commerce, has been assigned a central position in the economic strategy of the NJM. He is the deputy Minister of Finance, chairman of the Cocoa Board, chairman of the National Commercial Bank (NCB), established by the NJM to galvanize domestic savings for developmental purposes, and a director of the Marketing and National Import Board (MNIB), another creation of the Bishop regime. Rahmdanny also plays an important role on behalf of the Caribbean bourgeoisie, having been elected as a member of the board of directors of the Caribbean Association of Industry and Commerce. The other prominent capitalist in the PRG is Norris Bain, who is a former member of the GNP and owns an important merchant house. He is presently the Minister of Health (*Caribbean Year Book* 1979–80; *Caribbean Monthly Bulletin* (CMB) April 1979). Other non-NJM members of the PRG include Dr Bernard Gittens, a medical doctor and president of the Grenada Council for Human Rights, and Sydney Ambrose, a teacher and another former member of the GNP.

The principal transformations carried out by the NJM at the level of state institutions are as follows. Legislation now takes place by the promulgation of 'People's Laws' which are announced over Radio Free Grenada and published in the official government gazette. These 'People's Laws' are basically amendments to the pre-existing laws of Grenada and have been designed to legitimize the events of 1979 and clear off the statute book most of the repressive and capricious legislation introduced by Gairy. The island's status as a member of the British Commonwealth has not been altered and the Governor-General who was appointed under Gairy, Paul Scoon, remains the titular head of state. However, PRG control over the Governor-General is effected by People's Law No. 18, which mandates the head of state to 'act in accordance with the advice of Cabinet'.

The changes that have taken place with regard to the judiciary are of a similar nature. People's Law No. 4 abolished the West Indian Associated States Supreme Court (WIASSC) in the island and established in its place the Supreme Court of Grenada. This consists of a High Court and a Court of Appeal and these are vested with the jurisdiction formerly enjoyed by the WIASSC. The Supreme Court is presided over by Archibald Nedd, the former WIASSC judge resident in Grenada. Most of the other judges in the island are also the same conservative figures who served under Gairy. However, People's Law No. 14 confers authority on the PRG to vary the number of judges of the Supreme Court and also gives the Prime Minister the power to advise the Governor-

General as to who shall be appointed judge. The grip of the PRG on the judiciary is further reinforced by the Privy Council (Abolition of Appeals) Law which (quite correctly) removes the right to appeal to the British Privy Council (People's Laws of Grenada; Burgess 1981). The *de jure* concentration of power in the hands of the PRG is finally buttressed by the People's Revolutionary Army (PRA), created by the NJM on the morrow of the revolution, and composed of numerous party militants and supporters who took part in the mopping up operations carried out against recalcitrant remnants of Gairy's security forces. Thus the NJM, the predominant organization in the PRG, is the determinant political force in Grenada today, and it is the class character of this party which provides the key with which to unlock the door to an assessment of the objective nature of the Bishop regime.

Globally, the NJM may be characterized as a 'revolutionary. petty bourgeois workers' party'. This seemingly contradictory formula is suggested in order to encapsulate the distinctiveness of the NJM's politics. In the first place, the party must be described as some sort of 'revolutionary' organization since from the very early days (1974) it cultivated an armed detachment and understood that revolutionary violence would be necessary to unseat Gairy. This was explained by Hudson Austin, the principal architect of the 13 March operation, in the Cuban-made film *Big revolution, small country* (n.d.). The reformism which the party evinced during the 1976 elections did not lead it to abandon an insurrectionary perspective. The 'petty bourgeois' aspect of the NJM stems from the class background of its leading personnel *and* the political programme which it currently espouses.[3] Of the nine NJM members who were designated posts in the original fourteen-member PRG (this figure was subsequently increased to twenty-three), three were barristers (Lloyd Noel, Kenrick Radix and Maurice Bishop), three held university and technical degrees (Bernard Coard, Unison Whiteman and Hudson Austin) two were public sector workers (Vincent Noel and Selwyn Strachan) and one was a locally trained teacher (George Louison) (CMB April 1979). It should be pointed out that some of these individuals can be characterized as petty bourgeois (if not bourgeois) in the full sense of the term in that they also have certain interests in property. For example, Maurice Bishop's father, Rupert Bishop, was a local merchant who made his money in Aruba, and Maurice Bishop presently owns an apartment block in a significant tourist area, Morne Rouge. Kenrick Radix, who is the Attorney-General and Minister of Legal Affairs, Agro-Industries and Fisheries, also has an important interest in real estate. Other members of the NJM, particularly those in the intermediate and lower echelons of the party, have modest landholdings.

Of more decisive importance, of course, is the *political programme* of the party. As we have seen, the 1973 manifesto was fundamentally petty bourgeois in its inspiration. The NJM's current usage of official communist formulae does not signify that it is now an orthodox CP. What one has here is a phenomenon which has been described by Gabriel in the case of Angola and the other revolutionary nationalist states of Africa (1978). That is, an attraction of the petty bourgeoisie towards certain tenets of official communism. The basically reformist and popular frontist policies pursued by the NJM in its early days are now couched in the phraseology of the CPs, but their content remains the same. The party's programme is still essentially one that is based upon an alliance with the local capitalist class. In a parallel fashion, the Castroist motifs, which also form part of the NJM's ideology, have simply been grafted on to the original political discourse. As we shall see, the Cuban model of popular organization, *poder popular*, has come to replace the Jamesian paradigm. Thus, the revolutionism of the NJM has been limited to the exigency of seizing state power, and is now confined to the arming of the masses in order to defend that power.[4] It has not entailed any substantive modification of the party's political platform. Finally, it is also necessary to lay emphasis on the 'workerist' nature of the party. In the first place, Grenada never developed any nationalist movement whatsoever. What one had was a movement *against independence under Gairy*, of which the NJM was perceived to be the principal protagonist. This was because of the energy exerted by the party in its mass campaigning and also the fact that it suffered the most tragic blows at the hands of Gairy's henchmen—Rupert Bishop was murdered and six leading NJM activists were brutally beaten. It is therefore very difficult to place the NJM in a taxonomy of nationalism. The term 'workers' party' is used here in recognition of the fact that the main organizational base of the party has been the public sector and service sector employees of the urban areas and that today it consciously seeks to expand and consolidate the mass organizations of the working-class and popular layers. The closest international political ties which the NJM has are with the Cuban workers' state, the Sandinista government in Nicaragua and the official communist parties of the Commonwealth Caribbean. The NJM is also a member of the Socialist International, but although this is significant in terms of the reformist nature of the party as a whole, the Cuban connection is far more important. In conformity with the party's overall programme, the NJM's relationship to the working class is fundamentally paternalistic and manipulative. Although the Bishop regime does at times call itself a workers' government the principal thrust of its policies is towards mobilizing the workers' movement as an auxiliary force with which to effect the moderate transformations it envisages. The economic power of the bourgeoisie and its political representation and influence on the state apparatus have not been broken.

As a 'revolutionary petty bourgeois workers' party', then, the NJM represents a new Grenadian Bonapartism. This is a Bonapartism of the petty bourgeoisie (cf. Löwy 1981) and despite the more rationalistic and democratic nature of the Bishop regime, it is in essence, like Gairyism, a mediated form of oligarchic rule. And as is always the case in such situations, the Grenadian ruling class see it as such. The 13 March overthrow was hailed by the Chamber of Commerce as 'a glorious opportunity for Grenada to build something new and different in the Caribbean' (*Express* 2 April 1979). Some weeks later Angela Smith, president of the Employers' Federation, sought to allay the fears of the Caribbean bourgeoisie at the annual general meeting of the Caribbean Employers' Federation. She pointed to the presence of a Rotarian and a former president of the Chamber of Commerce in the PRG and denied allegations that there were Cubans involved in the armed takeover (Caribbean Employers' Federation 1979). Since then a number of antagonisms have developed between the NJM and these organizations. However, these differences have their basis in disagreements over style (the spectacle of Grenadian teenagers walking around the place carrying rifles is somewhat anathema to these people, and Angela Smith specifically does not think that the fact that Vincent Noel is the Interior Minister and also the president of two important trade unions 'makes for good industrial relations') and the reluctance of certain capitalists to embrace the PRG's developmental efforts wholeheartedly. Indeed, there is also a conflict of interests but only to the extent that the interests of the petty bourgeoisie and those of the oligarchy/comprador bourgeoisie are not identical.

Economic and social policies

During the first three years of the revolution the PRG increased recurrent revenues by raising company tax, closing off a number of tax loopholes, imposing new licence fees on large and medium traders and introducing a withholding tax of 25 per cent on any profits sent out of the island by the subsidiaries of foreign companies. Total government recurrent revenue increased from EC$45 million under Gairy in 1978 to EC$53 million in 1979, EC$59 million in 1980 and EC$54 million in 1981 (January–February).[5] With the increased revenues, the PRG carried out a number of reforms in favour of the working class. Some 30 per cent of Grenadian workers were exempted from paying income tax, increases were made in family allowances and an entirely new educational allowance was formulated to help offset the costs incurred by the parents of children studying abroad, free secondary education was introduced and free uniforms and schoolbooks provided for the lowest income families, and finally health facilities were greatly improved and free basic physical and mental health care made available. Since the performance of the agricultural sector and wholesale and retail trade was somewhat desultory during this period (see table 9.3) and therefore government revenue from import and export duty (the main source of recurrent revenue) registered no appreciable increase, these measures led to current account deficits of EC$526,000 in 1979, EC$600,000 in 1980 and well over EC$6 million in 1981.[6] Thus all capital expenditure during this period came from loans or grants made available by either the foreign-owned commercial banks or international agencies and foreign governments.

TABLE 9.3   Grenada: economic growth (1979–81) (%)

	1979	1980	1981
Real GDP	2.0	3.1	2.0
Agriculture, fisheries and forestry	3.0	− 1.5	5.0
Manufacturing	3.4	− 3.3	n.a.
Electricity and water	5.5	5.5	0.4
Construction	n.a.	208.0	14.5
Wholesale and retail	2.9	2.0	− 2.2
Hotel and restaurant	n.a.	− 6.2	− 6.0

Note: n.a. = not available.
Source: *Report on the National Economy* 1982: 6.

The sums made available were quite impressive[7] and have provided a vindication of the NJM's claims to be able to mobilize funds from these sources. Capital spending increased from EC$8 million in 1978 to EC$15 million in 1979, EC$32 million in 1980 and EC$67 million in 1981.

The largest slice of these funds was earmarked for the construction of the new international airport at Point Saline. Table 9.4 shows the sources of funding for this project in 1981. It shows the large amount of untied finance provided by Cuba and also the important role which is being played by Arab capital. It also highlights the negligible sums that have been raised locally. Since then EC$6 million in assistance (i.e. loan) has been obtained from the lending arm of the EEC, the European Development Fund (EDF)—despite a US-inspired attempt to prevent funding—and a credit line of some EC$28 million has been provided by the British company, Plessey Airport, which was given the contract

TABLE 9.4   Grenada: expenditure on new international airport, Point Salines (1981)

	EC$m
Grants (external)	27.1
Algeria	0.9
Syria	3.2
Cuba: materials	9.0
labour	14.0
Loans (external)	10.8
Libya	10.8
Total external	37.9
Local finance	0.8
Total	38.7

Source: *Report on the National Economy* 1982: 22.

to supply communication and electronic equipment (*The Weekly Gleaner* (TWG) 30 September 1981; FT 20 May 1982). The airport project is central to the plans of the PRG to boost the island's tourist and agricultural industries. It also has strategic implications. The existing airport at Pearls cannot accommodate large aircraft and does not have lighting facilities for night landing. Travellers to Grenada have therefore been obliged to trans-ship in either Trinidad and Tobago or Barbados and this has deterred potential tourists from visiting the island, and enabled the governments of these two countries to exert political pressure on the Bishop regime. The other main economic projects initiated by the PRG include the planned feeder road construction programme, which will facilitate the transportation of agricultural produce, schemes for the rehabilitation and development of cocoa, sugar and bananas, and other technical and infrastructural programmes designed to assist the agricultural and fishing industries. The funds for these projects have come from a variety of sources including the IMF, World Bank, CDB, EDF, OPEC, Iraq, Algeria, Syria, Canada and the USSR. The EDF and the foreign aid institution of Canadian imperialism, the Canadian Industrial Development Fund (CIDA), have been the most important donors.

The economic strategy of the PRG is based upon the mobilization of international sources of finance in order to develop the productive capacity of Grenada. The class structure of the island is to remain intact while the predominant role played by local and foreign capitalists is to be modified but not eliminated. Grenada is also to remain a member of the Caribbean association of neo-colonial states, Caricom, which the NJM perceives to be an important avenue for economic integration. However, the PRG's ability to secure capital inflows from foreign governments and lending agencies has given it a certain leverage which it is using to cajole the private sector into becoming more productive and efficient. Only in this sense is it possible to go along with the description of the NJM's development strategy which has been made by Bernard Coard, the Minister of Finance, Industry and Trade:

As Comrades are aware, we are developing our economy on the *mixed economy model* [emphasis in the original]. Our economy as a mixed economy will comprise the state sector, the private sector and the co-operative sector. The dominant sector will be the state sector, which will lead the development process (*Report on the National Economy* 1982: 64).

Table 9.5 shows how far the NJM needs to go before the state sector is 'dominant'. In terms of overall economic activity (the figures on consumption) the private sector continues to play the decisive role. It is only in the sphere of domestic investment that the state sector is today predominant, and this is merely an illustration of the parasitism and unproductive character of the Grenadian capitalist class. A consideration of the principal areas of government intervention will show how economic policy is subordinated to the logic of capital accummulation.

The PRG's efforts in the agricultural sector have been centred around

TABLE 9.5   Grenada: selected national accounts data

| | EC$ million | | | % changes | |
	1979	1980	1981	79/80	80/81
Gross domestic expenditure	232.9	324.3	352.8	39.2	8.8
Consumption	205.4	267.0	272.4	30.0	2.0
Central government	53.9	59.6	66.0	10.6	10.7
Private sector	151.5	207.4	206.4	36.9	−0.5
Domestic investment	34.5	46.3	77.9	34.2	68.3
Central government	30.5	41.5	73.8	36.1	77.8
State enterprise	1.2	2.1	2.1	75.0	0
Private sector	2.8	2.7	2.0	−3.6	−25.9
GDP (at current prices)	211.5	254.5	284.2	20.3	11.7

Source: *Report on the National Economy* 1982: 9.

improving the performance of the twenty-five estates which it inherited from the Gairy regime. These estates occupy only 4,000 acres out of a total farm acreage of 34,243 acres. The PRG has so far only succeeded in reducing the operating losses of these estates from EC$3.75 million in 1978 to EC$800,000 in 1980 (*Grenada is not alone* 1982: 100–101). As regards the vast acreages that remain at the disposal of the oligarchy (probably around 15,000 acres) government policy has been particularly moderate. It was not until mid-1980, following a workers' rebellion on the River Antoine estate owned by the de Gale family (see pp. 216–217) that the question of agrarian reform was broached. The PRG set up a National Land Reform Commission to investigate the availability and potential use of land which had remained uncultivated over a long period of time. The commission held public hearings in each parish, calling on people to give evidence of idle and unused lands, and soliciting pledges of land for lease or purchase from big landowners. Some 7–8,000 acres of idle land were identified, which represents nearly 25 per cent of the total farm acreage. The PRG then went on to promulgate a Land Utilization Law which gives the Minister of Agriculture the power compulsorily to lease idle lands of any estate over 100 acres. The law also includes clauses to prevent the breaking up of the big estates into small unproductive lots (*Grenada Bulletin* vol. 3, no. 1). While it is too early to draw any balance sheet of the effects of this law one can already see that it is essentially devised to induce the oligarchy into becoming productive capitalist farmers. It clearly does not amount to an expropriation and contains a number of provisions that can be used by landowners to prevent the acquisition of their property. In this respect it is similar to the ill-fated Land Lease Project of the Manley regime (see chapter 4 of this book).

In April 1980, with a fund of a mere EC$1 million the PRG launched the National Co-operative Development Agency (NACDA) which was charged with implementing the 'idle lands for idle hands' programme by stimulating the formation of agricultural co-operatives. Nineteen months later George Louison, the Minister of Agricultural, Rural Development and Co-operatives, reported that twelve agricultural co-operatives had been set up (there are a further eleven co-operatives involved in fishing and handicrafts), involving 160 youths working on 146 acres of land (*Grenada is not alone* 1982: 99). Given that this is considered to be the main programme designed to alleviate unemployment the number of people and the acreage involved are quite inadequate. The PRG itself admits that there are some 7,000 persons unemployed in the island. This represents a quarter of the labour force, and of those unemployed, 65 per cent are below the ages of 16–25 (*News Release* 2 July 1982). The PRG has thus failed to eradicate mass unemployment—even though it has reduced it from 50 per cent under Gairy—and the agrarian policies it has adopted so far would seem to offer no real solution to this problem. The Cuban revolution has shown that rural unemployment can be eliminated within the space of one year. However, in order to accomplish this the expropriation of the big landowning class and other rural exploiters is a prime necessity (cf. Boorstein 1969: 130).

In keeping with the 1973 manifesto, the PRG has greatly increased credit facilities available to the Grenadian peasantry. The MNIB also provides a market for non-traditional crops. However, the MNIB merely competes with the existing trading firms and its role in terms of foreign trade is restricted to importing a few basic commodities (sugar, rice, cement and powdered milk) and identifying external markets for local produce (*Free West Indian* (FWI) 13 February 1982). The distributive trades sector is still dominated by local merchants and the marketing of nutmegs, cocoa and bananas has been unaffected. In fact, by restoring the elective principle to all three of the statutory marketing boards these bodies have in practice been handed back to the oligarchy. The MNIB too, it should be pointed out, is run by local capitalists. The Grenadian peasant still suffers from the extreme parcellization of his holdings and land hunger. An indication of the failure of the PRG qualitatively to transform the plight of the rural poor is provided by the Agriculutral Census conducted in August 1981. It was found that praedial larceny and labour shortage were the two most important problems facing farmers (*News Release* 11 November 1981). Grenada's unemployed youth are still obliged to steal agricultural produce as a means of survival and refuse to work for low wages on the fragmented plots of the peasants or the 'primitive' estates of the oligarchy.

The PRG's respect for private property is equally apparent in the tourist industry. The manifesto pledge to nationalize all foreign-owned hotels has been abandoned and the Bishop regime has devoted its attention to developing the three hotels and four restaurants which it appropriated from Gairy. The largest hotel in the island, Holiday Inn, which accounts for 33 per cent of all hotel rooms (50 per cent of the first-class ones) and contributes over 50 per cent of the foreign exchange earned from visitors each year, is still owned by foreign capital. The remainder of the eighteen hotels and six guest houses are still in the hands of local and foreign capitalists (*News Release* 28 October 1981; *Grenada is not alone* 1982: 35). Thus the reference which Dr John Watts, the founder of the GNP and presently the chairman of the Grenada Tourist Board, has made to Grenadian tourism being similar to the tourist industries of Eastern Europe and Cuba, is quite misleading. State ownership of the principal means of production in these countries ensures that tourism is integrated into an overall economic plan. The profits from the industry remain inside the country and the leakage of visitor expenditure into imports is insignificant.[8] The reluctance of the NJM to take full control of the Grenadian economy will make it difficult for *it* to effect such a transformation. In fact, Watts's interviewer, Sebastian Clarke, pointed out that the Grenadian hotels were still selling imported fruit juices, despite the abundance of tropical fruit on the island (*West Indian Digest* November 1980: 60–61).

Apart from the question of ownership there are a number of other problems with regard to the NJM's attitude towards tourism. The current world recession is having a serious impact on the tourist industry throughout the Commonwealth Caribbean and the number of visitors to the region has dropped substantially. In particular, the weakening of the US dollar has induced American tourists to take their holidays closer to home and in countries where the currency is linked to that of the US—i.e., the Bahamas, Puerto Rico and the US Virgin Islands. Added to this general trend has been the adverse publicity which Grenada has attracted in the North American media—most of which, of course, has been consciously fostered by forces hostile to the revolution. These factors led to a 15 per cent drop in the number of stay-over visitors in 1981 and the replacement of the US by the countries of the Caribbean as the principal source of stay-over visitors to Grenada (see table 9.6).

TABLE 9.6 Origin of stay-over visitors to Grenada (1981)

Country or region	%
Caribbean	33.0
US	21.0
UK	11.5
West Germany	11.2
Canada	8.0

Source: *Report on the National Economy* 1982: 27.

A greater diversification of the Grenadian tourist industry has in fact been consciously promoted by the NJM as part of its campaign to foster a 'new type tourism'. However, the tourist arrivals from the Caribbean have not been sufficient to replace the visitors lost from the US. And given the high-class nature of the Grenadian industry it is very difficult to see how they could. These difficulties must raise doubts as to the viability of the NJM's pursuit of tourism as a locomotive of economic growth. For not only does the industry continue to suffer from significant excess capacity but even with the completion of the new airport there is very little likelihood that Grenada will be able to compete with Barbados, which has a greater variety of tourist accommodation and resources. Grenada is also going to face serious competition from Jamaica, whose tourist industry has recently been given special treatment by US imperialism, and Cuba, which is now the cheapest holiday resort in the whole Caribbean basin. As regards the expansion of the tourist industry the new international airport project could well turn out to be a great white elephant (FT 19 September 1981, 6 December 1980).

The NJM's solution to the domination of the island's banking system by foreign capital has been the establishment of the NCB. The facilities for this operation were obtained by purchasing the local branch of the Canadian Imperial Bank of Commerce, which had announced its intention to cease operations. According to Bernard Coard the NCB is now the second largest bank in Grenada (Barclay's is first), has deposits exceeding EC$40 million and is now lending more to agriculture and other productive areas of the economy than any other bank operating in Grenada (*Grenada is not alone* 1982: 42). The NCB is in the hands of prominent capitalists and the basic strategy seems to be to displace the foreign banks by competition rather than nationalization. This represents a further retreat from the 1973 manifesto. The foreign banks themselves are undeterred by the NJM's monetary policy. As a 'local bank manager' (probably from Barclay's) explained to Lucien Pagni:

... we enjoy a large freedom and good relations with the government. There are no restrictions on foreign transactions and the new bank set up with state participation is only a fellow-competitor as far as we are concerned (*Courier* 1980).

Indeed, the foreign-owned banks are playing a significant role in the NJM's development programme, having, for example, provided most of the money for the PRG's house repair scheme. And of course, most of the finance received from international agencies and capitalist governments is deposited with Barclay's Bank. Like the foreign-owned banks, the NCB maintains a clearing account with the East Caribbean Currency Authority, the monetary authority of the Caricom sub-group of East Caribbean states. Thus, Grenada continues to have no foreign exchange reserves of its own, no central bank and thus no direct means of government management of internal credit. The island is still exceptionally open to trends in the capitalist world economy.

The NJM's agro-industrialization policy is based upon a combination of state initiatives and incentives to private businessmen. Government enterprises have so far been the most important with the PRG having established for the first time in the island's history the following range of products: saltfish, smoked herrings, nutmeg jellies, and the juices and nectars of mango, soursop, tamarind and other fruits (*Grenada is not alone* 1982: 44). The private sector is being prodded in the direction of industrial development by the greater availability of loans being made available by the Grenada Development Bank (GDB) and a new taxation measure introduced in 1982. The taxation law was designed to increase private sector investment by providing for big reductions for businesses which reinvest profits in Grenada. In June 1982 Bernard Coard expressed satisfaction with the increase in the number of requests for loans made to the GDB. According to Coard, requests for loans jumped from EC$291,000 in 1978 to EC$1.6 million during only the first five months of 1982. The areas of intended investment include the expansion of the local bottling plant, the repair of hotels, the construction of a garment factory and other factories for making jams, jellies, macaroni and spaghetti (*News Release* 2 June 1982).

In summary, it is clear that while the economic policies of the Bishop regime have given a new stimulus to the Grenadian economy and brought about important improvements in living standards, they have not challenged the basis of oligarchic rule and foreign domination of the island. These policies are in conformity with the main body of the 1973 manifesto. The retreat of the NJM from some of the radical aspects of this programme provides a confirmation of its idealistic character. The proposals to nationalize foreign-owned hotels, banks and insurance companies have proved to be incompatible with an economic strategy based upon securing inflows from capitalist governments, lending agencies and foreign firms, and which accords pride of place to tourism. In order to mobilize funds from the international bourgeoisie the NJM has been obliged to temper its revolutionary ardour and provide an economic (i.e. capitalist) climate in which these resources could be made available. In like manner, the NJM's departure from the manifesto pledge to establish a state monopoly of foreign imports is the result of a more sober appreciation of the realities of Grenadian capitalism. As has been pointed out, the tentacles of the Grenadian ruling class extend into the three main areas of the island's economy—agriculture, tourism and distribution. The NJM's disinclination to expropriate merchant capital is part and parcel of its strategy of alliance with the bourgeoisie, and since in Grenada the comprador bourgeoisie = the oligarchy = the hotel owners and tourist operators, the NJM has refrained from moving into any of these areas. Grenada thus provides a further illustration of the dictum proffered by Trotsky that in the countries of belated capitalist development any strategic alliance with the bourgeoisie could only be made at the expense of the agrarian and anti-imperialist tasks of the revolution.

At this stage it is necessary to clear up a certain misconception which has appeared in certain quarters. The recourse to capitalist governments, lending agencies and banks for development expenditure does not in and of itself determine the class nature of a given society and neither does it necessarily entail the subordination of society to the law of value. What is decisive is the amount of capital involved in relation to the size of the economy in question and the role which this capital plays in the economic life of that society. In Grenada today economic activity is dominated by the private sector and the vast majority of central government and departmental expenditure consists of funds borrowed from the local and international bourgeoisie. This is not the case in the USSR, or the 'People's Democracies' of China, North Korea, Vietnam, Cuba. It is true that Western capital plays a growing role in most of these countries, and has, due to gross·miscalculations on the part of the privileged castes which govern most of them, added an element of disequilibrium (alas Poland!). However, these societies are cushioned from the more debilitating effects of world capitalism (i.e. mass unemployment and crises of overproduction) by collective ownership of the means of production, central planning and a state monopoly of foreign trade. None of these things exists in Bishop's Grenada.

Relations with the masses

The most celebrated aspect of the Grenadian revolution has been the impetus that it has given to the self-organization of society at large. Due to legislation and initiatives spearheaded by the NJM there has been massive growth in the organizational strength of trade unions, the National Women's Organization, youth and student bodies, parish councils and the militia. Working-class representatives sit on the boards of management of state enterprises and profit-sharing is being encouraged. Although most of these bodies and institutional arrangements are obviously led by NJM activists and sympathizers, they appear to enjoy a certain amount of autonomy from the PRG. There is no denying the fact that in terms of mass participation in the political process, trade union and women's rights, Grenada under Bishop is the most democratic country in the English-speaking Caribbean (cf. *In the spirit of Butler* 1982). The tirades of Messrs Tom Adams and Edward Seaga etc. concerning the alleged totalitarianism of the Bishop regime are sheer hypocrisy. None of these leaders enjoys anything like the same amount of popular support that is evident in Grenada today, while Tom Adams has recently provided an illustration of what he means by 'democracy' by paying homage to the terroristic regime of Forbes Burnham during a visit he made to Guyana in January 1982 (cf. *The Nation* 29 January 1982). Nevertheless, it is necessary to adopt a sober attitude to the popular institutions which exist in contemporary Grenada. As has been explained above, all legislative power resides in the hands of the PRG. The parish councils and other mass organizations simply deliberate on and suggest amendments to options which have already been chosen by the NJM leadership. Popular participation is also effected through mass rallies and demonstrations. In this respect there is a certain parallel with *poder popular* in Cuba and the organization of power which is currently espoused in Nicaragua. Now while it is plausible and correct to argue that given the novelty of the Grenadian process, its continued vulnerability to imperialist sabotage and the low educational and cultural level of the population, a move towards immediate proletarian rule is out of the question, one ought not make a virtue of necessity and elevate the present institutional forms into a model of socialist democracy. This criticism has been made by Weber with regard to the Sandinista regime and it bears equal relevance to Grenada (see chapter 5 of this book). The statements of NJM leaders and their supporters do not speak of the present arrangement as a transitional form which will be superseded by an ultimate devolution of power to the popular institutions (see in particular, *Grenada is not alone* 1982; Bain 1980; *Is freedom we making* n.d.). This represents a further retreat from the 1973 manifesto, which, despite the spontaneous way in which the question was posed, did lay down guidelines for such a transition. One should mention in passing the absence of genuine party democracy in the NJM itself—for example no party congress has been held since the revolution. A similar attitude should be adopted with regard to the banning of the island's principal bourgeois newspaper, the *Torchlight*, and the subsequent introduction of People's Law No. 81 which prohibits the production of newspapers apart from the government-owned *Free West Indian*. Considerations of space do not permit me to make a detailed examination of these measures. What can be pointed out, however, is that the PRG has still not published a media policy, despite a pledge to do so, which guarantees the right to freedom of expression and explains categorically that the abrogation of this right can be undertaken only in a number of specified conditions and for a determinate period of time (cf. *Caribbean Contact* August 1981).

A more decisive criticism concerns the limitations on proletarian democracy which are the inevitable concomitants of capitalist relations of production. There is a qualitative difference between the parish council system in Grenada and *poder popular* in Cuba, in that Grenada, unlike Cuba, is still a dependent capitalist country. And as is the case in all countries where capital holds sway, the PRG's ability to eliminate unemployment, improve the living standards of the masses and increase their political participation (which is what democracy is all about) is constrained by its respect for private ownership of the means of production. As we have seen, the PRG's policies consist of various measures designed to induce the owners of capital to become more productive and benevolent. But it is these owners who ultimately decide what is to be the fate of the country. Grenadian democracy is therefore a form of bourgeois democracy, albeit one with certain distinctive characteristics. For what has clearly been omitted from the agenda of the parish councils and other popular gatherings is the tremendous extension of democratic rights and popular control over society that could be brought about by an expropriation of the bourgeoisie and a redefinition of Grenada's relationship with the capitalist world market. And in the final analysis it is the refusal of the NJM to embark upon this path which constitutes the gravest danger to the embryos of popular control which presently exist. It is the very economic power of the bourgeoisie and the failure of the PRG to eliminate unemployment which is providing the basis for cynicism and a right-wing opposition to grow. And this will undoubtedly lead to even greater restrictions of democratic rights. This development has already occurred in countries such as Algeria, Ethiopia, Angola and Mozambique which underwent similar political transformations to that of Grenada.

Various leaders of the NJM have pointed to the peasant character of Grenadian society and the low level of class consciousness as a justification for their 'softly softly' approach. What these explanations fail to point out is that the growth of class consciousness is a dialectical interaction between an objective maturation of proletarian and plebeian disquiet and the conscious intervention of a political vanguard. Numerous studies of revolutionary upheavals in the Third World have laid stress upon the critical role played by leadership (see in particular, Wolf 1969; Alavi 1965; Petras 1978; Löwy 1981). The NJM has never organized a popular campaign against the big property-owning class as a whole and today its 'anti-imperialist' mobilizations are confined to denunciations of US foreign policy and expressions of solidarity with national liberation movements—worthy activities in themselves but wholly insufficient in terms of liberating the island from imperialist tutelage. The NJM currently uses the pretext of 'Gairyism' to create an ideological prop for its deification of private ownership of the means of production. As Bernard Coard proclaimed to the Chamber of Commerce 'with the revolution has come the end to the forceable seizure of people's property' (1979). Thus, in keeping with its intrinsic class character, the NJM today plays a Bonapartist role in the class struggle. This can be illustrated by a brief consideration of two events.

As previously mentioned, in February 1980 agricultural workers protesting about bad working conditions and low pay occupied the River Antoine estate owned by the de Gale family, one of the biggest landowners in the island. The NJM condemned this move and linked the workers' action to an alleged CIA plot. It also opposed the demand for the legalization of marijuana, which had been made by NJM and PRA members linked to the occupation, and dubbed the protesters 'marijuana capitalists'. Whether there was CIA involvement in these events or not two things are clear. First, having set up a commission of enquiry which more or less vindicated the workers' complaints, the estate was handed back to the de Gales. Second, there has never been any large-scale trafficking in marijuana in Grenada so the NJM assertion that the actions of these youths were 'diverting substantial areas of land away from agricultural production' was something of a red herring, especially when one considers the vast acreages which are idle. The objective nature of the NJM intervention becomes evident when one considers the letter sent to *The Times* by David de Gale on behalf of his family and his class:

... it is relevant to record publicly that when, in February 1980, our family estate was peremptorily taken over by a village commune and renamed 'The People's Collective Farm' government support was immediately forthcoming for the manager's protection and the estate was returned (eventually) to normal working.

It is by judicious, well regulated behaviour that Mr Bishop—like Mr Mugabe—hopes to transform his small nation into a homogenous structure of living communities (*The Times* 13 February 1981).

(The comparison with Mugabe is quite pertinent.) The second event concerns the Coca Cola bottling plant which is owned by W. E. Julien and Co., whose pre-eminence has already been mentioned. In August 1979 the workers at the factory went on strike to protest against the unfair dismissal of two workers. After the dispute dragged on for five weeks with management refusing to reinstate the workers, the PRG stepped in and took over the running of the plant in accordance with the workers' demands. In March 1982 it was announced that Julien's had resumed management of the factory and all funds which the PRG had collected during the two years of its control would be handed over to Julien's (FWI 6 March 1982).

An interrupted popular revolution

In a comprehensive and illuminating survey of revolutionary upheavals in the capitalist periphery in which he attempts to assess the validity of Trotsky's theory of permanent revolution, Michael Löwy advances the concept of an 'interrupted popular revolution' (1981). The chief characteristic of this genre of revolutionary transformation, he argues, is its failure to 'grow over' into a fully fledged socialist revolution and consequently its inability to resolve all three of the national democratic tasks which classical Marxist theory assigned to the bourgeois democratic revolution (i.e., national liberation, democracy and a solution to the agrarian question). He defines the interrupted revolution as follows:

... where the popular masses, workers and/or peasants burst onto the scene of history, smash the old political structures, but are eventually neutralized by bourgeois or petty bourgeois forces who usurp leadership and 'institutionalize' the revolution. Classic cases include: Mexico (1910–20) Bolivia (1952–5) and Algeria (1954–65) (Löwy 1981: 164).

Löwy identifies a group of countries (South Yemen, Afghanistan, Angola, Mozambique, Guinea Bissau, Ethiopia) which have recently undergone momentous upheavals but whose ultimate fate, he considers, remains to be arbitrated by history. These countries are characterized by a stated allegiance to Marxism and strong political and economic ties with the Soviet Union and Cuba. Grenada can therefore be seen as the latest entrant into this grouping of countries, which the official communist movement and its supporters consider to be embarked upon a path of 'socialist orientation' or 'non-capitalist development'. I have argued in this paper that the Grenadian process conforms to the scenario of the interrupted popular revolution and would suggest that a similar conclusion can be reached with regard to all the countries isolated by Löwy. Certainly

Gabriel, who writes from the same theoretical tradition as Löwy and the omission of whose work is therefore somewhat surprising, has provided sufficient data concerning the 'Marxist' states of black Africa (1978, 1980, 1981). Halliday and Molyneux (1981) have recently presented evidence with regard to Ethiopia which would again indicate a process of petty bourgeois usurpation. However, these authors prefer to leave the matter open-ended principally on the basis that the socialist proclamations of the Derg should be taken seriously. One can therefore see quite clearly the precise role which the theory of socialist orientation plays in the ideological armoury of the official communist movement, and the objective nature of Cuban intervention in the so-called non-capitalist countries. For Cuban policy in Grenada is fundamentally the same as its policy in Ethiopia and Angola.[9] It focuses on the *military* preservation of the Bishop regime. The Cuban leadership has endorsed the cosmetic changes that have been made in the bourgeois state apparatus and is vigorously promoting the illusory notion of a mixed economy and socialist orientation.[10] It is undoubtedly true that Cuban aid to Grenada is qualitatively and quantitatively superior to that received from any other source, and that this is inherently progressive in that it demonstrates concretely to the Grenadian masses the non-rapacious and collectivist nature of Cuban society. It also entails certain risks for the Cuban leadership in that it is its intervention in Grenada and other countries of the Third World which remains the principal stumbling block to any normalization of relations with Washington—a move that would have important economic benefits to the Cuban state. However, the Cuban leadership, in tandem with the Soviet bureaucracy, is not prepared to bear the full economic and political responsibility which the birth of a new post-capitalist society in the Caribbean would entail. It is quintessentially a conservative influence on the Bishop regime.

This does not mean that Grenada in the hands of the workers and poor peasants would inevitably find itself bereft of any economic assistance whatsoever. One should remember that it was not the Soviet bureaucracy, nor indeed the PSP (the Cuban communist party), that told Fidel Castro to carry through the socialization of the Cuban economy. It is also evident that a major economic realignment of Grenada with Cuba and Eastern Europe would necessitate numerous political compromises, and would give rise to a certain amount of domestic upheaval. But such is the reality of world economy and world politics today and those who obscure this with talk of 'scientific stages of growth'[11] simply foster illusions among the Grenadian and Caribbean oppressed.

Finally, it is a truism to state that Grenada's size and natural resource endowment do not present ideal conditions for an economic transition to socialism. But there is no material reason why Grenada should not be able to feed itself (food imports still constitute well over 40 per cent of total imports and increased from EC$45.1 million in 1980 to EC$57.5 million in 1981), eliminate unemployment, develop authentic organs of proletarian rule and progressively raise the living standards of *all* its people. These are tasks that a socialist revolution in Grenada could accomplish.

NOTES

1 The term Bonapartism is used here and elsewhere in the text to describe a situation in which political power is based upon a relatively small fraction of the ruling class.

2 Information on the disturbances of 1973–74 is contained in Jacobs (1974).

3 Let me stress, at the outset, that the principal criterion I have used to characterize the NJM as a petty bourgeois party is its *political programme*. The sociological background of the leading personnel of a governing party is undoubtedly relevant in all cases. However, in a situation in which capitalist relations of production prevail and no steps have been taken to curtail the reproduction of these relations, this factor assumes an added significance. The experiences of Egypt and Algeria have shown that it is the petty bourgeois elements who occupy the state apparatus that have the most to gain from a process of dependent capitalist development. They become a new bourgeoisie. The chapter by Thomas in this book provides an examination of how this development has taken place in Guyana.

4 The establishment of a popular militia by the NJM, is, of course, a radical initiative. However, the militia is tightly controlled by the NJM, plays a limited and decreasing role in the political process, and does not stand in contradiction with the class nature of Grenadian society.

5 All figures in this section, unless otherwise stated, are taken from *Report on the National Economy* (1982)

6 The sharp jump in the current account deficit in 1981 was due to the fall in receipts from import and export duty and tourism.

7 Grenada has the largest capital development programme out of all the Less Developed Countries of Caricom.

8 This is not to suggest that tourism does not have its problems in these countries; it does. But they are of a different character. They are mainly to do with the stimulus that tourism provides to the black market and the deleterious consequences which it has for proletarian class consciousness, in the context of a higher productivity of labour in the imperialist metropolis and the administration of these countries (Eastern Europe) by a bureaucratic caste.

9 For a discussion of Cuban policy in Africa see Halliday and Molyneux (1981: 250–256), Gabriel (1978: 185–190) and Mestiri (1980).

10 Reports that the Castro leadership has been advising the FSLN in Nicaragua, and by implication the NJM, to maintain the private sector were contained in *FT Survey, Nicaragua* (FT 28 July 1980), *The Economist* (6–12 December 1980) and *Latin American Regional Reports— Caribbean* (5 December 1980). The Cubans published the book by Jacobs and Jacobs (1980) in which the thesis of 'non-capitalist development' is spelt out, and the Cuban film *Big revolution, small country* (n.d.) expressly refers to the NJM pursuing a 'non-capitalist path'. Finally, confirmation of all of this has recently been provided by Michael Manley (1982), who in spite of his proclivity towards obscurantism does appreciate the difference between a 'mixed economy' and a centrally planned economy.

11 In an out of hand dismissal of an earlier study which I made of Grenada (Ambursley 1982), Jacobs, who wrote the editorial introduction in the same publication, accused me of 'ultra-leftism'. Providing no information with which to substantiate this claim, nor even making a coherent response to the critique

Grenada: the New Jewel Revolution

I made of his analysis of the revolution, he again writes of 'the scientific necessity for stages of growth'. Perhaps his response to this essay will be a little more erudite. Another proponent of 'stagism' in Grenada is Gonsalves (1979). Finally, in an amazing exercise in sophistry, Clark (1980) has come to the conclusion that the Bishop regime does not really mean what it says when it talks about a mixed economy etc., and that what is taking place in Grenada is a socialist revolution. A similar methodology also seems to have informed the analysis of Martin (1982).

REFERENCES

Alavi, H. 1965, 'Peasants and revolution', *Socialist register*, pp. 241–277
Ambursley, F. 1982, 'Whither Grenada? an investigation into the March 13th revolution one year after', in S. Craig (ed.), *Contemporary Caribbean: a sociological reader*, vol. 2, Trinidad and Tobago, Susan Craig, pp. 425–463
Bain, F. J. 1980, *Beyond the ballot box*, St Georges, Grenada Publishers Ltd
Big revolution, small country, film made by El Instituto Cubano del Arte e Industria Cinematográficos
Bishop, M. and Carrera, J. 1982, 'Grenada has chosen its road: interview and afterword', *World marxist review*, vol. 25, no. 4, pp. 82–88
Boorstein, E. 1969, *The economic transformation of Cuba*, New York, Monthly Review Press
Brierley, J. S. 1974, *Small farming in Grenada*, Winnipeg, University of Manitoba, Department of Geography
Brizan, G. n.d., *The nutmeg industry: Grenada's black gold*, pamphlet
Burgess, A. 1981, 'Review of the laws of Grenada: March 1979–March 1981', *Bulletin of Eastern Caribbean affairs*, vol. 7, no. 1, pp. 20–25
Caribbean Contact August 1981
Caribbean Employers' Federation 1979, *Proceedings of nineteenth annual general meeting held in Jamaica on 25th, 26th, 27th April 1979*
Caribbean Monthly Bulletin (CMB) April 1979
Caribbean Year Book 1979–80, Caribrook Ltd
Clark, S. 1980, *Grenada: a workers' and farmers' government with a revolutionary proletarian leadership*, New York, Pathfinder Press
Coard, B. 1979, *Address by Minister of Finance, Mr Bernard Coard at the annual general meeting of the Grenada Chamber of Commerce*, 24 May
Coard, B. n.d., *Grenada: let those who labour hold the reins: interview with Bernard Coard of the revolutionary government of Grenada by Chris Searle*, London, Liberation & Class
Courier, The May–June 1980
Current economic position and prospects for Grenada 1976, Latin American and Caribbean Regional Office, World Bank
Current economic position and prospects for Grenada 1979, Latin American and Caribbean Regional Office, World Bank
Dabreo, D. S. 1979, *The Grenada revolution*, Castries, MAPS
Demographic and economic trends for the Eastern Caribbean 1976, United Nations Development Programme, Physical Planning Project, East Caribbean Region
Economist, The 6–12 December 1980
Epica Task Force 1981, *Grenada: the peaceful revolution*, Washington
Express 2 April 1979
Ferguson, T. 1974, 'Potential for increasing agricultural production in Grenada', in *Independence for Grenada: myth or reality? proceedings of a conference on the implications*

of independence for Grenada, Institute of International Relations, University of the West Indies, Trinidad and Tobago

Financial Times 25 August 1971; 28 July 1980; 6 December 1980; 19 September 1981; 20 May 1982

Free West Indian (FWI) 13 February 1982; 6 March 1982

Gabriel, C. 1978, *Angola: le tournant africain?*, Paris, Editions La Breche

Gabriel, C. 1980, 'In defence of the Angolan masses', *Review of African political economy*, no. 19, September–December, pp. 69–74

Gabriel, C. 1981, 'Y a-t-il un "modèle de partis léninistes" en Afrique noire?', *Quatrième internationale*, year 39, vol. 3, no. 5, pp. 71–78

Gomes, P. I. 1978, *The marxian populism of C. L. R. James*, Working Papers on Caribbean Society, series A, no. 1, Department of Sociology, University of the West Indies, Trinidad and Tobago

Gonsalves, R. 1979, 'The importance of the Grenadian revolution to the Eastern Caribbean', *Bulletin of Eastern Caribbean affairs*, vol. 5, no. 1, March–April, pp. 1–11

Grenada Bulletin vol. 3, no. 1

Grenada Chamber of Industry and Commerce n.d., *List of members with their main classified listings*, mimeo.

Grenada is not alone: speeches by the people's revolutionary government at the first international conference in solidarity with Grenada, November 1981 1982, St Georges, Fedon Publishers

Grenada Statistical Abstract 1979, St Georges, Government Printery

Halliday, F. and Molyneux, M. 1981, *The Ethiopian revolution*, London, New Left Books

In the spirit of Butler: trade unionism in free Grenada 1982, St Georges, Fedon Publishers

Is Freedom we making, n.d., St Georges

Jacobs, W. R. 1974, 'The movement towards Grenadian independence', in *Independence for Grenada: myth or reality? proceedings of a conference on the implications of independence for Grenada*, Institute of International Relations, University of the West Indies, Trinidad and Tobago

Jacobs, W. R. and Jacobs, B. I. 1980, *Grenada: the route to revolution*, Havana, Casa de las Américas

James, C. L. R. 1969, *State capitalism and world revolution*, Detroit, Facing Reality

Latin American Regional Reports—Caribbean 5 December 1980

Löwy, M. 1981, *The politics of combined and uneven development*, London, New Left Books

Manifesto of the New Jewel Movement for power to the people and for achieving real independence for Grenada, Carriacou, Petit Martinique and the Grenadian Grenadines n.d., pamphlet

Martin, M. 1982, *Volcanoes and Hurricanes: revolution in Central America and the Caribbean*, London, Socialist Challenge/Revolution

Manley, M. 1982, Interview with Michael Manley conducted by Winston James, London

Mestiri, E. 1980, *Les Cubains et l'Afrique*, Paris, Editions Karthala

Nation, The 29 January 1982

News Releases, Government Information Service, St Georges, Grenada, various dates 1979 – to date

O'Loughlin, C. 1968, *Economic and political change in the Leeward and Windward Islands*, New Haven and London, Yale UP

Payne, A. J. 1980, *The politics of the Caribbean Community, 1961–79: Regional integration amongst new states*, Manchester, Manchester UP

People's Laws of Grenada, St Georges, Grenada

Petras, J. 1978, 'Socialist revolutions and their class components', *New left review*, no. 111, September–October

Report on the National Economy for 1981 and the prospects for 1982. Presented by Bro. Bernard Coard, Deputy PM and Minister of Finance and Trade, People's Revolutionary Government of Grenada, St Georges, Grenada, 29 January 1982

Singham, A. W. 1968, *The hero and the crowd in a colonial polity*, New York, Vail-Ballou Press

Small farming in the Less Developed Countries of the Caribbean 1980, Caribbean Development Bank

Smith, M. G. 1965, *Stratification in Grenada*, Berkeley and Los Angeles, University of California Press

Strachan, S. 1979, Interview with Selwyn Strachan, *Intercontinental Press/Inprecor*, vol. 17, no. 42

Thomas, C. Y. *et al.* 1968, *Economic and social development of Grenada*, Institute of Social and Economic Research, University of the West Indies, Jamaica

Times, The 13 February 1981

Trinidad and Tobago Review May 1979

Weekly Gleaner, The (TWG) 30 September 1981

West Indian Digest November 1980

Wolf, E. 1969, *Peasant wars of the twentieth century*, London, Faber & Faber

TEN

The Changing Pattern of
State Control in St Vincent
and the Grenadines

Philip Nanton

The first part of this chapter examines the pattern of colonial economic and political repression in St Vincent and illustrates what may be called the transition from 'coercive' to 'incorporative' policies. These changes have involved the handing over of political and economic control to a local populist and middle-class elite, a change from colonial political domination to economic dependence on the metropolis and a greatly expanded role for the state.

In the second part of the study I pose the questions 'Is there a crisis of the state? Is it apparent at the economic or political levels? What form does the crisis take?' In seeking to answer these questions, I examine the extent to which those in command of the post-colonial state have reverted to new forms of established coercive policies. The conclusion reviews my argument and evidence that the expanded role of the Vincentian state has increased its instability and deepened its dependence on outside support.

The legacy of the plantation

Prior to 1951 the state in St Vincent was typical of a number of colonial states on small islands in the region. Essentially it served to maintain law and order, to preserve the political hegemony of the metropolitan power and to repress the labour force. This repression was effected in the interests of the planter class who governed in close association with the colonial authorities.

In fact, plantation society took longer to establish in St Vincent than in the other islands because the Caribs refused to give up their lands. Following two Carib wars (the first concluded in 1773 and the second lasting from 1795 to 1796) the Carib population was defeated, their lands expropriated and 5,080 Caribs banished to Ruatan (off Honduras). By 1829 St Vincent contained 98 sugar estates totalling 37,842 acres. The structure of the society mirrored the individual plantation. At the base was the mass of the slave population, numbering 20,025 in 1825. A small stratum of 2,845 free coloureds separated the slaves from the even smaller number of white planters and attorneys who numbered 1,301 (Shephard 1945). In 1848, only 12 of a total of 100 proprietors were resident on the island (Davy 1854); and by the end of the nineteenth century the bulk of cultivable land was in the hands of five owners. Further land concentrations occurred. In 1882 an estimated two-thirds of the island (some twenty-two estates) was owned by D. K. Porter & Co., while a further sixteen estates were owned by three other planters. Over the next half-century, the patterns of land ownership of the planters and small-holders moved in opposite directions. Whereas the planters managed to increase their average acreage from 392.1 in 1896 to 495.9 in 1961, the average size of smallholdings fell from 6.8 acres to 1.5 acres over the same period; with the total number of smallholders (with less than 10 acres) increasing from a low of 46 to 10,928 (see table 10.1).

TABLE 10.1   St Vincent: land concentration (selected years)

	10 acres		10–100 acres		100 acres	
	No.	Acres	No.	Acres	No.	Acres
1896	46	311	123	3,942	129	50,584
1946	n.a	1,056	n.a	77,578	n.a	22,114
1961	10,928	15,954	390	7,650	32	15,871

Note: n.a = not available.
Sources: Royal Commission 1897; *Census of Agriculture* 1946; 1961.

The declining fortunes of the smallholders placed them, in many respects, in the same category as other dominated classes. Indeed, 'small farmers', 'peasants', 'proletarians' or 'marginalized workers' often combine 'peasant' and 'proletarian' features as a number of Caribbean scholars have noted (Norton and Cumper 1966; Frucht 1967; Mintz 1974). In the context of St Vincent, I use the term 'agricultural labour' to describe the bulk of the rural work force, despite the fact that most rural labourers mix paid agricultural labour with land cultivation. The term is appropriate because although agricultural labourers hold a mixed status, they stand in opposition to the planters, both insofar as they regularly sell their labour power to the big landowners and because the agricultural labourer is unable to compete successfully for control of the remaining cultivable land.

The position of the agricultural wage labourer has long been precarious. As far back as 1897, when members of the Norman Commission visited St Vincent following the collapse of the sugar industry, they received 'an unusual number of letters and petitions alleging distress among the labouring class' (Royal Commission 1897: 53). The major causes of distress were limited employment and low wages. In evidence to the commission, one witness alleged that workers in agriculture were employed only eight to ten days per month and many were unable to earn even as little as 4 shillings a month. A deputation of estate workers complained that on some estates wages were withheld and at some estate shops debts were extracted before wages were paid. Prior to the commission's visit, wages had actually fallen and it was not until 1937 that a minimum wage was introduced, though this became the norm rather than the minimum on most estates. Two years later, a visiting commissioner noted that in St Vincent '1,000 people lived on charity and 400 on poor-relief grants while large numbers existed on intermittent earnings augmented by garden produce and wild food' (Orde Browne 1939: 154).

Between 1946 and 1978 the numbers of unemployed grew dramatically. Of a labour force totalling 22,773 in 1946, an estimated 4.4 per cent were unemployed. The proportion increased to 12.6 per cent of a labour force of 24,596 in 1960 (Shurcliff *et al.* 1967) and to 18 per cent of a total labour force of 32,050 in 1977 (Chernick 1978). The seasonal nature of paid agricultural employment leads to substantial numbers of employees being laid off between one crop and another. The number laid off can be as many as half of the employed labour force. On the twenty-four largest estates during the November to May 1958/59 crop season, for example, 6,000 people were employed on the land and a further 300 in the processing of agricultural products. During the slack period, however, employment fell to 3,000 and 100 respectively (*Census of Agriculture* 1958; 1959; 1961).

In the 1970s the possibilities of wage employment were further reduced by the planters, whose estates became more capital-intensive. In 1972, out of 24,405 people employed in agriculture, 15,729 were farm operators and their dependants, 2,004 were unpaid workers while only 6,672 were paid workers. Of these paid workers, 30 per cent were employed by plantations while 59 per cent were employed by smallholders. In the same year, the ownership of tillage and cultivating equipment was exclusively registered among those farmers owning 50 or more acres (*Census of Agriculture* 1972/73).

The adverse effects of land concentration on the smallholder have already been noted. In his study of the role of government in St Vincent's agricultural development from 1896 to 1961, Martin argues that the state has attempted to help the small farmer, but that its policies have been largely unsuccessful because of the *ad hoc* manner of state intervention. Land-settlement policies tended to be prompted only in response to a crisis, while efforts to increase incomes through agricultural research and extension have lacked co-ordination (Martin 1967). There is evidence to suggest, however, that there was more behind the failure to implement policies than ill luck or miscalculation. The attempts by agricultural labourers to obtain land have, rather, been frustrated by long-established policies favouring the large landowners. When the La Soufrière volcano erupted in 1902–3, for instance, the colonial authorities preferred to organize emigration to Jamaica for the dispossessed rather than initiate an equitable land-redistribution scheme. Again, when the first land-settlement schemes were organized in 1902 (supposedly for the unemployed landless labourers) they were allocated only the poorest lands characterized by steep slopes, soil exhaustion or an inaccessible location. The conditions attached to later settlements were an equal deterrent. Whereas by 1910 settlers were allowed a five-year period of grace before paying for freehold settlement, in 1932 no such terms were permitted and interest rates were doubled (Giuseppi n.d.). The post-1932 schemes simply failed to cater for the landless. Shephard (1945) illustrated that prior to 1933, 75 per cent of those who took up offers of land were already cultivators on their own account; in the post-1932 schemes only 11 per cent of allottees did not already own land, a pattern that later schemes also followed.

In attempting to reorganize the settlement schemes in 1945, the Administrator openly stated his preference for the estate system which he regarded as 'the most economic method of producing our main exports' (Gibbs 1947). In a like manner, the Land Settlement Board, which was designed to 'control, regulate and develop land settlement' operated the two estates it bought (Wallilabou and Richmond Vale in 1946 and Fancy, bought in 1961) as traditional plantations. In reality, therefore, the tenants were no more than labourers who were also allowed food gardens for an annual rental. In its 1963 report the board repeated its commitment to estate agriculture: 'For the majority of crops, the West-Indian estate system is more efficient than any other and thus desirable from every other angle except the political one' (Land Settlement Board 1963).

Coercion to incorporation: political changes

Colonial and planter interests thus effectively prevented the possibilities of an economic challenge by the labour force of the colony. The years 1951 to 1961, however, marked the start of an important period of change in the relationship of the colony to the metropolis which caused a decline in the overt political influence of the planters. The attainment of mass enfranchisement in 1951 and a change to local management of the colony budget in 1961 were key features of this period.

Prior to the first moves towards enfranchisement in 1925 and to its full fruition in 1951, rule by decree and co-optation were the two most marked features of the political process. The Governor, who was the effective ruler, was helped by a personally chosen Council which acted in an advisory capacity. Qualifications for nomination to the Council were, however, so high that they virtually excluded everyone but planters. Although in 1925 a minority of the council seats were open to election, until 1943 only those who owned 50 acres of land or one lot in town valued at £50 per annum qualified for membership of the Assembly. By 1945 the franchise qualifications had changed to either ownership of property valued at £100 or more, payment of rent of £12 per annum on property, payment of direct taxes of 15 shillings, or income worth £30 per annum. But for nomination to the Legislative Council, ownership of real property to the value of at least £500 or an income of £200 per annum were required (Moyne 1945: 379).

Members were effectively appointed to represent white planter and business interests: prior to 1925 the planters A. M. Fraser and L. L. Punnett served alongside the journalist and newspaper proprietor J. E. Sprott.

The introduction of the restricted franchise had little effect on this bias, as the 1925 Legislative Council still comprised five Colonial Office officials and four merchants and planters whose interests represented no more than 7 per cent of the colony's population (John 1979: 170).

Agitation for enfranchisement had started as early as 1919 when the Representative Government Association (RGA) was established. As an essentially black middle-class organization, the RGA was preoccupied with electoral change. When this was partly granted in 1925, the RGA won the only three seats that were open to contest, but soon declined when its founder, George McIntosh, established the first trade union and political party, the Workingmen's Co-operative Association (WMA), in 1936. With the departure of its founding member and the start of electoral reforms, the RGA was rapidly eclipsed.

Because the WMA was open to membership by rural and urban labour alike, its growth was rapid and within the first few months of its formation 4,000 members were enlisted: by 1939 it had a membership of 10,000. In the general election of 1937, the WMA won four out of the five available seats, a result which was repeated under a Labour Party banner in 1940 (John 1971).

The planters responded to the political challenge of the WMA by forming the Planters' and Peasants' Association (PPA) to fight the 1937 election. Whereas the WMA based its election campaign on land distribution, the PPA, led by the planter Eric Hadley, defended the inviolability of private property. The planters were defeated at the polls in 1937, 1940 and again in 1951. As the results of these elections indicated, the planters were unable to maintain their access to political power in open competition and on a popular front. With the help of the colonial administration, a variety of strategies were then pursued to maintain their political presence.

Despite its showing in the 1937 election, none of the elected WMA candidates was invited to hold nominated posts on the Executive Council, the Governor's advisory body where *ex-officio* and nominated planter members outnumbered elected members by 6:5. Planters thereby managed to retain control over nominated seats to the Legislative Council until 1961 when all seats had to be contested.

The arrival of a contested electoral system initially offered the electorate the choice between the populism of the People's Political Party (PPP) led by E. T. Joshua, who had made his name through his trade-union activities, or the more conservative middle-class leadership of the St Vincent Labour Party (SVLP) under the lawyer R. Milton Cato. Joshua had broken with the short-lived but grandly named political party, the Eighth Army of Liberation, and its trade union, the United Workers', Peasants' and Ratepayers' Union, after it had successfully defeated the WMA and the planters' New Era Party in the 1951 election. In order to establish his own trade-union credentials, Joshua interceded in issues about pay and conditions in the sugar industry and fought to have his trade union, the Federated Industrial and Agricultural Workers' Union

(FIAWU) recognized as the bargaining agent for sugar-industry employees. The planter management were unwilling to accept FIAWU and with the resulting deadlock strikes were called annually between 1951 and 1957. The strikes provided Joshua with the prestige of a radical, one willing to challenge the power of the planters. The direct benefits of these strikes were questionable as they were invariably broken without agreement being reached, but the electoral benefits accrued to Joshua's PPP, which grew in popularity. In 1954, the PPP returned three of the eight elected members to the Legislative Council. In 1957, 1961 and 1966 the PPP won convincing electoral victories (5–3, 6–3 and 5–4 respectively) against the SVLP.

At its inception in 1955, the SVLP was the only political party without a trade-union base in the West Indies. Its programme emphasized law and order and gradual constitutional change. This conservative outlook was maintained by a black middle-class leadership, most of their political contestants being drawn from a group of local professionals. The party's first vice-president, H. F. B. Davis, who was one of the early leaders of the RGA, was a merchant and hotel owner. The president, O. D. Brisbane, another former RGA leader, was also a merchant, while Cato, who was elected the political leader, was a barrister. In the 1979 election, five lawyers, two businessmen, an accountant and an engineer were among the thirteen SVLP candidates for election. As Gonsalves (1977) has pointed out, the SVLP has consistently played an anti-working-class role, particularly in the industrial relations crisis which brought about the closure of the sugar industry in 1962. On this occasion, the SVLP denounced the strikers as law breakers, accused Joshua and the workers of wrecking the economy and supported the planters and the police in their efforts to break the strike.

Kenneth John has argued that despite their different origins and styles, it is difficult to distinguish any significant differences between the PPP and the SVLP. While both parties presented themselves as 'labour' movements and thus claimed to represent the same constituency, they were both dominated by the patronage of planters and by the individual opportunism of their members. The lack of strong ideological differentiation is shown by the fact that in a six-year period between 1961 and 1966 (in a nine-seat legislature), the 'floor' was crossed at least eleven times (John 1971).

The pattern of two-party politics with the movement of individuals from one party to another became more complex with the growth of other political parties after 1972. In that year, the independent candidate and leader of the New Democratic Party (NDP), James 'Son' Mitchell, won the Grenadines seat, thereby gaining the balance of power between the PPP and the SVLP. After establishing an alliance with the PPP to form a government, Mitchell was rewarded with the premiership, while Joshua retained the post of minister of finance. However, Joshua soon resigned, claiming that his position was being undermined, and a vote of no confidence in the alliance government was passed.

Joshua's departure led to a good deal of political manoeuvring as the 1974 election approached (Duncan 1975). Among the developments was an agreement between Joshua's faction of the PPP and the now more powerful SVLP that candidates were to be jointly supported to ensure Mitchell's defeat. In the event, the SVLP was returned with ten out of the twelve seats. As part of his pre-election agreement with them, Joshua was given a post in the SVLP government. The other PPP seat was held by Mrs Joshua who, after the election, declared that she would sit in the opposition. With the support of the SVLP behind her, Mrs Joshua was appointed leader of the opposition. Duncan (1975) suggests that these bizarre developments were probably designed to reduce the effectiveness of Mitchell, whom Joshua identified as a radical threat to the more-established parties. In 1978 Joshua left the alliance, but this did not affect the significant majority held by the SVLP government.

Other newly established parties were also seeking alliances in a bid for power. The Democratic Freedom Movement (DFM) was formed from a nationalist and intellectual fringe-political group, the Educational Forum of the People (EFP). Other splinter groups from the EFP—the Organization for Black Cultural Awareness, the Young Socialist Group, and others —formed the core of a Marxist-Leninist party, YULIMO, which did not feel itself sufficiently strong to contest the 1974 election. By 1982 a total of seven political parties were in existence. Leaders of YULIMO and the NDP were manoeuvring towards an alliance, individual defections from opposition parties were again taking place, while the SVLP had lost at least one member to the opposition (*The Vincentian* 18 September 1981; 5 February 1982). The SVLP was, however, firmly in control as a result of its victory during the 1979 election when it won eleven of the thirteen seats.

Coercion to incorporation: economic dependence

Whatever the vagaries of local political alliances and divisions, the political life of St Vincent is firmly constrained by the country's high level of economic dependence on the metropole. The pattern of dependency has, however, changed. Britain has continued to meet the growing levels of budgetary expenditure and has also institutionalized market protection for the banana industry. This development has greatly extended the role of the state which, as I shall argue, has produced its own dilemmas.

In the colonial period, a major concern of the administrators who controlled the finances of the colony was to maintain a balanced budget. Between 1925 and 1944, total expenditure was $9m (£1.9m) and total revenue $9.3m (£2m) (Gibbs 1947: xii). Until 1953 there was no demand for direct-grant aid to the colony, for deficits that accrued were eased by the Colonial Development and Welfare Fund. After 1955 budgetary deficits were met by grants, which more than doubled between 1955 and 1956 to meet an expanding government service and increased wages and salaries.

Although in 1961 the responsibility for the island's finances was placed under local control, the effective result was an increase in external financial dependence. In 1969 a Mission Report from the University of the West Indies noted that for the period 1960–68, internally generated revenue grew at an annual average rate of 5.9 per cent while total government expenditure grew at 8.2 per cent (UWI 1969: 44). By 1968 over 42 per cent of total spending was budgeted to come from overseas aid.

Another important feature of increased dependence has been the change from an open economy to market protection. Sugar, arrowroot, cotton and bananas have each, in turn, risen to prominence as export crops and then declined. During the first half of the twentieth century, St Vincent attempted to remain competitive by shifting from one crop to another as prices for its produce on the market fluctuated (Spinelli 1973). After the 1950s, however, a pattern of monoculture emerged, with bananas becoming the island's economic mainstay. Banana exports grew from 2.9m lb in 1950 to 36m lb in 1957 (O'Loughlin 1967). By 1976 the banana industry was estimated to account for 60 per cent of the total value of St Vincent's exports and 50 per cent of the island's total economic activity. Most of the island's 6,000 banana farmers depend on this crop alone and growers with less than 10 acres account for 50.4 per cent of the acreage devoted to the crop. Another 5,000 Vincentians are employed indirectly in the industry (Banana Growers' Association 1977). The survival of the industry depends on two features over which there is no local control—British market protection and shipment and distribution by Geest Industries (WI) Ltd.

All bananas shipped to Britain are transported by Geest Industries (WI) Ltd, a subsidiary of Geest Industries Ltd. The price at which bananas are imported into Britain is determined through negotiation between the producers, represented by the West Indian Banana Association (WINBAN) and the shippers. WINBAN is bound annually by contract to supply all exportable bananas to Geest, the latter also accepting and classifying the bananas into various grades at the dockside. Geest, then, are in a strong position to determine the price paid to the grower. In 1976 a British Government Select Committee investigating UK trade with small countries noted of St Vincent that: 'It is not surprising to find that in this situation the consumer has benefited at the cost of the grower' (Select Committee 1976: xvii).

While the price to the producers is largely under Geest's control, the level of banana exports is protected by a trading agreement with Britain in which St Vincent, along with the other Windward Islands and Jamaica, have guaranteed access to the British market. Protection is afforded by the 'Dollar Area Quota', which ensures that bananas from the dollar area, i.e. the larger and more efficient low-cost producers of South and Central America may enter the UK market only under licence. The Select Committee claimed success for this arrangement because of the relatively inexpensive nature of the scheme in supporting ailing economies like that of St Vincent. It was recognized that Britain paid more for the fruit and obtained a poorer quality than it could otherwise obtain, but that there were 'good overall political and social reasons for keeping up the banana trade from the Caribbean' (Select Committee 1976: 145).

The manifest and continuing dependence on the goodwill of the former colonial power has provided the ostensible reason for the government to intervene in many areas of the economy. Official government policies have included the stabilization of smallholder cash-crop production, the encouragement of crop diversification, import substitution and the operation of a policy of price controls on essential commodities. The sugar industry has also recently been revived, foreign capital has been encouraged to enter the tourist industry, while, since 1978, special efforts have been aimed at encouraging capital to enter the manufacturing sector. Cato, the Prime Minister, has argued that state intervention is required to provide 'centres of entrepreneurial activity'. He has also claimed that 'we want the private sector to continue, not merely to exist but to flourish' (*West Indian Chronicle* 1979: 25). As I shall demonstrate below, the general effect of this intervention has been to swell the state bureaucracy at the expense of growth in the productive sector, while also laying the groundwork for a crisis in the capacity of the state to manage the economy effectively or ensure political and social stability.

The nature of the crisis: economic pressures

Despite the complex patterns of political conduct and the increased economic dependence on Britain, there is little indication of a crisis in the sense of a profound rupture or qualitative change in the political and economic life of St Vincent society. Economic and political developments since 1976 appear to support this view. The government appears to be popularly elected and embarked on a substantial public-investment programme in a small but confident mixed economy.

In recent years gross domestic product has increased from EC$59.8m in 1975 to EC$117.4m in 1979. During this same period, the contribution of the manufacturing sector quadrupled, though admittedly from a low base of EC$4m to EC$16m. Government participation in the economy in 1980 accounted for 60 per cent of a public investment sum totalling EC$100.7m. In 1978 and 1979 the government obtained higher levels of overseas aid than in previous years of the decade. Tourism, another indicator of stability, showed substantial growth in the late 1970s. From 1970 to 1975 visitors to St Vincent had averaged 15,000 per annum, but this figure increased to 17,177 in 1976 and by 1979 it had reached 42,000 (St Vincent Tourist Board 1980).

Appeals for foreign-capital investment were backed by an aura of optimism and stability. By 1980 six new foreign firms were being established, increasing the numbers employed in manufacturing from 1,400 in 1977 to 3,200, with prospects of a further 1,000 jobs expected to follow (Coopers & Lybrand Associates 1980). With a few reservations, World

Bank studies equally support this encouraging outlook. The 1979 World Bank Report indicated that the island's economic performance had shown an improvement since the period 1976–78. The World Bank identified St Vincent's poor resource endowment as the major factor inhibiting its medium- and long-term prospects. The World Bank's 1980 Report argued that the country is capable of maintaining an economic growth rate of 5 per cent per annum on the strength of its performance between 1975 and 1978 (World Bank 1980).

A number of contrary developments, however, suggest that it is necessary to be wary of these signs of optimism and stability. Widespread but ineffective economic intervention by the government, its heavy-handed response to the revolt in the Grenadines, the mushrooming of new political forces on the left and a growing fear of organized labour, all cast doubt on the assumed stability of the country, while the state itself shows a return to coercive policies in the form of repressive legislation and a concern to tighten and activate more aggressive local and regional security measures. Let me turn first to the mounting economic pressures affecting the performance of the government, dealing in turn with its ineffectual agricultural policies, the problems arising from the alliance with foreign capital and the difficulties of meeting its recurrent and capital expenditure.

Intervention in agriculture

The decline in direct political involvement by planters after 1961 has resulted in a loss of confidence in land ownership among this class. The increased political pressure on the planters, together with the declining receipts from agriculture, have coincided with their gradual movement into the retail and service sectors of the economy and an increased, but not wholly beneficial, intervention by the government in acquiring declining estates. I have conducted a survey on the fate of seventeen major estates belonging to landowners who held political influence in the 1950s. By 1979 various government administrations had bought 30 per cent of the total acreage of the seventeen estates comprising 14,125 acres. Some estates have been sold privately to local smallholders while others are being sold for residential and agricultural use.

Cato justified the SVLP government policy of land acquisitions as follows (Cato 1976):

In agriculture, there is no doubt that the large farmers, the so-called planter class, with a very few significant exceptions, have failed to make a proper contribution to St Vincent. The estates were acquired by their ancestors, but the children have either migrated or if they have not are not interested in cultivating their lands. It is therefore becoming necessary for government to take over these lands and try to develop them.

As I have previously argued, the advantages of these acquisitions for the smallholder and for landless agricultural labour are questionable.

Estates acquired by the government operated successfully for a time, but soon suffered neglect and economic losses. Wallilabou and Richmond Vale, together comprising 4,004 acres, were acquired in 1946 for £60,000. By 1971, when the St Vincent Development Corporation took over the administration of these two estates, they had a surplus of $51,495 and a cash holding of $54,068. But two years later, as a result of various party-political appointments, loss of equipment and inadequate management, deficits stood at $131,861 and $146,392 for Wallilabou and Richmond Vale respectively. As other examples I can cite the cases of the Fancy and Lauders estates. Fancy, bought by the PPP administration in 1961, was never broken up or reorganized on any official leasehold basis. The neglect of this estate led the residents of Fancy village to sub-divide the land among themselves and many now squat on the land without legal rights. Lauders (one-half of Union Estate), a family-owned estate totalling 1,686 acres before sale, was purchased in 1972 and, like Fancy, neglected. In 1981 the SVLP government attempted to institute a leasehold system but agricultural workers refused to co-operate and demanded the right to freehold ownership.

In all, the fate of these recent acquisitions has shown that government intervention has succeeded neither in raising production levels nor in releasing the energies of smallhold agriculturalists. The latter have acquired some land, at times illegally, and have been confronted with government agricultural policies that have proved to be an impediment to economic production, whether by the government's active participation or by its neglect.

The shortcomings of other recent innovations have also started to become apparent. The government-controlled Marketing Corporation was instituted to encourage diversification of crops and to stabilize the supply and price of smallholder crops to the market. Far from stabilizing the supply of produce during its first decade of operation in the 1970s, the corporation has presided over alternating gluts and shortages. Between 1974 and 1975, the production of sweet potatoes for export declined from 3.6m lb to 2.3m lb, but rose to 4.9m lb in 1976. This rise did not, however, represent the full growth in production as 'several thousand pounds' of sweet potatoes had to be bought and dumped by the corporation to prevent a collapse of the market. In 1975 the corporation had to intervene to save ginger growers who over-responded to high prices and shortages in the previous year. A glut of carrots in 1976 was followed by farmers refusing to grow carrots in 1979 as a protest over the low price offered to farmers by the Marketing Corporation (St Vincent Marketing Corporation 1975; 1976; 1977).

Between 1972 and 1977 the agricultural sector received a constant annual share of 3 per cent of total recurrent expenditure (*Estimates* 1973–78). In 1979/80 recurrent expenditure on agriculture totalled $1.5m. In contrast, capital expenditure on prestige projects to re-establish sugar-cane growing and a sugar factory, and to set up a new dairy-milk plant, took $6.9m and $1.5m respectively from a total of $16.7m set aside for capital expenditure on agriculture for 1979/80 (*Estimates* 1979/80). Yet these two projects have proved notably unsuccessful. In 1971 the Caribbean Development Bank (CDB) commissioned a study on the restoration of sugar in St Vincent and found that the industry was unlikely to prove commercially viable (CDB 1971). Nevertheless, in 1977 the CDB agreed to finance the project, estimated then to cost $11.8m over the first three years, on the grounds of its 'social soundness' rather than for its expected economic benefits (CDB 1977). In its first year, costs exceeded planned expenditure by $2m. After the factory became operational, no further accounts were published. As to the dairy, most of the raw materials for the plant need to be imported and the nutritional benefits of its produce are uncertain given the known high incidence of 'lactose intolerance' among black populations. Complaints about the products have been numerous, and again for the first two years of operation no accounts from the plant have been made public.

The state and foreign capital

Ineffective intervention by the state in local production has been paralleled by the dubious benefits conferred by the import of foreign capital. The PPP and SVLP governments of the 1960s both negotiated generous sale and lease terms to establish luxury tourist enclaves in the Grenadine islands (which are 'wards' of St Vincent). Mustique and Petit St Vincent were bought by foreign companies, while Mayreau, another in the Grenadine chain, is owned by a local landlord. Some 775 acres, 17.5 per cent of Bequia's 4,420 acres, are owned by one US company, Windward Islands Plantation Inc. Three of the five major hotels in Bequia are US-owned. In 1974 around 65 per cent of employment and over 70 per cent of hotel income was generated by ten foreign-owned hotels in St Vincent. By that year, foreign investment was estimated at $6m (Llewellyn-Davis 1974). Common features of the agreements to establish enclave enterprises included 12.5 per cent free share capital for the St Vincent government and the right to nominate one board member. The foreign companies obtained permission to import technically qualified staff and to repatriate profits. Mustique Company Ltd obtained the added advantage of being excluded from paying company tax as well as customs' duties for twenty years. A 99-year lease for Palm Island was agreed for a total rental of a mere $99.

The benefits of these developments have by no means all been positive for St Vincent. Although the industry was estimated to provide some 400 jobs in 1974, enclave tourism has exacerbated a dependence on imports and disrupted small communities to little local advantage. Since 1953 the St Vincent economy has carried an imbalance in its visible trade. In 1954 a gap of $1m existed between the value of imports and exports. In 1957 the Frampton Report laid the blame for this deficit on government expenditure on wages and salaries which put more money into circulation (Frampton *et al.* 1957: 81). By 1977 the trade gap had increased to $55.1m and, despite being a food-exporting country, food imports were the largest single import item, comprising 28 per cent of total imports. A major cause for the rise in food imports has been the attempt to meet tourist tastes and demands, a factor that has made the possibility of St Vincent feeding itself a remote prospect.

Bryden has argued that enclave tourism weakens other sectors of small economies because of its competition for scarce island resources. He has estimated that some 80 per cent of tourist expenditure is repatriated, thus providing little lasting benefit locally (Select Committee 1976: 156). Enclave tourism has also given rise to a number of social tensions on islands with permanent local populations. On most of these islands, housing and wages compare favourably with those on the mainland, but food costs are substantially higher. In Mustique, for example, locals who have been tenants for generations have to continue leasing their accommodation because the Mustique Company owns rights to the entire island. Locals are also denied burial rights and the right to give birth on the island (St Vincent Christian Council 1980) on the grounds that issuing these rights would lead to a permanently based local population which would create long-term responsibilities for the company and limit the possible range of sites for new housing developments and other projects. In Canouan in 1980, friction between local shopkeepers and the Martiniquan developers of a yachting marina became so intense when the developers set up a shop taking away trade from local residents that an outside investigation was deemed necessary (St Vincent Development Corporation 1980).

Other than in tourism, foreign capital has also become dominant in manufacturing. But between 1963 and 1972 growth in St Vincent's manufacturing sector stagnated. During these ten years the sector contributed 4 per cent annually to the island's GDP (Llewellyn-Davis 1974). But in 1978 a major change occurred when the services of a British consultancy were obtained to promote foreign capitalized investment in St Vincent. The result of 'marketing' St Vincent caused the manufacturing sector to more than double its contribution to GDP, increasing from $5.9m to $12.7m between 1977 and 1978.

The advantages offered to incoming foreign capital by the St Vincent government include low labour rates, company tax holidays for the first ten to fifteen years, duty-free raw materials and machinery, access to land for building and the entitlement to full repatriation of profits (St Vincent Development Corporation 1977). Even these concessions, however, were insufficient for some firms. Two companies, Maidenform and Bayliss Bros, persuaded the government to break its own minimum-wage legislation by demanding and obtaining a 'training rate' at 30 per cent less than the current statutory minimum wage.

At least two of the companies, Maidenform and Jamerican Inc., seem to have been persuaded to locate in St Vincent as much by the absence of US-quota restrictions on items assembled in St Vincent as by concessions offered by the St Vincent government. Under pressure from the US unions, the US Customs have enforced quotas on imports of selected items from offshore manufacturing locations, notably the Dominican Republic and Haiti in the Caribbean. Quotas on apparel and electrical goods are of particular concern to the companies involved. After having already established itself in the Dominican Republic, Maidenform was thus forced to seek a new location without such quotas, while Jamerican Inc. expressed a similar concern over the same restriction when applying to establish its plant in St Vincent. Bayliss Bros, another newcomer faced with increasing labour costs in Barbados, agreed to move to St Vincent only when the government proved pliable over minimum wages.

Overall, these factors suggest that the St Vincent government is in a weak bargaining position when it comes to influencing the arrival of foreign capital and will have little influence in retaining these companies should external conditions change or tax holidays expire. The generosity of the terms offered in both the tourist and the manufacturing sectors indicate the strength of pressure on the government to create employment, no matter how uncertain the prospects and/or how unclear the benefits of their presence.

The budgetary crisis

The manifest failures in supporting the agricultural sector, together with the limited returns from the encouragement of foreign capital, have deepened the difficulties of the government in meeting its expenditure. These difficulties are compounded by two further factors—the increased size of the government service in relation to the productive sectors of the economy and the increased reliance on Britain to meet capital and recurrent expenditure.

The swelling of the state bureaucracy can best be illustrated by comparing it with the agricultural sector. In 1942 agriculture accounted for over three times the value of St Vincent's government services (Gibbs 1947). By 1961 the agricultural sector had doubled its contribution in value, from $3.4m to $6.9m, but the value of the government-services sector had quadrupled, from $1.1m to $4.8m (*Development Plan 1965–70*). By 1966, 50 per cent of government expenditure was spent on civil-service salaries and personal emoluments (UWI 1969: 47), while by 1975 public administration had become the largest single sector in the economy, representing 22 per cent of a total GDP of $59.8m (World Bank 1980). The state bureaucracy is equally the largest single employer. In 1960, 1,600 civil servants were employed (Shurcliff *et al.* 1967); by 1978/79 the total had increased to 3,221 (*Estimates* 1979–80). This represented an increase from 6.4 per cent of the labour force in 1960 to 10.7 per cent of the labour force in 1978/79. In recent years, up to five new statutory corporations have been established, which have themselves spawned a para-statal bureaucracy.

The difficulties in meeting the increased salary bills are made worse by St Vincent's increasing reliance on overseas aid. While St Vincent has been in receipt of growing external aid in the form of recurrent and capital funds, there is no local influence over the relative quantities received. In 1969 inflows of recurrent and capital sums from Britain were of similar proportions, $2.1m and $2.9m respectively. From 1970 to 1979 cash inflows for recurrent expenditure were held down while capital receipts increased significantly. In 1972 and 1973, receipts for recurrent expenditure supplied by Britain totalled $1.2m each year. In the same two years, capital receipts were $3.4m and $4.3m respectively. These amounts represented 17.5 and 18.3 per cent of total budget expenditure. In 1979 capital expenditure receipts totalled $46.9m, of which Britain's contribution was $10.9m. Again in 1979, capital expenditure exceeded recurrent expenditure, and assistance of $3.7m was required to meet recurrent costs (*Estimates* 1970/71–1979/80).

This pattern of greatly increased capital dependence assumes that existing recurrent costs for depreciation, loan repayments, wages and other costs can be met by local revenue and that increased levels of capital aid can be productively utilized. The experience of the last twenty years suggests, however, that these requirements cannot be easily met. Table 10.2 shows local revenue as a percentage of recurrent expenditure for selected years from 1960 to 1979. Only in one year, 1978, did local revenue meet recurrent expenditure. However, between 1978 and 1979 capital expenditure increased from $29.7m to $47.3m, increasing the likelihood of continued shortfalls in required recurrent funds.

TABLE 10.2 St Vincent: local revenue and recurrent expenditure for selected years (EC$'000s)

	1960	1965	1970	1975	1978	1979
Local revenue	3,872	5,429	10,450	21,334	32,368	39,420
Recurrent expenditure	5,869	8,025	13,183	23,894	31,322	43,166
1 as % of 2	65.9	67.5	79	89		91.3

Sources: Estimates of St Vincent 1960; 1965; 1970; 1978; 1979.

The problems produced by these shortfalls in recurrent expenditure were graphically illustrated by Sir Bruce Greatbatch, the head of the British Development Division in Barbados, who stated:

In the Eastern Caribbean we have to consider the acute difficulties which these small states face through having to cover all the trappings of a state ... it is difficult sometimes to appreciate how desperately acute the budgetary problems are in the small associated states. I personally elsewhere have never seen anything like this. Literally the situation is such that the extension worker has not got any petrol to put in his Land Rover to go out and look at a farm because the vote has run out, and the hospital has not got the drugs because there is not money to support it. There is a very acute shortage of recurrent funds (Select Committee 1976: 17).

Insufficient cash to meet the wage demands of the numerous public servants has, as I shall show, provided the cause of labour unrest and has directly contributed to recent efforts to introduce more repressive legislation to circumvent their demands.

The nature of the crisis: political challenges

The crisis at the economic level consequential on state intervention in the agricultural, manufacturing and para-statal sectors has been paralleled by the growth of a significant political opposition on the left, an increase in labour unrest and, on one of the Grenadines, a revolt directed at the government. These political challenges are described in turn, together with the nature of the government's response.

Behind the 1979 election

The election of 1979 appeared to give the SVLP a landslide victory, but the formal result concealed the development of new forces on the left. The election was fought between four political parties, the SVLP, the PPP, the New Democratic Party (NDP) and the left alliance of the United People's Movement (UPM). The SVLP won eleven seats, while the NDP won the remaining two. Three features were significant in the election —the PPP was defeated as a political force having failed to win a single seat, the SVLP appeared to dominate the political arena and a new challenge by the left in electoral politics took the form of the UPM alliance.

The three political parties which comprised the UPM were (a) ARWEE, which was described as 'a workers' and peasants' organization from the rural areas' (much of its support came from the Georgetown area of the island); (b) the People's Democratic Movement (PDM), decribed as 'the democratic socialist party led by politically aware professionals, workers and businessmen' (this organization was essentially the old DFM which had fought the previous election in 1974 with little success), and (c) the Youlou United Liberation Movement (YULIMO), described as 'a working-class party which fights for the cause of the working people' (UPM 1979: 2).

Formed in 1974, YULIMO became active in support of organized labour and a critic of the establishment through its newspaper, *Freedom*. Its leadership was, at first, partly influenced by the American Black Power styles of the late 1960s (some adopted 'African' names) and by the race-conscious language of black America. Others adopted a pro-Soviet stance, defending Soviet and Cuban policies and the recent Grenadian revolution in public debate, in *Freedom* and in the mainstream newspaper, *The Vincentian*. YULIMO is led by the Marxist lawyer and former university teacher Ralph Gonsalves. The party became a sufficient irritant to the SVLP government to provoke intermittent state harassment: police raids on homes and arrests of some leaders were documented in *Freedom* (28 July 1977). Occasional attempts were made to dismiss leading members who were in public employment.

The UPM contested the election by arguing the need for land reform, by opposing large-scale land ownership and foreign capital interests, by demanding closer control over the private sector and by arguing for the development of a co-operative sector in the economy. At public meetings, its attempts to raise support (directed mainly at young people) emphasized that the UPM was free of the corruption to which other parties had succumbed when in office.

But the UPM failed to win a single seat in the election. One reason for this was that the alliance had been formed primarily as a convenience. This became apparent, for example, over the difficulties encountered in choosing a leader: at first the General Secretary of YULIMO, Renwick Rose, was announced; later Ralph Gonsalves was declared the electoral leader of the alliance. Both YULIMO and the PDM continued to issue their own newspapers and it was an open secret that Parnel Campbell, one of the leaders of the PDM, was unenthusiastic about the alliance. Soon after the election the alliance was dissolved, though ARWEE and YULIMO stayed together under the name of YULIMO. Although the UPM failed to win a seat in the election, the party obtained 13.4 per cent of the vote (as against the SVLP's 53.6 and the NDP's 27.1 per cent), faring slightly better than the DFM had done in the 1974 election.

The SVLP's electoral result was also helped by the sudden eruption of the La Soufrière volcano which started on 13 April 1979. In pre-election addresses, Cato made much of the international support that his government commanded and of the 'special relationship' St Vincent maintained with its 'friends' in the region, particularly Trinidad and Barbados (two countries that had helped in relief work and that were approached for help with rehabilitation loans). Cato also identified St Vincent's 'special friends' Canada, the United States and Great Britain. Their relief efforts, which included dramatic air lifts of some refugees and regular visits by ships, were presented as signs of tangible support which the SVLP was able to tap when in need. There was also the threat that less aid would be forthcoming should St Vincent take the path of Grenada; a revolutionary trajectory with which the UPM was labelled.

The other major advantage accruing to the SVLP was its opportunity to lavish expenditure on the independence celebrations. As part of an independence aid agreement with Great Britain, total aid receipts increased to 47.3 and 56 per cent of the 1978 and 1979 budgets. These amounts represented substantial increases on earlier budgetary aid which, in 1973 for example, had been as low as 18.3 per cent of the budget. An early election, brought forward by six months, cashed in on these events and greatly contributed to the SVLP's eleven-seat victory.

Nevertheless, despite its apparently clear electoral success, nearly 32,000 people (or 47 per cent of the electorate) did not support the

SVLP and approximately 38 per cent of the electorate failed to vote. The combination of the low poll and pre-election developments apparently helped the SVLP maintain its dominance, but with less support than would be expected given the advantageous turn of events. Apart from the new electoral challenges, other signs of dissent became apparent including the development of labour unrest on the mainland and the threat of secession caused by neglect of the Grenadines.

Labour unrest

Labour disputes have arisen around two issues: government delays in agreeing new contracts with public employees and the unwillingness of employers to recognize trade unions. The absence of recurrent funds to meet the public-wage bill led to numerous delays in agreeing new contracts after existing employment agreements had expired. Between 1970 and 1978 there were no salary increases in real terms for public employees, though the purchasing power of the EC dollar had fallen by 50¢. By 1978 the dollar was worth 40¢ of the 1970 dollar.

The largest union, the Commercial Technical and Allied Workers' Union (CTAWU), with a membership of around 1,900, had to wait from 1975 until 1977 for government decisions on contracts for health workers, water-authority workers, airport personnel and sanitary workers. In 1975 the government's stalling tactics were challenged by the teachers' union which took strike action. An ensuing demonstration and march were declared illegal and police fired tear gas on the marchers and arrested a number of teachers. After a negotiating delay of twenty months, water-authority employees came out on strike for four weeks between April and May 1981 before an agreement could be reached.

Recognition of the trade unions as bargaining agents has long been a source of industrial conflict in St Vincent, but the intensity of recent clashes seems now to be bringing the issue to a head. Although both the 1950 Trade Union Ordinance and the St Vincent constitution permit rights of association and grant workers the right to join the trade unions of their choice, there is no legal requirement on employers to recognize a trade union if they choose not to do so. Employees do have a right of appeal but only to the government-appointed Labour Commissioner. Such an appeal is less than helpful when, for example, the government itself is disinclined to recognize a union. At the government-owned Richmond Vale agricultural estate it took a ten-week strike and five months of negotiations in 1981 for the majority of workers to obtain recognition of the union of their choice, the Workers' and Peasants' Union. The union was led by a member of the opposition in the House of Assembly, Calder Williams, and this may well have accounted for the delay.

Many local businesses refuse to recognize trade unions and it is not uncommon for workers who raise the issue of representation to be dismissed. A number of disputes have arisen around this issue. The July and August 1978 strike by Texaco employees was a response to the management's refusal to recognize a newly formed union (the Farmers' and National Workers' Union) which was supported by 63 per cent of the employees. Similarly, the 1979 strike by Royal Bank of Canada employees and the January 1981 strike at the St Vincent Container Corporation, both resulted from a refusal to recognize the CTAWU.

Neglect of the Grenadines

The record of neglect of the Grenadines is not recent. In 1965 O'Loughlin wrote that: 'Nearly all public services are below the standards of all but the remotest parts of St Vincent itself', and in the southern Grenadines she found 'an isolation not often met with in the West Indies' (O'Loughlin 1965). Lewis (1968) noted that in the Grenadines 'the sense of grievance, of being passed over, is real'. In recent years the islands have been forced to depend on the mainland for fresh-water supplies. Of the seven permanently inhabited islands, Mayreou and Canouan are without electricity. No islands contain more than an outline of a road system. Educational standards on most of the islands remain low and emigration is accepted as a way of life.

Neglect is also shown by the lease or sale of a number of islands to foreign private companies at almost giveaway rates, in order to develop tourism. The miserable returns to the treasury from some of these private developments have been noted above. One result has been the growth of strong partisan political support for the leader of the NDP, James 'Son' Mitchell (from Bequia) who has regularly held the Grenadines seat since 1967.

The sense of grievance also surfaced, although in a different form, a few days after the 1979 general election. A revolt was staged by fifty-four young people intent on leading Union Island in secession from the state of St Vincent and the Grenadines. The revolt, led by Lennox 'Bumber' Charles, had a modicum of support in both Union Island and from a few young Vincentians. Charles had lived abroad for some years and had returned to Union Island where he set up a few small-scale, but unsuccessful, projects. He was involved in a local newspaper and had plans for a farming scheme. In 1978 he made representation to the Caribbean Council of Churches concerning neglect of Union Island's community, over-fishing of the waters, drug smuggling (in which some locals claimed he had participated) and foreign exploitation of the island's resources by the tourist trade (*Caribbean Contact* 17 February 1980). The revolt, which lacked organization, equipment and sufficient support on the island, was quickly put down by the St Vincent police aided by a section of the Barbados Regiment. Charles and a few of his associates managed to escape to Carriacou (a 'ward' island of Grenada), where they were later detained and returned to St Vincent to face criminal charges.

The government response

These events may appear relatively insignificant when they are viewed separately, but the accumulation of political challenges from an organized political party of the left, the growing labour unrest, the Grenadines revolt in 1979 and the doubtful and, at times, negative consequences of government interventionist economic policies, have resulted in efforts to obtain tighter control over local and regional security and to attain an increased level of local control through legislation.

Efforts to tighten security have taken various forms. Following the revolution in Grenada and the Union Island revolt, Cato approached Great Britain with a request for intervention. When this was denied, his concern over security took other forms. The police force was strengthened (in 1979 it numbered 473 in a total population of 90,000, forming the third-highest item of public expenditure) and rumour of an attempted coup in August 1981 led to plans for the formation of a citizens' militia. Despite the brevity and ineffectiveness of the Union Island revolt (it lasted no more than a few days), a state of emergency was declared which lasted from December 1979 until June 1980.

The presence of troops from Barbados was a practical demonstration of mutual support, later to be formalized by the establishment of the Organization of Eastern Caribbean States. Moving away from traditional regional concerns of trade and economic development, the organization has introduced the idea of establishing a regional coastguard for the seven eastern Caribbean members: to this end Great Britain has donated a coastguard cutter to St Vincent.

The issuing of wider-ranging legislation became an increasingly common response to what were perceived as threats to the stability of the country. In April 1970 the St Vincent government responded to the growing radicalism on the campuses of the University of the West Indies, and to their fear of visits from 'Black Power' activists, by banning entry to 20 people from America and around the region, including Stokely Carmichael and the academics Emmanuel and Rodney. In the same year, the St Vincent government hurried through an enactment of a new Public Order Bill to replace the colonial Emergency Power Order in Council of 1939. The new Act gave the government wide powers of arrest, detention and expulsion from the island.

In an attempt to curb the political influence of the Educational Forum of the People (an informal grouping of returned university graduates who held public meetings critical of local conditions), a Public Service (Conditions of Employment) Act was introduced in 1971. This Act prohibited any public officer from publishing or expressing an opinion on any matter of a political or administrative nature—a number of the Educational Forum's leaders were in government service, teaching or other government employment. In the event though, the Act proved unworkable for at least four electoral candidates in the 1979 election were public employees.

By 1981 the SVLP had returned to imposing tighter security and repressive legislation to stifle labour demands, while attempting to obtain wider powers of public control in response to growing trade-union activities. Two new bills, the Essential Services (Amendment) Bill and the Public Safety and Public Order Bill, were introduced. The former, intended to remove the right of those in essential services to strike, declared that the final arbitrator in a dispute would be a government minister and gave the government the right to declare any service essential. Powers were to be made available for the government to 'issue any direction' or to 'take any action as may be appropriate' to avoid threatened inconvenience to the public (*The Vincentian* 12 June 1981).

The Public Safety and Public Order Bill attempted to introduce twelve emergency regulations similar to those imposed under the State of Emergency in 1979. The Bill incorporated powers to outlaw peaceful demonstrations and made it an offence 'to bring hatred or contempt or to excite disaffection against the constitution or the government by law established or the House of Assembly' (section 9). One critic argued that the proposed Bill was so loosely worded that citizens had more protection under the State of Emergency provisions than they did under the proposed Bill. Sentences of up to fourteen years and fines of EC$40,000 were proposed for contravention.

Both Bills faced widespread opposition when an attempt was made to give them a second reading in the House of Assembly. Backed by trade unions and other representative groups, a National Committee in Defence of Democracy was formed in May 1981 to oppose the legislation. A 15,000-strong demonstration, combined with a general strike in June, brought further pressure against the Bills. At first the government agreed to introduce amendments. Later the passage of the Bills was defeated by the proroguing of the House of Assembly.

Conclusion

This chapter has described the long-term changes in the pattern of state control in St Vincent and the Grenadines. Until 1951 the state was characterized by economic repression, intervention, confined characteristically to law-and-order issues and to the exercise of metro-politan political hegemony in alliance with planter interests.

The post-1951 era saw a significant expansion in the role of the state. Two features appear to have been linked to this development. One of these was fierce competition for access to state power and to the attainment of political power. Much of the competition was between black-populist and middle-class elements who rotated dominance among themselves while claiming to represent the masses. Initially, this competition took the form of political individualism within two-party politics. This was followed by new political-party formations and, most recently, by the development of unstable party alliances. The newly emerging challenge from the left has been unable to avoid this latter feature. The second element linked to the expanding role of the state is the increasing external dependence of the Vincentian economy. The British government and other sources regularly supplement government expenditure. Geest controls transportation and marketing of produce and the terms extracted by foreign capital leave little room for manoeuvre. An increase in the state's activity has thus been combined with increased dependence on external support.

In addition to this major contradiction in the exercise of state power, government intervention in the agricultural sector reveals that intervention can have unintended and not necessarily beneficial consequences. Where price controls obtained, they have seriously weakened the industry concerned, land acquisitions have been poorly managed and recent capital expenditure on agricultural improvements appears to have been ill considered. In a small dependent island like St Vincent, the negative effects accruing from the exercise of expanded state power seem to suggest that as expansion occurs so dependence increases. The more the state has intervened in the economy, the more its effectiveness has declined.

At the same time, state ineffectiveness and economic mismanagement have produced tensions which have been expressed in labour unrest, separatist challenges and signs of a political challenge from the left. The state sees these developments as problems requiring more legislation and tighter security. Its return to repression shows how limited are the options available to the state in its quest for stability.

REFERENCES

Banana Growers' Association 1977, *Annual Report for St. Vincent*, St Vincent, BGA
Caribbean Contact 17 February 1980
Caribbean Development Bank (CDB) 1971, *Re-establishment of the sugar industry in St. Vincent: a preliminary report*, London, Bookers Agricultural & Technical Services
Caribbean Development Bank (CDB) 1977, *Appraisal report on the sugar factory in St. Vincent*, London, Bookers Agricultural & Technical Services
Cato, M. R. 1976, *Feature address delivered at the golden jubilee dinner of the St. Vincent chamber of industry and commerce*, typescript, 27 March
Census of Agriculture for St. Vincent 1946; 1958; 1959; 1961, 1972/73, London, HMSO
Chernick, S. F. 1978, *The commonwealth Caribbean*, Economic Report, Washington, World Bank
Coopers & Lybrand Associates 1980, *Creating employment opportunities in St. Vincent*, Final Report, vol. 1, phase 2, London, C & LA
Davy, J. 1854, *The West Indies before and since slave emancipation*, London, Cass, reprint 1971
Development Plan 1965–70, St Vincent, Government printery
Duncan, N. C. 1975, *The Vincentian elections 1974*, Occasional paper no. 3, Barbados, ISER (Eastern Caribbean)
Estimates of St. Vincent 1960; 1965; 1970; 1973–78; 1979/80, St Vincent, Government printery

Frampton, A. de K. *et al.* 1979, *Report and recommendations for the development of St. Vincent by a team of experts, November 1957*, Barbados, Colonial Development & Welfare Organization

Freedom 28 July 1977

Frucht, R. 1967, 'A Caribbean social type: neither "peasant" nor "proletarian"', *Social and economic studies*, vol. 3, no. 3

Gibbs, B. (ed.) 1947, *A plan of development for the colony of St. Vincent*, St Vincent, Government printery

Giuseppi, A. H. n.d., *History of land settlement in St. Vincent*, Kingston and St Vincent, St Vincent Archives

Gonsalves, R. E. 1977, *Who killed sugar in St. Vincent?*, St Vincent, YULIMO

John, K. R. V. 1971, *Politics in a small colonial territory: St. Vincent: a report*, Ph.D., University of Manchester

John, R. 1979, *Pioneers in nation-building in a Caribbean mini-state*, New York, United Nations Institute for Training and Research

Land Settlement Board 1963, *Annual Report*, St Vincent, Department of Agriculture

Lewis, G. K. 1968, *The growth of the modern West Indies*, London, Macgibbon & Kee

Llewellyn-Davis and Partners 1974, *The development of tourism in St. Vincent*, independent report, London

Martin, C. I. 1967, *The role of government in the agricultural development of St. Vincent*, M.Sc. thesis, UWI, St Augustine, Trinidad

Mintz, S. W. 1974, 'Rural proletariat and the problem of the rural proletarian consciousness', *Journal of peasant studies*, vol. 1, no. 3, pp. 291–325

Moyne 1945, *West Indian royal commission report (the Moyne commission)*, Cmd. 6607, London, HMSO

Norton, A. and Cumper, G. 1966, '"Peasant", "plantation" and "urban communities" in rural Jamaica: a test of the validity of the classification', *Social and economic studies*, vol. 15, no. 4

Orde Browne, Major St J. 1939, *Labour conditions in the West Indies*, Report, Cmd. 6070, London, HMSO

O'Loughlin, C. 1965, *Report of a committee to advise on the establishment of free ports in the St. Vincent Grenadines*, St Vincent, Government printery

O'Loughlin, C. 1967, *Capital needs of Leeward and Windward islands and Barbados*, London, HMSO

Royal Commission 1897, *Report of the West Indian royal commission*, London, HMSO

St Vincent Christian Council 1980, *Grenadines consultation*, Bequia, 22–24 April, author's notes

St Vincent Development Corporation 1977, *Incentives for investors*, St Vincent, Government printery

St Vincent Development Corporation 1980, Report by the author, unpublished

St Vincent Marketing Corporation 1975; 1976; 1977, *Reports for the board of management*, St Vincent

St Vincent Tourist Board 1980, Author consultation of files in Tourist Board

Select Committee on Overseas Development 1976, *The relationship between UK investment and trading patterns and development with reference to the specific problems of small LDCs*, Second report, London, HMSO

Shephard, C. Y. 1945, *Peasant agriculture in the Leeward and Windward islands*, London, Imperial College of Tropical Agriculture

Shurcliff, A. W., Wellameyer, J. F. and Henry, L. 1967, *Development in the eastern Caribbean islands*, series 4, Manpower Survey, Government of St Vincent, mimeo.

Spinelli, J. G. 1973, *Population change and economic growth in St. Vincent 1764–1960*, Ph.D., University of Florida

UPM 1979, *The 1979 election manifesto of the united people's movement*, St Vincent, mimeo.

UWI Development Mission 1969, *The development problem in St. Vincent: a report*, Kingston, Jamaica, UWI

Vincentian, The 12 June 1981; 18 September 1981; 5 February 1982

West Indian Chronicle December–January 1979

World Bank 1980, *Economic memorandum on St. Vincent and the Grenadines*, Report no. 2995–CRG, May, Washington, World Bank

ELEVEN

State Capitalism in a Petroleum-Based Economy: the Case of Trinidad and Tobago*

José Miguel Sandoval

Introduction

The conceptualization of the state in post-colonial societies has been modified somewhat in view of the different historical experiences of these societies. Alavi (1976), in analysing the cases of Pakistan and Bangladesh, proposed three theses as an attempt towards re-conceptualization. First, historically, the state apparatus created by a metropolitan bourgeoisie is bequeathed to the indigenous class or classes at independence. The state, therefore, is not the creation of an indigenous class in post-colonial society. Second, the state in post-colonial societies is characterized by a 'multi-class' relationship. And third, Alavi contends that the state assumes a relatively autonomous *economic role* with the appropriation of a large portion of the economic surplus, which is allocated to economic activities for the stated purpose of promoting economic development.

Alavi's propositions are useful for the conceptualization of the state in the case of Trinidad and Tobago. It is obvious that the state apparatus was inherited by a local petty bourgeoisie which was mobilized and which emerged as a significant class in the 1950s. The second multi-class relationship thesis is also relevant, as the state in Trinidad and Tobago has acted as a promoter of the overall interests of the indigenous bourgeoisie. It can be argued that at the time of independence there was no indigenous bourgeoisie in Trinidad and Tobago (Sudama 1980). However, there was unquestionably some kind of bourgeois stratum in the form of commercial capital linked to international trade and some agricultural activities. It is important to note that the bourgeoisie, which emerged after independence as a result of specific state policies, has hardly ever taken an independent position on any fundamental political question up to 1981. It can be stated that the local bourgeoisie subjected itself to petty-bourgeois political rule in Trinidad and Tobago as the latter was making every effort to maintain a capitalist orientation as well as to act as a liaison between foreign capital and the local bourgeoisie.

Alavi's third proposition is even more relevant in the case of Trinidad

* All figures cited are in Trinidad and Tobago (TT) dollars. The exchange rate in 1973 was US$1.00 = TT$2.4.

and Tobago for, as it became obvious after independence, the state was the only means of re-directing economic surplus in view of the then-accepted strategy for economic development.

Alavi concludes that this phenomenon is accompanied by a specific form of class formation in post-colonial society. Poulantzas (1976) makes a similar point in referring to the emergence of a 'state bourgeoisie' in some developing countries, through the bureaucratic control of economic surplus. In discussing the Tanzanian situation, Shivji (1976) considers the state bureaucracy a 'bureaucratic bourgeoisie' because of its control over economic activity. On the other hand, Saul (1979) postulates that there is some uncertainty as to whether the bureaucracy is a class distinct from the petty bourgeoisie. Although bureaucracy represents a new phenomenon in countries where state control of economic activity becomes overwhelming, it is still part of the petty bourgeoisie.

This chapter focuses on the autonomous economic role of the state in Trinidad and Tobago after independence. There are three basic assumptions underlying the arguments presented here. First, this is a social formation in which capitalist relations of production are dominant; and, as will be seen, state intervention has in no way challenged the permanence of the capitalist system. Second, the case of Trinidad and Tobago does not correspond to any advanced capitalist economy but to a dependent one in which a trend towards monopoly capitalism is observed. Third, no global conclusions about state capitalism are attempted in this chapter. The purpose of the argument is to analyse the case of state capitalism in Trinidad and Tobago and relate its evolution to the capacity of the state to control and manage an enlarged economic surplus.

Petras (1978) has argued that in the Third World 'private capitalist and classical petty-bourgeois classes' have shown no inclination to develop dynamic national economies. He also argues, however, that 'it does not follow that there exist no other forces which are capable of tackling the job'. The consequence of this is that once that class system or coalition is in control of economic management, the model which is implemented is one of national state capitalism.

This chapter makes no attempt to analyse the complexities of the social and political formations under state capitalism, nor does it defend or criticize a position wherein the bureaucracy constitutes a separate class with defined political, economic and social interests. In addition, there is another dimension, that of race, which is not included here. Sudama (1980) has correctly argued that the race dimension has to be incorporated into the analysis of the state in a racially heterogeneous society such as Trinidad and Tobago. As political and social complexities are touched upon only marginally in this chapter, the issue of race has, however, been ignored as a conditioning factor in class formation and ideological concerns.

Background

In Trinidad and Tobago, post-colonialism marked not only the beginning of autonomous administration, but also the initiation of development strategies which resulted from the intellectual response of the local intelligentsia. When the local political elite took over the administration of the country from the Colonial Office, it became apparent that the role the state had to play would be quite different from its earlier one. West Indian intellectuals had the opportunity to implement a national project of their own: a situation that demanded fundamental changes in development strategy as well as modified state policies.

The pre-Second-World-War colonial period was marked by the virtual absence of industrialization in the West Indies. The official colonial view was consistent with the process of capital accumulation which was taking place in the metropolis. Industry was almost exclusively confined to the metropolis, whereas the colonies were compelled to produce primary goods. West Indian territories had no choice but to produce sugar, coffee, cocoa, copra and other similar products for export to the metropolitan centre, where economic surplus found its accumulation in the industrial sector. Through its Colonial Office, the colonial state orchestrated the process of capital accumulation in the metropolis by either forbidding or by discouraging manufacturing activities in its colonies.

By the end of the nineteenth century, liberal ideas were superseding the earlier mercantilist approach. Less active state interference in economic affairs was preferred, at least in the metropolis. In the colonies, the official view continued to discourage West Indian governments from entering into manufacturing activities (Norman Commission 1897), unless projects were established in co-operation with British capital (Moyne Commission 1945). The colonial state, therefore, consistently tied economic activities in the West Indian colonies to the capitalist interests of the metropolis. At the turn of the century, the policy towards Trinidad and Tobago consisted of reactivating the sugar industry, agricultural diversification, land settlement, encouraging emigration and economizing in public expenditure and welfare services.

The discovery of oil in 1907 added new dimensions to an agricultural economy whose incorporation into the capitalist system consisted of exports of tropical products to the metropolitan centre. The incorporation of oil contributed towards diversifying the economy, but of paramount importance was the fundamental change which took place in the generation of economic surplus. The oil industry was to become the basis for economic prosperity and, most importantly, the fundamental factor underlying the emergence of an 'interventionist' state.

Since its inception in the Trinidad and Tobago economy, the oil industry needed regulation and protection. The state had to intervene on both counts and legislation had to be enacted to stimulate activity. Thus there followed various ordinances which attempted to foster the oil industry: authorization of geological surveys on private lands, supervision of work in the fields, and definition of conditions for the erecting of oil refineries (Thomas 1981). Similarly, the state had to intervene to protect the industry from industrial unrest by keeping organized labour at bay.

From the beginning, the oil industry was a highly profitable venture. In 1910 three oil companies operated in the country and by the late 1930s there were fourteen. The industry soon exhibited a trend towards concentration and by the late 1930s, six of these companies were producing 90 per cent of Trinidad and Tobago's crude oil. Apart from providing economic surplus to metropolitan capital, this sector was of strategic importance to the British Navy which had replaced coal with oil in 1919.

The war years gave the colonies their first opportunity to industrialize, albeit rather tentatively. Unavailability of supplies, together with the growing demand for manufactured goods, stimulated an embryonic form of industrialization. Additionally, oil output doubled during the late 1930s and the presence of US military bases in the country stimulated the growth of infrastructural activities (St Cyr 1981).

The post-war crisis forced the colonial state into adopting an ambiguous position towards industrialization in the colonies. On the one hand, it was clear that the magnitude of the crisis in the metropolis prevented the return to a 'mercantilist' approach, for the manufacturing sector in the metropolis itself needed revitalizing. On the other hand, it was officially argued that once the crisis was over, the 'principle of comparative advantage should weigh more in determining long-term policy' (quoted by St Cyr 1981). In other words, the colonial state intended to revert to a pre-war situation after a return to 'normality' in the metropolis. But this did not occur, for political events were drawing the metropolis towards decolonization.

Trinidad and Tobago were granted universal adult suffrage in 1946 and, in 1950, a semi-autonomous government undertook to rule the nation. The fact that the government became answerable to the public and that elected leaders had the opportunity to exercise their powers in the interests of the electorate, marked the beginning of party politics in Trinidad and Tobago.

The People's National Movement (PNM) led by a historian, Dr Eric Williams, was elected in 1956 and given the opportunity to implement an economic programme that had resulted from the debate that challenged the official view on industrialization in the colonies. Arguing in favour of industrialization in the West Indies, W. Arthur Lewis became a leading voice and his policy recommendations were adopted by Dr Williams in Trinidad and Tobago.

Development strategies and the state

Industrialization has become an undisputed, universally accepted means of fostering economic development. Colin Clark (1941) established the link between manufacturing and economic and social prosperity. Manufacturing soon became accepted as the prime instigator of development, calling for and stimulating changes in consumption, trade, education, infrastructure, urbanization and so forth.

R. Prebisch (1951) argued the case for industrialization in Latin America as a necessary step in avoiding further inequality in the distribution of the benefits of technological progress. The strategy he suggested advocated greater concern for local conditions, namely specific economic resources and the abundance of non-productive labour: 'It is understandable that domestic production should be substituted for imports in order to increase employment when there are unemployed factors' (Prebisch 1951: 13). Prebisch's thesis provided the framework for a phenomenon taking place in Latin America even before the war.

Similarly, W. A. Lewis argued the case of industrialization in the Caribbean as the unquestionable direction for the islands to follow: 'The policy which seems to offer most hope of permanent success is for the islands to follow in the footsteps of other agricultural countries in industrialization' (Lewis 1939: 44). Lewis went even further by naming the industries he considered had good prospects: sugar refining, chocolate manufacturing, copra processing, dairy products and other resource-based industries. In the early 1950s Lewis repeated his conclusion that the islands had to industrialize, though the strategy he suggested this time was a different one. He proposed a combination of regional import substitution and export-promotion industrialization (Lewis 1951).

After the war, industrialization became an issue of such importance that development strategies were designed to achieve in one or two decades what had taken more than one hundred years in countries that had first industrialized. Although the state's role in the implementation of strategies had differed widely in accordance with each country's specific political, social, cultural and economic background, the following four types of strategy can be identified as a basis for model formation in industrialization:

Resource-based industrialization

Here manufacturing is founded on the stock of available natural resources. Every industrialized country has unquestionably gone through resource-based manufacturing in one way or another. Embryonic manufacturing evidently started from primary production. It is a different matter, however, to base a process of industrialization on available resources only. W. A. Lewis suggested this strategy for the Caribbean in the late 1930s and, at present, countries such as Belize, Guyana and Suriname have partially followed this path. It will be seen later that in the case of Trinidad and Tobago, the thrust that the state has given to the development of energy-based industries is based on this strategy, due to the abundant availability of natural gas.

Export-promotion industrialization

Here the emphasis is placed on the use of some economic factors whose abundant availability directly affects their costs, as is the case of labour. But most important for the success of this strategy has been the influence of 'non-economic' factors, such as the location of the country with respect to industrialized centres, transport and communication facilities and so forth.

The limitations of the domestic market have also been used to argue in favour of this type of 'outward-oriented' industrialization. The Caribbean found a pioneer in this type of strategy in Puerto Rico during the early 1950s.

Import-substitution industrialization

The success of this strategy depends on the availability of favourable factors of production, as well as an accessible market for manufactured goods. This was the pattern followed by most Latin American countries after the war. R. Prebisch justified this strategy in Latin America on the grounds of its greater labour-absorption potential.

Import-substitution industrialization at the regional level

This was a follow-up from the previous strategy which attempted to overcome the limitations of producing manufactured goods for markets which soon exhausted their demand. Well-known case studies of strategy in Latin America are provided by LAFTA, the Andean Pact and Caricom.

In the many countries where the above strategies or combinations of them have been attempted, the state has been able to select from a wide range of options regarding active intervention. There are cases where state intervention has been overwhelming—as in some African countries—and others in which a 'mixed economy' has emerged. Regardless of the size of the state sector in developing countries after the war, the fundamental factor in explaining its presence has been the need to regulate the process of capital accumulation in pursuing defined national interests. Class formations that preceded the implementation of industrialization strategies provided refined definitions of 'national interests'. Countries with a strong landowner class in control of and/or with access to a substantial part of the economic surplus had a different range of options for state intervention from those of countries in which colonial domination or immediate post-war events had made room for rapid social and political adjustments in the light of expectations raised by the onset of independence.

Thus, unless some kind of revolutionary change in the power structure preceded implementation of the strategy, the direction and involvement of the state was determined by phenomena linked to the previous process of capital accumulation.

In Trinidad and Tobago, the process of capital accumulation was characterized by the presence of foreign companies, in both the petroleum and sugar sectors, whose purpose was to extract economic surplus for subsequent accumulation in the metropolis. Local capital was concentrated in trade, internal distribution and provision of services.

The owners of local capital are found in a class of former planters and migrants established in trading activities whose influence in the colony came to be of secondary importance—though complementary—to the foreign capital which dominated petroleum and sugar. The rest of the social spectrum consisted basically of members of the urban middle class engaged in the service sector and in the civil service, farmers, sugar and oil workers, and other agricultural and industrial workers. This complex of social forces comprised the national constituency which, after decolonization, came to define the meaning of the 'national interest'.

Development plans and state intervention

The transitional period between the end of the war and the beginning of a degree of autonomous direction in economic and political affairs (1950) marked the beginning of a period in which state intervention was geared towards encouraging indigenous activity in the manufacturing sector. A set of policies was suggested by the Shaw Committee (meeting in 1949) whose main objectives were to stimulate the expansion of existing industries and to create some new ones. These emphasized the need for the indigenous accumulation of capital through providing a number of generous fiscal incentives—duty-free imports of plant and equipment; protective tariffs to allow for the capitalization of new industries; removal of export barriers and income-tax exemptions.

In addition, measures were taken to ameliorate conditions created by the post-war adjustments in Britain, such as the release of foreign exchange for purchasing plant and machinery, and assistance in obtaining new materials for the manufacture of export goods (St Cyr 1981: 7). The 'Aid to Pioneer Industries Ordinance' was enacted in 1950 to put these recommendations into practice by providing duty-free concessions on imports of capital equipment, exemption from payment of income tax for five years, unlimited carry-over of losses, and tax-free distribution of profits.

In other words, before decolonization, the regulatory role of the state was geared towards stimulating private accumulation in industries that offered some potential, namely citrus, lumber, biscuits, industrial alcohol, spirits, cosmetics, pharmaceuticals, caustic soda, woven goods, bagasse-based goods and others. In addition, special treatment was given to industries in which sizeable investments had been made, such as cement.

It should be noted in relation to the industrialization strategies outlined above that state policies were attempting to combine import substitution with some export promotion, as can be seen from the industries listed above. The capitalist nature of these measures was unmistakable; they represented the first attempt to attract indigenous capital into manufacturing, a trend that continued.

The First Development Plan, 1958–62

Under the charismatic leadership of Dr Williams, the new group of decision-makers introduced a more formally presented development programme. Williams was highly critical of the previous administration which had inherited an official programme approved by the metropolitan power. In particular, he criticized the previous programme for failing both to provide productive jobs and to modify the economic structure in which oil and sugar continued to predominate (Williams 1981: 6).

Williams's interpretation of W. A. Lewis's strategy led him to the conclusion that the provision of jobs could only come from industry in the long run and from tourism in the short run. Traditional activities were no longer absorbing sufficient labour, while the labour force was expanding quite considerably. Lewis had already earmarked a list of the most favoured industries—hosiery, leather, garments, footwear, china, paper trades, glass, building materials, food processing and textiles. These light industries were to be provided with facilities for the importation of raw materials, as well as incentives to foreign investment for their establishment. This part of the programme was to be 'export oriented'. As Williams himself put it: 'the British West Indian industrialization programme must follow the example of Puerto Rico and produce for export rather than for the limited domestic market' (Williams 1981: 7). State intervention was justified on the grounds that the programme needed support: 'Notwithstanding the emphasis on the private investor, there is a case for government initiative in starting industries' (Williams 1981: 7).

The First Five-Year Development Plan, 1958–62, dubbed 'The People's Charter for Economic and Social Development', was prepared during 1956–57. Professor Lewis and Mr Moscoso from the Economic Development and Administration of Puerto Rico assisted the government in formulating the plan which mobilized an unprecedented amount of resources through direct government action (approximately $218.5m over the five years). Complementary to the plan was the enactment of additional legislation which formalized the incentives created to attract private capital into the foreign industries and institutionalized the state's presence through the Industrial Development Corporation.

This plan differed from the previous programme in terms of the actors participating in its formulation. The nationalist approach taken by Williams and his party added a West Indian dimension to a programme that did not attempt to challenge capitalism in the country, but rather to develop it. The state was to instrumentalize the 'People's Charter' through regulating economic surplus in favour of private capital and through direct participation in infrastructural development and education.

The Second Five-Year Plan, 1964–68

The combination of import-substitution and export-promotion strategies attempted in 1958 was never implemented as planned. Manufacturing activity remained committed to supplying the local market, while the export-oriented manufacturers were centred in establishments which became enclaves under total control of foreign capital, as was the case of the fertilizer industry.

During this period, the state attempted to consolidate its position in the control of public utilities. Electrical power which was originally supplied by different companies became amalgamated into one company, now fully owned and managed by the state; the establishment of the Water and Sewerage Authority came to unify under one department this basic utility. The establishment of the Port Authority sanctioned total state control over the management of the ports, and the creation of the Public Transport Service Corporation added new involvement in public transportation. The overall function of the state in the above area was institutionalized with the creation of the Public Utilities Commission which acted as a planning and advisory body for activities now under total state control.

In addition to its involvement in activities traditionally accepted as 'nationalist monopolies', the state continued to support private capital by providing financial assistance to industries starting manufacturing activities. This was carried out by purchasing minority holdings in private companies that welcomed the needed inflow of funds. For the period corresponding to the Second Five-Year Plan, it is clear that the state acted as a supporting institution for private capital—which evolved subsequently into powerful economic conglomerates—as well as consolidating a nationalist approach with regard to public utilities and local distribution of petroleum products. Over the period 1958–81, the state invested in some sixty-five commercial enterprises, owning thirty-five outright, having a majority stake in fourteen and a minority share in the remaining sixteen enterprises.

The Third Five-Year Plan, 1969–73

By the mid-1960s, it became clear that the original strategy of import substitution, combined (rather unsuccessfully) with export-oriented industrialization, was stalling. The state did not possess the resources required for adding new dynamism to the original programme, as the incentives policy had reduced the tax base and the inflow of petroleum revenues had slowed. On the other hand, because of the expanded role of the state in the social and economic infrastructure, public expenditure had reached a high level.

As in the case of the Latin American countries, the exhaustion of the process of import substitution was seen to result from the small size of the local economies. In 1968 the region sought to formalize an expansion in the local market by creating the Caribbean Free Trade Association (Carifta), which later evolved into the Caribbean Community (Caricom).

The development strategy underwent modifications which made import substitution at the regional level the preferred approach. This meant that governments had to act accordingly to pave the way towards regional expansion of those activities that had already shown 'comparative advantages', at least at the local level. This was formally institutionalized through the harmonization of fiscal incentives to industry throughout the region. As will be seen later, local groups in positions to expand regionally took advantage of this policy by creating subsidiaries or by consolidating their presence in other territories.

Despite continued revenue constraints, the state continued its trend towards direct intervention in activities and this further consolidated its control over public utilities, as in telecommunications and broadcasting. In addition, the state extended its control into the areas of banking and finance by nationalizing a foreign bank and by taking a majority shareholding in various insurance companies.

By mid-1973, however, the state was in a precarious financial position. The foreign and internal debt had escalated, new sources of revenue were faltering (due to the fiscal incentives programme) and the state's commitment to social and economic expenditure was perceived of as a 'national goal' in which reduction or cuts were considered synonymous with failure. This critical situation was alleviated by the events in the Middle East and the resulting policies pursued by OPEC.

The oil-boom period, 1974–80

The Third Five-Year Plan was the last explicit programme ever to be formally presented by the state. There has been no need for another plan, for since 1974 the state has focused precisely on implementing the strategy of import substitution at the regional level, combined with export-promotion industrialization. Confirmation of the first type of strategy through expansion and growth has been left to private capital. Export-oriented industrialization has been taken over by the state as part of its own involvement in commercial ventures, since the main focus of this sector is on activities where the energy component (natural gas) plays a strategic role.

The recent establishment of energy-based industries would not, however, have been possible without the participation of foreign capital, through the presence in Trinidad and Tobago of multinational corporations. Despite its unprecedented bonanza in terms of tax revenues collected after 1973, the state entered into partnership with foreign multinationals, in the form of joint ventures, with the objective of securing know-how and access to foreign markets for the new products. Local capital has been totally absent in these new links between the state and private external capital. Nevertheless, it was agreed by both the state and local capital that economic activities related to the installation and servicing of energy-based industries opened up additional avenues for indigenous sharing of the unprecedented economic surplus which resulted from the oil-price increases.

Accordingly, the state expanded towards energy-based activities, namely, steel, fertilizers, petro-chemicals and liquefied natural gas. In addition, as a form of improving social services, the state has created autonomous enterprises for administering activities as diverse as school nutrition, hospital administration, road repairs and solid-waste collection and disposal. In response to the regional institutionalization of import substitution, the state has entered partnerships at the international level in activities geared towards integration and co-operation in the context of Caricom.

The state's role has been expanding and changing according to modifications in development strategy. It has been an 'in crescendo' trend, both quantitatively and qualitatively. At the beginning, when political conditions were rather uncertain for the ruling group, the state adhered fairly strictly to rules set out in the development plan. As the ruling group began its consolidation into a one-party-type government, the state acquired more equity and started to participate more in productive activities. The unprecedented increase of economic surplus, regulated by the state after 1973, provided the opportunity to implement a strategy already favoured in the 1950s which gave 'natural direction' to a small and open economy possessing energy resources.

Finally, the size of the public sector in the economy as a whole and commercial enterprises in particular, may be evaluated through the following:

1   The overall size of the state can be seen in table 11.1. It is clear that there is an important quantitative change both in public expenditure and revenue after 1973. The ratios of total expenditure to GDP and current revenue to GDP reached their highest levels of 42.4 per cent and 43.9 per cent respectively in 1980. Even more significant is that the current surplus has been accumulating steadily, which provides additional resources still not used productively in the economy.

2   State participation in companies during the period January 1973 to June 1980 reached the amount of $2,941m, which is equivalent to 21 per cent of the GDP for 1980 or slightly more than the total GDP for 1973.

TABLE 11.1 Trinidad and Tobago: the public sector in the economy

Year	GDP	Current revenue	Capital receipts	Current expenditure	Current surplus	Capital expenditure	Total expenditure	Total expenditure: GDP	Current revenue: GDP
1951	308.3	62.6	—	49.6	13.0	—	—	—	20.3
1960	865.9	138.2	—	100.9	37.3	—	—	—	16.0
1970	1,630.9	324.2	3.3	273.2	51.0	111.2	383.5	23.5	19.9
1971	1,796.3	355.9	7.9	340.6	15.3	118.9	459.5	25.6	19.8
1972	2,039.4	413.8	1.5	408.7	5.1	140.9	549.6	26.9	20.3
1973	2,554.7	493.9	0.9	476.3	17.6	130.5	606.8	23.8	19.3
1974	4,101.5	1,306.9	80.8	637.6	669.3	341.8	979.4	23.9	31.9
1975	5,496.7	1,816.0	31.2	773.3	1,042.7	428.9	1,202.2	21.9	33.0
1976	6,502.3	2,302.6	0.3	979.1	1,323.5	891.8	1,870.9	28.8	35.4
1977	8,552.2	2,981.0	6.0	1,162.9	1,818.1	1,094.0	2,256.9	26.4	34.9
1978	9,501.6	3,083.2	2.5	1,483.0	1,600.2	1,409.6	2,892.6	30.4	32.4
1979	11,499.7	4,037.0	0.1	2,247.5	1,789.5	1,943.6	4,191.1	36.4	35.1
1980	14,081.9	6,179.4	48.2	2,818.9	3,360.5	3,155.9	5,974.8	42.4	43.9

Source: Review of the Economy 1980.

Industrial expansion and concentration of capital

Since the beginning of the incentives programme, governments before and after Dr Williams have intended to create an industrial sector able both to create employment and to provide foreign exchange. They have done this through the use of fiscal incentives aimed at accelerating the rate of capital accumulation in favoured activities. The 'Pioneer Industries Acts' formalized this mechanism.

Between 1950 and 1955, 101 manufacturers were granted pioneer status. In 1950 the new thrust given to industrial diversification through the Industrial Development Corporation meant that the number of establishments expanded to include 158 new factories by 1969. During the 1970s the number of establishments continued to grow, though at a slow rate. Between 1951 and 1961 the manufacturing sector grew at an average annual rate of 9.7 per cent; the following period (1963–68), corresponding to the Second Five-Year Plan, showed a rate of growth of 7.1 per cent per annum. The subsequent period and throughout the 1970s witnessed a slower rate of growth at an average of 6 per cent per annum.

In global terms, the growth of the manufacturing sector cannot be termed spectacular. Taking into account the significant changes in the value of petroleum after 1973, the manufacturing sector's contribution to GDP did not change substantially during the 1970s. Table 11.2 shows, in percentages, the evolution of GDP during the 1970s; it is clear that manufacturing activities have not gained significant weight in relation to other sections of economic activity.

TABLE 11.2 Trinidad and Tobago: GDP at factor costs (%)

	1970	1971	1972	1973	1974	1975	1976	1977	1978	1979	1980
Petroleum	22	20	20	27	45	48	46	43	38	36	35
Manufacturing	9	9	10	9	7	6	7	6	7	7	7
Construction	6	7	8	7	6	5	6	7	7	7	8
Finance	8.5	8.4	8.0	7.8	6.8	8.1	8.2	8.3	10.5	11.2	11.3
Government	8.4	10.0	10.3	9.1	7.1	7.7	7.3	6.9	7.6	9.1	8.2
Rest: transport, distribution, etc.	46	46	44	40	28	25	26	29	30	30	31

Source: CSO, *The Gross Domestic Product of the Republic of Trinidad and Tobago. Review of the Economy* 1980.

The Industrial Development Corporation (IDC) is the state institution that has been behind industrial expansion in the country since 1957. It has determined the eligibility of enterprises for 'pioneer status' and has also earmarked areas in which new enterprises should be established. In addition to facilitating the establishment of rather large enterprises, the IDC embarked on a campaign for promoting 'small businesses'. In short, the IDC has been instrumental in creating a capitalist-based manufacturing sector whose structure has tended unequivocably towards concentration, as explained below.

During the 1970s the state placed special emphasis on the development of the 'small business sector', i.e. enterprises in which total employment does not exceed six workers or investment does not exceed $150,000. The IDC created a 'Small Business' division in 1970 which (between 1970 and 1979) granted soft loans for $20.90m to 1,171 small businesses of which 483 were engaged in manufacturing (Industrial Development Corporation 1980).

This small business sector, created with the help of the state, has become a satellite type of activity with respect to the rather larger establishments in the manufacturing sector. Table 11.3 shows the distribution per activity of a total of 977 small establishments in 1978. It is significant to note that 44 per cent of the total corresponds to manufacturing activities.

TABLE 11.3 Trinidad and Tobago: distribution according to sectors of small businesses (1978)

Sector		No. of businesses
3	Petroleum industries—service contractors	1
4	Food processors and drinks	24
5	Textiles, garments, footwear and headwear	72
6	Printing, publishing and paper correctors	84
7	Wood and related products	70
8	Chemicals and non-metallic minerals	19
9	Assembly type and related industries	122
10	Miscellaneous manufacturing	37
12	Construction	61
13	Distribution (wholesale trade)	26
	(retailsale trade)	17
15	Transport, communication and storage	13
15	Finance, insurance, real estate and business services	34
19	Personal services	397
Total		977

Source: Industrial Development Corporation, *Register of Small Business* 1980.

Table 11.4 shows the number of large establishments by industry for the years 1974 and 1977 with their respective employment numbers. From tables 11.3 and 11.4 it is possible to conclude that the expansion in manufacturing favoured the following activities in order of importance: assembly-type and related industries, food processing and drinks, textiles, garments, headwear and footwear and wood and related products.

Moreover, it is also possible to conclude from both tables that a centre-satellite type of structure has been formed, particularly in the assembly-type and related industries sector. It becomes evident that a greater degree

TABLE 11.4 Trinidad and Tobago: employment in large
establishments by industry

	No. of establishments		No. employed	
	1974	1977	1974	1977
Food processors	86	92	7,200	8,000
Textiles, garments, headwear, footwear	86	89	4,500	5,900
Printing, publishing and paper converters	46	47	2,400	2,800
Wood and related products	79	74	2,200	2,200
Chemical and non-metallic products	51	62	3,200	3,900
Assembly-type and related industries	83	88	5,900	8,200
Other manufacture	27	32	1,500	1,100
Total	458	484	26,900	32,100

Source: Review of the Economy 1980.

of interdependence has been established, as small businesses provide some inputs for and demand some inputs from the larger establishments.

Concentration of capital by 1981

The strategy of import substitution combined with export promotion followed by the state since 1950 generated a concentration of capital based in trade activities carried out by an indigenous bourgeoisie. With the exception of the petroleum sector and of export-promotion activities, both almost totally controlled by foreign capital, the presence of indigenous capital in the favoured manufacturing sector is overwhelming. Furthermore, the incentives policy launched by the state has reinforced the significance of local capital by making use of 'pioneer status' which has brought about rapid capital accumulation, at least for some local companies.

Most of the economic groups formed during the 1970s have their historical origins in trade, some in traditional export activities such as cocoa, coffee, sugar and copra. Needless to say, the holding of lands and real estate also helped companies consolidate their positions, which enabled them to establish themselves as bases for further accumulation when they embarked on manufacturing.

By 1981 four large economic groups had become established in the country. These have ramifications which extend horizontally into various national and multinational economic activities in the Caribbean region, both through subsidiaries and through associations with local companies in other territories.

The two largest of these groups have based their process of capital accumulation on assembly-type manufacturing, particularly automobile assembly. The growth of a third group is based on trading, particularly in the import of equipment, machinery, foodstuffs and hardware and, more recently, on the manufacture of building materials and on construction. The fourth group has expanded through retail distribution which has extended to local manufacturing in the light-industries sector.

All four groups have expanded their operations into other Caribbean territories and, because of the particular type of manufacturing that each group has undertaken, there exist obvious links with foreign capital. Almost every manufacturing activity carried out by each group involves a licensing contract or agreement with a foreign company to provide technology and/or inputs. A brief account of each of the four groups follows.

The Neal & Massy Group

The Neal & Massy Group is the largest indigenous economic group in the Caribbean. It started with the merger of two private companies (Neal and Massy) which, in 1923, came together to become the sole agents in Trinidad and Tobago for automobiles (both British and American) and also for agricultural and industrial machinery. After becoming the sole agents and assemblers for Nissan Motors (Datsun) in the mid-1960s, the group expanded rapidly. Obviously the company made use of the 'pioneer status' incentives provided by the state and, at the beginning of its assembly operations in 1966, it received an influx of funds from the state, thus forming a partnership. Further expansion took place in the 1970s through various mergers and/or absorption of established enterprises. By 1981 the group, under the global control of Neal & Massy Holdings Ltd, comprised six sub-groups and a total of fifty-one companies, twenty of which are registered in other Caribbean countries and fifteen of which are majority-owned. Their degree of diversification is quite considerable, ranging from motor-car assembly, building materials, machinery, wholesale and retail distribution and supermarket chains to finance and real estate. Needless to say, most of the manufacturing companies controlled by the group had made use of 'pioneer status' at the beginning of their respective operations.

The Neal & Massy group has been most dynamic in responding to the expansionist changes that have taken place in the economy as a whole. From 1970 to 1973 its sales grew at an average rate of 20 per cent; from 1974 to 1979 the rate of growth jumped to an average of 55 per cent, with a peak in 1975–76 when sales reached an unprecedented 138 per cent (Neal & Massy 1979). These figures show that expansion of the group has corresponded with the expansion of the economy in general and with state revenue in particular.

The McEnearney Alstons Group

The McEnearney Alstons Group resulted from a merger of two companies, Charles McEnearney & Co. Ltd, and Alstons Ltd. The first company had been in operation since the 1920s as agents for an automobile company (Ford) and as importers of industrial and agricultural machinery. The second company had been linked to international trade and local distribution since the beginning of the century. The merger took place in the 1960s and, as in the previous case, the focus of dynamic expansion was in automobile assembly, through a company named Amalgamated Industries Ltd which assembles vehicles of different makes—namely Ford, Mazda, Vauxhall, Renault and, formerly, Austin.

The merger facilitated horizontal diversification which ranged from building materials, engineering services and supermarkets to finance and publishing. The group participates in the holdings of thirty-two companies, of which ten are totally owned, sixteen are majority-owned and six are minority-owned. An additional five companies are registered which operate in other Caribbean territories (McEnearney Alstons 1981). As with the previous economic group, McEnearney Alstons grew substantially during the 1970s, especially after 1974.

The Geddes Grant Group

The Geddes Grant Group is the most international of the four. It operates subsidiaries in five Caribbean countries, apart from Trinidad and Tobago, and also in the United Kingdom. Although the expansion of this group in the Caribbean and in Trinidad and Tobago has been quite considerable, Geddes Grant is the only economic group whose president is a British citizen. This is related to the origins of the group and also to the nature of their activities—basically international trading—which the parent company had carried out from the early years of the century (1917). The group is made up of a total of forty-seven subsidiaries, thirty of which operate outside Trinidad and Tobago. In addition, the group participates as a minority shareholder in the holdings of ten other associated companies.

The main activity of the group is trading (approximately 90 per cent), manufacturing accounting for only 4 per cent of total turnover. Overseas operations account for 45 per cent of total sales, the remaining 55 per cent corresponding to operations carried out in Trinidad and Tobago (Geddes Grant 1981).

In Trinidad and Tobago the group's manufacturing activities are concentrated in building materials and in construction contracting. Because its activities are concentrated mainly in trading, expansion has followed a different pattern compared with the two previous cases. Over the last ten years (1972–81), total group sales have grown at an average annual rate of 47 per cent. It is, however, interesting to note that the period 1976–79 was more or less stagnant, which is quite the opposite of the previous two cases. This can only be attributed to depressed activities in other territories, particularly Jamaica, and to loss of trading to competitors.

The Kirpalanis Group

Strictly speaking, Kirpalanis is not an economic group as are the previous three cases. The difference lies in the fact that the previous three economic groups are 'public companies', that is to say, companies whose capital is owned by more than sixteen shareholders. These companies have issued shares which have been sold to the general public. Kirpalanis, on the other hand, is a private company which is almost totally owned by one family. Kirpalanis Ltd has, however, expanded into manufacturing— mainly light industry—through 'affiliated' or 'associated' companies which in most cases are owned by the same shareholders.

Kirpalanis Ltd, which started in the 1920s as a retail store, has expanded considerably into a chain of department stores as well as into light manufacturing. The figures contained in table 11.5 correspond only to the operations of Kirpalanis Ltd, therefore when comparing them with other companies shown, one must estimate a much larger size of operations both in absolute and relative terms to take into account their numerous affiliated companies.

TABLE 11.5 Trinidad and Tobago: total sales and their relation to GDP*of four selected economic groups (in '000 TT$)

Group	1979 Sales†	Sales/GDP* (%)	1980 Sales	Sales/GDP* (%)	1981 Sales	Sales/GDP* (%)
Neal & Massy	662.9	6.02	824.5	5.91	1,066.7	6.76
McEnearney	522.0	4.74	743.0	5.33	798.9	5.08
Geddes Grant	370.3	3.36	477.7	3.43	523.8	3.33
Kirpalani's‡	97.4	0.88	108.5	0.77	110.6	0.70
Total	1,652.6	15.0	2,153.7	15.44	2,500.0	15.87

NOTES

* The GDP used here corresponds to the non-oil GDP plus non-oil imports for each year.

† The figure for total sales corresponds to sales to third parties for each group. This value includes sales made in other countries by subsidiaries belonging to the group. This corresponds to less than 10 per cent of total sales for each group, except T. Geddes Grant.

‡ These figures correspond only to Kirpalanis Ltd. Data was not available for the group of companies controlled by Kirpalanis Holding Ltd (the rest of the affiliated companies).

Source: Annual Reports, Neal & Massy, McEnearney-Alstons, T. Geddes Grant and Kirpalanis Ltd. Government of Trinidad and Tobago, Review of the Economy 1981.

The activities of these affiliated companies include drugstores, footwear and textile manufacturing and finance. It is also worth noting that Kirpalanis Ltd operates retail stores in other Caribbean territories under the same name. By December 1981 the total number of 'affiliated' companies had reached eighteen.

The degree of concentration of capital by the four groups presented above is quite considerable. Table 11.5 shows the total sales of each group and its relative weight with regard to the non-oil GDP plus imports for the years 1979–81. Considering the large proportion of overseas operations carried out by Geddes Grant, and the operations of affiliated companies of the Kirpalanis Group, the figures still reflect the immense impact of the four groups in the total economy of Trinidad and Tobago. Total sales of the four groups account roughly for 14 per cent of the non-oil GDP plus imports.

This figure involves double accounting because of transactions between the groups and because of the impact of imported inputs. It is, however, still useful for depicting the size reached by the four groups overall. Another method of estimating the size of the conglomerates is to relate their taxation to total non-oil corporation tax collected by the state. For the year 1979, with an estimated total of $294m in non-oil corporation tax, the proportion contributed by each group was, according to official sources, as follows: Neal & Massy 10.26 per cent, McEnearney Alstons 6.91 per cent, T. Geddes Grant 3.70 per cent and Kirpalanis Ltd 0.70 per cent. In other words, in 1979 these four economic groups contributed 21.57 per cent of the total company tax collected in the country. This figure confirms the impact and relative size of these groups in the economy.

Individual group significance, on the other hand, provides a better picture for visualizing the degree of concentration reached by each conglomerate. Unquestionably, these figures show the presence of strong oligopolies whose formations in recent years have been associated with the general expansion that the economy has undergone since 1973.

It is also quite obvious that the rapid concentration of capital has been due, partially, to a deliberate state policy of supporting private ventures in manufacturing activities. This has obviously been a net consequence of the industrialization strategy which the country has pursued since 1950. Clearly, the companies that have benefited most from the policy have been those that were linked to capital accumulation prior to the industrialization period. It could not have been otherwise, as capitalist accumulation in the country has traditionally been linked to petroleum, sugar and trading. Since petroleum and sugar were under the control of foreign capital, at least before the nationalization of the sugar industry, indigenous capital that expanded into manufacturing and other sectors could only come from traditional trading activities. In other words, what has taken place in Trinidad and Tobago in the last thirty years is the qualitative transformation of commercial capital into productive capital under oligopolistic conditions. This has been obtained with the very explicit support of the state.

Conclusions

Over the last thirty years, the economy of Trinidad and Tobago has undergone important changes. From a monoculture of two staples, petroleum and sugar, the economy has evolved into a more diversified structure where local industries producing for the internal and external market now play a more significant role.

The process of industrialization followed strategies that were favoured by the ruling groups which inherited political power from the metropolis. In the absence of dynamic bourgeois forces, the model followed was one of national state capitalism. The state, as we have seen, contributed fundamentally towards creating and consolidating an indigenous bourgeoisie which, although dependent on foreign capital, has managed to expand locally and regionally despite the absence of firmly established economic linkages.

The state, for its part, has expanded into diverse areas as a partner to foreign capital and as a mediator between the indigenous and the foreign bourgeoisie. The fundamental factor underlying the model has been the availability of economic surplus and the capacity of the state to negotiate its case with regard to sharing the surplus with multinational enterprises operating in the petroleum sector.

As the triumvirate formed by the state, the local and foreign bourgeoisie has evolved without major friction up to 1981. Each part has found room to manoeuvre at the economic level. This has been possible because of the availability of economic surplus which has so far remained buoyant in terms of volume and value. The prospects for continued buoyancy are, however, not clear. The production of crude petroleum reached its peak in 1978 and there have been no new discoveries which could slow down or stop the decline in production. The refining of oil has dropped substantially—in 1980 it was 40 per cent lower than in 1973—and with downward trends for the rest of the 1980s. This is a net result of a change of policy in the main refinery operating in the country (Texaco) which has shifted its operation back to the United States. Asphalt production has also declined dramatically over the last seven years.

On the other hand, the production of natural gas has increased substantially (65 per cent between 1973 and 1980) and since 1973 fertilizer manufacture has increased steadily. This shift is consistent with the strategy of energy-based industries which the state and foreign capital have jointly embarked on. What is not clear, however, is whether the shift from traditional oil production and refining to the use of natural gas in export-oriented manufacturing can equal the amount of economic surplus which was made available after 1973. The most significant aspect behind the availability of surplus was the dramatic change in oil prices, which affected the value of total exports and therefore the government revenue position.

The shift towards the utilization of natural gas does not seem to foreshadow a similar bonanza as the one enjoyed between 1974 and 1980. This may well add new dimensions to the so-far non-frictional relationships between the state and local capital and the state and foreign capital. The first relationship may be affected if the state reduces the amount of surplus enjoyed by the indigenous economic groups through taxation or cuts in incentive measures. On the other hand, the relationship between the state and foreign capital can also become more antagonistic if the former imposes measures to ensure that a larger portion of the economic surplus is re-accumulated in the country.

Whether or not the state will continue trying to keep a portion of the economic surplus aside for activities consistent with the economic strategy under implementation, there are no signs that the model of national state capitalism, which has been followed, will change. This seems to be confirmed, at the political level, by the consolidation of the political groups in control since 1956 into a situation that is similar to the Mexican case.

Import-substitution industrialization combined with export promotion has been viable in Trinidad and Tobago only because of the availability of an economic surplus coming from the oil sector. In contrast to other Latin American countries which have attempted a similar pattern of industrialization, Trinidad and Tobago has been privileged in having access to a surplus in foreign currency. The prospects of a renewed surplus in the form of foreign exchange are uncertain. This may well prove the decisive factor in determining the survival of the model of state capitalism as well as the maintenance of relatively trouble-free relationships which have given political stability to a country where the inherent contradictions of the capitalist system have, for the time being, been attenuated.

REFERENCES

Alavi, H. 1976, 'The state in post-colonial societies: Pakistan and Bangladesh', *New left review*, no. 74

Clark, C. 1941, *The conditions of human progress*, London, Macmillan

Geddes Grant Ltd, T. 1981, *64th annual report*, Trinidad and Tobago

Industrial Development Corporation 1980, *Newsletter*, vol. 1 January–March

Lewis, W. A. 1939, *Labour in the West Indies: the birth of a workers' movement*, London, Fabian Society. Republished by New Beacon, 1977

Lewis, W. A. 1951, *Industrial development in the Caribbean*, Caribbean Commission, reprinted from Caribbean Economic Review

McEnearney Alstons 1981, *Annual report*, Trinidad and Tobago

Moyne Commission 1945, *West India royal commission report*, London, HMSO

Neal & Massy Ltd 1979, *Annual report end 1979 accounts*, December

Norman Commission 1897, *Report of the West India royal commission*, London, HMSO

Petras, J. 1978, 'State capitalism and the third world', in *Critical perspectives on imperialism and social class in the third world*, New York, Monthly Review Press

Poulantzas, N. 1976, *Political power and social classes*, London, New Left Books

Prebisch, R. 1951, *The economic development of Latin America and its principal problems*, ECLA Bulletin

St Cyr, E. B. A. 1981, *Industrial development strategies in the Caribbean countries: the case of Trinidad and Tobago*, Department of Economics, the University of the West Indies, St Augustine, Trinidad, March

Saul, J. 1979, *State and revolution in eastern Africa*, New York, Monthly Review Press and London, Heinemann Educational Books

Shaw Committee 1949, *Report of the economics committee*, London, HMSO

Shivji, I. 1976, *Class struggle in Tanzania*, New York, Monthly Review Press
Sudama, T. 1980, *Class, race and the state in Trinidad and Tobago*, Department of Government, University of the West Indies, St Augustine, unpublished paper
Thomas, R. 1981, *The profit situation in the Trinidad oil industry circa 1937*, Department of Economics, University of the West Indies, St Augustine
Williams, E. 1981, 'Economic problems of Trinidad and Tobago', in E. K. Sutton (compiler), *Selected speeches of Dr Williams*, Longman Caribbean

List of Abbreviations

Alcoa	Aluminium Company of America
ATC	Asociación de Trabajadores del Campo (Rural Workers' Association, Nicaragua)
BITU	Bustamante Industrial Trade Union (Jamaica)
Bomika	Bond van Militair Kader (Union of Military Cadres, Suriname)
BPR	Bloque Popular Revolucionario (Revolutionary Popular Bloc, El Salvador)
CACM	Central American Common Market
Caricom	Caribbean Community
Carifta	Caribbean Free Trade Area
CAUS	Central de Acción y Unidad Sindical (Federation of Trade Union Action and Unity, Nicaragua)
CCAA	Caribbean–Central American Action
CCK	Comité Christelijke Kerken (Committee of Christian Churches, Suriname)
CDB	Caribbean Development Bank
CDC	Comité de Defensa Civil (Civil Defence Committee, El Salvador)
CDS	Comité de Defensa Sandinista (Sandinist Defence Committee, Nicaragua)
CIDA	Canadian International Development Agency
CIS	Central Inkoop Suriname (Central Purchasing Agency of Suriname)
CLO	Centrale van Landsdienaren Organisaties (Federation of Unions of Public Servants, Suriname)
CNT	Christian–Social Trade Unions (Nicaragua)
CONDECA	Central American Defence Council
COSEP	Consejo Superior de la Empresa Privada (Higher Council of Private Enterprise, Nicaragua)
CRM	Coordinadora Revolucionaria de Masas (Revolutionary Co-ordinator of the Masses, El Salvador)
CST	Central Sandinista de Trabajadores (Sandinista Workers' Federation, Nicaragua)
CTC	Confederación de Trabajadores Cubanos (Cuban Workers' Federation)
CUS	Consejo de Unificación Sindical (Council of Trade Union Unification, Nicaragua)
DFM	Democratic Freedom Movement (St Vincent)
DRU	Dirección Revolucionaria Unificada (United Revolutionary Leadership, El Salvador)
EDF	European Development Fund
EFP	Educational Forum of the People (St Vincent)
ERP	Ejército Revolucionario del Pueblo (People's Revolutionary Army, El Salvador)
FAPU	Frente de Acción Popular Unificada (United Popular Action Front, El Salvador)

List of Abbreviations

FARN	Fuerzas Armadas de Resistencia Nacional (Armed Forces of National Resistance, El Salvador)
FDR	Frente Democrático Revolucionario (Revolutionary Democratic Front, El Salvador)
FDS	Frente Democrático Salvadoreño (Salvadorean Democratic Front)
FECCAS-UTC	Federación Católica de Campesinos Salvadoreños–Unión de Trabajadores del Campo (Christian Federation of Salvadorean Rural Workers)
FIAWU	Federated Industrial and Agricultural Workers' Union (St Vincent)
FMLN	Frente Farabundo Martí para la Liberación Nacional (Farabundo Martí National Liberation Front, El Salvador)
FPL	Fuerzas Populares de Liberación (Popular Liberation Forces, El Salvador)
FSLN	Frente Sandinista de Liberación Nacional (Sandinista National Liberation Front, Nicaragua)
GAWU	General Agricultural Workers' Union (Guyana)
GDB	Grenada Development Bank
GHRA	Guyana Human Rights Association
GMMWU	Grenada Mental and Manual Workers' Union
GNP	Grenada National Party
GPP	Guerra Popular Prolongada (Prolonged People's War, El Salvador)
IDC	Industrial Development Corporation (Trinidad and Tobago)
IMF	International Monetary Fund
JUCEPLAN	Cuban state planning agency
JLP	Jamaica Labour Party
KTPI	Kaum Tani Persuatan Indonesia (Indonesian Peasants' Party, Suriname)
LAFTA	Latin American Free Trade Association
LP-28	Ligas Populares – 28 Febrero (Popular League – 28 February, El Salvador)
MNIB	Marketing and National Import Board (Grenada)
MNR	Movimiento Nacional Revolucionario (National Revolutionary Movement, El Salvador)
NACDA	National Co-operative Development Agency
NCB	National Commercial Bank (Grenada)
NDP	New Democratic Party (St Vincent)
NJM	New Jewel Movement (Grenada)
NMC	National Military Council (Suriname)
NPK	Nationale Partij Kombinatie (National Combination of Parties, Suriname)
NPS	Nationale Partij Suriname (National Party of Suriname)
NWU	National Workers' Union (Jamaica)
OAS	Organization of American States
OPEC	Organization of Petroleum Exporting Countries
ORDEN	Organización Democrática Nacionalista (National Democratic Organization, El Salvador)
PALU	Progressieve Arbeiders en Landbouwers Unie (Progressive Workers' and Peasants' Union, Suriname)
PCF	Parti Communiste Français (French Communist Party)
PCG	Parti Communiste Guadeloupéen (Guadeloupan Communist Party)

List of Abbreviations

PCM	Parti Communiste Martiniquais (Martiniquan Communist Party)
PCN	Partido Comunista Nicaragüense (Nicaraguan Communist Party)
PCS	Partido Comunista Salvadoreño (Salvadorean Communist Party)
PDC	Partido Demócrata Cristiana (Christian Democratic Party)
PDM	People's Democratic Movement (St Vincent)
PNC	People's National Congress (Guyana)
PNM	People's National Movement (Trinidad and Tobago)
PNP	People's National Party (Jamaica)
PNP	Progressieve Nationale Partij (Progressive National Party, Suriname)
PNR	Partij Nationalistische Republiek (Party for a Nationalist Republic, Suriname)
PPA	Planters' and Peasants' Association (St Vincent)
PPP	People's Progressive Party (Guyana)
PPP	People's Political Party (St Vincent)
PRA	People's Revolutionary Army (Grenada)
PRG	People's Revolutionary Government (Grenada)
PSN	Partido Socialista Nicaragüense (Nicaraguan Socialist Party)
PSV	Progressieve Surinaamse Volkspartij (Progressive People's Party of Suriname)
RGA	Representative Government Association (St Vincent)
RVP	Revolutionaire Volkspartij (Revolutionary People's Party, Suriname)
SKM	Surinaamse Krijgsmacht (Surinamese Army)
SML	Stichting Machinale Landbouw (Foundation for Mechanized Agriculture, Suriname)
STC	State Trading Corporation (Jamaica)
SVLP	St Vincent Labour Party
TNC	Transnational Corporation
TUC	Trade Union Congress
UDN	Unión Demócrata Nacionalista (National Democratic Union, El Salvador)
UNO	Unión Nacional Opositora (National Union of Opposition, El Salvador)
UPM	United People's Movement (St Vincent)
UPP	United People's Party (Grenada)
USAID	United States Agency for International Development
USWA	United Steelworkers of America
VHP	Verenigde Hindoestaanse Partij (United Hindustani Party, Suriname)
VP	Volkspartij (People's Party, Suriname)
WINBAN	West Indian Banana Association
WMA	Workingmen's Co-operative Association (St Vincent)
WPA	Working People's Alliance (Guyana)
WPJ	Workers' Party of Jamaica
YULIMO	Youlou United Liberation Movement (St Vincent)

Index

Index

Index

Index